The Life of
Geoffrey Chaucer

B

BLACKWELL CRITICAL BIOGRAPHIES

General Editor: Claude Rawson

The Life of
GEOFFREY CHAUCER
A Critical Biography

Derek Pearsall

BLACKWELL
Oxford UK & Cambridge USA

First published 1992
Reprinted 1993

Blackwell Publishers
108 Cowley Road
Oxford OX4 1JF
UK

238 Main Street
Cambridge, Massachusetts 02142
USA

British Library Cataloguing in Publication Data

A CIP catalogue record for this book is available from the British Library.

Library of Congress Cataloging-in-Publication Data

Pearsall, Derek Albert.
The life of Geoffrey Chaucer : a critical biography / by Derek
Pearsall.
p. cm. —— (Blackwell critical biographies : 1)
Includes bibliographical references and index.
ISBN 1–55786–205–2
1. Chaucer, Geoffrey, d. 1400——Biography. 2. Poets. English-
Middle English, 1100–1500——Biography. I. Title. II. Series.
PR1905.P43   1992
821'.1——dc20
[B]

Typeset in 11 on 12 pt Baskerville
by Photo·graphics, Honiton, Devon
Printed in Great Britain by T.J. Press Ltd, Padstow, Cornwall

This book is printed on acid-free paper

Contents

Illustrations

Plates

Tables

Maps

Preface and Acknowledgements

I have attempted, in the introduction below, to explain my motives in writing this critical biography of Chaucer. It is, nevertheless, hardly possible to imagine embarking upon such a biography without the invaluable *Chaucer Life-Records* of Martin M. Crow and Clair C. Olson. Their work is employed extensively throughout, though cited only when directly quoted or when the information being used is not to be found in some obvious place in the volume. No reference is normally made to earlier biographical scholarship absorbed into and superseded by annotation in the *Chaucer Life-Records*; or to sources for historical information that is available in standard works of history, such as May McKisack's volume on *The Fourteenth Century* in the Oxford History of England, or in standard works of reference such as the *Dictionary of National Biography*. Nor is reference commonly made to sources for such information on Chaucer's life and poetry as is readily accessible in the annotation and other apparatus of *The Riverside Chaucer* (which is used for Chaucer reference and quotation throughout).

In quotations from non-Chaucerian Middle English, the letters thorn and yogh are replaced by their modern equivalents. In referring to famous historical figures, such as John, Duke of Lancaster, and Henry, Earl of Derby, I have tended, though not always, to use the names that are familiar from Shakespeare (Gaunt and Bolingbroke), rather than follow what is often a confusing succession of titles. On the whole I have tried harder to be clear and unambiguous than to be historically and consistently proper.

I have talked about the matter of this biography with friends, colleagues and students, and gained much from such discussions, as from the questions and comments of audiences to whom I have spoken about it. I have had help with specific questions from a large number of people, and I am very grateful to all of them. Martha Driver, A. S.G. Edwards and Jeremy Griffiths generously made available to me materials and information that helped greatly with the compilation of the appendix on the Chaucer portraits.

I am grateful to Everyman's Library and its editor Peter Washington for permission to reprint, in a slightly different format, the Chronological Table from the introduction I have prepared for the reissue of the Everyman edition of *The Canterbury Tales*, due out in 1992. I also wish to acknowledge the support of the Hyder R. Rollins Publication Fund, administered by the English Department at Harvard University, in defraying the costs of the photographs for the appendix on the Chaucer portraits.

I particularly want to thank Barrie Dobson, Richard Firth Green, Henry Ansgar Kelly and Paul Strohm, who all read through nearly the whole of the book in draft and made many valuable suggestions for improvement. I have also profited greatly from their published work in the field. I want finally to thank my wife, who read through all of the book at different stages, and made many perceptive comments on its style and manner of argument.

Abbreviations

BIHR	Bulletin of the Institute of Historical Research
BLJ	British Library Journal
CFMA	Classiques Français du Moyen Age
ChauR	Chaucer Review
E&S	Essays and Studies
EETS	Early English Text Society
ES	Extra Series
OS	Original Series
EHR	English Historical Review
ELH	English Literary History
ELN	English Language Notes
ES	English Studies
JEGP	Journal of English and Germanic Philology
JMRS	Journal of Medieval and Renaissance Studies
JWCI	Journal of the Warburg and Courtauld Institutes
LQR	Law Quarterly Review
LSE	Leeds Studies in English
M&H	Medievalia et Humanistica
MLN	Modern Language Notes
MLQ	Modern Language Quarterly
MLR	Modern Language Review
MP	Modern Philology
MS	Mediaeval Studies
N&Q	Notes and Queries
NM	Neuphilologische Mitteilungen
NS	New Series
P&P	Past and Present

PMLA	*Publications of the Modern Language Association of America*
PQ	*Philological Quarterly*
RES	*Review of English Studies*
SAC	*Studies in the Age of Chaucer*
SATF	Société des Anciens Textes Français
SB	*Studies in Bibliography*
SP	*Studies in Philology*
STS	Scottish Text Society
Text	*Text: Transactions of the Society for Textual Scholarship*
UTQ	*University of Toronto Quarterly*
YES	*Yearbook of English Studies*
YLS	*Yearbook of Langland Studies*

Introduction:
Writing a Life of Chaucer

The evidence for Chaucer's existence is very sound. There are 493 documentary records of his life brought together in the *Chaucer Life-Records* of Martin M. Crow and Clair C. Olson, and they witness to a long career as a page, as an esquire of the royal household, and as a government and civil servant.[1] More is known about his public or official life than about Shakespeare's, and there is a solid substantiality in the documentary record that contrasts with the shadowy life that is all that can be imputed to his great contemporary, William Langland, or of course to the totally unknown '*Gawain*-poet', if such there was, or were.

Furthermore, there is no reason not to attribute the poems known to be by 'Chaucer' to the Geoffrey Chaucer whom we know to have existed, even though there is no document that could be said to 'prove' that they were the same person. Chaucer mentions 'Chaucer, thogh he kan but lewedly / On metres and on rymyng craftily', in the Introduction to the Man of Law's Tale (*Canterbury Tales*, II.47–8) as the author of the legends that make up *The Legend of Good Women*; in the Prologue to *The Legend of Good Women* he acknowledges himself to be the author of *Troilus and Criseyde* (F. 332), *The House of Fame*, *The Book of the Duchess*, *The Parliament of Fowls* and other works (F. 417–30); and in the Retraction at the end of *The Canterbury Tales* he adds to all these *The Canterbury Tales* themselves.[2] Though he did not supervise a chronologically ordered 'collected edition' of his poems as did his French predecessors and contemporaries, Machaut, Froissart and Deschamps, Chaucer secured the canon of his major works and their attachment to himself with a care only less remarkable for being less obtrusive than that of his friend John Gower, who went to the length of adding a Latin colophon at the end of his *Confessio Amantis* in which he listed and described his three major works. There are no conceivable authorship disputes in the case of Chaucer's major works, though there remain some disagreements about the attribution of the translation of *The Romaunt of the Rose*, the prose *Equatorie of the Planetis*, and a few minor poems.

Given the existence of such a quantity of material evidence, the writing of a Chaucer critical biography, or 'Life and Works', might seem a reasonable thing to attempt. However, there are many who would think not, arguing one or more of the following: that it cannot be done, that it is not worth doing and that it has been done.

Those who argue that it cannot be done would point to the very different role of the biographer of a recent or living writer. Such a biographer can talk to people who knew the writer, visit places that were important to him, consult diaries and journals and private letters, and do a great many other things that may be useful in the attempt to identify the elusive alchemy through which 'life' becomes 'works'. None of these resources is available to the Chaucer biographer. There are the documentary records of his life, none of them intimate and many of them extremely uninformative, a few comments from contemporaries and, for the rest, Chaucer's own 'autobiographical' references in his poetry, where he is elusive at best. The prospect is that these slim pickings will be eked out with such speculation – Chaucer 'must have' done this, Chaucer 'would have' done that – as may be found in quantity in Howard's recent Chaucer biography, an admirable work in many other respects.[3] The danger of this kind of speculative grammar is that a semi-fictional biography will be fabricated which will then be used to endorse views of the poems that the biographer has arrived at by no other means than the usual one of reading them. It might be better to have no biography at all, it seems, than such evident putting of the cart before the horse.

The argument against a Chaucer biography might be pressed further by those who point out that a biographer has in any case a great deal less to work with in pre-Romantic times when there was less emphasis, or maybe no emphasis at all, on 'self-expression', and still less opportunity for it in narrative poetry, which is what Chaucer mostly writes. While accepting this as a practical problem, the biographer of Chaucer would want to repudiate the old idea that medieval writers were essentially anonymous, or the strangely similar new idea that they lacked individualized subjectivity.[4] Whatever may have been the case in earlier centuries, by the time of which we are speaking poets had no desire at all to be anonymous, and would have thought it rank bad luck if they had become so.

Nevertheless, given these differences between pre-Romantic and later poets, Chaucer remains remarkably silent even on those everyday matters to which contemporary poets, poets of his own day, customarily attach their writings, which is one reason why the chronology of his writings is such a spider's web of hypothesis. There is more reference to the poet's own life and the day-to-day events of which he was part in the writing of Langland, albeit that we know nothing of him, while Froissart and Deschamps give us a perhaps representative picture of the medieval poet-about-court at his characteristic business of self-advertisement. Froissart is constantly weaving the events of his real life into his poetry, and writing little poems, like postcards, to mark occasions, or to give as gifts, as he goes about in France and England. Why could not Chaucer have done the same? There are no doubt some good answers to this question, but he certainly did not make the biographer's task any easier. Like Cervantes, he seems to have anticipated modern verdicts on 'the death of the author' by prudently absenting himself, leaving only his creations to deputize for him.[5]

There are, however, those who would argue, more radically, that a biography of Chaucer is not difficult but pointless. What difference does it make to our reading of *The Book of the Duchess* to know who John of Gaunt and Blanche were, and why Chaucer should have been writing about them; or to know whose marriage plans *The Parliament of Fowls* refers to? The people are all dead: the poem remains, and their significance within it, if any, will be solely and sufficiently conveyed through the text of the poem. The force of this argument has to be allowed, especially the manner in which it can hold up for derision those comparatively superficial associations between Chaucer's life and writings that have figured so large in traditional biographical scholarship. The emphasis on Chaucer's presence within his poems has often been no more than a convenient fiction for those who wished to attribute their own interpretative activity to his supposed intentions.[6]

These are cogent arguments, then, against a certain kind of 'bad' biography, but they are taken further by writers like Roland Barthes and Michel Foucault, who consider the idea of the author to be a post-medieval myth, and look forward to the acknowledgement of what they call the 'author-function' as an element in the text. 'A text', says Barthes, 'is not a line of words releasing a single "theological" meaning (the "message" of the Author–God) but a multi-dimensional space in which a variety of writings, none of them original, blend and clash.'[7]

Barthes and Foucault have their own agenda, which is to get rid of the *author* as being the principal representative of textual *authority*: the idea of the author, says Foucault, is 'the principle by which . . . one limits, excludes, and chooses' ('What is an Author?', p. 159). Medievalists are understandably sceptical about a project to get rid of authors whom they find difficult enough to locate in the first place, but it must be admitted that modern scholars working on the rise of the concept of the 'author' find many resemblances, fortuitous or not, between medieval theory of authorship and the post-modern textualization of the 'author-function'.[8] The medieval *accessus ad auctores* (introductions to the works of certain authors) and the *vidas* (lives) of the troubadours think of their subjects not so much as persons with lives and feelings which will be 'expressed' in their writings, as representative 'roles' which help to identify the nature of their discourse within its tradition. In the *intentio auctoris* section of the *accessus*, says Minnis, 'there was rarely any attempt (at least, not until very late in the Middle Ages) to relate a person's purpose in writing to his historical context, to describe an author's personal prejudices, eccentricities and limitations' (*Medieval Theory of Authorship*, pp. 20–1). Minnis acknowledges that there were changes taking place in the fourteenth and fifteenth centuries and that the idea of the author as an individual was becoming stronger, but it is important to point out that the phenomena being described, and the changes taking place, are phenomena of perception, of the way in which medieval scholars viewed the relation between an author's life and his writings, not evidence of the actual relation that existed.

The third argument, that the biography of Chaucer has been done, and done again, in every style ranging from the meticulously factual (in the *Life-Records*) to the frankly, indeed licentiously fictional (in John Gardner's biography) is perhaps the strongest disincentive of all to the prospective biographer.[9] He may agree that much has been done, and done well, and may feel that a new 'Life and Works' comes in any case too close upon the heels of the very ample 'Life, Works and World' of the late Donald Howard. What more is there to say?

In answering this question, and at the same time addressing the other arguments against literary biography, I have to assert at the beginning a firm belief, without which presumably no literary biographer would set finger to word-processor, that the experience of writers' lives, outer and inner, is the matter of their writings in a most significant manner. Knowledge of a writer's life does not 'explain' his writings, and there is probably much that is bound to remain mysterious in the process by which those writings come into being, but it does provide an important context for understanding them. I do not imagine that MM. Foucault and Barthes, for all their desire to obliterate the author, would wish, or would have wished, to think of their own texts as detached from their own persons, floating in a sea of author-functions, and they would acknowledge how what they write is the product of what they themselves are and have been and are desirous of being.

But the relationship between 'life' and 'works' may take many forms. It may be very obvious, as in the case of Byron, Oscar Wilde and Sylvia Plath, where the writings are almost an appendage of the life; or it may be very subtle, as with some of the quieter women poets of the nineteenth century such as Emily Dickinson. With Chaucer, the relationship seems, unexpectedly, to be very close: although he tells us little about himself, or about his attitudes to the great events of his day, the quality of his poetic presence is such that he stimulates in us an unusually powerful desire to know what he was 'really' like.

Chaucer is not alone in his time in cultivating an interest in himself, the poet, as an individual: it was a developing trend in the fourteenth century, and Machaut, Froissart, Deschamps and Christine de Pizan represented themselves, in their poetry, in a manner quite different from that of their predecessors, such as Guillaume de Lorris and Jean de Meun. Hoccleve, meanwhile, taking his cue from his master Chaucer, moves towards the directly autobiographical. Yet Chaucer, though not alone in the interest he creates in himself, remains exceptional: he conveys an unmistakable and consistent sense of identity, not just as a poet or even a persona, but as a person, and makes one feel that he would have been worth knowing, and his views worth hearing. It is not so much the 'real' Chaucer that one can go in search of, though that must be the desire that provides the motive for searching, as the manner in which he constructed his poetic self, or had it constructed for him.[10]

At the same time, given these arguments for the importance of a literary biography of Chaucer, and the rationalness of the desire to write one, there must be some qualifications concerning the kinds of biographical and historical data that are deemed to be important to the understanding of his poetry. There are things in a writer's life that are important to his writing and there are things that are not; there are also private matters of which we know nothing and upon which it would be idle to speculate, such as whether Chaucer's marriage was a happy one. But the impact on Chaucer of his experience of life in court and aristocratic households, of his journeys to Italy, of his own ambiguous station in life, and of living in London at a time when the capital was at the centre of rapid economic change, was clearly of profound significance for his poetry. It will be much of the substance of this book.

An account of such experiences takes as much from general historical sources as from the known facts of Chaucer's life. But it is better to accept the necessity of imprecision in the pursuit of what is acknowledged to be significant than to look for those neat matches between literary text and biographical or historical event which have been the substance of so much biographical scholarship. Such interpretations, whether plausible or not, are reductive in their view of both text and event, and their lack of significance is revealed as soon as the question is asked, So what? They treat the relationship between text and event as a relationship between fixed and objectively known data, ignoring the complex networks and processes of which they are both part. Discovering the 'occasion' for which a poem was written is only a preliminary stage in finding out how it is embedded in those networks and processes.[11]

The study of Chaucer's life and writings is inseparable from the study of the history of his time, but again there is a history that is important to the understanding of his poetry and a history that, by and large, is not. The traditional matter of political, military and constitutional history is on the whole of lesser importance: the great constitutional crises of 1376–77, 1386–89 and 1399 affected Chaucer's life profoundly, in that they determined how he was employed, where he lived, how well-off he was, but they do not find their way into his poetry. Nor does Chaucer make any significant mention of the Peasants' Revolt, despite the sometimes desperate efforts of his admirers to extract something appropriate from him. Yet it should be understood that the changes taking place in economic relationships within society, changes of which the Rising is a violent symptom, are indeed richly documented and explored by Chaucer in *The Canterbury Tales*. To the conflicts

between social classes, the increasing permeability of rank-div-
isions, the realm of negotiations opening up within the marriage
contract, and the new ways of interpreting other kinds of vow and
oath and promise, his fictions bear urgent witness.

The study of this kind of history, in which Chaucer's writings,
like his life, are seen to be embedded, does not, however, supersede
or make irrelevant the more traditional study of power relations,
and of the actions of kings and commanders, which define the
arena and determine the circumstances within which social and
economic changes take place. Richard II's own character is
important here, as is the role he developed for himself as a cultural
patron, not so much because of individual acts of patronage or
expressions of taste, but because he made money available and
created an impression of expansiveness. When he resumed his
regal power in 1389, the money to pay for the building of the
Great Hall of Westminster Palace, which had been diverted by
the Lords Appellant to pay for things like the Earl of Arundel's
pathetically dogged attempts to wage a naval war against the
French, began to flow again. Chaucer, probably not by coincidence, also found himself once more in employment.[12]

One final point has to do with the position of the biographer,
and the extent to which he must recognize constantly how he
builds himself into the biography of his chosen writer and recreates
his subject according to his own preconceptions. One need only
mention the long history of snobbery among English biographers,
from Speght to Godwin and on, and their determination to make
the most of the Lancastrian connection, and the tendency of
American biographers, by contrast, to make a point of democratiz-
ing Chaucer. Both J. R. Hulbert and J. M. Manly are eager to
emphasize that Chaucer got where he did by hard work and not
by receiving special favours from king or aristocracy: in so doing,
while making Chaucer an honorary American, they give an even
more distorted picture of the patterns of social and cultural patronage in the fourteenth century.[13]

Being conscious of potential bias in this way is of course valuable; even something admirable like enthusiasm for one's subject
may be dangerous in a biographer, though it might well be preferable to the claim to an unachievable 'objectivity'. In studying the
lives of other people it is impossible to think of them objectively,
as objects, or to pretend that they can be understood without
imagination, participation, moral concern and therefore bias.
Maybe a frank declaration of interest in finding Chaucer to be a

decent sort of fellow is the most honest course of action. But everyone who has written a Chaucer biography has found him thus, whether the interest has been acknowledged or not.

Perhaps one could adopt a differently prejudiced view of Chaucer, and represent his life, and its importance in his writings, as that of a time-serving opportunist and placeman, who pictured his own pliability in all that he saw. He might be seen as one who had outlived the idealisms of chivalry and faith but found nothing to fill the vacuum that they left; who exposed the meretriciousness of institutionalized religion, but retreated into its most inflexible dogma when his humanity was exhausted; who recognized no central social value in law and other forms of contract, but saw only what was hollow and saleable; who made many generous gestures towards women, but returned generally to a conventional misogyny; who viewed life in a spirit of pessimism interspersed with irrepressible hilarity.

This at least is an image of the man that may serve as a coordinate in refiguring certain expectations, and bringing it to mind may give an impression of novelty, if not of impartiality.

1

Beginnings:
c. 1340–1360

The Date of Chaucer's Birth

On 15 October 1386, Geoffrey Chaucer was called before the High Court of Chivalry, meeting in the refectory of Westminster Abbey, to make a deposition, as witness number 22, in the dispute between Sir Richard Scrope and Sir Robert Grosvenor as to the right to bear certain arms, namely, *azure a bend or*. Chaucer said that he saw the said coat of arms borne by Sir Richard and (with a label) by Sir Henry Scrope (Richard's cousin, bearing the label as the mark of difference of an eldest son) when he was himself in arms before the town of 'Retters' (Rethel, near Reims) in France, and saw them frequently on this expedition, on which he himself was taken prisoner. In reply to subsequent questions, he affirmed that it was common knowledge that these were the Scrope arms, and that the family's right to bear them dated back to ancient times. As to the claim of Sir Robert Grosvenor, Chaucer tells a little story: he was walking down Friday Street in London one day when he noticed a new sign with the Scrope coat of arms outside a *herbergerie* (inn, in the sense of the town house of a family from out of town). When he asked who had hung out the Scrope arms thus, he was told that they were not the Scrope arms but those of Sir Robert Grosvenor, a knight of the county of Cheshire. This, as Chaucer says, was news to him.

The proceedings relating to this celebrated controversy, which were held in various places around the Abbey and Palace of Westminster, had begun the previous year, after Scrope had challenged Grosvenor, when they were both in northern England on the Scottish expedition in August 1385, on his right to bear the arms. They went on until 1390, when they were determined in favour of Scrope. Sir Richard Scrope (*c.* 1327–1403) had served prominently in Edward III's wars, and was an equally prominent figure in Richard II's administration, sometime chancellor and later builder of Castle Bolton in Wensleydale. This was not the first time he had had to defend his exclusive right to bear the arms *azure a bend or*, which were unfortunately rather simple and therefore prone to crop up independently elsewhere. Sir Robert Grosvenor (d. 1396), though he had a good war record (he fought beside Scrope at the battle of Najera in 1367), was a much less distinguished personage, and it was a surprise to no one when he lost the case.

The importance of this record of Chaucer in 1386, apart from the glimpse it gives us of one of the main talking-points of upper-class London in the late 1380s, and the indication it gives of Chaucer's accepted status and evident pride in his status within this society (his friends Sir Peter Bukton, Sir John Clanvowe and Sir Lewis Clifford gave testimony four days later), is that it offers the best evidence for the date of Chaucer's birth. He declares his age to be 40 years and more, and says that he has been 'armeez' (that is, commissioned to bear arms in the king's service) for twenty-seven years: 'Geffray Chaucere esquier del age de xl ans et plus armeez par xxvii ans' (*Life-Records*, p. 370). (The record is of course in French, or at least that form of French used in official documents in England, though this does not imply that the proceedings were not, in part at least, in English.) The vagueness of 'forty years and more' has usually been improved upon by scholars, who suggest it means about 42 or 43, with added evidence coming from the age he is likely to have been, that is, not less than 16 years old, when he was first 'armed' in 1359. So 1343 emerges as the projected hypothetical date of Chaucer's birth, superseding the earlier accepted date of *c.* 1340, which was just an honest guess and a round number, and the earlier date still, accepted till late in the nineteenth century, of 1328. This date, which has the precision of pure invention, became established in the early biographies of Chaucer, perhaps for no better reason than that it gave Chaucer extra time to write the many spurious pieces that he was then loaded with, or opportunities to be active on the occasions which were wrongly supposed to have inspired poems that he did not write.

The chief difficulty with a date like 1343 is that it is likely, by its air of precision, to create a sense of authenticity. It becomes the year in which Chaucer was born. A date two or three years earlier could certainly be equally well argued for: 16 was in any case very young to be 'armeez', and 'xl ans et plus' could well mean, with the leniency that a middle-aged man would be likely to allow himself, 45 years or even more. One cannot be certain, of course, that 'xl ans et plus' is any more than a guess at Chaucer's age made by the court clerk who was responsible for recording such things. The same formula ('xl ans et plus', 'lx ans et plus') is used in the record of the testimony of many other deponents, and the equivalent Latin form ('etatis xl annorum et amplius' (of the age of 40 years and more)) was usual in legal documents. Furthermore, where a deponent's age is given exactly, as is often the case in the record of the inquisition, and can be checked against more accurate historical records, it is often out by several years. However, the date of first service in the field, which is always given where appropriate, is nearly always exact and often not given in years but in reference to a particular campaign, siege or battle. Such references are likely to be accurate. This is not too helpful in Chaucer's case, since we still cannot be sure how old he was in 1359, when he was first armed. A brief analysis of the depositions of the witnesses in the Scrope–Grosvenor inquisition shows the age of first being armed, as deduced from total age, where both are given exactly, to vary from 12 to 31, but in a random sample of thirty witnesses, only four were armed before the age of 15 and only two over 23. The average age for being armed, for what it is worth, comes out at 19.

Since it is wise not to be too specific about matters where there can be no certainty, the early 1340s would be the best estimate for the date of Chaucer's birth.[1]

PARENTAGE

Geoffrey Chaucer names his father as John Chaucer, vintner of London (' . . . me Galfridum Chaucer filium Johannis Chaucer vinetarii Londonie'), in a legal deed of 19 June 1381, in which he gives up his rights to a tenement in Thames Street, formerly his father's, to Henry Herbury, vintner of London (*Life-Records*, p. 1). The property had probably come to him very recently on the death of his mother, to whom it would first have been left. (It is interesting to reflect that the document was drawn up and dated just five days after the final acts of the spectacular drama of the Peasants' Revolt had been played out at Smithfield on Saturday 15 June: thus smoothly, we might think, does everyday life resume its routines.) This deed of quitclaim is the only document that associates Geoffrey with either of his parents, but it is enough to give access to a good deal of knowledge about them and the rest of the Chaucer family.

The family came originally from Ipswich, where Geoffrey's great-grandfather, Andrew de Dynyngton, also known as Andrew le Taverner, maybe kept a tavern (see table 1). His son, Robert de Dynyngton, also known as Robert Malyn, Robert Malyn le Chaucer and Robert le Chaucer, made the move to London, and eventually established himself there as a mercer or vintner and a solid citizen. His adoption of the name Chaucer is very plausibly explained in a recent study by Lister Matheson. Robert was an apprentice in the service of a London mercer called John le Chaucer, and when his master was killed in a brawl in 1302 Robert found himself a beneficiary of his employer's will. As a mark of his esteem and of his determination to carry on the business, and perhaps also as a proclamation of his new status upon coming into his windfall inheritance, he adopted his master's surname.[2]

Robert le Chaucer was in the king's service in 1305. He married Mary, the widow of John Heyron (Heron), a pepperer, by whom she had already a son, Thomas, who also became a vintner; after Robert's death, Mary married his cousin Richard Chaucer, another vintner. Robert and Mary had a son, John Chaucer (*c.* 1312–1366), who married Agnes, daughter of John de Copton, probably in the late 1330s. Geoffrey was their son, the only child born to them of whom there is definite knowledge, though there is seventeenth-century evidence of a sister called Katherine (*Life-Records*, p. 289). Agnes survived John, marrying Bartholomew Chappel within weeks of her husband's death in 1366; she probably died in 1381.

John Chaucer was a figure of some prominence in London, a vintner and an active member of the London business community. His adventures began early, for in 1324, when he was about 12, his mother being by now married to Richard, he was abducted by his aunt Agnes de Westhale (sister of Robert) in order that he should marry her daughter Joan. The abduction had to do with the securing of John's inheritance from Robert, now that his mother

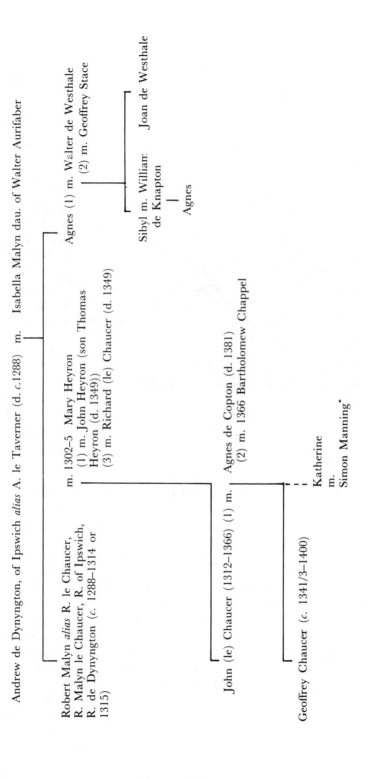

Andrew de Dynyngton, of Ipswich *alias* A. le Taverner (d. *c.*1288)   m.   Isabella Malyn dau. of Walter Aurifaber

Robert Malyn *alias* R. le Chaucer,
R. Malyn le Chaucer, R. of Ipswich,
R. de Dynyngton (*c.* 1288–1314 or
1315)

m. 1302–5   Mary Heyron
(1) m. John Heyron (son Thomas
    Heyron (d. 1349))
(3) m. Richard (le) Chaucer (d. 1349)

Agnes (1) m. Walter de Westhale
       (2) m. Geoffrey Stace

Sibyl m. William   Joan de Westhale
      de Knapton

Agnes

John (le) Chaucer (1312–1366) (1) m.   Agnes de Copton (d. 1381)
                                       (2) m. 1366 Bartholomew Chappel

Katherine
m.
Simon Manning*

Geoffrey Chaucer (*c.* 1341/3–1400)

* See chapter 5, p. 204.

Table 1. The Chaucer family tree *(1)* (with acknowledgements to Lister M. Matheson)

had remarried, but it was fortunately, for Geoffrey's sake and ours, unsuccessful, and John was awarded damages in 1330. Meanwhile, he had been involved in the inglorious Scottish expedition of 1327 and was active in the London disturbances of 1328 that were prompted by the Earl of Lancaster's opposition to the regency of Isabella, Edward II's widow, and her lover, Roger Mortimer, Earl of March.

In all these adventures, John was closely associated with his stepbrother Thomas Heron, who had earlier shown his friendly interest by pursuing John's kidnappers to Ipswich and robbing Agnes, as she said, of £40. Thomas was also close to his stepfather Richard, and had many business interests in common with him. Richard lived in the house in Watling Street, in the Cordwainer Street ward, which had originally belonged to his wife's first husband, John Heyron, the pepperer (see map 1). The close-packed alleys of this ward, just to the north of the Vintry, where Geoffrey's father settled, were the home and business places of the pepperers, who dealt in all kinds of expensive spices, such as ginger and cinnamon, as well as pepper, and had much of their trade with Italian merchants and in Italian ships. The Watling Street house was where John Chaucer was living with his mother and stepfather (Richard) when he was kidnapped, and where he was later brought up by his stepfather in the wine-trade; it was where Richard's brother Simon was brought to die in 1336 after a street-fight in which he was struck on the head by a door-bar; and it stood to Geoffrey, in his earliest years, as the house of his grand-parents, where he would have been a frequent visitor. All this side of the family was wiped out in the plague of 1349.[3]

By 1337, John Chaucer was established as a London wine-merchant, and he became a prosperous citizen; he was appointed to the important position of deputy in the port of Southampton to the king's chief butler (the man who looked after the royal wine-cellar), John de Wesenham, in 1347. There he would look after shipments of wine from Bordeaux destined for the king's cellars. In 1349 he gave up this appointment, probably because a number of family properties came into his hands in that year as a result of the death in the plague of Richard Chaucer, Thomas Heron and his wife's uncle and cousin. John Chaucer subsequently became a freeman of the city of London, and was prominent in its affairs, standing surety, for instance, with others in 1364 that Richard Lyons, vintner, would cause no harm to Alice Perrers (later, or perhaps even already, Edward III's mistress), or prevent her going

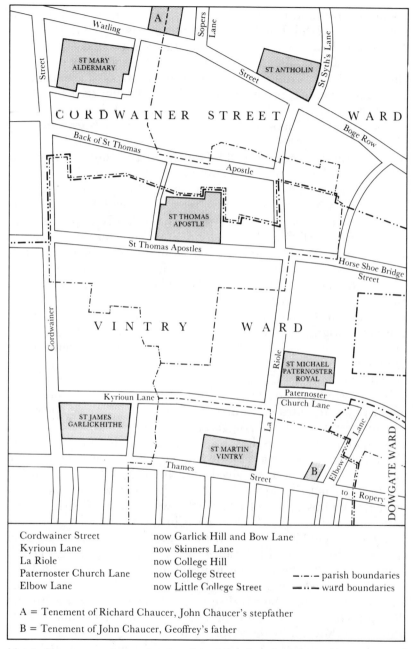

Cordwainer Street now Garlick Hill and Bow Lane
Kyrioun Lane   now Skinners Lane
La Riole   now College Hill
Paternoster Church Lane now College Street —·—· parish boundaries
Elbow Lane   now Little College Street —··— ward boundaries

A = Tenement of Richard Chaucer, John Chaucer's stepfather

B = Tenement of John Chaucer, Geoffrey's father

Map 1. Chaucer tenements in the city of London (based on the map in the Redstones' essay, cited in chapter 1, note 3)

about her own and the king's business. Richard Lyons was one of the most powerful London merchants of his day: Geoffrey had dealings with him too, for Lyons was the collector of customs when Geoffrey was appointed controller in 1374 and thus effectively Chaucer's boss. Lyons was attacked in the 'Good Parliament' of 1376 for customs profiteering, and briefly imprisoned; much hated, he died at the hands of the rebels in 1381.

The surname 'Chaucer', from the Old French *chaucier*, originally identified a person as a maker of shoes or boots or other (leather) wear for the feet or legs (Old French *chauces*), but occupational surnames had very often become merely hereditary by the fourteenth century, and in any case the original family name is likely to have been Malyn, as we have seen. Geoffrey Chaucer's father was, in fact, a vintner, as were nearly all his relations. The first discovery of this fact by John Stow, the busy Elizabethan antiquarian, caused some embarrassment to Chaucer's early biographers, who would have much preferred an aristocratic pedigree for the father of English poetry. Thomas Speght, who wrote an important life of Chaucer for his edition of Chaucer's *Workes* in 1598, was not the man to disguise the unpalatable fact of Chaucer's bourgeois origin, but he did nevertheless declare stoutly his belief that the family was no doubt wealthy 'and of good account in the commonwealth' and probably descended from some ancient but decayed noble line ('Chaucer's Life', sig. b. ii)

But it would be quite wrong for a modern biographer, who might prefer the idea of an open society in which merit could win its way despite birth, to exaggerate the lowly nature of Chaucer's origins. It is worth stressing that Chaucer was not only exceptionally fortunate in having a settled home when he was young and in having parents who survived until he was well into manhood, but he also had the advantage of a father who was in one of the most prestigious forms of trade, who was extremely well-off and quite influential, and who had been in the king's service in both military and civil capacities. Furthermore, the careers of a number of others associated with Chaucer as esquires in the king's household suggest that he was not unusual in moving from what looks to us like a background in 'trade' into an aristocratic household and eventually into the royal service. Merchants with wealth and the right connections – and John Chaucer was such a one – could provide or buy for their offspring the privileges associated with gentility even though they themselves might not be 'gentle'.

The fundamental distinction in society was between those who were 'gentle' and those who were not: the distinction remained important in English society until quite recently (it remains perceptible still) and many of Trollope's novels derive their impetus from fine but vital questions concerning who is and who is not a gentleman, and whether the children of commerce qualify for polite society. 'The one great difference in our society', says Owen Fitzgerald, in *Castle Richmond* (1860), 'is between gentlemen and ladies, and those who are not gentlemen or ladies.' But neither in the fourteenth nor in the nineteenth century was the distinction of class based on the possession of a systematic set of 'qualifications', though birth, title, estates and wealth were all variously important. To be 'gentle' one had to be seen to be gentle, to be so regarded and accepted. Hence the frustrations of Chaucer's Franklin, who has all the qualifications for gentility except the universal recognition of his fellows.

The fourteenth century did see an increasing mobility in society, and the rise of the de la Pole family from Hull merchants to the earldom of Suffolk in two generations is commonly cited as a spectacular example of such mobility. Langland complained about shoemakers buying knighthoods and other such violations of the natural hierarchy of society (*Piers Plowman*, C. V. 72), but Chaucer, perhaps conscious that he himself had been a main beneficiary of increased social mobility, shows a keen and open-minded interest in questions of *gentillesse*, and the closeness of its connection with birth and breeding, particularly in the Wife of Bath's Tale, the Squire's Tale and the Franklin's Tale. Paradoxically, but not surprisingly, mid-fourteenth-century mobility was followed by a period in which the newly enlarged class of the nobility and gentry became increasingly stratified and difficult to get into.[4]

LIFE IN LONDON

The Thames Street house was probably the one in which Geoffrey Chaucer was born and brought up. Like many properties in London, it stood on land owned by a religious order: a rent of 60s. per annum was payable to the prioress and convent of Cheshunt. It was not a small house: Henry Herbury, a citizen and vintner of high standing, was happy to live there when he came into possession in 1381. Comparable houses of which details are known had a large central area called the hall, which would be the main dining and reception area and where much of the wine-merchant's business would be conducted; a handsome living-room with windows, called a solar, opening off, perhaps up some stairs at the side of the hall; a small parlour or two, for the women of the household, and the children; a kitchen, and a privy. Upstairs, in the roof-space, there were two or three bedchambers. Within the house there would be the requisite tables, chairs and chests, but wills indicate that beds, bed-hangings and plate were the most valued part of a citizen's property, the other furniture being merely functional and much of it built-in.

Down below were extensive cellars, not the least important part of these houses in the Vintry, the ward of the city where the wine-merchants had their businesses. Like most trades, they tended to congregate in a certain area: so leather-workers were to be found in Cordwainer Street, and scribes and others concerned in the making of books in the area round Paternoster Row. The area of the Vintry, especially around Thames Street and Royal Street (La Riole), was also a favourite resort and residence of alien merchants in medieval London, including those Italian wine-traders from whom, along with the pepperers a few streets away, Chaucer probably first picked up the language that was to be so important in his public and poetic career.

Thames Street ran east–west, north of and parallel with the Thames. Little alleys, with cellars and overhanging solars and bakehouses and shops and yards, ran back to the Thames, and to the quays where wine was unloaded. On the north side of Thames Street the houses, with their outbuildings, stretched back to Walbrook, still then an open stream used to carry off sewage to the Thames (it was not vaulted until 1462). The most desirable latrines were those that stuck out over it. The Chaucer family home was one of these houses on the north side. Its site was that of a property known as 177 Upper Thames Street in the eighteenth and nineteenth centuries; in the late nineteenth century the area was levelled and redeveloped and in 1940 it was levelled again by bombs during the Blitz.

Thames Street was in the heart of the city of London, which, with a population of perhaps 50,000, was by far the largest city in England (York and Norwich, the next largest, each had about 10,000). The early fourteenth century had been a period of spectacular growth for the city, especially as a port. It had overtaken Boston as a wool-exporting port by 1306, and took control of the wine-trade from French importers in 1324–7. By 1334 it was five times richer than its nearest trading competitor, Bristol, and in the 1350s it took over the banking monopoly from the Lombards. Yet London was still small compared with Paris or Hamburg or the big Italian cities such as Genoa, Venice and Florence, where the population might reach 100,000, and tiny compared with Baghdad, which had close on a million. (England, we should always remember, was, in global terms, a backwater of a backwater.)

Most of the inhabitants of London still lived within the square mile of the walled city, which extended up to about half a mile north of the Thames from the Tower of London in the east to Blackfriars in the west (see map 2). The seven main gates included Aldgate, above which Chaucer had his dwelling during his years at the customs (1374–86), and these gates were still closed at night. Within the city there were warrens of stinking alleys, but also streets of quite substantial houses and business premises (like Thames Street) and fine broad avenues and open spaces around the mansions kept up by the nobility. There were parish churches everywhere, four in the Vintry ward alone, and perhaps seventy or eighty in all within the city. There were also, in and around the city, about thirty religious houses, hospitals and colleges, including the houses of the Grey Friars and the Black Friars: their newly built preaching churches, of which nearly all visible trace disappeared at the Reformation, rivalled St Paul's Cathedral in size.

It is hard for us to get a mental picture of fourteenth-century London. Most of the streets and alleys were unpaved; there would be animals, animal dung, refuse, offal everywhere; the smells would be strong, though most of the noise would come from church bells. Parts of the city would look little different from a farmyard, though there would also be spacious tree-lined gardens, and some magnificent town houses, public buildings and churches. Thirty years ago, one could find provincial towns in the less frequented parts of Spain that had something of the atmosphere of medieval London; now one would have to go to Morocco.

London was at the same time an important intellectual and cultural centre. The great mendicant and other religious houses of London had their schools and libraries: the London Carmelite house was the *studium generale* for the entire order in England, while the library of the Grey Friars probably supplied Sir Thomas Malory, when he was in prison in Newgate, with essential reading for his reworking of the Arthurian story. There was also the

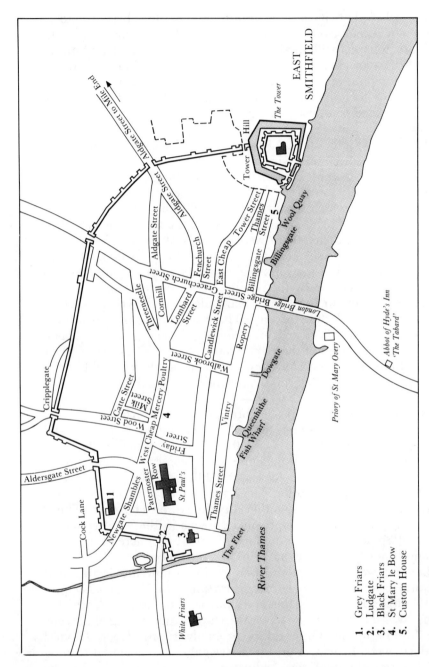

Map 2. The London of Chaucer's time

1. Grey Friars
2. Ludgate
3. Black Friars
4. St Mary le Bow
5. Custom House

EAST SMITHFIELD

The Tower

Tower Hill

Aldgate Street to Mile End

Aldgate Street

Aldgate Street

Fenchurch Street

Cornhill

Threeneedle

Gracechurch Street

Lombard Street

East Cheap

Candlewick Street

Tower Street

Thames Street

Billingsgate

Billingsgate Street

Ropery

Wool Quay

London Bridge

'The Tabard'

Abbot of Hyde's Inn

Priory of St Mary Overy

Dowgate

Walbrook Street

Vintry

Mercery Poultry

West Cheap

Milk Street

Catte Street

Wood Street

Friday Street

Thames Street

Queenhithe

Fish Wharf

Cripplegate

Aldersgate Street

Cock Lane

Newgate Shambles

Paternoster Row

St Paul's

White Friars

The Fleet

River Thames

cathedral school at St Paul's, which took older students up to the age of 30 as well as younger pupils of 7–14 at the Almonry School, and monastic schools at Westminster and St Saviour's, Southwark, outside the city. Scholars of international repute were working in London: Robert Holcot (d. 1349) and William of Ockham (d. 1349), important and controversial figures in the new theology, spent time here, and Nicholas Trivet, whose commentary on Boethius provided many glosses for Chaucer's translation of the *Consolation of Philosophy* and whose Anglo-Norman history supplied the material of the Man of Law's Tale, was lector in the Dominican priory of Black Friars during the 1320s. Thomas Bradwardine, Archbishop of Canterbury and the redoubtable exponent of divine predestination, to whom Chaucer refers in the Nun's Priest's Tale (*Canterbury Tales*, VII. 3242), was chancellor of St Paul's from 1337 to 1349. The London households of the great bishops, such as John Grandisson, Bishop of Exeter (d. 1369), and Richard de Bury, Bishop of Durham (d. 1349), often had distinguished masters attached to them; these households were to be found in the spacious surroundings of the great episcopal residences which were being built up, beside abbatial and aristo-cratic palaces, along Fleet Street and the Strand, between those leafy lanes and the river. The city itself meanwhile was swarming with canon lawyers servicing the episcopal and archdiaconal courts of the London diocese, as well as the Canterbury court of appeal at the Court of the Arches. There were bookshops, book-makers and book-dealers (though not nearly as many as in Paris), and grocers and other London tradesmen are recorded as owning books.[5]

London was also full of rich and ambitious merchants who were eager to imitate the manners and customs of their aristocratic superiors. Guild meetings would often be the occasion for elaborate feasting in courtly style. John Shirley describes how Henry Scogan's *Moral Balade* was delivered to the four teenaged sons of Henry IV around 1407 when they were 'at a souper of feorthe merchande in the Vyntre in London at the hous of Lowys Johan', while John Stow, in his *Survey of London*, tells how Henry Picard, vintner, mayor of London 1356–7, feasted four kings on one day at his house in that same Vintry. Much later, in 1429, Lydgate wrote a 'Mumming' of quite an ostentatious and learned kind, such as he was accustomed to present at court at Christmas and other festive occasions, to be put on by the silk-merchants before Mayor East-field at an Epiphany feast in that year; he wrote another to be

put on by the goldsmiths before the same Mayor Eastfield at the
following Candlemas; and a Mumming at Bishopswood, 'sente by
a poursyvant to the Shirreves of London, accompanyed with theire
bretherne upon Mayes daye at Busshopes wod, at an honurable
dyner, eche of hem bringginge his dysshe'.[6]

At an earlier date, there was also the *puy*, a kind of bourgeois
eisteddfod, an annual merchant feast with a 'prince' presiding, at
which a prize would be awarded for the best poem in praise of
loyal love and virtuous ladies. The records for such gatherings are
much better for France than they are for London, but a Guildhall
record of the early fourteenth century does seem to suggest the
setting up of a ceremonial occasion of the kind, perhaps under the
influence of French immigrants or visitors. It has been suggested
that Gower may have written for such a *puy*, and Chaucer's
Complaint to his Lady has been considered undistinguished enough
to be associated with a similar occasion.[7]

Across the river from the city by London Bridge, the only
bridge over the Thames until 1750, was the thriving borough of
Southwark, where Chaucer's pilgrims stayed at the Tabard Inn
before beginning their journey to Canterbury, and where prosperous merchants like William Walworth, mayor of London and hero
of 15 June 1381, had a lucrative sideline in brothels, forbidden
within the city. Boats plied a busy trade. Outside the walls of
the city, to the east and north, were the shacks and shanties
of unsuccessful new immigrants, the chronic poor, and the less
prosperous of the criminal classes: these were the 'suburbes' of the
city, as Chaucer's Canon's Yeoman terms them, describing where
he lives:

> Lurkynge in hernes and in lanes blynde,
> Whereas thise robbours and thise theves by kynde
> Holden hir pryvee fereful residence.
> *(Canterbury Tales*, VIII. 658–60)

But the country was not far away, and every day carts came in
through the gates from the farms and fields around, bringing
produce for London's markets. It is such a 'fare-carte' that Troilus
mistakes for the conveyance bringing back Criseyde, as he looks
out from the walls of Troy (London was, after all, 'New Troy'),
'by hegge, by tre, by greve' (*Troilus and Criseyde*, v. 1144), and asks
the porters, though it is late in the evening, to delay closing the
gates a little longer.

To the west of the city there was more extensive development. The Inns of Court were there, and the roads around them and leading to Westminster, a mile and a half to the west, were becoming built-up. The Strand, formerly a riverside path, was increasingly popular with those who wanted more space, and a bigger distance between themselves and the potentially unruly inhabitants of the city. John of Gaunt, who had reason to want a bigger distance than most, had his great palace of the Savoy there (it was burnt to the ground by the rebels in 1381). Beyond, to the west, was Westminster, the seat of government and the London home of the king when he chose, as he mostly did, not to entrust himself to his subjects in the city by residing in the Tower.

THE BLACK DEATH

It would be impossible to convey in a few words, or indeed in a great many, what 'life was like' in the 1340s and 1350s, while Geoffrey Chaucer was growing up. The modern practice of attributing a certain 'character' to a decade, arbitrary as it is, is probably even less relevant to the fourteenth century, when things changed slowly, if they changed at all, and nothing more slowly than the economic circumstances which determine the basis for change. The thirteenth century, broadly speaking, had been a time of economic expansion and population growth in England and Western Europe; that era had long passed its peak, and the unprecedented series of fierce winters and poor harvests of 1315–17 marked a stage in this economic decline rather than caused it. People in London would in any case not have been so much aware of these principally agricultural and rural changes, except insofar as they noticed that more people from the country were coming to live in the city. Commerce was prospering, especially trade with the rapidly growing commercial centres in Flanders and Italy, and England was beginning to make its mark as an exporter of finished cloth, having been for centuries merely an exporter of raw wool.

No doubt, too, some invigoration was given to commerce, as well as to general morale, by the success of Edward III's early expeditions to France in pursuit of his claim to the French crown. It is very difficult to assess the economic advantage to the country as a whole of such wars: they provided quantities of loot and ransom money, but most of this came into the hands of a small class of professional soldiers, and meanwhile the costs of the war fell, inordinately as they thought, upon the money-making classes and the clergy, the 'winners' as opposed to the 'wasters', as they are called in the witty and lively alliterative poem of the 1350s, *Winner and Waster*. Most businessmen, if they had made a cool and rational assessment of the situation, would have concluded that war was a net loss, but cool and rational assessments are at a premium when news is coming home of such brilliant victories as those of Crecy (1346) and Poitiers (1356), both of them fought by retreating English armies, more than eager to leave the country, against greatly superior French forces. At such times, Edward and his son, the Black Prince, must have looked good for business as well as for the righteous claim of England in France and the high nobility of chivalry.

One event, however, cannot be passed by, since it reshaped England, along with most of Europe and Asia, and contributed, we must believe, to some reshaping of the mentality of the age. A boat returning from a Genoese trading post in the Crimea put into the Sicilian port of Messina in October 1347 with a crew of dead and dying men, their bodies swollen and blackened. The mysterious disease that afflicted them, which had already swept through India and the Middle and Near East, spread rapidly via the trading routes that the great Italian mercantile cities of Genoa and Venice maintained with the Levant. So began, in Europe, the outbreak of bubonic plague called in its own day 'the death' or 'the great pestilence', but now commonly referred to as the Black Death, from an adaptation into English in the nineteenth century of a Continental term originating in seventeenth-century Scandinavia. The term is sometimes extended to cover the further major outbreaks of plague in England in 1361 (particularly severe), 1368–9, 1371, 1375, 1390 and 1405; for it must be remembered that every summer brought with it a threat of the recurrence of plague, as of other epidemics. But the Black Death of 1348–9 was altogether exceptional, and in terms of loss of life it may well have been the greatest natural catastrophe ever to strike Europe and Asia. The plague first came ashore in England in June 1348, probably at Melcombe (now part of Weymouth) in Dorset, spread from there and from other South Coast ports during the late summer and early autumn, and then after a brief lull burst with full fury in the early months of 1349, striking London as early as January. Of England's total estimated population of 4–5 million, probably 1.5–2 million died, most of them in the next eight months.

The affliction began with swellings in the groin and armpits which grew to hard lumps the size of a small egg. These swellings caused intense pain, and soon began to ooze blackened blood and pus, while the rest of the body broke out in boils and black blotches and crusted suppurating sores. Death, after shivering fits, violent pain, increasing feebleness and vomiting of blood, usually came within three days, often much sooner; few who became infected by the disease survived. The bacillus that caused the disease lived in the black rats which came in the boats from the East, and was transmitted by fleas, though this of course was not known or suspected by medieval physicians. The disease could spread in two ways, by flea-bite and by respiratory infection, the latter being more virulent though less common. Everything issuing from the body of the victim in the throes of plague – breath, sweat, blackened blood, urine and excrement – was exceptionally foul-smelling.

Those who lived in poor and close-knit communities were hardest hit, and whole villages and religious communities disappeared. The poorer parts of towns fared no better: in London the ceremonies of burial were abandoned, and hastily dug mass-burial pits soon began to overflow. It was said that there were not enough living to bury the dead, and there were certainly not enough priests to give all the dying the last sacraments: one bishop gave permission for laymen, and even laywomen, to hear the confessions of the dying. Those who were wealthy tended to have better chances of survival: they did not live so close to their neighbours, or in straw-thatched dwellings infested by rats, and they had the means to isolate themselves and to escape from danger. So Machaut, in *Le Jugement dou Roy de Navarre*, describes the plague in Reims from the comparative security of his town house, while the ten young ladies and gentlemen of Boccaccio's *Decameron* leave Florence, where plague is likewise raging, to spend the time in villas and gardens in the country around. There they concentrate on eating and drinking well, amusing themselves, telling stories, having picnics, and generally doing all the things that the plague tracts (practical pamphlets with survival hints) quite sensibly advised – for those who could afford it – to keep the plague at bay. The pope didn't succumb to the plague, perhaps because he took to sitting between two roaring fires in his palace at Avignon: this was supposed to protect him from putrid vapours, but its effectiveness was probably in keeping away the fleas. Two arch-bishops of Canterbury, on the other hand, whether from bad luck or bad management, died of plague, John Offord in May 1349, after an incumbency of only eight months, and his successor, Thomas Bradwardine, on 26 August of the same year.

It was a year that ought to have shaken English society to its foundations and left an indelible mark on all who lived through it. The comparatively muted nature of the response in England to the Black Death of 1349, its lack of impact, for instance, on the themes and images of writers and painters, is therefore puzzling, though modern writers have done their best to make things more exciting, indulging themselves with vivid accounts of a general decline into debauchery, feverish outbreaks of penitence, pro-cessions of flagellants, and a descent into morbid and diseased imaginings which eventually led to the Waning of the Middle Ages. Philip Ziegler, in one of the standard books on the Black Death, is a historian who has contributed to the '1349 and all that' version of history: 'The sharp fall in moral standards which was noticed in so many parts of Europe in the years after the Black Death was nowhere more striking than in London.'[8] His evidence for this comes from monastic chroniclers, in other words, it is non-existent, since monastic chroniclers had a vested interest in sharp falls in moral standards: history, properly speaking, con-sisted of nothing else.

Millard Meiss, in his classic study, *Painting in Florence and Siena after the Black Death*, argues, on the contrary, that the plague led, not to excesses of debauchery and morbidity, but to a renewed sense of the value of the religious life, an increase in sobriety and asceticism, and a flood of religious endowments. Even the famous fresco of *The Triumph of Death* in the Campo Santo at Pisa, fam-iliarly cited as an example of the influence of the Black Death in promoting morbidity, has been authoritatively redated to a decade or more earlier, and probably before 1333.[9]

In England, the rapid growth of chantry chapels, where priests were endowed by bequest to say masses in perpetuity for the soul of the deceased, argues for a similarly undebauched and pious response. More striking, though, in England, is the continuity which is to be seen in institutions and communities, customary observances, law and civil government. There was no breakdown in public order, no halt in the collection of taxes, no significant cessation of religious appointments and observances. The routines of existence showed their customary tenacity. As for debauchery, quite the reverse: Langland complains in *Piers Plowman* about the number of marriages for money rather than love that have been contracted 'sethe this pestelences' (C. X. 269), suggesting something of the scramble for inheritances unexpectedly fallen in. The grandiose plans for the rebuilding of Winchester Cathedral may have gone by the board because of the plague, but Edward III's massive programme for the renovation and refurbishing of the royal palace at Windsor hardly faltered, and the elaborate feast of the Order of the Garter was held as usual on St George's Day, 1349, with 300 knights and 300 ladies present at the jousts and festivities.

We should be warned, therefore, against thinking of 1349 as a time of apocalypse, or even as a watershed in the economic history of England. Indeed, Alan Macfarlane has argued that the 'peasant society', which is traditionally supposed to have begun to break up after the Black Death, had long disappeared in England (if it had ever existed) and that both individualism and capitalism were well advanced (it was 'a capitalist-market economy without factories').[10]

But England did become for a time definitely more prosperous: even if one cannot see in the mid fourteenth century an abrupt break with the past, one can see at least an acceleration and consolidation of existing trends. The general economic effect of the Black Death was to loosen manorial ties by encouraging estate workers to go off in search of the higher wages which were now available because of the shortage of labour. The authorities deplored this wicked mobility and self-seeking, and enacted Statutes of Labourers in 1351 and frequently thereafter to freeze wages at pre-Black Death levels, but without much success: the generally increased social mobility of the second half of the fourteenth century is in an important way one of the consequences of the Black Death. The labour market was becoming more powerful than the webs of customary obligation that had characterized the old manorial economy, and the increasing practice of commuting estate services for money rents assisted in the process. While wages rose because of the shortage of labour, prices fell, and then stabilized, because of the surplus in production. The acreage under cultivation shrank, but it was the best land that remained, only the marginal land which had been ploughed during the days of overpopulation being abandoned. There was for a time a windfall of unexpected inheritances such as made John Chaucer rich and gave Geoffrey, eventually, his opportunity for social elevation. One would not wish to make too much of this paradox, as for instance in claiming that it was the Black Death that made Chaucer's poetry possible, but recent research has revealed how much new wealth was created, for people who were not traditionally very wealthy, by the Black Death.[11]

The Chaucer family was in Southampton, we recall, during the plague year and did not return to London until the autumn of 1349, by which time the worst was over. Chaucer no doubt heard a lot about the plague in subsequent years, but its impact on his poetry is small. He says of the Reeve of the General Prologue that the estate servants were 'adrad of hym as of the deeth' (*Canterbury Tales*, I. 605), but the effect of this is no more than trivialising hyperbole. In the Pardoner's Tale, though death is a potent presence throughout, it is the rioters who become animated and indignant about the ravages of the false traitor Death in 'this pestilence' (VI. 679). The Old Man of the tale has a different understanding of death, and the story as a whole rests on those contrasts of bodily and spiritual life and death that inspire the Gospels and inspire too the austere didacticism of the Danse Macabre (as in John Lydgate's poem of that name), which has nothing to do with morbid obsessions about death. If there were no Chaucer biographers looking for the significant impact of the Black Death in his poetry, no one would think of these allusions as needing explaining. It certainly does not look like evidence of memories so terrible that they had to be erased.

How does one explain the comparatively muted response to the Black Death, and the speed with which normal life was resumed, in England at least? Familiarity with disaster, in the form of famine and epidemics, was one factor, and the lack of global communication was another: the full nature of the visitation took a long time to make itself known. Prosperity helped, and so did religion. The Christian faith is not outstandingly good at dealing with the psychological impact of disasters that are due to human weakness and wickedness, like world wars, or the Holocaust, but it is unrivalled in its capacity to give meaning to the inexplicable, to console where nothing is to be done but suffer. There is also a more fundamental and pragmatic quality in human beings which helps explain the reaction, or lack of it, to the plague. The disease had this character: those who contracted it died; those who did not were not ill. It was not generally 'lowering'. To survive some natural disaster is a source of invigoration, whatever the pain of bereavement and of being a witness to suffering. It was good, and unexpected, to be alive. 'Historians often argue that the horrors of pestilence made late medieval men and women preoccupied with death and filled their art and literature with fantasies of mortality,' says Du Boulay, 'but the most striking historical consequence of the Black Death seems to have been a sharper appetite for a better life.'[12]

CHAUCER'S EDUCATION; CHAUCER'S LATIN

For Chaucer's early biographers it was, of course, very desirable that the poet should have attended one or other of the ancient universities; conscious of the invidiousness of choice, they compromised by sending him to both. Another tradition has grown up more recently, again largely based on wishful thinking, that Chaucer was a student at the Inner Temple. It is derived from a passing comment made by Thomas Speght in the life of Chaucer prefixed to his 1598 edition of the *Workes*, where, speaking of the friendship of Chaucer and Gower, he says:

> It seemeth that both these learned men were of the inner Temple: for not many yeeres since, Master *Buckley* did see a Record in the same house, where *Geoffrey Chaucer* was fined two shillings for beating a Franciscane fryer in Fleetstreete. ('Chaucer's Life', sig. b. ii)

William Buckley was indeed the person to have seen such a record, if it existed, since he was in Speght's time a bencher of the Inner Temple and the official responsible for the preservation and care of the Inner Temple records. The records themselves have disappeared, but comparable records from Lincoln's Inn, another of the Inns of Court, survive from 1422 onwards and do regularly show fines, ranging from 1*s*.3*d*. to 3*s*.8*d*., for fighting and other disorderly conduct. Fleet Street bounds the Inner Temple on the north.

It is clear that no general education, and probably not much systematic legal education, was provided in the fourteenth century at the London Inns of Court (Lincoln's Inn, Gray's Inn, Middle Temple, Inner Temple), which were principally lodging-houses for law students. The Inns of Chancery provided basic legal training for chancery clerks, but Chaucer was not a chancery clerk, and his poetry reveals none of the specialized knowledge that might be expected if he had had such a training. What he knows of the law is what someone with his combined mercantile and court background would be likely to have known. He may have had some informal *ad hoc* tutorial association with an individual lawyer, such as might be the occasion of his appearing in a Temple record. But Chaucer could not have received the kind of general formal education at the Inns of Court that his modern biographers tend to wish upon him. From early in the fifteenth century, it is true, the Inns of Court were beginning to provide a quasi-university education, not specifically directed towards the law, for the sons of the aristocracy and gentry who did not want the specialized, primarily theological education provided by the universities. But there is no evidence that the Inns of Court performed any such function before about 1400, and it is therefore extremely unlikely that Chaucer received anything corresponding to a 'university education' at the Inner Temple.[13]

Meanwhile, one must reckon with Master Buckley's awareness of the prestige that might accrue to his society from Chaucer's alleged association with it, with Speght's inclination to find early evidence of Chaucer's crypto-Protestant hostility to the religious orders, and with the desire of modern scholars to find something useful for Chaucer to be doing during the blank years of the biographical record, 1361–5. No doubt there is also a certain satisfaction in picturing a Chaucer so youthfully energetic and unruly, as well as so properly disposed towards friars.

But all this would have to do with the 1360s. As far as the earlier period is concerned, the great desire to get Chaucer properly educated has also produced much speculation about schools he might have gone to in the city. The favourite, because it was the biggest, and best equipped with the books that scholars would like Chaucer to have had early access to, is the Almonry School of St Paul's Cathedral, about three minutes' walk from the house in Thames Street. It was run by the almoner, who supervised the cathedral's distribution of charitable gifts. The list of books given to the school in 1328 by the late almoner and master, William de Tolleshunt, contains grammars and encyclopaedias and books of philosophy, logic and law that Chaucer might have known, while the very large collection of eighty-four books (actually eighty-four items in forty-three volumes) bequeathed in 1358 by William Ravenstone, late almoner and master, includes standard classical authors (Ovid, Virgil, Statius), late Latin writers whom Chaucer knew, or knew of, such as Claudian and Maximian, and some miscellanies and *florilegia* of classical authors ('flowers from the great poets') such as a non-specialist reader might use to extend his reading without too much painful effort. Chaucer's time at St Paul's, if he ever went there, would have finished well before the books entered the school library in 1358, but he could presumably have had access to them before then.[14]

What can be said for certain, to leave aside such hypotheses for a moment, is that the children of a family like Chaucer's would, while still at home and quite young, have learnt the alphabet from a *tabella* of wood or horn, and then learnt to read and write the Hail Mary, the Our Father, the Creed and the Ten Commandments, in English, from a primer. Geoffrey, as a boy, would then have gone at the age of about 7 to a 'grammar school', that is, one that taught Latin, and received there his early formal education. All cathedrals and some collegiate churches had such schools, usually with just a single clergyman in charge, and more and more parish churches, especially the bigger ones in the cities, were setting them up. There was one, as we have seen, at St Paul's, a preparatory establishment for the cathedral school, and it may have served also as the song-school, where young boys were trained as choristers and meanwhile were taught elementary Latin. There is such a school in the Prioress's Tale, where the 'litel clergeon' (*Canterbury Tales*, VII. 503) goes when he is 7 years old. There were also grammar schools attached to some of the parish churches, and the foundations of this kind at St Martin's-le-Grand, near Aldersgate, and St Mary-le-Bow, in Cheapside (neither of them far away from where Chaucer lived), though formally recorded in the reign of Henry VI, were probably already flourishing in the fourteenth century. Founders of chantries, the newly fashionable form of religious endowment in the fourteenth century, often made provision for the chantry priest to keep a grammar school.

The education in such schools began with the learning by heart of the Latin Ave Maria, Paternoster and Creed (probably long before they were well understood, as with the 'litel clergeon' and his *Alma redemptoris mater* in the Prioress's Tale), followed by rote-learning of Latin paradigms, translation of set sentences from and into Latin, practice in simple Latin composition, and some reading of literary texts, principally from the point of view of grammatical explication. These texts included Aesop's *Fables*, the *Distichs* of Cato (short verse moral apophthegms), Virgil's First Eclogue, and student anthologies of 'gems from the poets' such as the *Liber Catonianus*. It was something of a grind. Nevertheless, it was taken seriously, and an alderman of 1312 has it on record that he wants his sons to stay at school until they can compose reasonably good verses in Latin.[15]

A word needs to be said about the extent of Chaucer's reading in Latin literature. The books he has been credited with a knowledge of by scholars enthusiastic that he should have read the books they have read (perhaps in the spirit of Chauntecler, in the Nun's Priest's Tale, VII. 3120–1) would have filled a good-sized monastic library, and clearly there has been some exaggeration. Chaucer was widely read, and used his reading intelligently, but he was not a scholar. Perhaps, if he had been, some of his characteristic independence of mind and audacity would have been knocked out of him. The mistake is to imagine Chaucer in the equivalent of a modern library, reaching down the collected works of the great Latin authors, or indeed possessing such books in any numbers. His acquaintance with books is likely to have been much more unsystematic than this, more reliant on borrowing and chance recommendations. Books were rare: if the Clerk of the General Prologue had 'twenty bookes' (I. 294) at his bed's head in reality rather than in his dreams, then he had a large library – and he, unlike Chaucer, was a professional scholar and a university man. Probably much of Chaucer's knowledge of classical writings came from anthologies and miscellanies containing extracts and purple passages, with or without authorship attributions, annotation and glosses. Characteristic of such manuscripts is Bodleian Library MS Auct. F. 1. 17, with extracts from Virgil, Ovid, Prudentius, Alan of Lille and the twelfth-century rhetoricians Geoffrey of Vinsauf (whose famous apostrophe to Friday Chaucer alludes to in the Nun's Priest's Tale, VII. 3347) and Matthew of Vendôme. Jankin's 'book of wikked wyves' in the Wife of Bath's Prologue (III. 685) is such a compilation, albeit one with a theme. Meanwhile, much of Chaucer's repertoire of Latin tags and *exempla* and miscellaneous general knowledge was derived from the moral and homiletic compilations of the friars, such as John of Wales's *Communiloquium*, and from encyclopaedias such as those of Vincent of Beauvais. It was an intelligent and busy man's short cut, the simpler syntax of medieval Latin prose presenting far fewer problems than classical Latin verse.[16]

Much of Chaucer's knowledge of the Latin classics was derived, further, from intermediaries: when he refers to Livy as his source in the Physician's Tale (VI. 1) he is using the version of Livy in the *Roman de la Rose*, which he does not refer to, and his knowledge of Claudian's *De raptu Proserpinae* is probably derived from the *Liber Catonianus*, already mentioned as an anthology of Latin used as a school reader. The stanza on the origin of dreams in *The Parliament of Fowls* (99–105) is closely parallel to a passage in another poem by Claudian, *De IV Consulatu Honorii*, but Pratt has shown that this too occurs in the *Liber Catonianus*. Pratt reminds us that such reading of the classics is not to be scorned: he suggests that Chaucer's knowledge of the *De raptu*, for instance, though less extensive, was more intensive than that of a professional scholar, was indeed 'natural, unpretentious and enduring' in a manner that makes allusion charming and effortless rather than forbiddingly learned.[17]

Nevertheless, Chaucer used French translations of Latin authors whenever he could: his knowledge of Ovid's *Metamorphoses* comes primarily from the *Ovide Moralisé*, with its ludicrous allegorizations, which no doubt gave him some amusement. He used French translations as a crib, going back to the original Latin, which he read with more difficulty, when he felt he needed to. This is how he translates Boethius's *De Consolatione Philosophiae*, following Jean de Meun's prose translation for the most part, but going back to the original Latin for the metres, where he suspects Jean de Meun may have been rather free. His translations of the metres are crabbed, literal and awkward, and show evidence of some labour in the working out and accurate communication of the sense of the Latin.

The implication of such an account of Chaucer's learning, and especially of his Latinity, is that modern scholars may have imposed upon him expectations more appropriate to a university-trained man. Likewise, the search for Chaucer's schools, of which we spoke earlier, may betray a modern preoccupation with formal education and a feeling that Chaucer must have had one. It neglects the importance of the wide-ranging but only partly formal education that boys received in the household of a great magnate, where they would have been sent to live and act as pages, like Chaucer, at quite an early age.[18]

If we look forward for a moment to Chaucer's future career as a civil servant, we find that the historian who has written most authoritatively on the growth of the civil service in the fourteenth century, and of the association of the new kind of civil servant with developments in education and literature, has this to say about Chaucer:

> How far a court training could under Edward III give a thorough culture to men, originating in the middle class of townsmen, and so remote from the clerical profession that the university had nothing to say to them, can well be illustrated by the career of that eminent civil servant, Geoffrey Chaucer.

And elsewhere: 'I am convinced that the excellent education which Geoffrey undoubtedly received was the education which the household of a king, or one of the greater magnates, could give to its junior members.'[19] Tout describes the fundamental changes that are taking place in the civil service, and the importance of Chaucer and his non-clerical background as symptoms of these changes. Though he acknowledges the importance that the Inns of Court were coming to have as the training-ground for the new breed of professional administrators, he takes it for granted that the foundation of Chaucer's own education was in the court and not in the Inns of Court, and dismisses the arguments of Manly and Rickert concerning the latter.

CHAUCER IN SERVICE AS A PAGE

The earliest documentary evidence of Geoffrey Chaucer's existence is contained on two leaves accidentally surviving, in the binding of another book, from the household expense accounts of Elizabeth, Countess of Ulster, wife of Prince Lionel, the second surviving son of Edward III (*Life-Records*, pp.13–18). The records cover two and a half years from July 1356 to January 1359. The first mention of Chaucer is of a payment of 4*s*. (about £80 in modern terms, multiplying, crudely, by 400) to 'Galfrido Chaucer' in 1357, after 4 April and before Easter (which fell that year on 9 April), for a paltock (a short cloak or cassock with sleeves such as pages wore) bought from 'cuidam paltokmakare Londonie', and another payment on the same day of 3*s*. for a pair of black and red hose and a pair of shoes. All this was to get young Geoffrey properly set up for the celebration of Easter, which was to take place that year in London. On 20 May there is payment of 2*s*. for expenses incurred in providing 'Galfrido Chaucer Londonie' with 'garniture' for the Sunday before Pentecost at Woodstock. On 20 December Chaucer receives 2*s*.6*d*. for necessaries in preparation for the feast of the Nativity, celebrated at the royal residence at Hatfield, a few miles north-east of Doncaster, in Yorkshire (not to be confused with the more famous Hatfield House in Hertfordshire). The house at Hatfield was at this time in the keeping of Queen Philippa, until her son Edmund of Langley should come of age.

Another guest at Hatfield that Christmas was the young Earl of Richmond, better known now as John of Gaunt (he was born at Ghent), who was to play an important part in Chaucer's life. He was 17, Chaucer 14, and imagination could easily become over-excited about the nature of the meeting that might have occurred between them. Richmond probably had other things on his mind: on the same day that Chaucer was paid for his 'necessaries', a servant of Henry, Duke of Lancaster, was paid for bringing letters to the countess from Henry's daughter Blanche. She was to marry Richmond on 19 May 1359. Was this their first meeting, or were the letters to say she couldn't come?

Chaucer may well have had his own preoccupations. The same accounts record payments 'pro factura garniture' and 'pro factura i corsetti' to one 'Philippa Pan.' (the fullstop stands for the elevated *punctus* which always appears after her name in these records), which show that she too was a member of the Countess of Ulster's household. It is not entirely clear who this person is. It is possible that 'Pan.' is an abbreviation for *panetaria* ('panter', the person in charge of the pantry, or bread-store), though the word is regularly abbreviated 'panet'', with a loop from the *t* as the customary mark of contraction, elsewhere in the records. It is possible that the reference is to Philippa, daughter of Sir Payne (Paon) de Roet, though again one might have expected 'de Roet' rather than 'Pan.' to be used to identify her. If so, this Philippa is the elder sister of Katherine, who was later to be John of Gaunt's mistress, and may be the Philippa who later became Chaucer's wife. She too was at Hatfield for the Christmas of 1357.

Queen Philippa, who presided over the Christmas festivities, was the daughter of William I, Count of Hainault, and had married Edward III in 1328, when she was 14 and he 16. She fulfilled, through her long life (she died in 1369), all the duties of a queen, even to the point of perhaps oversupplying the kingdom with heirs to the throne (see table 2). Her eldest son, Edward of Woodstock, later called the Black Prince, was born in 1330 when she was 16,

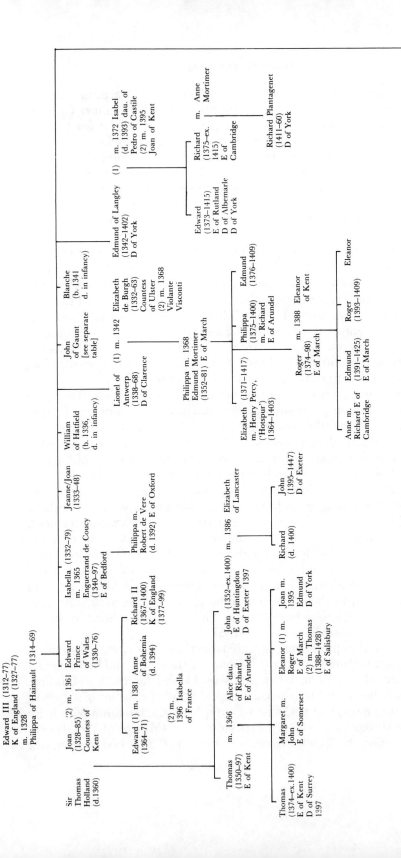

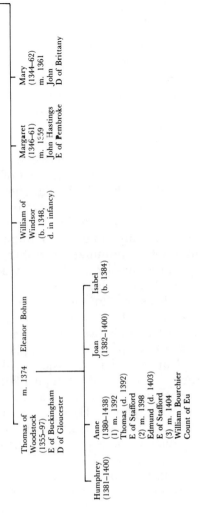

Table 2. The House of Edward III, Plantagenet

and she had twelve children in all, of whom the last, Thomas of Woodstock, was born in 1355, when she was 41. Of the five daughters, three survived to be married, but, with so many brothers, none had even a sniff at the succession. Of the seven sons, five survived infancy and variously affected the course of history, though none became king. Lionel of Antwerp (royal sons were familiarly called by the place of their birth until granted their first official title), the second son to survive, though actually the queen's fifth child, was betrothed in 1342 at the age of 4 to one of the great heiresses of England, Elizabeth, daughter of William de Burgh, Earl of Ulster, herself then 10 years old. Lionel became Earl of Ulster by right of marriage in 1347, and was created Duke of Clarence in 1362. His only child was Philippa, born in 1355, whose marriage in 1368 to Edmund Mortimer, Earl of March, created the circumstances that led to the eventual 'Yorkist' claim to the throne and the Wars of the Roses.

The Countess of Ulster had at this time a separate financial provision from that of her husband, and kept a separate household, with several female attendants (*domicellae*), one or more clerks, esquires, yeomen (*valetti*) and pages, and a chaplain. The surrounding records make it clear that Chaucer, whose rank is not specified, was not at this time a *valettus*, or yeoman of the chamber (an attendant somewhere between an esquire and a page in the hierarchy of the *familia* or household). He was most probably a page, like the Thomas who is called a page in the records and, like Chaucer, received payment for a paltock. A page was a boy or youth anywhere between about 10 and 17 years old who was engaged as a servant and personal attendant in the household of a person of rank, to work there, in many quite menial kitchen and household tasks, and to be brought up, if he were lucky, in the usages of polite society. By this means he would acquire a patron, and so become part of the system of patronage which was the only secure avenue to a career in the public service in the Middle Ages. A page got his board and lodging free and was given clothing and other necessaries or else reimbursed for expenditure on such items. His pocket money came from his own family, and there could be great differences in both rank and disposable cash among the young attendants thus thrown together. The best household to be in, from the point of view of career prospects, was of course that of the king, but Chaucer, considering his background, did very well.

Life in the countess's household was marked by frequent travelling, chiefly to do the rounds of the estates and to keep royal feasts. In the few years covered by the records, the household was at Reading, London (for Easter, 1357), Windsor (for St George's Day, 1357), Woodstock, near Oxford (for Pentecost, 1357), Doncaster (in July 1357), Hatfield, Anglesey, Bristol and Liverpool. There were outings to the Tower of London to see the lions whose keeper was paid 6*s*.8*d*. on 6 November 1358, to the tournament at Smithfield for which the countess had cushions of tapestry made, and perhaps to see the magnificent entry into London laid on in May 1357 for King John of France, captured at Poitiers and arriving in England as the Black Prince's prisoner, riding towards Westminster on a great white horse, the Black Prince at his side on a humble palfrey. Preparations for the betrothal of the countess's baby daughter to the Earl of March would bestir the household, as would the arrangements for the funeral of the queen mother Isabella at the Franciscan church of Newgate, in London, on 27 November 1358, or for attendance at the splendid wedding of Richmond and Blanche of Lancaster, at Reading on 19 May 1359, and the great three-day tournament that accompanied it.

The period of Chaucer's service as a page is not known, but it probably began not long before the records of 1356 commence, and ended certainly not long after they break off. By the autumn of 1359, when Lionel came of age, his and the countess's households were merged and Chaucer became officially one of the prince's attendants. Meanwhile, he passed many of his formative years closely involved in the day-to-day activities of a royal household. Much of his time would be spent working in the kitchen and the household and in learning the routines of courtly life, such as how to wait on the superior members of the household at table and how to attend them on formal and ceremonial occasions without picking his nose and scratching himself and otherwise betraying his inattention. There would be much physical and military exercise, including hand-ball (*jeu de la paume*), riding and elementary swordsmanship, and we should not assume that Chaucer found all this boring. There were music and dancing lessons, singing and some poetry, though not much, for a person of Chaucer's background. Richard Firth Green is probably right to emphasize the comparative menialness of the life of the 'page' (Chaucer is never specifically said to have been one), and to suggest that we set aside 'romantic notions we may have harbored of pages as sprightly young gentlemen with neat tunics and bobbed hair'. Kate Mertes draws attention to the variety of roles performed by these *pueri* or *pagetti* in a fourteenth-century noble household, and the further difficulty of extrapolating much that is definite about the mid fourteenth century from the predominantly fifteenth-century evidence.[20]

There would of course be differences in the duties assigned to different young attendants, in accordance with their abilities, inclinations and social background. Chaucer surely impressed himself on others at an early stage as outstandingly literate, and was steered towards a career as a secretary and junior diplomat. Education at court was not a formal and self-conscious activity, even though one of the household clerks might be given the task of knocking some Latin into the heads of the pages. There was no regular school or school hours, and a boy or girl (girls were as much part of the household as boys) learnt as much as he or she was willing and able to learn. A clerk who was a good scholar, and who would 'gladly teche', could do a lot with a bright and eager pupil. So Chaucer had the chance to improve his Latin and to extend his knowledge of Latin literature while he was a page at court. He would also acquire, if he did not have it already, complete fluency in French, which was the language of formal or polite intercourse in the household, with English used more in off-duty moments. He would become familiar with French books of religious instruction and books of chivalric and courtly etiquette, and above all with the fashionable French love-allegories and romances, as well as with the somewhat less fashionable English romances imitative of the French, such as those in the Auchinleck manuscript (Edinburgh, National Library of Scotland, Advocates' MS 19. 2. 1).

CHAUCER'S SERVICE AS A *VALETTUS*; THE CAMPAIGN OF 1359–1360

There is record of a payment from the king's wardrobe on 1 March 1360 for the ransom of Geoffrey Chaucer after his capture in France: 'Galfrido Chaucer capto per inimicos in partibus Francie in subsidium redempcionis sue' (*Life-Records*, p. 23). The sum paid was £16, which seems to have been the going rate for a *valettus*, and quite a large sum of money. The king would be responsible for ransoming those who were in the service of his lieutenants, so the record does not indicate that Chaucer was at this time in the king's service. It is clear, in fact, from a later record that Chaucer was in the company which Lionel, Earl of Ulster, led to France in September 1359 for the 1359–60 campaign. It was in 1359, we recall from his evidence at the Scrope–Grosvenor trial, that Chaucer was *armeez*, and it was at this time too that he must have been raised to the rank of *valettus*, or yeoman.

Prince Lionel's was not a large company, consisting of six knights, thirty-two esquires, forty archers and an unspecified number of *valetti* and other attendants. The Earl of March, by contrast, had 600 men of the specified ranks, and Richmond 400. Knights received 4*s.* a day while on active service overseas, esquires 2*s.*, archers 12*d.* and *valetti* 6*d.* Judging from Chaucer's evidence in his testimony at the Scrope–Grosvenor trial, it must have been on this very campaign that he saw the Scrope arms displayed at Rethel, near Reims. Reims had great symbolic importance as the city in which the kings of France were traditionally crowned, and Edward III made it the major target of the 1359–60 campaign, intending to have himself crowned there. Lionel's company was in the division led by the Black Prince that took the route from Calais to Reims via Rethel, a town commanding the crossing of the Aisne. There was action there, to which Chaucer refers, during a holding operation by the French, but he does not say where he was captured. He could have been involved in the fighting in the area during the siege of Reims, or in the advance into Burgundy after the siege had been abandoned on 11 January 1360. Both Machaut and Deschamps, incidentally, the former an old man, the latter a very young one, were in Reims during the siege, though it was hardly the ideal occasion for literary conversations with the young Chaucer. A truce was made on 10 March, soon after Chaucer's release, and most of the English army was back in England by the end of May. So ended Chaucer's eventful first trip abroad.

The campaign of 1359–60, in which Edward reasserted his claim to the throne of France, was prompted by the failure of the French to keep to the terms of the treaty agreed after the battle of Poitiers in 1356, especially in respect of the colossal ransom demanded for the return of King John II of France, captured at Poitiers and held as a prisoner in England. The English commanders were not unconscious, too, that France was in some disarray after citizen uprisings in Paris and the fierce peasant rebellions known as the *Jacquerie,* and with the continuing havoc caused by the unemployed mercenary soldiery of the so-called

'Free Companies'. They were perhaps anticipating some easy pickings. But things did not work out as they expected: the absence of the chivalrous and certifiably high-minded John II was a real advantage to the French armies, who were now under the command of the Dauphin Charles. His strategy was to avoid pitched battles, which the English at this time had a tendency to win, and to deprive the enemy of supplies by laying waste the territory through which they advanced. The English armies on this occasion by-passed Paris, laid unsuccessful siege to Reims, drifted rather aimlessly south-east into Burgundy, plundering and burning, suffered a very cold and wet winter, and were eventually, in May 1360, glad to settle for the terms of the Treaty of Bretigny – a reduced but still large ransom for King John and large territorial concessions to England in the west and south-west of France. Edward meanwhile gave up his claim to the throne of France.

Chaucer was back in France in the autumn of 1360 for the formal ceremonies accompanying the ratification of the Treaty of Bretigny at Calais on 24 October. The Earl of Ulster, along with the Black Prince and Henry, Duke of Lancaster, was present at the formal signing, having left England around 13 October. In the financial accounts of the expedition that happen to survive, compiled by Andrew de Budeston, a member of Lionel's household, there is record of a payment of 9*s.* to 'Galfrido Chaucer' (*Life-Records*, p. 19) for carrying letters to England. This would be a characteristic employment for a *valettus*: they were probably private rather than state letters, the carriage of which would have been paid from royal funds. Chaucer presumably left Calais before the main party, but he would have followed the same itinerary that Lionel took on 31 October–3 November, and which Andrew specifies: Calais, Deal, Canterbury, Boughton, Ospringe, Sittingbourne, Dartford and Rochester. This was not the first time, nor was it to be the last by any means, that Chaucer travelled the route by which he sent his pilgrims to Canterbury some years later.

CHAUCER AND WAR

The modern view of medieval war and chivalry is likely to be touched by scepticism, but we should not imagine Chaucer taking our rather jaundiced view of proceedings such as those of 1359–60, or think of his enthusiasm for soldiering as being necessarily half-hearted. The modern reader tends to look for the cynical element of *realpolitik* in the theatrical gestures of medieval chivalry, and to succumb too readily to the apparent risibility of much of it. Edward III, for instance, made a habit of being persuaded by Queen Philippa not to take ruthless vengeance on those who had displeased him, like the unfortunate carpenters whose wooden grandstand collapsed at a tournament in Cheapside in 1331, or the burghers of Calais who had so inconsiderately refused to surrender their besieged town in 1347. We might think there was a good political reason for acquiring a reputation as a ruthless war-leader who on appropriate occasions might be merciful; perhaps there is a similar staginess in Theseus's submission to the pleas of the queen and her ladies in the Knight's Tale (I. 1748). There seems to us, too, a large amount of contrivance in chivalric warfare: Froissart's story of the blind King John of Bohemia trying desperately to take part in the battle of Crecy and ending up, inevitably, cut to pieces, along with those devoted knights who had hitched their horses to his, provokes more bewilderment than admiration, as do the almost comical attempts of John of France at Poitiers to get himself captured by the right class of English person. But the demands made by the modern reader upon medieval chivalry are as unhistorical as the similar demands made upon medieval religion. There is something prim in the modern reader's insistence that the age should live up to ideals which the same reader would consider the greatest nonsense in themselves. There is a misunderstanding too of the pageant-like ritualistic element in both chivalry and religion, which had a practical and ideologically cohesive function, even though it may not look very sensible to us.

In an important sense, war was indeed a game, engaged in partly to prevent the principal participants from getting up to other kinds of mischief. Edward III's comparatively trouble-free reign was in some measure due to his success as a war-leader in keeping his barons busy and profitably employed in France. There was also a close social bond between persons of rank who were opponents in the game, far closer than that between knights and ordinary soldiers on the same side, especially when so many of those who did the actual hand-to-hand fighting were mercenaries. The practice of ransoming prisoners was a mark of the well-regulated relationship that existed between the English knights and their French opponents. Next to looting, looking for ransomable prisoners, or for suitable captors to surrender to, occupied much of their energy during battle. Ransomable prisoners, once captured, could be traded for immediate advantage among the captors, though there was the danger of the prisoners, on a good day, beginning to outnumber their captors and having to be ransomed quickly. Ransoms were important for personal advancement and could be the foundation of the fortune of a successful soldier; they were a vital resource for those who did not receive the traditional support of a feudal liege lord.

The camaraderie that existed between the opposing knights did not stop them from engaging on occasion in ritual exchange of insults, but it meant they could also cooperate in making plans to find a convenient level site for a battle, where the horses could have a good run. The action of Lord Burghersh in inviting the French commander of the besieged garrison at Cormicy to come and inspect the mines that would blow up him and his castle, if they did not surrender, seems very civilized. Froissart, who probably never actually saw a battle in his life, writes always of battles as a connoisseur speaks of works of art: he is not so much interested in military strategy and its consequences, or even in who won, as in fine feats of arms and displays of chivalry. When he cannot find any, he invents them, as in his account of the brave exploits of Sir Robert Salle during the Rising of 1381. The whole story is a complete fabrication.[21]

Chaucer is not Froissart, but to some extent he absorbed and was influenced by the ideology of chivalry, with its snobbish disregard for the lives of the non-gentle, its theatricality, its occasionally powerful idealism. He may in later years have favoured a policy of peace with France (as is perhaps suggested in *Melibee*), but this is because it was the policy of the court party, not because of disillusion with military chivalry. It is an anachronistic modernism that makes of Chaucer's Knight a ruthless and cold-blooded mercenary killer, a view that takes its origin not from history but from the modern horror of war and the determination to make Chaucer share the views of his modern admirers.[22] The portrait of the Knight in the General Prologue, on the contrary, breathes the spirit of the old chivalry, perhaps with a self-conscious nostalgia, and his exploits have many points of correspondence with those of Henry, Duke of Lancaster, Edward's most loyal commander and comrade-in-arms. Geoffroi de Charny, who bore the French oriflamme at Poitiers and died rather than yield it up, writes in his *Livre de Chevalerie* of the almost religious dedication of the true *chevalier*. In fact, he says, knights are more truly dedicated than monks, who can eat and sleep regularly.

Car qui voudroit considerer les pains, travaux, doulours, mesaises,
grans parurs, perils, froisseures et bleceures, que li bon chevalier,
qui l'ordre de chevalerie maintiennent ainsi comme il doivent, ont
a souffrir et seuffrent mainte fois, il n'est nulle religion ou l'en en
souffre tant comme font cil bon chevalier . . . [23]

For whoever thinks about the pains, labours, sufferings, discomforts,
tedious preparations, perils, freezings and woundings that the good
knight, who maintains the order of chivalry as he should, has to
bear and often does bear, there is no religious order where one
suffers so much as does the good knight.

One recalls how closely Chaucer's Knight, with his austerity of
life and dedication to the Christian cause, approximates to the
condition of the ideal monk, while Chaucer's real Monk (also one
who 'rides out', an *outridere*) lives the life of self-indulgence and
dedication to 'venery' that characterize a decayed knighthood.[24]

There are also qualities to admire in Chaucer's Squire, who is
portrayed in the very springtime of his chivalry, and it is clear
from the Knight's Tale that Chaucer could share and catch the
spirit of the tournament, whether the fervour of expectation, and
the desire to be one of the day's chosen participants (I. 2106–16),
or the morning's excited anticipation of the day's events, with
armourers hammering, horses' hooves clattering, common
people gawping, and the experts out in force guessing the likely
winners:

> The paleys ful of peple up and doun,
> Heere thre, ther ten, holdynge hir questioun,
> Dyvynynge of thise Thebane knyghtes two.
> Somme seyden thus, somme seyde 'it shal be so';
> Somme helden with hym with the blake berd,
> Somme with the balled, somme with the thikke herd.
>
> (I. 2513–18)

The fighting itself is described with great vigour, Chaucer
employing the heavy alliteration (2602–16) which he considers
specially suitable for battle poetry and uses elsewhere only in the
description of the battle of Actium in the legend of Cleopatra
(*Legend of Good Women*, 635–49). It has been argued, by those who
wish Chaucer to share their distaste for fighting, that there is an
element of parody or of self-conscious preciousness in this deliberate use of an alien style, but such readers would be likely to find
all traditional English alliterative poetry parodic, and do.

How easy it is to find parody in Chaucerian allusions where there is none can be demonstrated in a familiar misreading of a passage in the Knight's Tale. Palamon and Arcite, fighting in the grove like fierce lions and tigers, are momentarily left in pitched combat while the narrative turns to Theseus:

> Up to the ancle foghte they in hir blood.
> And in this wise I lete hem fightyng dwelle,
> And forth I wole of Theseus yow telle.   (I.1660–2)

Laughter has greeted the apparent ridiculousness of this (how can the narrator *afford* to leave them for a moment if they are already . . . ? and so on), and it has been construed as evidence of a parodic and subversive tendency throughout this story of war and chivalry. We are told, says Howard, 'that they are fighting up to the ankles in their own blood – a circumstance that would be alarming enough if they were standing in a tub. Chaucer, having made the remark, hurries on, leaving them in this ridiculous posture'. The misreading is simply explained: they are not up to their ankles in blood in a field that is all ankle-deep in blood, but up to the ankles in blood in their *chausses* or metal shoes. This, allowing for an element of conventional hyperbole, was a common and grisly circumstance in medieval battle, when blood from any leg wound would run down into the shoe, where it would quickly accumulate. Froissart gives us a report on just such a circumstance, in a perfectly matter-of-fact way.[25]

War and chivalry are not Chaucer's favourite subject, admittedly, and there may be an implied critique in this comparative silence, but there is no doubt that when, in the Franklin's Tale, he describes Arviragus leaving Brittany to spend a year or two in England in chivalric pursuits (*Canterbury Tales*, V. 811–12) he expects us to cheer him on, and not complain that he is neglecting his wife.[26]

2

Early Career:
The 1360s

Lionel, Earl of Ulster, was appointed as the king's viceroy in Ireland, by virtue of the earldom he had inherited through his wife, on 1 July 1361, and landed in Dublin in September of that year. He remained in Ireland, on and off, until November 1366, mostly frustrated in his dutiful attempts to subdue the Irish to English rule. The Countess Elizabeth went with him, but died in 1363. There is no record of Chaucer, whom we last saw attached to Lionel's household in October 1360, having been with him in Ireland, nor is it clear when he was transferred to the king's service, where he is recorded as a *valettus* on 20 June 1367. These are the lost years in the Chaucer biographical record, apart from the Spanish record of 1366, and it is impossible to know what precisely Chaucer was doing during this period, though it is likely to have been some service in a royal household, in England or in Aquitaine. It is important, however, to try to convey some impression of the general nature of his experience during these years, as a young man in service in a royal household, and it is a task that can be reliably undertaken. But first, there are the facts of his life and journeys.

Chaucer's Service as a *Valettus* and Esquire to Edward III

On 20 June 1367 Geoffrey Chaucer was granted a life annuity of 20 marks (£13.6s.8d.) payable at the exchequer, in Westminster

Palace, in half-yearly instalments at Michaelmas and Easter.* The
granting of a life annuity was a normal means of remuneration for
royal servants. There is an interesting difference between the Latin
of the enrolment of the patent for the grant (that is, the formal
registration for the official record) and the Anglo-French of the
writ authorizing the sealing of the patent at the office of the Privy
Seal (that is, the instrument of enactment), which is given the
same date but may well be later. In the former, Chaucer is styled
'dilectus vallectus noster', in the latter 'nostre ame esquier' (*Life-
Records*, p. 123). It would be usual to presume that the former is
correct, the usage of the French being more casual and informal,
though there remains some ambiguity in the matter. It is not until
the entry of the half-yearly payment on 2 June 1372 that Chaucer
is styled, in Latin, 'armigero regis', that is, king's esquire, and this
is long after he has been styled *esquier* in other records, and quite
clearly was one.

Payments of the annuity were kept up with exceptional regularity until Chaucer transferred it to John Scalby in 1388, though
this regularity was due, as the editors of the *Life-Records* point out
(p. 534), not to special royal favour but to Chaucer's own care in
having payment assigned to safe and convenient sources and to
his own personal knowledge of the complexities of exchequer practice. Nor do the terms 'dilectus noster' and 'nostre ame' have
anything to do with any special affection that Chaucer was held
in by Edward III, as is supposed in popular biographies of
Chaucer:[1] they are the standard bureaucratic phrases, no more
than the relic of the previous existence, as domestic offices of the
royal household, of what were now government agencies. The king
probably had about as much knowledge of the phrasing of such
documents as he did of Chaucer.

The grant of 20 June 1367 may mark Chaucer's promotion to
the rank of *valettus*, or yeoman of the chamber, in the king's
household, but it is more likely, in the light of other evidence, and
since it is granted 'pro bono servicio', that it is a recognition,
in the form of more generous or more secure and permanent
remuneration, of past service in that rank and perhaps an earnest

---

* Financial records of the time refer to either marks or pounds (a mark is two-
thirds of a pound, that is, 13*s*. 4*d*.), though detailed accounting is done in £. *s.*
d. The survival of marks, a much less flexible unit for computing purposes, is
analogous to the survival of roman numerals after the introduction of arabic.

of promotion to esquire. How long Chaucer had been in the royal service, and when he transferred from the household of the Earl of Ulster, is not known. What seems in Chaucer's case a rather long drawn-out process contrasts sharply with the meteoric rise of Arcite, in the Knight's Tale, who spends only a year or two as 'page of the chambre' to Emelye (I. 1427) before Theseus, recognizing his great merit, promotes him to be a squire of his own chamber, 'And gaf hym gold to mayntene his degree' (I. 1441). Arcite skips a whole rank in the usual promotional ladder, and Chaucer is perhaps reflecting ruefully on the difference between fiction and reality.[2]

As an esquire of the king's household, Chaucer was entitled not only to financial remuneration but also to gifts of clothes to wear at special court festivals (*Life-Records*, pp. 94–103). Such clothes were not only useful to the recipient and a valuable perquisite of office: they were also, as a livery, a visible and distinguishing mark of a great lord's patronage, an assertion of his power, and a means to ensure that his servants did not wear anyone else's. In November 1368, 'Geffrey Chaucer' is one of forty 'esquiers', among nearly 600 other members of the royal household (including thirteen 'valletz de la chambre du roi', fifty-eight 'valletz des offices', and thirteen 'damoiselles', one of them 'Philippa Chaucer'), to be granted robes for Christmas, to be delivered by the clerk of the great wardrobe. In the following year, a payment of 20*s*. is recorded for a summer robe ('roba estivalis') for Chaucer, among the fifty-five esquires of the royal household, for Whitsun, which fell on 20 May. Esquires are called 'scutiferis et servientibus hospicii' in this record, 'scutiferis' (shield-bearers) designating one of the traditional military roles of esquires. Later in the same year, on 1 September, there is a writ of allowance for liveries of mourning at the funeral of Queen Philippa, who had died on 15 August. Chaucer appears here among eighty-eight 'esquiers de meindre [less] degree' and not among sixty-three 'esquiers de greindre estat': whatever distinction of rank is implied here, it did not affect the entitlement to funeral garb, which was set for both groups at three ells of black cloth. Meanwhile, 'Phelippe Chaucere', among the 'damoiselles', got six.

Philippa Chaucer, who may or may not be the 'Philippa Pan.' of the Ulster records described earlier, was married to Chaucer before 12 September 1366, when she is named as receiving a life annuity on the exchequer of 10 marks (£6.13*s*. 4*d*.) as a *domicella* of the chamber to Queen Philippa. That she was at some time

Geoffrey Chaucer's wife is clear from later records of 1374 and 1381 (*Life-Records*, p. 68), and the fact that she is given her husband's surname in the 1366 grant rather than, as was common for young married women, her maiden name (unless it, also, was Chaucer) may indicate that she was well established and well known by this time as Chaucer's wife. She later received the gifts of clothing already mentioned.

If Philippa Chaucer is indeed the 'Philippa Pan.' of the Ulster record, and if that 'Philippa Pan.' is indeed the daughter of Payne (Paon) de Roet of Hainault, Guienne King of Arms, then Chaucer clearly made a 'correct' marriage. A young unlanded esquire did well to marry a lady of the queen's household and the daughter of a knight. On the other hand, his bride's father was himself a person of little account in England, and heralds and Kings of Arms, despite their resonant titles, were little higher than messengers and minstrels in terms of their status in the household. As to the children of Geoffrey and Philippa, the only one of whom we can be more or less certain is Thomas, who was born soon after the marriage, probably in 1367.[3]

If Philippa was, as we have assumed, the daughter of Sir Paon de Roet, then her sister was Katherine de Roet, who first married Sir Hugh de Swynford and later, after being his mistress for many years, John of Gaunt. By his marriage, it would appear, Chaucer's family connections were certainly to be interestingly enlarged. Such a consequence may well have been in the mind of the first person to make the connection between Philippa and Katherine, Robert Glover, Somerset Herald 1571–88. A great advantage of the connection, and one that was seized upon by Thomas Speght, in the Chaucer pedigree he concocts for his 1598 life of Chaucer, is that it enabled Chaucer's rather sparse family tree to be gloriously divaricated. Not only is the vintner's son now equipped with a very respectable set of descendants, including a son, Thomas, who enjoyed a distinguished career as a public servant and a granddaughter, Alice, who married the future Duke of Suffolk, but he has also acquired a spectacular collateral line through his relationship, ambiguous as it may have been initially, with John of Gaunt. Speght expounds these matters with some circumstance and satisfaction and has the Glover pedigree incorporated also in the decorative 'Progeny' page drawn up at his request (as he explains in 'Chaucer's Life'), with appropriate coats of arms displayed, by John Speed (see plate 3). The only link, it should be stressed, between Philippa Chaucer and Paon de Roet, apart from the record of 'Philippa Pan.' and the speculations of Glover and Speght, is the tomb of Thomas Chaucer at Ewelme, where the arms of Roet are found quartering those of Burghersh (Maud Burghersh was Thomas's wife). Even this is an odd substitute for what one might have expected and never appears, namely, Chaucer/Roet. Nevertheless, the Glover pedigree is now generally accepted, except by those who maintain that Thomas 'Chaucer' was really John of Gaunt's bastard son by Chaucer's wife.[4]

JOURNEYS ABROAD

Until recently, nothing was known of Chaucer's life between October 1360 and 20 June 1367. Then, in 1955, attention was drawn to documents from the royal archives of Navarre at Pamplona, which included a safe conduct, enrolled in the chancery register of Charles II of Navarre, issued to 'Geffroy de Chauserre escuier englois en sa compaignie trois compaignons' to cover the period from 22 February to Pentecost (24 May) 1366 (*Life-Records*, p. 64). The document had been first published in 1890, but escaped the attention of Chaucer scholars because the name was rendered as 'Chanserre': *n* and *u* are frequently indistinguishable in medieval manuscripts.[5]

It is possible that Chaucer and his three companions were on pilgrimage: pilgrims on their way to the shrine of St James of Compostella, in Galicia, the greatest shrine of medieval Europe, had to cross the Pyrenees at Roncesvalles and pass through the kingdom of Navarre, and they commonly received such safe conducts. But Lent was not the high season for pilgrimages. If Chaucer had been on official business, it is likely that it would have been specified on the safe conduct, but the possibility remains that he was on an unofficial, even secret mission connected with the affairs of Pedro (Peter) of Castile, who was about to figure large in English policy.

Pedro I had succeeded his father, Alfonso XI, on the throne of Castile and Leon in 1350, but his father also left him a number of bastard half-brothers, one of whom, Enrique (Henry), Count of Trastamare, set himself up as a rival claimant to the throne. He secured the support of the French, who disliked the way Pedro had been treating his French queen, Blanche of Bourbon, and of the pope, who was very eager to offer a paid diversion to the Free

Companies then threatening Avignon. Enrique entered Castile at the head of his army, with the formidable Bertrand du Guesclin as his field commander, early in 1366. On 22 March he was proclaimed Enrique II. Pedro fled to Bayonne, where he enlisted the support of the Black Prince, who was usually willing to do anything to annoy the French. On 16 February 1367, an army led by the Black Prince passed Roncesvalles, and on 3 April was fought the battle of Najera, in which the Black Prince won a decisive victory, the climax of his career as a military commander. Lancaster too won some fame as one of his lieutenants, and is fulsomely praised, like everyone else, in the *Life of the Black Prince* written in French by Chandos, the domestic herald of Sir John Chandos, one of the Prince's most stalwart followers:

> Et d'autre part li noble ducz
> De Lancastre, plein de vertuz,
> Si noblement se combatoit
> Qe chescun s'en merveilloit
> En regardant sa grant prouesce.[6]

Pedro was reinstated, and the all-conquering English returned to Bordeaux in August 1367.

But all was to no avail: Pedro betrayed his promises to his allies and his conduct as king was worse than ever (his nickname was Pedro the Cruel); when Enrique invaded again, his army once more commanded by du Guesclin, Pedro was comprehensively defeated at the battle of Monteil on 14 March 1369. During the siege that followed, Pedro was invited, on 23 March, to du Guesclin's tent, ostensibly to discuss a deal that would allow him to escape, and there slain by his half-brother and Olivier de Mauni. Chaucer knew enough about this to make a reference to du Guesclin's coat of arms and a punning translation of de Mauni's name in his two stanzas on Pedro in the Monk's Tale: 'The wikked nest [= *mau ni*] was werker of this nede' (*Canterbury Tales*, VII. 2386). Chaucer's interest in the subject, though, was nothing compared to that of Lancaster, who married Pedro's daughter Costanza (Constance), the legitimate heiress of Castile and Leon, in September 1371, and styled himself 'Roy de Castille et de Leon Duc de Lancastre' in all documents from 1372 to 1388.

The question remains as to what Chaucer was doing in Navarre in the spring of 1366. Events then unfolding in Castile, and the possible subsequent involvement of England in Spanish affairs, make it likely that he was there on some kind of secret diplomatic mission. It may have been to dissuade some of the English knights of the Free Companies from joining the cause of Enrique; or it may have been – and this seems more probable – that he was carrying promises to Charles of Navarre in the hope of securing him as an ally, or at least not an enemy, in any future English military activity in the peninsula. Chaucer's presence in Navarre is proof that he had been earlier in the Black Prince's domain of Aquitaine, and a strong suggestion that he had spent some time there in the prince's service. This would be an occupation for the 'lost years'.[7]

After his expedition to Spain in 1366, Chaucer was on more familiar ground a couple of years later. There is a warrant from the royal privy seal, dated 17 July 1368 at Windsor, for the issue of a licence for 'nostre ame vallet Geffrey Chaucer' to pass at Dover across the sea, with two hackneys (horses), 20 shillings in sterling for his expenses, and £10 'en eschange' (*Life-Records*, p. 29). The warrant is the medieval equivalent of a passport, and the sterling allowance will be familiar to English travellers abroad in the 1950s and 1960s. It was paid at the exchange tables at Dover, while the £10 would be in the form of a letter of exchange, like a traveller's cheque, payable at Calais, which of course was an English possession.

The sum that Chaucer received in alien currency was enough to take him almost anywhere in Western Europe, even as far as Rome. It could conceivably have taken him to Milan, where his former patron, Lionel, now (since 1362) Duke of Clarence, was celebrating his marriage to Violante, daughter of the ambitious Galeazzo Visconti, lord of Pavia. Galeazzo wanted to upstage his more famous brother, Bernabò Visconti, lord of Milan (whose court Chaucer was to visit in 1378), and for this purpose was eager to ally himself with the English royal house as he had earlier allied himself with the French, through the marriage of his son, Gian-Galeazzo, to Isabella of France. The marriage of Lionel and Violante turned out very unluckily, Lionel dying on 17 October 1368, without ever returning to England, after a five-month whirl of feasts and tournaments. Chaucer had just enough time to be in Milan for the marriage celebrations, since he is not known to have been back in England before the end of October, when he received the Michaelmas instalment of his annuity. With the four-week or five-week one-way journey, it would have been a whirlwind visit, and he is unlikely to have made it, but it is pleasing to picture him there, in the company of Froissart and the venerable Petrarch. No business is specified in the warrant.

Chaucer was abroad again in the following year, on record as having received from the keeper of the king's wardrobe the sum of £10 as a 'prest' (a prest was an advance of money to cover the costs of an undertaking or expedition), probably in September 1369 (*Life-Records*, p. 31). Chaucer was being paid as an esquire of the king's *familia*, or household, for his services in relation to the expedition of John of Gaunt to Artois, Picardy and Normandy (July–November 1369) on the renewal of war with France. In subsequent records, from 1373 and 1374, Chaucer receives his 'quietus' or release from responsibility for having to account in detail for the spending of the £10 (*Life-Records*, pp. 106–9); this is all routine red tape.

The expedition of 1369, like almost every military enterprise that Lancaster engaged in, was a failure. The reason for the renewal of hostilities lay in the South, where the Gascon nobles of Guienne were becoming increasingly impatient with the Black Prince's high-handed rule there as Prince of Aquitaine, especially his demand that they should subsidize his Spanish expedition of 1367. Many decided that vassalage to Charles V might be preferable, and Charles took the opportunity of demanding that the Black Prince, as his vassal, should account in person for the unsatisfactoriness of his regime. The prince haughtily refused, and took his revenge by persuading his father to renew his claim to the throne of France. Edward wearily agreed, but his fighting days were over, and he appointed his next oldest son to conduct the campaign. Lancaster landed at Calais in July 1369, plundered aimlessly in northern France for a while, but had little policy except to hope that the French would accept pitched battle. On the one occasion that the hoped-for confrontation seemed about to come to pass, the leader of the French forces, Philip, Duke of Burgundy, the king's youngest brother, quietly decamped in the middle of the night, leaving camp-fires burning to cover his removal.

In the following year, Chaucer received letters of protection on 20 June 1370 for going abroad, yet again, in the king's service ('in obsequium regis ad partes transmarinas' (*Life-Records*, p. 31)). Such letters were issued to travellers who wished to protect themselves from lawsuits during their absence; they were a form of travel insurance. Chaucer's was one of many such 'litteras de regis proteccione' being issued at this time for those taking part in the annual expeditions to France. Lancaster was in Aquitaine, taking over the responsibilities of the ailing Black Prince and improving his acquaintance with Katherine Swynford, but Chaucer's letters cover only the period until Michaelmas (29 September), which suggests that he was not intending to go so far from home. He may have been with the diversionary expedition in northern France, led by Sir Robert Knollys, which left Calais on 22 July, or he may have been involved elsewhere with the preparations for the treaty with Flanders signed on 4 August.

COURT LIFE IN THE 1360s

Chaucer spent some considerable part of the 1360s in a large and splendid royal household. One of the other members of this household was the lady-in-waiting who, probably at some time before 1366, became his wife, though marriage made less difference to the day-to-day routine of his life than we might expect, since he and his wife were obliged to live separately for a great part of the year and had no independent establishment or home of their own until 1374.

The life of a *valettus* or of an esquire of the royal household was still much tied, like that of a page, to the daily rhythms of feasting, sport, practice in the martial arts, hunting, music, dancing and song, and to the annual cycle of festivals, visits and campaigns. There were fewer menial tasks, less waiting on table and running errands, and more time to cultivate the arts of poetry and conversation. For Chaucer and the group of esquires to which he belonged, a kind of lay secretariat, there would be more time to concentrate on the development and practice of their professional skills.

In fact there was more leisure than usual for all these activities in the 1360s. The upheavals caused by the nomadic existence of the royal household, and the continued need to spread the burden of provisioning such a horde over as many grateful subjects as possible, should not be underestimated. But things were changing. Until recently, the whole national administration, which in effect was what the king's household was, had habitually followed the king on his peregrinations: now the great offices of state (Chancery, Wardrobe, Exchequer) stayed more permanently in London or in Windsor. The king, furthermore, was showing an increasing

inclination to stay for longer periods with his private household
(*secreta familia*) in his favourite country houses at Eltham, Sheen,
Langley, Havering or Moor End, which he had recently spent a
great deal of money on refurbishing. In addition, all was comparatively quiet on the French front, and was to remain so for most of
the decade. So, with less travelling about and no campaigning,
there was actually nothing for all these people to do except amuse
themselves in a brilliant and civilized fashion.

It could be argued that the English royal court in the early
1360s was an exceptionally splendid one. The absence of the Black
Prince, who was never happy unless he was fighting, was a positive
asset. He spent most of these years in south-west France, where
as Prince of Aquitaine, a title he was granted in 1362, he kept
great state in Bordeaux and governed virtually as an absolute
monarch. Lionel, the king's second son, was mostly in Ireland,
and the king had betaken himself to a quieter life and, well before
the death of his queen in 1369, the pleasures of attendance upon
Alice Perrers. So the dominant figure at court was the young John
of Gaunt. His marriage to Blanche had turned out spectacularly
well: her father, Henry, Duke of Lancaster, died in the second
visitation of plague in 1361, leaving her as co-heiress with her
sister Maud to the vast Lancastrian estates, and then Maud died
without issue in 1362. John, who had become Earl of Lancaster
in 1361 by right of his wife, was now (1362) created Duke of
Lancaster, and was for the rest of his life the richest man in
England, with his own splendid household in his father-in-law's
palace of the Savoy.

The royal court, in which he and his wife Blanche exerted now
an important influence, was a mobile and flexible grouping of
knights, squires, ladies, *valetti*, pages and assorted attendants, in
addition to members of the royal family and the lords of the realm.
Some resided permanently within the household, while some had
lodging elsewhere and attended as duty bade, and others were
present at the great festivals. There were offices to perform, of an
administrative and diplomatic kind, and Chaucer had his share of
the latter. There was physical and martial exercise, including
tournament jousting on great occasions, and jousting at the quintain for practice and fun. London apprentices also engaged in this
sport, and Chaucer's Manciple compares the Cook's angry gestures, which threaten to throw him from his horse into the mud,
to those of someone preparing to ride at the quintain or *fan* (vane):
'Now, sweete sire, wol ye justen atte fan? (*Canterbury Tales*, IX. 42).

Then there was hunting, the major leisure activity of the upper classes, and a sport pursued with fanatical devotion. Of Gaston Phebus, Count of Foix, and one of the most vivid characters in Froissart's *Chronicles*, it might be said that he was possessed by the hunt as by a fever; he met his death, appropriately enough, on a bear-hunt in the woods of Sauveterre de Bearn in 1391. He wrote the most famous of all medieval books of the chase, *Le Livre de Chasse*, in 1387–89, and declares roundly in his Prologue that hunters, of all men, live the life most pleasing to God and most joyful. Since idleness is the source of all sins, the hunter, by eschewing idleness, avoids sin; he is indeed so busy that he has no time for sin, and returns home so exhausted that he has no energy for it. He concludes: 'Donc di je que veneurs s'en vont en paradis quand il meurent, et vivent en cest monde plus joyeuse-ment que nulle autre gent.'[8] 'So I declare that hunters go to paradise when they die, and live in this world more joyfully than any other people'. C. S. Lewis once said that rhetoric was the greatest barrier between us and our ancestors.[9] I am sometimes inclined to think that hunting is a greater barrier still, though again Trollope reminds us, in the inordinate delight he takes in chapter after chapter on the subject in *Phineas Finn* or *The American Senator*, that the obsession with hunting has only recently become less general.

It is appropriate, therefore, that Chaucer's first poem, *The Book of the Duchess*, should begin with the poet waking up, in his dream, to find that everyone else has gone out hunting (the story of my life, one can hear him say) and that the poem as a whole should turn on the pun of the hunting of the heart/hart (see line 1313). Chaucer knows about hunting, as did any man of accomplishment of his time, and it has its place in the aristocratic background of appropriate later poems, for instance the Knight's Tale (I. 1687), the Clerk's Tale (IV. 234) and *Troilus* (iii. 1780). But he does not choose to parade its language of technical expertise before us, as does the author of *Sir Gawain and the Green Knight*. There is a confidence in Chaucer, a lack of anxiety, or of the need to assert a knowledge of court life and manners that is so importunate in some provincial poetry and indeed also in the London romances of the Auchinleck manuscript. It is in one of the latter, *Guy of Warwick*, that we find the heroine dutifully instructing her maid in the properly stand-offish behaviour required of a courtly mis-tress, and in one of the Northern romances, *Sir Tristrem*, that the author feels constrained to tell his audience that a correct knowl-

edge of the technical terms of hunting is what distinguishes a
gentleman from a common man. Chaucer never shows any sign
of this widespread English anxiety, which argues for his sense of
his own centrality in English culture, for what that culture was
worth.[10]

Indoors, there was chess and backgammon, the ubiquitous
'ches or tables', which usually figure in Chaucer in a rather
negative way: they are what a courtly person might be expected
to be satisfied with as a pastime, but what Dorigen in the
Franklin's Tale (V. 900) and the dreamer in *The Book of the
Duchess* (51) are not. Books are what the dreamer wants, and he
takes up 'a romaunce' (48), that is, a book of narrative poetry
in French, to while away his sleepless hours. French romances,
in verse or prose, were the staple reading of court society, and
surviving lists of books owned by members of the aristocracy
are dominated by romances such as those of *Lancelot* and *Tristan*.
Chaucer, in the Nun's Priest's Tale (VII. 3212), rather mischievously characterizes a liking for the story of 'Launcelot de
Lake' as a female taste.[11]

Romances, like the French love-vision allegories such as *Le
Roman de la Rose*, could be read privately but more commonly there
would be a small listening group with someone reading aloud,
such as we find in Criseyde's 'paved parlour' (*Troilus*, ii. 82). Love-
poems and love-songs, by contrast, though they could be read
in anthologies and collections, were more the currency of social
intercourse, and every man about court would be expected to be
able to sing or breathe forth some well-known piece, or a new
piece to an old tune (like the *roundel* at the end of *The Parliament
of Fowls*) or at least to show his prowess in composition. Amans,
in Gower's *Confessio Amantis*, the model of the aspiring courtly
lover, confesses that he has often tried out 'Rondeal, balade and
virelai' and composed 'Caroles with my wordes qweinte' (*Confessio
Amantis*, I. 2727, 2730) in his desire to advance his purpose with
his mistress, and sung them forth loudly in hall and chamber; but
to no avail, since his mistress refuses to listen or, if she listens, to
believe that they are made for her sake. Not only men, one might
remark, engaged in writing these love-songs: women probably took
a larger part in such activities than the record shows.

Love was the theme, and the 'game of love' included all the acts
and scenes of fashionable flirtation, allusions to secret *amours*, hints
of assignations, scandalous imputations, as well as the rhetorical
outpourings of unrequited love. Of the former we hear something,

appropriately enough, in the Squire's Tale, where Cambyuskan's birthday feast is the occasion of much amorous play-acting:

> Who koude telle yow the forme of daunces
> So unkouthe, and swiche fresshe contenaunces,
> Swich subtil lookyng and dissymulynges
> For drede of jalouse mennes aperceyvynges ?
> No man but Launcelot, and he is deed.
>
> (*Canterbury Tales*, V. 283–7)

Of the latter we hear more than enough in the Franklin's Tale, where the squire Aurelius pours forth the love that he dare not speak in volley upon volley of love-lays: 'Songes, compleintes, roundels, virelayes, / How that he dorste nat his sorwe telle' (*Canterbury Tales*, V. 948–9). There is amusement here, of course, at the excesses of lovers, but we should not confuse mockery with satire, nor insist that there are behavioural norms that Chaucer is recommending as the corrective for such social deviancy. He is fully able to share zestfully in what he also finds amusing and maybe slightly ludicrous.[12]

There was more to the 'game of love', though, than these amorous vapourings. It was the emotional focus of some sophisticated intellectual activity – debates on subtle and improbable questions of conduct, conundrums of behaviour, exemplary stories of what might happen to an overeager suitor or an unresponsive mistress, games and quizzes of all kinds. A favourite game at court was to divide into parties so as to debate, no doubt with much ingenious sophistry, questions such as, Does a *clerc* or a *chevalier* make the better lover? Collections of such *demandes d'amour*, with appropriate responses, were available to assist those who were anxious to learn the art of amorous conversation. In the 1380s, both English and French courtiers gained amusement at the May Day festivities in declaring themselves adherents of the amorous orders of either the Flower or the Leaf, and debating the relative merits of the two: Chaucer alludes to the custom in the Prologue to *The Legend of Good Women* (F. 72).

Associated with these questions and debates is the game of *Le Roi qui ne ment*, in which one person in a group is given temporary absolute authority to ask and answer all questions concerning love, as Fiammetta is in Boccaccio's *Filocolo*. This is perhaps not so much part of courtly education and an introduction to the refinements of polite behaviour as 'stylized flirtation and erotic sparring', a way of providing 'an acceptable vehicle for bringing young people of both sexes together and allowing them a degree of social, even sexual, intimacy'. Formal games often perform this function in strictly regulated communities. It is a form of sex education.[13]

When stories were told or read out, they provided not merely pastime and entertainment but also themes for discussion. Romances are often contrived so as to pose interestingly difficult questions of amorous behaviour, upon which the assembled knights and ladies can then display their skill in conversation and casuistry. Boccaccio's romance of *Filocolo* has as one of its episodes a courtly gathering where various questions of love are presented in the form of stories and debated under the presidency of Fiammetta, who acts as the queen of a 'court of love'. One of the stories, that told by Menedon, formed the basis of Chaucer's Franklin's Tale, which likewise ends with a *demande d'amour*: 'Lordynges, this question, thanne, wol I aske now, / Which was the mooste fre, as thynketh yow?'(*Canterbury Tales*, V. 1621–2). Chaucer cannot, of course, go on with the debate as Boccaccio does, since the fictional framework of his story is different. A debate on such a question among the Canterbury pilgrims would soon get out of hand, with real-life equivalents of the goose and cuckoo of *The Parliament of Fowls* chipping in unhelpfully.

Discussion of such questions, high-minded or licentious as it might have been, was part of the 'love-talking' which was so much prized as a courtly skill. One of the first questions Criseyde asks of Pandarus, when he has broached the matter of Troilus's love for her, and allayed her first fears, has to do with love-talk: '"Kan he wel speke of love?" quod she; "I preye / Tel me, for I the bet me shal purveye"' (*Troilus*, ii. 503–4). At the feast before the great tournament in the Knight's Tale, Chaucer hesitates to speak of the bestowal of gifts, or the order of precedence on the dais, or who is accounted best at singing and dancing, 'Ne who moost felyngly spekyth of love' (*Canterbury Tales*, I. 2203). In *The Parliament of Fowls*, the three suitors expect and are expected to be judged on the basis of the eloquence with which they speak of their love for the formel eagle. It is, inevitably, a highly formalized and artificial eloquence. When Gawain arrives at Hautdesert, in *Sir Gawain and the Green Knight*, the people of Bercilak's household grow very excited at the prospect of having someone from court staying at the castle:

Now schal we semlych se sleghtes of thewes

And the teccheles termes of talkyng noble.
Wich spede is in speche unspurd may we lerne. (916–18)

Now shall we most becomingly see skilled demonstrations of cour-
teous manners and the faultless phrases of the art of courtly conversation. Now we can learn, without asking, what sort of thing success
in conversation is.

Mostly what is expected of Gawain is the polite language of
dalliance and flirtation, as is made clear a little later: ' "I hope
that may hym here / Schal lerne of luf-talkyng" ' (926–7). 'I believe
anyone who has the opportunity of listening to him will learn
something of the art of conversing about love.' He certainly needs
all the skill he has on the following days, as he tries to keep his
relationship with the lady of the castle on a strictly linguistic basis.
Conventionally, of course, it would be the lady who would be
doing the fending off.

Love was thus a principal theme in the drama of court life.
Other things would be talked about, especially when women were
not present, and Froissart has a description of his arrival with his
companion Sir Espaing du Lyon at the court of the Count of Foix,
where the conversation, as with Uncle Toby much later, is all of
attacks, surprises, sieges, assaults, skirmishes and battles, and the
amusements are tournaments, games of strength and physical skill,
and the chase. This male bonding was of course a more constant
part of male experience of chivalric reality than relationships with
women, and we should always remember that what men and
women talked about was not an index to what was uppermost in
their minds or most important in their lives. Froissart even remarks
at one point, in reference to a dispute that grew up between two
men concerning a woman, that companions in arms should have
overlooked such a problem. So much for Palamon and Arcite.[14]

But love was certainly a rich and comprehensive subject for
talking about, and the one that most truly identified the court as
the court. The high-minded cult of love was inseparable from the
life of chivalry: the book of instruction supposedly written at the
behest of Edward III for his eldest son recommends, first, *léauté*
in all things, as the foundation of a knight's honour, and then the
service of women:

A pain verrés nul home vaillant
Qu'il n'aime ou ait amé avant.[15]

For we hardly ever see a valiant man who does not love or has not
one time loved.

'The craft of fyn lovynge', as Chaucer calls it in the Prologue to
The Legend of Good Women (F. 544), the ability to love and speak
of love with fine feeling, was the distinguishing mark of the true
knight, what separated him from the commoner. Chaucer, with
an audacity that he found hard to sustain, was to claim in *Troilus*
that love was the principle of value not just in chivalrous knights
but in human beings:

> God loveth, and to love wol nought werne,
> And in this world no lyves creature
> Withouten love is worth, or may endure.   (iii. 12–14)

But, in the mean time, courtly love was of course exclusive
in a more practical way, for only courtly persons had the leisure
to indulge in an activity so ostentatiously unprofitable. It is the
maiden Idleness, we recall, who opens the gate of the garden of
love to the dreamer in the *Roman de la Rose* (*Romaunt*, 593).

Chaucer was deeply and inseparably part of this world. All his
longer poems up to the time of *The Canterbury Tales* have love as
their central theme – as distinct, for instance, from the predominantly non-court poems of the so-called 'alliterative revival', where
love is chiefly a delusion and women a snare, and where the
implied systems of value, if they are not explicitly religious, are
ethical rather than social.[16] Even a poem so sophisticated in its
understanding of court culture as *Sir Gawain and the Green Knight* is
bringing that culture to the bar of a moral and religious inquisition.
Chaucer has some questions to ask, too, about the place of love
in people's lives, but the agenda to which he speaks is already set
by the court culture which created him. He is, in this respect,
quite different from Gower and the *Gawain*-poet, who speak from
a predominantly 'clerkly' viewpoint, like Langland. Only Chaucer,
among all English poets of the Middle Ages, could have taken a
love-affair as the subject-matter of his poetic masterpiece, *Troilus
and Criseyde*.

FRENCH AT COURT

So Chaucer, even if he was not 'syngynge ... or floytynge, al the day', like the Squire of the General Prologue (I. 91), was certainly surrounded by a good deal of such singing and fluting. Like the Squire, he accepted the importance of being adept at poetic composition: 'He koude songes make and wel endite, / Juste and eek daunce, and weel purtreye and write' (General Prologue, I. 95–6). Some of these love-poems and love-songs may have been of use in the pursuit of his own affairs and flirtations. One remembers how Sir John Paston, who had lent his copy of Lydgate's *Temple of Glass* to a friend, asked for it back in a hurry in 1461, when he was wooing Anne Haute, probably to lift good lines from it to incorporate in one of his own love-epistles. Other love-songs were for public occasions: Froissart records that Gaston, Count of Foix, not only listened to instalments of Froissart's romance of *Meliador* that the poet read out to him every evening after supper, but also took great pleasure in music and song, and having rondeaux and virelays sung to him. At the English court, too, where he was secretary to Queen Philippa from 1361 to 1369 and, like Chaucer, part of the larger household of Edward III, Froissart tells how he ingratiated himself by composing love-poems to amuse the queen: 'à laquelle en ma jeunesse je fis clerc et la servoie de beaulx dittiers et traittiés amoureux.'[17]

There can be little doubt that Chaucer too was composing similar 'beaulx dittiers' and 'traittiés amoureux' in the 1360s. Gower's Venus, in commending Chaucer to Amans in the *Confessio Amantis*, says that Chaucer 'in the floures of his youthe' filled the whole land full 'Of ditees and of songes glade' (VIII. 2943, 2945). And they were among the many 'enditynges of worldly vanitees' for which, in another mood and another age, Chaucer asks forgiveness in the 'retracciouns' at the end of the Parson's Tale, but which he has no exact memory of: 'and many another book, if they were in my remembrance, and many a song and many a leccherous lay' (*Canterbury Tales*, X. 1087). Probably none of these poems survive, it being unlikely that any of the short love-poems accepted in the Chaucer canon, such as *The Complaint unto Pity*, *To Rosemounde* or *Womanly Noblesse*, belong to this period. The reasons commonly put forward for regarding such poems as early work – that they are artificial in style and derivative in content – carry no weight at all.

An important question remains: if Chaucer was writing fashionable love-poems during his service in the royal household in the
1360s, as he surely was, what language was he writing them
in, French or English? With Gower, who like Chaucer says he
abandoned his youth to the writing of foolish ditties of love – 'Et
les fols ditz d'amours fesoie / Dont en chantant je carolloie' (*Mirour
de l'Omme*, 27340–1) – we can be quite sure: they were in French,
even if they were not the surviving and inordinately sober *Cinquante
Balades*. But, to answer the question properly, it is necessary to
look at the historical situation of the two languages, or rather
three, since Anglo-Norman is also part of the question.

During the thirteenth century, the prestige vernacular in
England was Anglo-Norman. In form, Anglo-Norman was a development of the Norman dialect of French spoken by the invaders
of 1066; it remained intelligible to French speakers but gradually
acquired a 'provincial' character which distinguished it further
from metropolitan French. It came to be laughed at, and Chaucer
expects his audience to laugh at the Prioress for knowing no better:

> And Frenssh she spak ful faire and fetisly,
> After the scole of Stratford atte Bowe,
> For Frenssh of Parys was to hire unknowe.
> (General Prologue, I. 124–6)

Nevertheless, during the period of its dominance, Anglo-Norman
was a lively and widely spoken vernacular: it penetrated deep into
the middle layers of English society, and was by no means confined
to the upper classes; certainly no one with any pretensions to
education or literacy would be without it. As far as literature was
concerned, there would be a broad distinction between writing in
Anglo-Norman, designed for the educated classes, and writing in
English, designed for the uneducated, mostly in the form of popular
romances and instructional and didactic writing. This broad distinction would be more true of London and the South-East than
of areas of the West and North further from metropolitan influence.

By the end of the thirteenth century, there were signs of change,
in the form of Anglo-Norman grammars and glossaries: Anglo-
Norman was becoming a useful acquisition for those in polite
society rather than a true vernacular. The fourteenth century saw
a sharp decline in spoken Anglo-Norman, though it retained its

hold in some fields, such as official and business records (as we have seen in some of the Chaucer records), in correspondence, and of course in law until the seventeenth century. The last major English writer to use Anglo-Norman was John Gower, in his *Mirour de l'Omme*, probably dating from the middle or late 1370s, and he there disguises what was fast becoming a narrowly provincial and backward language by writing in a much closer approximation to Continental French. He uses English for his major poem, however, the *Confessio Amantis* (begun about 1387), and Chaucer apparently uses nothing else. Circumstances conspired to favour the English language, which reoccupied the heights of royal and aristocratic patronage from which it had been excluded since Anglo-Saxon times. Richard II's was the first English-speaking court since that of Harold Godwinsson.

The period of Chaucer's early poetic career is thus a critical one in the history of the shifting relationship between English, Anglo-Norman and French (which I shall not hereafter distinguish unless the distinction is important). English naturally remained the sole language of a large proportion of the population, while in the middle and upper strata of society there would be a good deal of bilingualism, with the dominance shifting towards English. There would be different patterns of speech behaviour in different linguistic contexts – whether in the North and West or around London, in high court or manorial court, on the street or at business, in great hall, kitchen or nursery – and the two languages existed side by side with a remarkable lack of resentment until propagandist remarks about 'English for the English' begin to be made about 1300. The author of the late-thirteenth-century popular English romance *Of Arthour and Of Merlin* puts it thus: 'Freynsche use this gentil man / Ac everich Inglische Inglische can.' By the end of the fourteenth century, when Thomas Usk was writing his *Testament of Love*, French was associated not with an English social class but with a foreign country:

> Let than clerkes endyten in Latin, for they have the propertee of science, and the knowinge in that facultee; and let Frenchmen in their Frenche also endyten their queynt termes, for it is kyndely to their mouthes; and let us shewe our fantasyes in suche wordes as we lerneden of our dames tonge.[18]

Popular prejudice meanwhile found an unexpected ally in the growing awareness among educated speakers of the 'provincial' nature of Anglo-Norman.

Nevertheless, the tenacity of Anglo-Norman in court and aristocratic households – the most important milieu for literature –
should not be underestimated. It had the advantage of being
spoken in the same form throughout England, where local dialects
might often present problems for the outsider, and the much
greater advantage of giving access to the lingua franca of Europe.
French was the written language of the more ephemeral kind of
official record throughout Western Europe (we saw an example in
the records of the kingdom of Navarre), as of correspondence
among the European aristocracy, and it was the spoken language
of the international set. When Anne of Bohemia came to England
in 1381 to be Richard II's queen, the language that she and her
retinue spoke, and would have spoken in Italy and Germany as
well as Bohemia, was French.

We can assume that, in the 1360s, there was a good deal of
interchange between English and French in court and aristocratic
circles, and speakers would slip from one to the other quite easily.
Edward III no doubt spoke English with his military commanders
and soldiers, and French with his Hainault-born queen and her
retinue. But it seems to have been still generally assumed that
anything formally committed to writing would be in French.
Henry, Duke of Lancaster, wrote in 1354 a devotional treatise in
Anglo-Norman called *Le Livre de Seyntz Medicines*, where, in making
a conventional apology for the crudity of his style, he explains: 'Si
le franceis ne soit pas bon, jeo doie estre escusee, pur ceo qe jeo
sui engleis et n'ai pas moelt hauntee le franceis'[19] (If the French
is not good, I ought to be excused, since I am English and have
not had much to do with French.) French was thus not his first
language but it was the correct language to write in. So it was, at
first, with Gower. Froissart, whose native language was the French
of Hainault, maintained himself as poet and secretary at the
court of Queen Philippa throughout the 1360s. He was certainly
surrounded by French speakers and writing for an audience who
expected to read and listen to others read in French. By 1395, the
same poet and chronicler, returning to England after a long
absence to offer a book of his verses to Richard II, finds it worthy
of note in his *Chronicles* that the king 'dipped into the book in
several places and read, for he spoke and read French very well'
(p. 408). Froissart was no doubt out of touch with the situation
in England after his long absence, but his remark surely records
a radical change in the status of French at court. Chaucer's poetry,

in its bulk and quality, is the main evidence for this change, its main product, and perhaps even its major precipitant.

Yet the court where he was a *valettus* and esquire in the 1360s was certainly, as I have said, predominantly French-speaking, and predominantly French, too, in its literary interests. The French wars conspired to make it, for a while, even more so, when the court was the home not only of a French-speaking queen and her followers but also of a large portion of the French royal family. Jean le Bon (John II of France) had been at the English court since 1357, having been taken prisoner at Poitiers, and his presence made for an increase both in the extravagance of court ceremonial, as Edward strove to demonstrate that the English court could be as splendid as the French, and also in its artistic and literary activities. Jean had been a patron of Machaut and had received Petrarch at his court, and he brought French artists and poets in his train to England, as well as French books. One of his painters, Girard d'Orléans, accompanied him to England and continued to work on commissions for him. His chaplain Gace de la Buigne began in England a long poem, *Le Roman de Deduis*, which manages to combine a debate about hunting with moral instruction on the vices and virtues: Jean had commissioned it for the edification of his youngest son Philip, the future Duke of Burgundy. Jean was also a great patron of book-dealers and book-illustrators while he was in London.[20]

After the signing of the Treaty of Calais in 1360, Jean returned to France, where he set about trying to raise the money for his ransom. The sale of his 11-year-old daughter in marriage to the son of Galeazzo Visconti was one such scheme. Meanwhile his place in England as security for the payment of the huge ransom imposed at Bretigny was taken by forty hostages, including the three younger royal princes, Louis, Jean and Philip, the future dukes of Anjou, Berry and Burgundy. Jean, Duc de Berry, was to be one of the greatest collectors and patrons of medieval France. His departure from his wife to go into exile in England was made the occasion of a delicate poem of farewell by Machaut, *Le Dit de la Fonteinne Amoureuse*, one of the models for Chaucer's *Book of the Duchess*. Jean de Berry stayed in England, with visits to France on parole, until 1367, but his two brothers negotiated their release privately in 1363. This so mortified their father that he returned voluntarily to captivity in England in January 1364: Froissart's second *pastourelle* celebrates his passage from Eltham to Westmins-

ter on this occasion. Jean died soon after at the Savoy palace on
8 April 1364.

French poetry at the English Court

The boat that brought the royal hostages from Calais in 1360 was
preceded by one carrying Geoffrey Chaucer, sent home early with
messages from Prince Lionel, and swiftly followed by another
carrying the young and ambitious poet–chronicler Jean Froissart.
Froissart himself dresses up the occasion in *L'Espinette Amoureuse*
as a heart-broken flight into exile in a strange land after an
unhappy love-affair, but the young Hainaulter, who like Chaucer
came from a bourgeois background, had already won himself,
perhaps through his facility in writing verses, a place in high
society and the promise of employment in the household of Queen
Philippa. There he stayed, as her 'clerc de la chambre', until 1367,
writing *poèmes d'occasion* and love-songs, and travelling indefatigably
to gather material for his continuation of the *Chroniques* of Jehan
le Bel. He was in Brussels, returning from a great tour through
Europe that had occupied him for two years (including attendance
at Lionel's marriage in Italy) when he heard news of Philippa's
death on 15 August 1369. He did not return to England until
1395.

Froissart mentions Chaucer in his *Chroniques* as being present at
the marriage negotiations in Montreuil in 1376, but there can be
no doubt that the two poets were well acquainted in the 1360s.
If Chaucer's wife was a Roet, this would have brought him closer
to the Hainault group at court. Froissart was a few years older
than Chaucer, and had made his way at court in a much more
aggressive style. It was inevitable that Chaucer's early poetry
should show the influence of Froissart: *Le Paradis d'Amours* is a
major source for the dream framework of *The Book of the Duchess*,
and *Le Temple d'Honneur*, probably written for the marriage of
Humphrey de Bohun and Joan of Arundel in May 1363, provided
some hints for *The House of Fame*. But the traffic was not all one
way, and it has been plausibly argued that Froissart's *Dit dou Bleu
Chevalier* is indebted to *The Book of the Duchess* and not, as is
conventionally taken for granted, the English poem to the
French.[21]

Chaucer learnt some of the apparatus of the courtly style and the *dit amoureux* from Froissart, though he learnt much more from Machaut. He may have learnt another kind of lesson from Froissart's example – not to attach his poetry too closely to the trivia of court life and personal quasi-autobiography. Froissart is incurably personal and gossipy, and it is one of the delights of his poetry. But it is also a limitation, and one that Chaucer recognized, to the benefit of his poetry and the despair of his biographer.

One other thing, potentially of significance, may be mentioned. Froissart has a way, especially in the *Chroniques*, of representing people and events without moral commentary, without the imposing, that is, of the moral grid upon experience that was the duty of the *auctor*. The effect of this is to extract his writing on war and chivalry from the realities of history and to make of it a kind of connoisseurship of fine feats of arms. In this way, war is 'civilized', made part of the aristocratic ideal of chivalry. The historical characters that people Froissart's writings are also, in a way, the material of connoisseurship: all have their interest for the assiduous admirer of courtly manners. Where there is a conflict between two members of the aristocracy, as between Derby and Mowbray in 1398, Froissart contents himself with an eclectic display of motives of the kind that gains for a dramatist or poet the reputation of being generously broad-minded. Froissart tends to speak well of everyone, except rustics and peasants, for whose disorderly conduct and presumption in daring to appear in the pages of his chronicle he has nothing but contempt. He finds something to admire in his beloved *seigneurs* even in displays of barbarous cruelty like the sack of Limoges in 1370. An axe is being ground, of course, on behalf of his aristocratic patrons, but the effect is one of geniality and courtesy.[22]

Chaucer caught this same courtesy very early. For him the portrayal of human behaviour became likewise a kind of connoisseurship, in which 'appreciation' substitutes for moral evaluation. Everyone, as we see particularly in the General Prologue to *The Canterbury Tales*, is best at something and can be admired in some way, and it is not a subtle reading that simply reimposes, through 'irony', the moral grid that Chaucer had found a way of removing for interest's sake. Only rustics and peasants are beyond the pale of such aesthetic courtesy, and Chaucer, except in such contexts as his portrait of the spiritualized Plowman, despises them as much as Froissart did. But even there Chaucer can sometimes assume a self-consciously patrician charm, as with the old widow at the beginning of the Nun's Priest's Tale: 'What a character . . .

dear old lady.' What was in Froissart part of an unsophisticated and uncritical absorption of the ideology of chivalry becomes in Chaucer a mannerism of style. This style carries always the potential of a smiling irony through which Chaucer can lay claim to a broader humanity, but there is no explicit repudiation of its essential snobbery. In this way, Chaucer can eat his cake and have it too.

But Froissart was not the only French poet who graced the English court with his amorous ditties, 'Rondiaus, balades, virelais, / Grant fuison de dis et de lais'.[23] Gace de la Buigne was there, as we have seen, and other poets in the employ of Jean le Bon. Jean de la Mote, who in 1339 had written an elegy on William of Hainault and dedicated it to the count's daughter, Philippa of England, was now in the queen's service. Probably in the late 1350s, he was the recipient of a poem ('De terre en Grec Gaule appellee' (Out of the land called Gaul in Greek)) of extravagant mock-diatribe from Philippe de Vitry, Bishop of Meaux (d. 1361), a famous poet–musician. Jean was accused of deserting his native land and devoting himself to the service of 'Albion de Dieu maldite'; he replied politely, in a poem ('O Victriens, mondains dieu d'armonie' (O man of Vitry, worldly god of harmony)) equally packed with mythological allusion, that service in England was not a disservice to poetry. This *Response* became quite famous, and Deschamps incorporates phrases from it in two ballades, one a lament for the death of Machaut, the other a tribute to Chaucer. He expected Chaucer to recognize the allusion to a famous literary *contretemps* of his youth. Jean de la Mote was probably a former pupil or disciple of the great 'Victriens'. Through him Chaucer would gain his first indirect acquaintance with the European literary world: Philippe was not only a close confidant of Jean le Bon, but also a friend of Petrarch and of the scholar Pierre Bersuire, who wrote an influential commentary on Ovid. It was not exactly the Renaissance, but it was an opening of horizons to a larger world of Latin and contemporary vernacular poetry.[24]

Jean, Duc de Berry, was at the English court for long spells between 1360 and 1367, and no doubt Chaucer got to know him too. Later in life, in 1389, Jean wrote a poem in the genre of the humorous 'Farewell to Love' ('Puiz qu'a Amours suis si gras eschapé' (Since I have escaped from Love so fat)), the first line of which directly echoes the first line of the third roundel of *Merciles Beaute* ('Sin I fro Love escaped am so fat'), a love-poem fairly reliably attributed to Chaucer, and possibly quite early. The amusement that the 60-year-old duke took in composing such a poem was perhaps the keener in that 1389 was also the year of his marriage at Riom to the 12-year-old Jeanne de Boulogne.[25]

Also at the court of Edward III, though he did not settle there permanently until after his return from the celebrations of Lionel's marriage in Milan in 1368, was Oton de Granson, the poet of Savoy. He was in the households of Edward III, then of Lancaster, and then of Richard II until 1387, when the death of his father compelled him to return to Savoy. He returned to England in 1392–96. He was a friend of Chaucer, and his poetry shows the influence of *The Book of the Duchess* in *La Complainte de l'an nouvel* and of *The Parliament of Fowls* in *Le Songe Saint Valentin*. Chaucer's *Complaint of Venus*, meanwhile, is a free adaptation, dating probably from the 1380s, of three ballades from a sequence by Granson: Chaucer makes the poetic narrator female instead of male, which might suggest some original occasional purpose for the composition of the *Complaint*. It is a remarkable testimony to the artificiality of these forms that Chaucer finds it so easy to make the change of sex. At the end, in the Envoy, Chaucer, unusually for him, makes a specific acknowledgement of his debt to Granson:

> And eke to me it ys a gret penaunce
> Syth rym in Englissh hath such skarsete,
> To folowe word by word the curiosite
> Of Graunson, flour of hem that make in Fraunce.

The remark about the scarcity of rhyme in English is of course intended to draw attention, in the right off-hand way, to Chaucer's skill in managing the difficult rhyme-scheme of his French original.

Only one manuscript has the Granson ballades in the order in which Chaucer obviously had them before him. This is University of Pennsylvania MS French 15, of about 1400, one of the largest collections of French poems in fixed forms on the subject of love. It is derived from exemplars put together in the 1350s or 1360s and can be taken to represent very fully what Chaucer would be growing familiar with and trying to imitate during that period. It includes a very large number of poems (310) by Machaut, twenty-seven by Granson, a few by Deschamps (who is mostly too late for the exemplars from which the Pennsylvania manuscript is derived), many anonymous poems, and, not coincidentally, the poetic exchange of Philippe de Vitry and Jean de la Mote. It also includes fifteen poems with the initials 'Ch' between rubric and text. It is the very kind of writing that a literate young courtier of the 1350s/1360s would have been engaged in, and no better explanation of 'Ch' has emerged than that it is a modest indication of Chaucer's authorship. The poems fill the gap in his poetic career with a neatness almost too perfect to be true.[26]

The 'Ch' poems are very representative of the collection as a whole and of the French lyric mode that prevailed at the time. They are awash with classical, mythological and Ovidian allusion, and play the game of love according to its set rules, aiming not to express passion but to mirror elegantly the high ideals of sensibility to which courtly society aspires. The poems purport to be spoken by a variety of personae – lover, lady, friend, wise commentator – and give ample precedent for the variety of 'voices' that Chaucer was later to take on as narrator. There are no startling parallels with his English poetry, though inevitably there are the similarities that one comes across in poems working so closely within common conventions. It is, to be truthful, not the French poetry one would have expected of Chaucer. Here he is, writing of love in the measured, civilized, high-minded style that is the staple of the collection:

> Entre les biens que creature humainne
> Puist acquerir pour vivre liement,
> C'est d'ensuir la vie souverainne
> D'Amours, qui est le droit commencement
> De toute honneur; et amoureusement
> Eslire dame honorable a maistresse.[27]

> One of the good things that a human being may do in order to live happily is to follow the sovereign life of Love, which is the true beginning of all honour; and in accordance with Love to choose an honourable lady as his mistress.

There is little vitality or idiosyncrasy, nothing that one could call characteristic of Chaucer: but then, is it to be expected that a poet's idiomatic style and tone of voice and general poetic 'character', especially when they are hardly formed, will survive translation to another language not his own? Is Milton's Italian poetry 'Miltonic'?

Among the Machaut poems in the Pennylvania manuscript, there are four that Chaucer definitely borrowed from in his later poetry, including two (numbered 110 and 182 in Wimsatt) that he used in *The Book of the Duchess*, and others that he echoed. Two anonymous ballades in the collection are closely related to poems by 'Ch', having the same or a similar refrain, and reworking the same subject-matter: they hint at informal writing competitions among the poets at court. Another ballade, warning of the tusked ox 'Cire Mire Bouf', who will devour badly behaved lovers, gives us an idea of the kind of humour that was enjoyed in such circles.[28] It is not much, and it was to be spectacularly improved upon by Chaucer when he got round to writing in English, as in his ballade *To Rosemounde*. The plight of the stricken lover was never so poignantly portrayed:'Nas never pyk walwed in galauntyne / As I in love am walwed and ywounde.' There is probably much topical and personal and occasional allusion in the poems of 'Ch'; the fixed forms and conventional style are ideal for masking such allusion. Much of the delight of such poetry must be lost with the inevitable loss of its social context.

CHAUCER'S ENGLISH INHERITANCE

Whether or not Chaucer wrote the poems of 'Ch', the only poems that he claims to have written or that are positively attributed to him in the manuscripts are poems in English. His decision to write in English, and subsequently exclusively in English, as far as we know, was an extraordinary decision for a writer attached to the English court of the 1360s. At least it must have seemed extraordinary at the time, though to us, with the benefit of hindsight, it looks a natural thing to have done. English, though it may have lacked the finesse in polite discourse of French and the abstract and conceptualizing vocabulary of Latin, was after all the mother-tongue, with more immediate access to the deeper well-springs of emotional experience. Chaucer reckoned shrewdly, at any rate, with the relative prospects of English and French, and may already have heard something of what Dante was doing with the vernacular in Italy. He made what we all agree, especially after reading the poems of 'Ch', to have been the right choice.

There were obstacles, though, to writing in English the kind of court poetry that Chaucer assumed he should write. A literary language capable of the sophistication associated with court poetry does not spring into existence because a poet of genius sees that it might be handy. It has to be hammered out, and in this instance it had to be hammered out from some unpromising materials. There were, in Chaucer's time, two sophisticated English literary languages, but they were confined to specific genres and regions, and unsuitable for Chaucer's purposes, if indeed he knew much or anything about them. There was the eloquent and expressive prose of the devotional and contemplative tradition, which was to reach something like perfection in the writing of Chaucer's contemporary, Walter Hilton (d. 1396), canon of Thurgarton in Nottinghamshire. This tradition was strongest in the North and West. So was the second tradition, that of alliterative poetry, which underwent an unexpected resuscitation in the second half of the fourteenth century. This poetry certainly had a sophisticated vocabulary of its own, most evident in the poems of the *Gawain*-poet, drawn eclectically from many sources, archaic English, French, Scandinavian and dialectal.

But, nearer London, French was more dominant, and as Chaucer looked around at what was available to him in the English prose and poetry of the South-East, written in the dialect of London with which he was familiar, he must have breathed a heavy sigh. There was some workmanlike prose of didactic instruction, most of it deriving from the church's attempt to educate the laity in basic Christian doctrine and in the principles of penitence so that they could make the annual confession enjoined upon them by the decrees of the Fourth Lateran Council of 1215 and Archbishop John Pecham's *Constitutions* of 1281. But most of what was written in English, for this purpose and others, was in verse, principally in the old long-line couplet, variously derived from Latin, French and native sources, or in the short octosyllabic or four-stress couplet, derived from French. The whole of the rapidly growing *South English Legendary*, which had been spreading from Gloucestershire since the 1280s as an accumulating compendium of saints' legends and other homiletic narratives, is in the former, while the remorselessly comprehensive poem of religious instruction, *The Prick of Conscience*, written probably about the time Chaucer was debating what language to write in, is in the short couplet. Popular romances in short couplet abounded, and there were others in the tail-rhyme stanza, the mechanical jog-trot of which Chaucer was later to catch with cruelly delightful precision in *Sir Thopas*. Much of this writing, religious and secular, could have come his way in a comprehensive manuscript of English poetry, almost a library in itself, such as National Library of Scotland, Advocates' MS 19. 2. 1 (the Auchinleck manuscript), which was made in London, probably for a rich bourgeois customer, in the 1330s. Indeed, it has been plausibly argued that this very manuscript passed through Chaucer's hands.[29]

He found in it, or in something very like it, a variety of lively verse narratives, told with brisk and undemanding ease, in the gossipy and diffuse style associated with traditional oral delivery, larded with expletives, asseverations and tags of all kinds. It was a language and style that could carry a story forward in a rapid and unemphatic manner, and provide for natural-sounding dialogue. Chaucer was no doubt aware of its insufficiencies as well as its virtues, and of a quality in it of 'informality which sometimes verges on inconsequence', and it has been argued that the characteristic informality of style in Chaucer and in other 'Ricardian' poets such as Gower is one of 'many improvisations and accommodations, ironies and silences' forced upon them by the inadequacy of English, its lack of a high style or of a poetry of ratiocination.[30] Chaucer, in other words, made a virtue of necessity, and created a personal style of witty self-deprecation that seems the best of all poetic languages out of a language that was capable of little more than being deprecated. It is characteristic of him to lament, and have his narrators lament, the insufficiency (Squire's Tale, V. 37, *Legend of Good Women*, Prologue, F. 67) or unworthiness (Man of Law's Tale, II. 778) of English to the narrative task in hand, though we should recognize that such comments, like the complaint about the scarcity of rhymes in English in *The Complaint of Venus*, are also a traditional way of drawing attention to the poet's skill in overcoming such obstacles.

There is more to the story of Chaucer's 'invention' of an English literary language than this, of course, and a long history of energetic supplementation of the resources of English with new words from French literature and court speech and learned borrowings from Latin. But what he began with is evident, and *Sir Thopas* can well be regarded not merely as a burlesque of the English popular romances but also as a back-handed compliment to them, its language and style representing 'the vigorous wild stock upon which were grafted Chaucer's other and more sophisticated styles'.[31]

It would be possible to underestimate the range of styles and power of language in the English romances, not merely in the carrying forward of narrative and in the exchange of dialogue, but also in the representation of moments of strong feeling. Here is a passage from *Sir Orfeo*, a poem in the Auchinleck manuscript that

Chaucer certainly knew, in which the faithful steward hears news
of his lord's death:

> 'Allas! wreche, what schal y do
> That have swiche a lord y-lore?
> A, way! that ich was y-bore,
> That him was so hard grace y-yarked,
> And so vile deth y-marked!'
> Adoun he fel aswon to grounde:
> His barouns him tok up in that stounde
> And telleth him hou it geth –
> 'It is no bot of mannes deth.'[32]

It would also be possible to exaggerate the extent of Chaucer's
indebtedness to them. Chaucer never falls into or aspires to a
language of such transparent simplicity as in the passage just
quoted. Already, where he writes of the emotion of bereavement
in *The Book of the Duchess*, he writes in a different way:

> My lyf, my lustes, be me loothe,
> For al welfare and I be wroothe.
> The pure deth is so ful my foo
> That I wolde deye, hyt wolde not soo;
> For whan I folwe hyt, hit wol flee;
> I wolde have hym, hyt nyl nat me.
> This ys my peyne wythoute red,
> Alway deynge and be not ded,
> That Cesiphus, that lyeth in helle,
> May not of more sorwe telle.　　　　(581–90)

There may be dramatic reasons for the mild inflation of style here,
in the desire to represent some quality of self-consciousness in the
black knight's show of grief, but the carefully pointed and elaborated use of antithesis, and the classical allusion, have been learnt
from Machaut, and are quite alien to the popular English tradition.

　　Yet, contrarily, as one reads the opening lines of *The Book of the
Duchess* –

> I have gret wonder, be this lyght,
> How that I lyve, for day ne nyght
> I may nat slepe wel nygh noght;
> I have so many an idel thoght
> Purely for defaute of slep
> That, by my trouthe, I take no kep

Of nothing, how hyt cometh or gooth,
Ne me nys nothyng leef nor looth.   (1–8)

– the debt to English and the difference from French are apparent.
One could compare the lines from 'Ch' quoted above, or indeed
the opening lines of Froissart's *Le Paradis d'Amours*, which Chaucer
is directly imitating:

> Je sui de moi en grant merveille
> Coument tant vifs car moult je velle
> Et on ne poroit en vellant
> Trouver de moi plus travellant
> Car bien sachiés que par vellier
> Me viennent souvent travellier
> Pensees et merancolies.[33]

I can only be amazed that I am still alive, when I am lying awake
so much. And one cannot find a sleepless person more tormented
than myself, for as you well know, while I am lying awake sad
thoughts and melancholy often come to torment me.

Instead of the polite and measured cadences of the French, every
word contributing to the impression of textuality and control, the
opening of the English poem has a conversational and gossipy
tone, the liveliness, the tags, the syntactical padding of familiar
address. The only words borrowed from French, despite the closeness of the imitation of a French poem, are the two in the fifth
line (*purely*, *defaute*). Already, too, the characteristic Chaucerian
'voice' is to be heard, not strikingly dissimilar from the voice of
the unsophisticated narrator in the English romances, and perhaps
partly therefore the consequence of some of those 'improvisations
and accommodations'.

THE ROMAUNT OF THE ROSE

The preceding discussion of Chaucer's poetic inheritance from
English has centred on *The Book of the Duchess*, but it would be a
reasonable assumption that Chaucer's first major poetic enterprise,
after some writing of love-songs in French and English, was the
translation of the French poem that above all others influenced
him, the *Roman de la Rose*. In this way, he was to make the poem

his own, absorb it in the fullest way into his imaginative life, and also assert for the first time the capacity of English to sustain the rhetoric of courtesy.

The *Roman de la Rose* survives in over 300 manuscripts, many of them finely illustrated, and it was by far the most widely disseminated and widely read secular poem of the Middle Ages. Guillaume de Lorris (d. 1237) wrote the first 4,058 lines, in which he virtually invented the courtly poetic genre that was to sweep all Europe before it, the allegorical love-vision in the form of a dream recounted by the poet–dreamer in the first person. His poem tells of a young man's first discovery of the fashionable courtly world of sexual love (the walled garden of 'Sir Myrthe', as he is called in the English version, *The Romaunt of the Rose*), his delight in its dancing and singing and flirtations, and his first experience of falling in love, represented allegorically in terms of seeing his lady's (his own) eyes in the well of Narcissus, and being struck by Cupid's arrows. There follow his allegorical encounters with the various obstacles to the pursuit of a successful love-affair, particularly the inhibitions placed upon the lady's natural warmth of response (*Bel Acueil*, 'Bialacoil') by her sense of social obligation and fear of what people may say (*Daunger*).

Guillaume's *Roman* is a poem of considerable erotic suggestiveness, with three descriptions of seductive young females already in the first thousand lines (Idleness, Gladness, Beauty), and the sweetly lascivious display-dancing of the two maidens, clad only in light summer dresses:

> That oon wolde come all pryvyly
> Agayn that other, and whan they were
> Togidre almost, they threwe yfere
> Her mouthis so that thorough her play
> It semed as they kiste alway.
> (*Romaunt*, 784–8)

There is a sense of summery freedom and the daring abrogation of the usual moral laws, of young people flocking to 'fleet the time carelessly, as they did in the golden world', in the Grecian idyll of *Daphnis and Chloe*, or in more modern terms in the film of *Camelot* or in an anthropologist's account of sex life in Samoa. Twelve-year-old Youth kisses freely in public with her *lemman* – 'They were ashamed never a dell' (1296) – and Richesse leads by the hand her lover, a young gigolo who loves living well (1129). After

dancing their *caroles*, the company retire to the shade, 'Undir the
trees to have her pley' (1318), where the grass grows thick and
velvet-soft, 'On which men myght his lemman leye / As on a
fetherbed to pleye' (1421–2).

There was great delight and a sense of audacity in seeing court
life presented in this uninhibited way, as there must always be in
the representation of general sexual pleasure as innocent of moral
and social consequence. There was delight, too, in seeing all the
stages of falling in love (a look, a word, a kiss are in turn all that
the lover desires, would be worth all the world to him, etc.)
given the dignity of literary-personification allegory, and military-
fortification allegory too: Bialacoil is to be imprisoned in a great
tower guarded by Daunger because he allowed the Lover to kiss
the budding Rose. Aspects of psychological and sexual experience
difficult to talk about directly in polite society, and perhaps inac-
cessible to other forms of discourse, can be hinted at covertly
through allegory. Much else can be suggested too – the mystery
and ambiguity and seamy side of sexual love as well as its vigour
and delight. There is much to scandalize and excite a courtly
audience and much to argue about and discuss.

Nor is Guillaume at all the prisoner of his fantasies; his poem is
much more than an artistic representation of heroically prolonged
sexual foreplay. He has a keen sense of the preening exclusiveness
of the social set he describes, and conveys it in the image of the
very upper-class young Amant 'basting' (sewing up) his sleeves
with a silver needle as he walks out on a May morning (*Romaunt*,
104), as well as in the pictures of those 'vices' excluded from
the privileged garden of love. They are shown to be excluded,
allegorically, by being painted on the outside of the garden wall.
There is Hate and Covetousness and Envy, all of them rather
down-at-heel, and also Vilanye, that 'litel coude of nurture' (179),
and Sorowe, made ugly by grief and with her hair disordered
(327), and Elde, an old woman, 'a foul, forwelked thyng' (361),
and Povert, clad in a patched old sack (457). Guillaume, that
is, through his allegorical imagery, recognizes something of the
narrowness of view and vulgar materialism that are implied in a
socially exclusive and exclusively social code of values. The brief
disquisition on mutability attached to the description of Elde
(369–99) also permits us to see the precariousness of the joys of
sexual love, poised as they are between innocence and decay.
There is humour too, and much that Guillaume makes us find
comical: the lover prowling around the wall and banging and

shoving at the little wicket-gate in his impatience to get into the garden (534), or the God of Love's instructions on the proper wallowing expected of a sleepless lover (2555–79).

Some forty years after Guillaume's death, his unfinished poem was 'completed' in a further 17,722 lines by Jean de Meun, a university-trained scholar. Jean de Meun does complete the allegorical 'love-story', in his last thousand lines portraying the lady, already distributed among her several faculties and totally depersonalized, as a fortress successfully stormed, in a passage notable for its violent sexual imagery; but he was less interested in continuing the allegorical love-story than in using the impetus and popularity of Guillaume's work as the opportunity for a display of learning, casuistry and scatological wit, and for indulging his sardonic ill-temper in university gossip and in abusing his fellow-clerics. His continuation, much of which is in the form of very long discourses by characters like Reason, Nature and Genius, is a kind of non-alphabetical encyclopaedia in the vernacular, in which everything gets mentioned somewhere. It is as if an unfinished novel by Jane Austen had been completed by Robert Browning. It is outrageous, but safely so, given the allegorical format and the multitude of voices that Jean deploys.

The *Roman de la Rose* is a book that Chaucer read with more than usual intentness; it became part of his mentality, perhaps more part of his experience than the experience of life itself. In particular, Jean de Meun's poem taught him all that he needed to know, to start with, of European culture, and it taught him too the liberating power of scepticism. Reading the *Roman* now is a constant revelation, a privileged visiting of the cellars and store-houses of Chaucer's literary imagination. Favourite passages, in which Chaucer seems to have encapsulated in a memorable way some special insight, are again and again found to have their inspiration in the *Roman*, especially in Jean de Meun: the Wife of Bath's lament for her lost youth, the proud sovereignty that the Franklin declares to be demanded by love, the Prioress's table manners, the poet's apology for the necessity of calling a spade a spade. Two of Chaucer's most subtle and characteristic creations, the Wife of Bath and the Pardoner, take their first being and much of their substance from Jean de Meun, from the long discourses of La Vieille and Faux-Semblant respectively. Chaucer was first introduced to some of the great commonplaces of the Western intellectual tradition through Jean de Meun: the nature of Fortune and her wheel, the debate about destiny and free will, the true nature of *gentillesse*. Poems for which he claims or seems to claim other sources, usually Latin, such as the Monk's Tale and the Physician's Tale, derive their inspiration in the first and sometimes the only place from the *Roman*.[34]

In the Prologue to *The Legend of Good Women*, the God of Love accuses Chaucer of being an enemy to love and love's servants:

> Thou maist yt nat denye,
> For in pleyn text, withouten nede of glose,
> Thou hast translated the Romaunce of the Rose,
> That is an heresye ayeins my lawe,
> And makest wise folk fro me withdrawe.
>
> (F. 327–31)

In the revised version (G) of the Prologue, he explains that the 'heresye' is the claim that the abandonment of the self to sexual passion, love *paramours*, is folly. This, by and large, insofar as it can be fished out from shoals of red herrings, is the theme of Jean de Meun's portion of the *Roman*, and the implication is therefore that Chaucer translated the whole poem. Deschamps clearly thought so, when he congratulated Chaucer on having 'planted the rose tree' (*planté le rosier*) in England, and called him 'Grand translateur, noble Gieffroy Chaucier.[35] And it is entirely natural that Chaucer should have translated the work, given that it was his practice to appropriate major texts of the European tradition to himself and his literary imagination by translating them. What he did with the *Roman* he did also with the *De Consolatione Philosophiae* of Boethius and the *De miseria condicionis humane* of Pope Innocent III (though his translation of the latter is lost) and a similar argument could be made concerning the purposes of translation in *Melibee* and the Parson's Tale.

However, all that survives is a fragmentary text of an English translation in the Hunterian Museum (Glasgow) MS V. 3. 7, which in its turn happens to be the copy-text for the first printing of the poem in the edition of the collected works of Chaucer published by William Thynne in 1532. Neither the manuscript nor the print marks any break in the 7,696-line text, but it does in fact consist of three distinct fragments. Fragments A (1–1705) and B (1706–5810) translate *Roman* 1–5154 and run continuously, but B is in a northern dialect, uses Northern and other non-Chaucerian rhymes, and from the start uses *bouton* as the trans-

lation for the key word *bouton* in the French, where Fragment A
had used *knoppe* consistently. Fragment C (5811–7696) translates
a completely separate portion of the French (10679–12360), uses
fewer non-Chaucerian rhymes than B but more than A, and differs
sharply from B in translating the French *Bel Acueil* as *Fayre-
Welcomyng*, where B had used *Bialacoil* throughout. The consensus
of opinion is that Fragment A is almost certainly by Chaucer, B
certainly not by him, and C probably by him. Chaucer, we must
assume, did his translation, whether he completed it or not, primarily for his own purposes of self-enrichment and practice in
versifying, and sought no particular public audience for the work.
Only a fragment came down to the fifteenth-century scribe of the
exemplar of the Hunterian manuscript, and the attempt to provide
a continuation, perhaps by setting two translators to work simultaneously at different points of the *Roman*, foundered. Scribal interest in providing extra material for poems left unfinished by
Chaucer is well evidenced for *The Canterbury Tales*.

As for Fragment A, it is certainly a translation of the best and
most readable part of the *Roman*, and it is itself very readable. If
Chaucer was learning his craft, he was learning among other
things to avoid the awkward inversions and clumsy padding that
become obtrusive as soon as one crosses over into Fragment B.
There are the beginnings too of the command of paragraph flow
through which Chaucer can avoid the jerkiness to which the
octosyllabic couplet is subject in English and through which he
can achieve something of the fluency of the French. Other antici-
pations of the future include a more personal tone in the narration,
sharper visual imagery, and a heightened quality of emotional
sensitivity.[36]

John of Gaunt and *The Book of the Duchess*

A long-established and tenacious tradition sees John of Gaunt as
Chaucer's early and perhaps principal patron. This view, which
is partly based on a desire to find a closer connection between
Chaucer and the most interesting public figure of his time, needs
some modification.

We have met John of Gaunt already, as Earl of Richmond, as
Earl and then Duke of Lancaster, at Hatfield in 1357, in Spain
at the battle of Najera in 1367, and on expedition to France in

1359 and 1369. Chaucer is likely to have met him on some of these and many other occasions, and in 1372 Philippa his wife and in 1374 Chaucer himself received annuities from Gaunt. The annuity most probably continued to be paid until Gaunt's death in 1399, the absence of record of payment after 1380 being due to the fragmentary and inconsistent nature of the relevant records, but there is no documentary evidence of any further personal connection between the poet and the prince. The desire to turn their association into a long-running soap opera, which has inspired two biographers of Chaucer to prove how every one of Chaucer's writings turns upon some event in his supposed patron's exciting life, must be regarded as wishful thinking.[37]

The ascription of an early date to Chaucer's *An ABC* may be similarly regarded. The poem is an alphabetical prayer to the Virgin, the twenty-three stanzas beginning with the letters of the alphabet in sequence (*j*, *u* and *w* are not regarded as separate letters of the alphabet). It is quite closely paraphrased from the Marian poem interpolated by Guillaume de Deguileville into his allegorical narrative of the *Pèlerinage de la Vie Humaine* (first brought out in 1331), with the twelve-line stanzas of octosyllabics of the French converted into ballade stanza, eight-line stanzas of pentameters rhyming *ababbcbc*, presumably because Chaucer could not face a twelve-line stanza with only two rhymes (*aabaabaabaab*). Chaucer's poem survives in sixteen manuscripts, an unusually large number for one of his smaller poems: six of these are manuscripts of the fifteenth-century English prose translation of the *Pèlerinage*, *The Pilgrimage of the Lyfe of the Manhode*, into which Chaucer's *ABC* was happily incorporated by the scribes. Space was also left for it in two of the four manuscripts of Lydgate's verse translation, *The Pilgrimage of the Life of Man* (the other two manuscripts are fragmentary), and Lydgate introduces it with some pomp (19751–90), but clearly the scribes had no copy.[38]

The poem itself celebrates, in each stanza, some quality or power of the Virgin, elaborating upon the traditional imagery with some skill, and Chaucer matches that skill in his English version. It is not fervent poetry of affective devotion, but formal celebration of the kind that was to become the norm of English Marian poetry in the fifteenth century, and of a kind that perhaps better suited Chaucer's rather formal piety. It was written at a time when Chaucer had begun to experiment with the pentameter, probably in the late 1370s. It appears at this point in our narrative because of Thomas Speght. As we have seen, Speght was very keen to enlarge upon Chaucer's Lancastrian connections, and, in introducing it into his 1602 edition of Chaucer's *Works*, he offered the explanation of the poem's occasion that it was 'made, as some say, at the request of Blanch, Duchesse of Lancaster, as praier for her privat use, being a woman in her religion very devout' (f. 347a). I think this is most likely Speght's or another's invention.

But, whatever the occasion of *An ABC*, there can be no doubt that *The Book of the Duchess* was written as a poem of consolation upon the death of the Duchess Blanche. She is called 'goode faire White' in the poem itself (948), in the cryptically allusive manner characteristic of court poetry, but in the Prologue to *The Legend of Good Women* Alceste, in defending Chaucer against the accusations of the God of Love, speaks of his having written 'the Deeth of Blaunche the Duchesse' (F. 418). Gaunt is also referred to in a cryptic manner at the end of *The Book of the Duchess*, where his poetic representative, the man in black, rides home to his castle: 'A long castel with walles white, / Be Seynt Johan, on a ryche hil' (1318–19). The punning allusion to John, Earl of Richmond, Duke of Lancaster, is not difficult to pick out, and it is quite unambiguous. The poem could hardly have been written without Gaunt's knowledge, and it is natural to assume that it bespeaks a certain intimacy. A young pipsqueak of an esquire would not have presumed to write on such a subject in such a way had he not been assured of a sympathetic reception.

At the beginning, the poet pictures himself as sorrowful and unable to sleep, because of some eight-year sickness that he mysteriously refuses to specify: Chaucer put this in as a talking-point, and it has certainly provoked a deal of talk. To pass the time, he takes up a book, where he reads the story of Seys (Ceix) and Alcyone, of Alcyone's grief at the death of her husband. Finally asleep, he dreams of a spring morning, a beautiful grove, and of finding a man in black alone in the wood lamenting the death of his lady. Not seeming to understand, perhaps because he is used to such complaints being merely a literary convention, the dreamer questions him about his loss, provoking first a rhetorical outpouring of mannered grief and then (759–1309) the story of the knight's love for 'White', her beauty and goodness, his attempts to woo her, his failure and final success, her death.

The Book of the Duchess is deeply indebted to the French poets: to the *Roman de la Rose*, to Froissart's *Paradis d'Amours* for its opening and dream-framework, as we have seen, to Machaut's *Le Dit de la Fonteinne Amoureuse*, written to console Jean, Duc de Berry, on being separated from his wife as he went into exile in England, and to Machaut's *Le Jugement dou Roy de Behaingne*.[39]

The *Jugement* is particularly important, and lines and phrases from it are echoed throughout *The Book of the Duchess*. It tells how the poet comes upon a lady and a knight lamenting, she because her true love has died, he because his beloved has proved faithless. In disagreement about who has the greater cause of sorrow, they refer the matter to the King of Bohemia (the one who was killed at Poitiers), who decides that the knight is worse-off. As a form of consolation for the black knight of *The Book of the Duchess*, this may seem a little tactless, but there is an occasion in Chaucer's poem when the comparison between the two kinds of loss is implicitly invoked. It is when the dreamer still seems to be under the impression that the knight is grieving over the loss of his 'Queen' at chess: the dreamer says that sorrowing for such a cause would be worse than the self-destructive acts of those who were betrayed in love – Medea, Phyllis, Dido, Echo and Samson (721–41). It is not as crude as 'It could have been worse', and it is a thought that must remain unspoken, but some hint of the 'manageableness' of death in comparison with other emotional catastrophes is apt enough.

References to Chaucer's debt to the French poets may suggest a cunning mosaic made out of their leavings, and Chaucer is not at all unwilling on occasion to encourage this fiction, as in the Prologue to *The Legend of Good Women* (F. 66–83). But in reality he makes all new and in so doing makes the French poets, rather unfairly, seem stilted and contrived.

The opening lines, as we have seen, imitate Froissart closely, but there is a world of difference, as there is between Chaucer's narrator and Machaut's, whose drollness is of a more calculated kind altogether. Chaucer's opening is strangely baffling, unsure, inexplicit, almost as if the poet were thinking aloud or talking to himself. The lassitude and perplexity seem to be what he is speaking out of, not about: it is very personal, not at all as if Chaucer were 'being a poet', which is the impression the French poets strive for, but as if he were being himself. The taking up and reading of the book is done in the same way, the sense of expectancy, of something important about to come our way, heightened by the rambling inconsequentiality of the exposition. Here is someone so devoid of artfulness, we must think, that we can be sure we can trust him. Only a lovable simpleton would speak thus of the subject-matter of the book he was reading –

> This bok ne spak but of such thinges,
> Of quenes lives and of kinges,
> And many other thinges smale   (57–9)

– or declare that reading of Alcyone's grief so upset him that he felt worse all the next day (99), or express surprise that there are so many gods in the story when he thought there was only one (237), or make such a hash of the connection between the story he read and his desire for sleep. He would have died, he says, for lack of sleep if reading this story had not kept him awake, but now, having heard tell of Morpheus, god of sleep, he will offer him a featherbed if Morpheus will help him to sleep.

The dreamer of the dream, when we finally get to it, has many of the traits of the poet, with the difference that he seems to be more at home with life in his dream than in reality. The arbitrariness of dream-experience – the horse that he suddenly finds in his bedroom (357), the hunt of (who else but?) the 'Emperour Octovyen' (368) – seems natural to him, though laying traps for future commentators may not have been too far from Chaucer's mind. He remains gentle, baffled, vulnerable, simple-minded, a true 'innocent abroad', and of course the ideal recipient for the black knight's confidences.

There has been a good deal of discussion of the role of the dreamer in *The Book of the Duchess* and in Chaucer's other dream-poems, and of the relation of the dreamer to Chaucer the poet. Terms like 'the dreamer', 'the narrator', 'Chaucer the poet', are commonly used, anything to avoid saying 'Chaucer' and laying oneself open to the charge of simple-mindedly confusing the two or three or four 'subjects' or 'subjectivities' involved. The 'Chaucerian persona' has had a particularly vigorous critical life, offering an opportunity for interpreters to substitute almost anyone they want for the unnameable prime suspect. Such interpretations masquerade as an open-minded approach to the text, one that does not wish to identify a single intentionality in the person of the author, but what they more often do is to substitute for the enigmatic and elusive intentions of the author the only too obvious intentions of the critic. The cult of the persona has thus become a technique for systematically ironizing the text and appropriating it to the service of particular kinds of programmatic interpretation. Some of the results have been very strange.

Another factor at work has been the assumption that roles appropriate to a writer in the age of private reading are equally appropriate to be assigned to a writer with a listening audience in mind, an audience, furthermore, listening to and watching the writer himself, present in person. Clear-cut divisions between the 'poet' and his 'persona' are specially unlikely in such a situation. But even with writers of our own day there has been a tendency to exaggerate the divisibility of the author's person. As Henry Miller said, when pursued by an eager critic arguing the extreme unreliability of his first-person: 'If he means the narrator, then it's me.'[40]

It is worth recognizing now, at the end of this historical episode in Chaucer criticism, that it is not simple-minded to talk of Chaucer as the 'I' of the poem, that the roles that can be played by the 'performing self' are infinite, and one role may merge into another in a word or a phrase, as in life in a wink or a gesture. There is nothing exceptional or specifically 'Chaucerian' about it, nor is this 'I' a mask that Chaucer deliberately assumed in order to cover the embarrassment and sense of alienation caused by his supposed social inferiority; on the contrary, the elusiveness of the 'I' is what we are used to delighting in in the story-telling of any skilled raconteur. Chaucer is simply very much better at it than anyone else. He is not someone somewhere else manipulating the 'I' for rationally explicable strategic purposes; he *is* the dreamer, as much and as fully as he *is* Chaucer. To recognize this is to recognize the essential fluidity of Chaucerian narrative, the way in which the reality represented constantly reshapes itself, so that everything is always on the edge of expectation or breakdown, and repeated journeys through the same narrative may register as different experiences. To suppress this true memory of the experience of reading Chaucer, in the interests of turning his poems into problems to be solved, is to mistake 'narrative' for 'text'.[41]

The dreamer is the way into the story, and it is the story that is above all important, in two principal ways, both of them having to do with emotional truth. The first beauty of *The Book of the Duchess* is the curve of consolation that it shapes, beginning in unbearable numbing misery and ending in the return to life. The misery is first of all hinted at as the poet's, but it is much more fully articulated in the story of Seys and Alcyone that he reads. Daringly punctuated with the hilarious comedy of the arrival of the messenger at the cave of Morpheus (178–85), it is nevertheless a story of inconsolable sadness and it is told with cruel brevity. The dead Seys appears at the foot of his grieving wife's bed, and says:

'My swete wyf,
Awake! Let be your sorwful lyf,
For in your sorwe there lyth no red;
For certes, swete, I am but ded . . .
And farewel, swete, my worldes blysse!
I praye God youre sorwe lysse.
To lytel while oure blysse lasteth !'

(201–4, 209–11)

All the deep grieving of the poem is concentrated here: it is worked out, in the security of fiction, and nothing can be as bad again.

The beginning of the dream is the first consolation – the sun streaming through the windows, the birds singing, the earth's joy after winter (410). The natural joyfulness of the season is the irresistible assertion of life against death, and it contains the hidden code of consolation. The hunt is another image of life abundant: the little dog's failure in the hunt (390) is a touching anticipation of the withdrawal from life of the man in black, as well as a hint of the therapeutic role of mindless innocence. The black knight's expression of his grief is at first self-dramatizing and operatically melancholic:

'For whoso seeth me first on morwe
May seyn he hath met with sorwe,
For y am sorwe, and sorwe ys y.'   (595–7)

He seems determined to strike postures, to dwell on his own self-absorbed present, to embroider and textualize his grief, and the dreamer's ridiculous mistake in thinking that he is *really* grieving over a lost chess-piece is in a way no more ridiculous than the knight's use of the chess image in the first place. The dreamer, with the polite and persistent naivety of his questions, draws out the knight, insists that he tells his story, and in telling his story the knight finds his consolation in the memory of his lady and the fulfilment of his service to her. His readiness to tell his story has much to do with his recognition of the innocence and good-natured sympathy of his interlocutor. The appropriateness of their relationship to the emotional success of the poem is no less clear than its appropriateness to the historical situation of poet and prince, with flattering consolation for the latter and tactful self-promotion for the former.

The poem, having laid such subtle siege to the barren self-absorption of grief, circles finally upon the central cause of consolation, not the usual Christian themes of the transience of life or the Better Place elsewhere, but the memory of Blanche's beauty and goodness. It is the heart of the poem, and much is drawn from Machaut, but Machaut's set-piece descriptive eulogies are here broken up and redistributed, with much questioning, prompting and exclaiming from the dreamer, so that the developing portrait of Blanche seems the natural result of reminiscence. The process of textual redistribution is also a process of psychological reintegration: the dismemberment which was the character of conventional medieval descriptions of women, as they inventoried each feature and limb, here gives way to a re-membering. Blanche's sweetness of nature comes through with a vividness that transcends time, her generosity of spirit, and the absence of the cold flirtatiousness that fashionable courtly ladies are expected to practise (862–77, 1020–33). There is even some suggestion of a moral depth of consciousness in her behaviour, of a freely willed quality in it which makes of it a kind of spiritual courtesy:

> And therto I saugh never yet a lesse
> Harmful than she was in doynge.
> I sey nat that she ne had knowynge
> What harm was, or elles she
> Had koud no good, so thinketh me. (994–8)

The knight's progress is a process of re-creation. He relives his love of Blanche, and emphasizes her still-living image within him (912, 1108, 1124). He also re-creates the woe of her first 'Nay' (1243), which he experienced as a kind of death: 'I nam but ded' (1188, cf. 204). The joy that followed her acceptance of his love is by contrast a return to life: '"As helpe me God, I was as blyve / Reysed as fro deth to lyve"' (1277–8). In this way the woe of bereavement is pre-empted and transcended, though the fact of loss must still be acknowledged: '"She ys ded!" "Nay !" "Yis, be my trouthe!" / "Is that your los? Be God, hyt ys routhe!"' (1309–10). It could be put as a platitude – ''Tis better to have loved and lost . . . ' or, more mundanely, She is not dead as long as the beauty of her life is remembered to give life to others – but the reawakening of life and the possibility of happiness comes about so spontaneously that it seems to be lived anew. Such is Chaucer's way with commonplaces, and this is how *The Book of the Duchess* comes to be a poem about death that is a celebration of life.

To interpret the poem, after this, as an encouragement to John of Gaunt to resume normal life and seek another partner may seem a little crass, and one hopes that both the poet and the prince had a subtler sense of the relationship between poetry and reality. The poem is deeply personal, but all our intimacy is with Chaucer; the sublimely idealized portrait of Blanche refuses that intimacy, as is only proper. Nor will the historical records answer our impertinent questions concerning the 'truth to real life' of the woman and the relationship so portrayed. Gaunt calls Blanche 'ma treschere jadys compaigne' in his will, which sounds like a specially poignant memory of his long-dead first wife; but he calls Constance, his Spanish wife, who also predeceased him (in 1394), the same. The phrases are, anyway, the routine commonplaces of inky clerks. He arranges for the annual commemoration of Blanche's death on the day she died, for ever, but a similar obit is guaranteed for Constance. He chose to be buried next to Blanche in St Paul's, but it was usual to be buried next to one's first wife, especially when she was the foundation of one's fortune.[42]

Or one could try the opposite tack. That Katherine Swynford was Gaunt's mistress before Blanche died seems very doubtful, though the customs of the time would not necessarily have frowned upon such a great lord if she had been. That she became a kind of foster-mother to his three young children after their mother died is clear, and, as Armitage-Smith puts it, in his charmingly Edwardian way, 'The Duke's "visits to the nursery" allowed the intimacy to ripen' (*John of Gaunt*, p. 391). Meanwhile, the duke was planning his great dynastic marriage to the heiress of Castile (see table 3); Constance was only 16 at the time of her marriage in 1372, and throughout her life as duchess she led a secluded life among her small Spanish retinue, pious and withdrawn, yet obstinately determined to return to Spain with her husband and reclaim her inheritance. She knew of Katherine and was probably quite content to be relieved of her husband's attentions. Gaunt was always, it must be remembered, a great lord, and a very busy man. On 14 January 1375 he arranged for a tun of the best Gascon wine to be sent to 'nostre tres cher et bien ame dame Katerine de Swynford' at her manor of Kettlethorpe in Lincolnshire; a few days later, on 26 January, he was making payment to Henry Yevele for Blanche's tomb at St Paul's, finally completed; and all this time he was actually married to Constance.[43]

That Gaunt paid attention to the commemoration of Blanche's anniversary, as he did every year, is no argument that Chaucer's

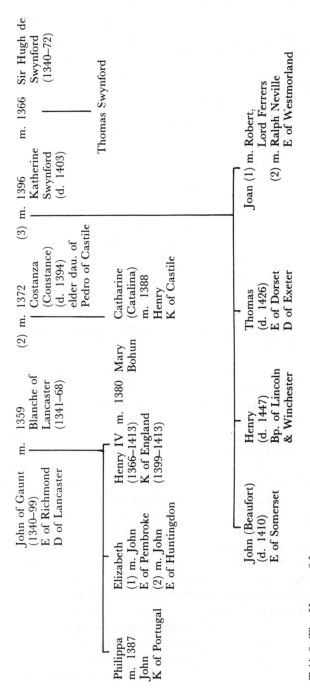

Table 3. The House of Lancaster

poem was written for one of these annual ceremonies. There seems
no good reason to deny the natural presumption that *The Book of
the Duchess* was written soon after Blanche's death in 1368, when
consolation would have been appropriate, and that it is an idealized account of the love of a lord for a woman of surpassing beauty
and goodness; it would be as nonsensical to suppose that the
account is true in all particulars as it would be to suppose that it
had no basis in a reality to which its early hearers and readers
had ready access.[44]

The delicacy of Chaucer's poem is a marvel, some worlds away
from Froissart's attempts to say what he presumably intends to be
the right thing:

> Ossi sa fille de Lancastre, –
> Haro! Mettés moi un emplastre
> Sur le coer! Car quant m'en souvient
> Certes souspirer me couvient,
> Tant sui plains de merancolie.
> (*Le Joli Buisson de Jonece*, 241–5)

Also his daughter of Lancaster – Alas! Put a plaster on my heart,
for when I think of it I cannot but sigh, so full I am of sadness.

But there remain some small awkwardnesses in Chaucer's poem,
particularly in his attempts to incorporate into it a range of classical learning and mythological allusion. This was something he
wanted to do as part of his ambition to enlarge and ennoble
English after the French model. All is well so long as the parades
of allusion can be ironically accommodated to the black knight's
self-conscious display of grief, even if Chaucer may not fully
deserve the benefit of such a doubtful accommodation. Later on,
when irony is out of the question, there are lists of those classical
heroes and heroines who are surpassed by the knight and his lady
(1054–87), or of the traitors whose treachery would be nothing
beside his treachery if he forgot his lady (1117–23), or the little
excursus on the invention of music (was it Tubal? or Pythagoras?)
that the knight makes in mentioning the songs he composed for
his lady (1160–70). Any 'dramatic' explanation for these would
be absurd: Chaucer has simply not yet learnt how to assimilate
the learning he feels he must display to his very personal way of
writing. The brilliant accommodations of the Wife of Bath's Prologue, or of Dorigen's complaint in the Franklin's Tale, or of the
whole of the Nun's Priest's Tale, are still a long way off. It must

be said too that Chaucer rather overdoes the dramatic trick by which the knight picks up the dreamer's words, or his own, in mock-outrage. What worked well once (1045) does not bear so much repetition (1052, 1075, 1115).

3

Advances:
The 1370s

From the point of view of the 1370s, the 1350s and 1360s must have looked like the good old days. Times had changed: the glories of Edward III's campaigns in France were now only a memory, and the superficial boost to the economy given by the labour shortages consequent upon the Black Death had long exhausted itself. Edward III himself was declining into senility, and his eldest son, the Black Prince, had returned from Aquitaine with the painful and debilitating gastro-intestinal disease, contracted in Spain, that was to kill him. Both he and his father were to die within just over a year of each other, the Black Prince on 8 June 1376, and Edward III on 21 June 1377. Lionel was already dead, as was the much-loved Queen Philippa. Of the younger princes, Edmund of Langley was never to make much of a mark, and Thomas of Woodstock was not yet old enough to have revealed the full troublesomeness of his disposition.

The Duke of Lancaster alone bore about him still something of the chivalric glamour of England's great days, but the decade for him was to be one embarrassing failure after another. His *chevauchée* of 1373 was a fiasco, the largest and best-equipped army ever sent by an English king to France wasting itself in a fruitless endeavour to bring the French to battle; his ambitions for the throne of Castile were, for the time being, frustrated; his interventions in politics, well-meaning or not, earned him only the bitter enmity of the London citizenry and the suspicion of his fellow-magnates. His private life, with a reclusive foreign queen and a publicly acknowledged mistress, was not entirely satisfactory either.

He remained, however, the most powerful man in the realm, and for a while Geoffrey Chaucer's fortunes were tied with his.

CHAUCER AS ROYAL ESQUIRE AND CUSTOMS OFFICER

Chaucer was still, at the beginning of the decade, an esquire of the king's household, and for a while he was something more. There is record of him among the sixty-two 'scutiferis camere regis' receiving winter and summer robes during the years 1371–3 (*Life-Records*, p. 100). An 'esquire of the king's chamber' was a member of the king's inner household, his *secreta familia*, which was in attendance upon him and travelled about with him. Chaucer's appointment at the customs in 1374 was clearly incompatible with regular attendance at court, and there is no further record of him as an esquire of the king's chamber. But he remained an esquire of the king's household, and is recorded in the wardrobe accounts for 1376–7 as being owed 40*s.* for winter and summer robes. Edward III also made him, on the feast of St George (23 April), 1374, the unusually handsome grant of a daily pitcher of wine for life (*Life-Records*, p. 112). This would be the equivalent of about a gallon a day, and Chaucer probably acted wisely in having it commuted in 1378 for an exchequer annuity of 20 marks.

Meanwhile, he continued to receive his regular annuity for the same sum, with occasional delays when he was abroad. Payment was assigned upon the customs in 1376, which was very convenient for all concerned, though the bureaucratic administration of such an exchequer annuity remained inordinately complicated, as the *Life-Records* show (pp. 133–43), especially when Chaucer was seeking an advance on his half-yearly instalment. When Edward III died, his grants had to be confirmed in the name of the new king, as was the customary practice; Chaucer's annuity was confirmed, with a block of others, on 23 March 1378, and his daily pitcher of wine commuted for a further 20 marks on 18 April. Nothing could illustrate more clearly the routine official nature of such records: the references to 'nostre ame esquier Geffrey Chaucer' in Richard II's privy seal writ of 18 April (*Life-Records*, p. 305) clearly have nothing to do with any personal regard in which he was held by the 11-year-old king. Annuities like Chaucer's were granted by the king through a warrant, to which was affixed the privy seal, authorising the issue of letters patent confirming the grant. The privy seal had originally been very personal to the king, in contrast to the great seal, but by the mid fourteenth century it no longer necessarily had any close connection with the king, and its use did not imply (though of course it did not exclude) any personal act on his part.

Whatever closeness of connection there had been between Edward III and Chaucer during the years 1371–3, when he was an esquire of the king's chamber (and also making his first visit to Italy), his career shifted decisively away from the immediate environs of the royal court in 1374. In that year he accepted an appointment as controller of the wool custom and wool subsidy and of the petty custom in the port of London. The letters patent authorizing the appointment are dated 8 June, and Chaucer took his oath of office on 12 June. No doubt he welcomed the addition of an annual £16. 13s. 4d. to his income, though the job itself was something of a chore, and not a usual avenue to promotion for an ambitious esquire. In accepting it, he probably had in mind a desire to get away from the court, where Alice Perrers and her favourites wielded considerable influence, and where there was a good deal of bitter squabbling. An intelligent man could see that trouble was brewing, that the financial connections between the king's circle and some of the more unscrupulous city merchants, such as Richard Lyons, were not only unsavoury but dangerous. The king possessed much potential personal authority, and his party through him, but he was expected to raise money in the traditional ways and to show himself to be publicly accountable. If Chaucer tried to remove himself to a position of neutral official-dom while the going was good, and thus avoid being drawn into the conflict betwen the 'Good Parliament' of 1376 and the court party, he acted both sensibly and characteristically. The dangers of the position of any royal appointee are well illustrated by the fierce attack on Richard Lyons at the 'Good Parliament' for customs profiteering. Chaucer kept a low profile in the political conflicts of his day, steering clear of potential trouble in his public life and never mentioning anything controversial in his poetry. In this way, with the instinct of the artist, he kept secure his poetic career.

A little before his appointment as controller, Chaucer had another piece of good fortune, when on 10 May 1374 he was granted the lease for life, rent-free, of a substantial dwelling above the city gate at Aldgate. His only responsibilities were to keep it in good repair, not to sublet it, and to be ready to have it garrisoned in time of emergency. Consisting of the rooms above the gate, a cellar, and perhaps also some former guard-house accommodation in the two large flanking towers, Aldgate was a very desirable residence; Chaucer's friend, the lawyer Ralph Strode, lived in the corresponding dwelling above Aldersgate between 1375 and 1382, and Aldgate went to a prominent royal esquire, Richard Forester, when Chaucer vacated it in 1386.

There are some interesting coincidences in this year of good fortune for Chaucer. The Aldgate lease is evidently connected with the appointment at the customs, and was intended to provide him with a house for himself and his wife now that he had left the court. It was probably granted to Chaucer, without rent, as a favour from the city to the king or other royal patron, since it was to the city that it belonged. The falling upon Chaucer of this heap of good things, not forgetting the grant of the pitcher of wine on 23 April, is difficult to think of as a sudden act of generosity on the part of the ageing king, from whom Chaucer had been growing more distant. But it was in April 1374 that John of Gaunt returned from his unfortunate *chevauchée*, and immediately set about re-establishing himself as a great lord and a generous patron. Richard Stury was restored to favour, and on 8 May Philip de la Vache and Lewis Clifford received grants from the Lancaster exchequer; all three were or were to become friends and close associates of Chaucer. On 13 June, the day after he took his oath of office as controller, Chaucer received the grant of an annuity of £10 from Gaunt, evidently to help in the maintenance of his new London establishment. On 6 July, Chaucer received two half-yearly instalments of his royal annuity, payment of which had become a little erratic in the past year or two, and his wife Philippa received five payments upon hers. A few days later Gaunt left for Tutbury and a tour of inspection of his Northern castles.[1]

An additional reason for what can be interpreted as Gaunt's favour towards Chaucer, apart from gratitude for *The Book of the Duchess*, is the very practical one that Chaucer was Philippa's husband. Philippa had been granted an annuity of £10 by Gaunt on 30 August 1372, for services to the Duchess Constance, to add to her royal annuity of 20 marks, and she had clearly become a valuable member of Constance's household. With others, she received special gifts on 1 May 1373, before Gaunt's departure for France, and was to spend nearly the whole of the following year at Tutbury Castle, in Staffordshire, with the duchess-in-exile. Gaunt had reason to be grateful, even more so if Philippa was Katherine Swynford's sister. However, what is certainly an interest on Gaunt's part in getting Chaucer well set up on this occasion cannot be extended into a general argument that he was, more

generally speaking, Chaucer's 'patron'. There is no further record
of favour shown to Chaucer, in records that reveal lavish generosity
on Gaunt's part to all kinds of servants, and Hulbert and Manly
are surely right in dismissing the older claim that Gaunt was
ubiquitous in promoting Chaucer's career.[2]

Chaucer was now back in the city where he had been brought
up, in a house of his own, surrounded by the bustle and noise of
the biggest manufacturing and commercial centre in the country.
His neighbours included fishmongers, butchers, potters, bakers,
chandlers, goldsmiths, saddlers, cordwainers, brewers, hatters and
spurriers, as well as some fripperers, arbalesters and fusters (*Life-
Records*, p. 147). All human life passed through the gate under his
dwelling, carts with iron-bound wheels carrying grain and other
victuals into the city from the countryside around, and others
leaving with loads of dung (like the 'dong-carte' about to leave at
the west gate of the town in the Nun's Priest's Tale, VII. 3036)
and the blood and entrails of slaughtered beasts. His daily walk
to work on the wool quay, between London Bridge and the Tower
of London, took him through some of the busiest parts of the city;
a slight detour took him past the end of Cornhill, where Langland
had his hovel and the second-hand dealers their stalls (*Piers Plowman*, C. V. 1); Friday Street, where Chaucer saw the unexpected
coat of arms outside the Grosvenor inn, was a little further west,
near Chaucer's old home in Upper Thames Street; to the north,
away from the river, was Paternoster Row, alongside the north of
St Paul's, which was the area of London where most of the book-
dealers and book-makers had their shops and offices. From here
Chaucer might have been seen hurrying home to Aldgate 'with
his second-hand torn copy of Macrobius (*Parliament of Fowls*, 110)
or a remainder volume of the old-fashioned tail-rhyme romances
that he was to parody in *Sir Thopas*; perhaps with *Piers Plowman*
itself'.[3]

Once home, he would escape with his books from the day's
business at the quay, and perhaps from his wife too, whose complaining voice seems to be heard through that of the eagle in *The
House of Fame*:

> For when thy labour doon al ys,
> And hast mad alle thy rekenynges,
> In stede of reste and newe thynges
> Thou goost hom to thy hous anoon,
> And, also domb as any stoon,

> Thou sittest at another book
> Tyl fully daswed ys thy look;
> And lyvest thus as an heremyte,
> Although thyn abstynence ys lyte.   (652–60)

It was the eagle too who reminded Chaucer of a familiar voice when trying to arouse him from his swoon:

> Me mette 'Awak' to me he seyde
> Ryght in the same vois and stevene
> That useth oon I koude nevene.   (560–2)

Perhaps we should think of *The House of Fame* as the poem in which Chaucer first showed not only the strains of coming to terms with European literature but also the pressures of unpractised cohabitation. There may even be a rude allusion, hidden away in lines 115–18, to the prison of married love and its effects on male potency. Whether Philippa in fact spent much time at Aldgate is doubtful. She would be most of the time in attendance at the court of Constance, her young son Thomas with her, at least until he was about 9 or 10.

Chaucer's job at the customs quay was no sinecure: it was not the kind of position that would be granted to a favoured poet to give him the leisure to write more poetry, but rather the kind that would give a good income and a respectable place in society to a worthy and hard-working court servant, and one from which he could readily be deputed if he were needed elsewhere in the king's service. The responsibility of the controller was to check the quantities of wool, wool-skins and leather-skins that were being shipped out, so that the proper export duty could be charged at the customs. The wool custom and the wool subsidy were different charges on the same kinds of goods; the petty custom covered a more miscellaneous range of goods (there is no certainty that Chaucer took this into his hands before 1382). Chaucer had to deal with about one thousand 'cockets' (documents relating to export goods) a year, on average, most of them relating to shipments to Calais, though Middelburg became the usual destination after the mid-1380s (see *Canterbury Tales*, General Prologue, I. 277). The work was much heavier during the winter, from November to May. The controller had to keep records, and he had to keep them in his own hand, which is why the job could be regarded as arduous and usually went to professional civil servants.

The plethora of records in Chaucer's own hand that we might have expected does not exist, because this batch of records happens not to have survived.

Something else does survive, however, from somewhat later in Chaucer's occupancy of the post. The custom-house, where Chaucer worked, was rebuilt in 1382 by John Churchman, a merchant and a collector of the petty subsidy (and one of the many who sued Chaucer for debt in later years). The tronage (weighing) hall, above cellars, was built at the seaward end of the waterfront quay at Billingsgate, and there was an extension added in 1383 with a counting-house and a small chamber over with a latrine. The site was excavated in 1973. 'Between the two buildings', we are told, 'was a timber latrine drain running south to the river; the excavators were proud to claim that Chaucer himself probably used it.'[4]

The main charge upon the controller was that he should be honest and careful. This was all the more important and difficult in that he was a mere nobody compared with the collector of customs, the person, usually a wealthy London merchant, who actually pocketed the customs duty. Farming out the customs in this way was a favourite royal method of repaying personal debts from what was by rights the national revenue. Merchants like Nicholas Brembre, William Walworth and John Philipot, who were collectors of the wool customs during Chaucer's term as controller, were quite unscrupulous in profiteering from their office (all three were knighted and became lord mayor of London), and the job of the controller, who was expected to keep a check on men of immensely greater wealth and power than himself, was no doubt awkward at times. What it demanded was acquiescence in doubtful practice, the perpetual turning of a blind eye, rather than outright venality. One can understand how a man like Chaucer could become accustomed to doing this, and understand too how he would like to forget about it at the end of the day, and how he would welcome opportunities to appoint a deputy and travel abroad on more interesting business.

One can understand too how, in a broader sense, Chaucer's elusiveness and indirectness in his response to the crises and conflicts of his day were encouraged by his situation. He had no power-base either in the aristocracy or in the church, and no rooted commitment to either. He received patronage because his father was rich, because he was useful, and in some measure, also, because he was clever, funny and inoffensive. It is not difficult to see why Langland, having or being none of these things, did not. Resentment in the one bred protest and sublime transcendence; comfort and satisfaction in the other led to those accommodations and silences which are as much the character of Chaucer's handling of his matter as of his handling of language, style and point of view. Similar kinds of accommodation in our own day, and the cultivation of a similarly dedicated lack of commitment, produce deconstructionist literary critics. It is not surprising that they like Chaucer.

Before turning to the journeys abroad which gave Chaucer so much pleasure in the 1370s, it is worth mentioning other records that indicate how well established Chaucer was becoming in the London of the 1370s, taking on those legal and often lucrative responsibilities that were the burden of a man in public office. He did not do as much as his father, but he did his share. In 1375 he stood surety or mainprize for John de Romsey, an old friend and fellow-esquire from court days (1367–73) who had become treasurer of Calais. Chaucer was guarantor or mainpernor that Romsey would appear before the exchequer to give a good account of the properties he had taken into his hand belonging to a man convicted of sedition. In 1378 Chaucer's mainprize was enrolled, along with that of John Beverley, another fellow-esquire, when the custody of Pembroke Castle and other lands was granted to Sir William Beauchamp during the minority of the Pembroke heir. Chaucer was supposed to guarantee that Beauchamp took proper care of the property and did not use it for personal profit. He would be glad to do this, or rather not do it too carefully, for a friend who was to be chamberlain of the royal household (1378–80), a witness in the Cecily Champain case (1380), and helpful in some capacity or other in Calais in 1387.

There are further actions of mainprize by Chaucer in the 1380s, but the 1370s also see him responding to the call to duty in another and much more profitable sphere. It was the custom for heirs of the king's tenants-in-chief, during their minority (that is, before they reached the age of 21), to be made wards of court, and for their property to be farmed or invested on their behalf. The king would sell these wardships (which included rights to the payments due to him on the marriage of the heir) or grant them to his favourites, and they would thus fall into the hands of people who had no personal connection with the ward, and who could easily use the office for their own profit; wards often had to go to law to get their property back when they came of age. Chaucer was granted the wardship of Edmund Staplegate, son and heir of Edmund Staplegate, a rich merchant of Canterbury, on 8 November 1375; he was also granted the marriage payment, which Edmund, who came of age a year or two later, bought back from him for £104. It is hard to know whether Chaucer behaved well or badly; these are simply financial transactions through which the king rewards his servants without incurring any actual expense to himself. In this case Chaucer was rewarded very generously. The wardship and marriage of William Soles, son and heir of John Soles, of Betteshanger and Soles in Kent, which Chaucer was granted on 28 December 1375, was much less profitable; the annual rent in the manor of Soles that formed part of the grant was only 5s., which Chaucer did not bother to collect, and there is no record of William getting married.

Chaucer had a couple of brushes with the law in 1379 and 1380; these will be dealt with in chapter 4.

Journeys Abroad

In late 1372, during his period of service as esquire of the king's chamber, Chaucer was sent with a trading mission to Genoa to discuss the appointment of a special seaport in England for the use of Genoese merchants. He received on 1 December 1372, the day he set out, the very substantial sum of 100 marks (£66. 13s. 4d.) as an advance on his expenses. After his return, Chaucer submitted to the exchequer a statement of receipts and expenses covering the period 1 December 1372 to 23 May 1373; the statement makes it clear that he had also been to Florence. The journey would have taken about a month each way, a few days longer if Chaucer took the Rhine route to avoid France (currently engaged in hostilities with England), so that he had about three months actually in Italy.

Chaucer was an important member of this commission, chosen principally because of his knowledge of Italian, which he had probably picked up as a boy from the Italian merchants with whom his father and his step-cousins, the Herons, had had business. His Italian was an added qualification for his later appointment at the customs, where many Italian merchants traded; Italy took a third of the total English wool export. But Chaucer was the least important of the three principals in the Genoese mission: the other

two, John de Mari (Giovanni del Mare) and Sir James de Provan
(Jacopo Provano), were Genoese of high rank in the service of
Edward III, the former having acted as an agent for the recruit-
ment of Genoese crossbowmen as mercenaries, and the latter as
an agent in the business of ship rental. It is not known whether
any formal agreement came out of the meetings in Genoa, but
Anglo-Genoese trade flourished in the years following and Genoese
ships made more than usual use of Southampton. As for the
journey to Florence, which was not mentioned in the original
commission, it was almost certainly to do with the king's private
business with the Bardi banking family, with whom he had close
contacts and from whom he had long been in the practice of raising
loans to finance his wars and his building extravagances.

This was Chaucer's first visit to Italy. He had been to France
and Spain, but Italy was the heart of Europe, physical witness to
the grandeurs of imperial Rome and the origins of the Christian
church, home of numerous kingdoms, dukedoms and principalities,
several of them individually richer than England, and perhaps
two centuries ahead of England in terms of artistic and literary
innovation. England, from an Italian point of view, was as remote
and poor and backward as it had been during the days of the
Roman Empire, and Chaucer must have felt it to be so. He would
be struck too by the development, in the Italian city-states, and
in Florence especially, of a sophisticated secular society, governed
by merchant oligarchies, in which the power of the traditional
aristocracy was much curtailed and in which the church, though it
had its place, was not allowed to interfere with the more important
business of making money and using it to provide the comforts
of life, including beautiful paintings. It would be an opening of
horizons on a humanist culture dominated neither by chivalry nor
by penitential religion, one that was rich and seemingly open
to all. The experience would be staggering, but also liberating,
somewhat comparable with the experience of those English aca-
demics and poets who spent time in the United States in the 1950s
and early 1960s, or, perhaps more immediately pertinent, the
open-mouthed response of Eastern Europeans when confronted in
the late 1980s with the wealth of the West.

There was, too, something that was more directly relevant to
Chaucer – the revelation to him of an acknowledged nobility in
the vocation of poet, in which he was in the service of neither
court nor church, neither an entertainer nor a propagandist. The
poet in Italy, above all in Florence, challenged for and was granted

a role in the community at large, in which he spoke as a philosopher and as a representative of the wisdom of the past, including
the classical past. Virgil was the great model, and Dante
(1265–1321) and Petrarch (1304–74) were the great inheritors,
with Boccaccio (1313–75) assiduously attentive to the reputations
of both. In truth, he could hardly have been more attentive to
Petrarch's reputation than Petrarch was himself: the latter had
himself crowned poet laureate in the presence of his patron, Robert,
King of Naples, when he was 36, and again in the following year
(1341) before the Roman senate on the Capitoline. He concocted
a ceremony in which he delivered an oration on the value of poetry
and the high status and fame in history of the poet, an oration
constructed on the principles of the medieval sermon but with
quotations from the classical writers rather than from the Bible.
It was, from one point of view, the beginning of the Renaissance;
from another, it was 'the most colossal feat of self-promotion in
literary history'.[5]

Above all, though Petrarch on these occasions spoke in Latin,
there was the fact that this dignity was granted to poetry in the
vulgar tongue. In the Latin *De vulgari eloquentia*, Dante had claimed
that the Italian vernacular had a potential for eloquence which
rivalled that of Latin, and he had reinforced this claim, with
additional arguments for the authority of the vernacular, in the
Italian *Convivio*. Here and in *La Vita Nuova* (XXV), the arguments
are made in the context of a discussion of secular poetry. In *La
Divina Commedia*, Dante not only lays further claim to a role for
himself as the vernacular poet of a great sacred poem (*Paradiso*,
xxv. 1–12) but also has the angelic host singing in Italian, as in
Paradiso, xxvii. 1–3. Thus Italian, through Dante's arguments and
his practice, had now occupied the commanding literary heights
previously reserved to Latin. Chaucer's career as a poet can be
seen, and very significantly seen, as the achievement of something
comparable for the English language, and equally as effecting, in
England, the transformation of the bard and *trouvère* into the 'man
of letters', the poet with a public voice in the commonwealth.[6]

Chaucer could have met Petrarch or Boccaccio on his way down
from Genoa to Florence, Petrarch at Arqua or Padua, Boccaccio
at Florence or nearby Certaldo, but it is extremely unlikely that
he did, or that he would have been well received if he had gone
out of his way to do so. They were old and crotchety, and very
distinguished, and did not have much time for young travellers of
no rank, and from England, of all places. In Florence, though,

Chaucer was at the centre of the literary cult of Dante; lectures on the poet had been established, and the next year's series were due to be given by Boccaccio. He had heard of the *Divine Comedy*, from Italian merchants and bankers in London; now he was able to take home a memory of reading the great poem, or even carry away a manuscript of it, or part of it, and so make his journey really worth while.

Chaucer's Italian and his experience of the Genoese were again in demand soon after his return, when he received a royal commission on 11 November 1373 to go down to Dartmouth, in Devon, and arrange for the restoration to its master of a Genoese merchant-ship, which had been over-enthusiastically 'arrested' by the port authorities. The ship's name was *La Seint Marie et Seint George* (*Life-Records*, p. 40) and there is every likelihood that Chaucer stored this away with his other impressions of Dartmouth, and came out with 'Dertemouthe' as the home of his Shipman, in the General Prologue, and *The Maudelayne* as the name of his ship (389, 410).

On 23 December 1376, Chaucer was paid 10 marks to go a journey on the king's secret business in the company of Sir John de Burley. It is not clear where he went, or why, except that it was 'in secretis negociis domini regis' (*Life-Records*, pp. 42–3). Sir John de Burley was the brother of Sir Simon Burley, an old associate and fellow-esquire of Chaucer's, who was to be tutor to the young Richard II, and one of the 'Chaucer circle' in the 1380s. The coincidence of the link through business acquaintance and kinship is no more than a mark of the comparative smallness of the court and London world in which Chaucer moved, something which we shall have occasion to mention again in reference to the account books of Gilbert Mawfield, from whom Chaucer took a loan in 1392.

Between 1377 and 1381, Chaucer made a number of visits to France on royal business, to do with negotiations for a peace-treaty and then for a marriage between Richard II and a French princess. It is not always clear where Chaucer went or when. He received his passport ('litteras regis de proteccione') on 12 February 1377 to cover the period until 29 September, and was advanced £10 on 17 February to pay for a journey to Flanders with Sir Thomas Percy (who was paid £33. 6s. 8d.), from which he returned on 25 March (*Life-Records*, p. 44). But the account of his expenses that he rendered on his return makes it clear that he did not go to Flanders but to Paris and Montreuil, where negotiations for a peace-treaty with France were in progress. On 11 April he received payment of £20 for unspecified journeys overseas. On 28 April he was given an advance of £26. 13s. 4d. for a journey to France 'in secretis negociis', etc. The account of expenses that Chaucer submitted on 26 June upon his return is for a journey lasting fourteen days. Since he is not on the list of those who received livery of mourning (money to buy funeral garb) when the old king died on 21 June, it is assumed he was out of the country on that day.

The flurry of diplomatic activity during the spring and early summer of 1377 has much to do with the disturbed state of England at the time – the death of the Black Prince, the impending death of the old king, the prospect of a new king who was no more than a boy, the continuing conflict in Parliament and the deep suspicions on the part of Londoners and others of the motives of the Duke of Lancaster – and the hope that peace with France might be secured at least for a time. That the negotiations were not entirely successful is indicated by the French raids on the South Coast which began as soon as the temporary truce expired, and the pillaging of Rye which took place on 29 June before Edward III was even in his grave (the funeral was on 5 July).

An unexpected side-light on the peace negotiations at Montreuil in 1377 is provided by Froissart. He tells us the names of the principal delegates on the French and English sides, assembled to treat of peace at Montreuil-sur-Mer, on the instructions of their respective governments. The three on the English side were Sir Guichard d'Angle, Earl of Huntingdon, a famous old veteran of the French wars, a Poitevin by origin who had thrown in his lot with the English after fighting on the French side at Poitiers; Sir Richard Stury, who like Chaucer was captured and ransomed in France in the campaign of 1359–60 and was an esquire of the king, and who went on to become a knight of the king's chamber and was certainly one of the 'Chaucer circle'; and 'Jeffrois Cauch-iés' (*Life-Records*, p. 50).

Chaucer received further payment of £22 on 6 March 1381 in respect of these journeys to France to treat for peace in the reign of Edward III and also in respect of another or others in the early part of Richard's reign to treat for marriage. Commissions to negotiate a marriage were appointed in 1378, 1379 and again in 1380, but Chaucer is not named in any of them.

However, Chaucer was certainly in Lombardy, on his second visit to Italy, between 28 May and 19 September 1378. He received his letters of protection on 10 May; the warrant for payment to himself and his senior companion, Sir Edward Berkeley, was issued on 13 May; Richard Barrett took the oath as deputy controller of the wool customs on 14 May, having been appointed by Chaucer in a memorandum in French which survives and may be in his own hand (*Life-Records*, pp. 158, 164); letters of attorney (to protect him against lawsuits during his absence abroad) were granted under the names of John Gower (the first appearance in the Chaucer records of the name of his friend and fellow-poet) and Richard Forester (who was to take over the Aldgate house in 1386) on 21 May; payment of £66. 13*s.* 4*d.* was made to Chaucer on 28 May; and a final payment of a further £14, to cover his actual expenses for a 105-day visit (computed at the regular rate of 13*s.* 4*d.* a day, with £4 added to the total to pay for the Channel crossing of himself, five men, and horses), entered in the records on 28 November 1380.

The purpose of the journey, on which Chaucer was as usual travelling as an esquire in attendance upon a knight (who was paid twice as much), was to take the king's greetings to Bernabò Visconti, lord of Milan, and to 'nostre cher et foial' Sir John Hawkwood, the English soldier who had made a reputation for himself as a mercenary adventurer in the wars between the Italian city-states, and to treat with them of business to do with the king's wars (*Life-Records*, p. 54). Both of these prospective allies were wicked and unscrupulous men, but international diplomacy has little time for the recognition of such niceties, and it was particularly important at this time to cultivate an Italian alliance. Peace-negotiations with France were not going smoothly, and there may have been some premonition of trouble in another quarter.

After being elected at the instigation of the French in 1309, the French pope Clement V decided that he would not be welcome in Rome, and settled in Avignon. A very luxurious 'Babylonian captivity' followed, during which the papal court at Avignon became renowned for extravagance and corruption. None of the succeeding six popes, all of them French, was eager to move back to Rome, which was full of old ruins and much less comfortable than modern Avignon, until Gregory XI decided to do so in 1376. When he died, on 28 March 1378, an Italian pope was elected, as befitted the mood of the Roman populace. (Froissart has a hilarious story, unfortunately untrue, of another Roman favourite being elected, a saintly old man aged at least a hundred years old who was so shaken up and exhausted by the jolting he received when he was sat on a white mule and paraded around the city that he died.[7]) Urban VI, the newly elected pope, promised to be receptive to French interests, but, having been elected, he changed his mind and became very obstructive. The conclave, consisting mostly of French cardinals, now elected an antipope, Clement VII, who was set up in Avignon. Thus began the Great Schism, in which the already tarnished reputation of the papacy suffered further as the two pontiffs waged war against each other and entered into competition in the sale of the spiritual prerogatives of their office, such as the power to annul the barren marriages of great lords on the grounds of consanguinity. The nations of Europe, its dukedoms and principalities, found themselves obliged to choose between Rome and Avignon, and inevitably England and France chose differently. Prospects of a lasting peace between the two countries seemed more remote than ever. Other alliances needed to be forged. Hence, probably, the mission to Italy.

Chaucer had heard much of Bernabò's splendid, violent and corrupt court, but it is unlikely that he had been to Milan before, despite the speculations, mentioned earlier, that he was there for Prince Lionel's marriage in 1368. The impressions he received contributed to the fine line which introduces Bernabò among the 'Modern Instances' in the Monk's Tale: 'God of delit and scourge of Lumbardye' (VII. 2400). At the end of the stanza, alluding to the fearful circumstances in which Bernabò was murdered at the instigation of his nephew and son-in-law Gian Galeazzo, in 1385, Chaucer scuttles for safety in his usual way: 'But why ne how noot I that thou were slawe' (VII. 2406).

Bernabò had a great library in Milan, which Chaucer surely saw during his six weeks there, if not the even greater library at Pavia of Bernabò's brother (and Petrarch's patron) Galeazzo Visconti, who died on 4 August, during Chaucer's visit. Chaucer, amid all his official engagements, was no doubt much exercised in acquiring copies of those writings of Boccaccio, as well as Petrarch and Dante, that were to be the creative inspiration of his poetry for the next ten years. Dante and Petrarch impressed him; Boccaccio was to be his meat and drink. It was in the Visconti libraries that he may first have gained extended acquaintance with the writings of Petrarch and Boccaccio; their influence is not evident in the poems he is presumed to have composed between 1373 and 1378, where the influence of Dante is by contrast very apparent. These library lists and book purchases may seem, to us, a good deal more important than the plans for a marriage between

Richard II and Caterina, Bernabò's daughter, which were the only thing the Milanese mission took back to England, and which came to nothing.[8]

Bernabò left a deep impression on Chaucer: he perhaps reflected upon the difference between the civic virtues of the Florentine state and the violent tyranny of Milan, and David Wallace argues persuasively that Chaucer's Clerk's Tale, in setting up a dialogue between the Petrarchan and Boccaccian versions of the story (the Visconti were Petrarch's patrons, whereas Boccaccio identified himself with Florence), has an important political implication. Like Boccaccio, Chaucer sets the tale in Lombardy, and like Boccaccio he is critical of Walter's 'tyranny', where Petrarch treats it as mysteriously proper. But it remains an implication.[9]

Chaucer's other explicit reference to the Lombard tyranny is in the Prologue to *The Legend of Good Women*, where Alceste tells the God of Love to be generous and merciful to Chaucer, as all lords should be to their subjects, 'And nat be lyk tirauntz of Lumbardye' (F. 374). The personalized and fictionalized context in which Chaucer introduces the allusion makes it appear, as usual, that he does not fully understand the implications of what he is saying.

It might be remarked further that, though he makes these characteristically diffused and oblique references to Bernabò, Chaucer makes no mention at all of the event which presumably took him to Italy in 1378. The Great Schism, especially before people got used to it, was a crisis for Europe and the church, and it provoked both Gower and Langland to express their shock and dismay. It was without doubt a major talking-point in government and diplomatic circles throughout the 1380s. Chaucer, himself involved in negotiations related to English foreign policy directly consequent upon the schism, says nothing. His silence on such a matter may be understandable, but it is also what we shall come to recognize as habitual.

THE HOUSE OF FAME

There was a long interval between *The Book of the Duchess*, written not long after Blanche's death in 1368 and certainly before Gaunt's second marriage in 1372, and *The House of Fame*, Chaucer's second attempt at independent and extended verse composition. *The House of Fame* cannot have been written before 1374, when Chaucer

began his work at the customs, which is clearly alluded to in lines
652–5, and it probably predates his second visit to Italy in 1378.
Though he acquired some knowledge of Dante, whose influence
is important in *The House of Fame*, on his first Italian visit (1372–3),
it is usually assumed that he had to wait until 1378 to make the
acquaintance of Boccaccio's writings, which had an impact on his
poetry of which there is no sign in *The House of Fame*. There is no
real temptation to place *The House of Fame* after *The Parliament of
Fowls*, since there is little likelihood that he would have gone on
working in the octosyllabic couplet, with all its limitations, after
he had 'invented' the pentameter, in *The Parliament of Fowls*.

The House of Fame comes out of or immediately after a period of
great activity and turmoil in Chaucer's life (1375–77), one in
which he was forced to recognize that the days of love and chivalry
were over, or at least sardonically compromised. After the radiant
certainties of *The Book of the Duchess*, it is a strange poem, full of
doubts and questions, characteristically diffracted in irony and
self-mockery. It is a poem that seems doubtful even of its own
existence, since it survives variously unfinished in all early witnesses, that is, three manuscripts and the prints of Caxton (1483)
and Thynne (1532). The small number of manuscripts suggests,
as with *The Book of the Duchess*, that Chaucer made no effort to
'publish' the work by having copies made by a professional scribe,
as he tells us he did with *Troilus* and *Boece* (in *Adam Scriveyn*). It
clearly comes from a time when he had no 'circle' and no established clientele of readers. Yet, beside the questioning and self-
questioning, which might suggest a time in his life when Chaucer
was debating the value of poetry, or, more painfully, the value of
his own poetry, there is also a sublimely carefree confidence that
makes the poem, with all its oddities, unmistakably Chaucerian.

If Chaucer was anxious about anything, it was about Dante and
Petrarch and their lofty notions of the poet's vocation. Fame was
their obsession, both the fame that the poet wins and the fame
that he confers on others. Fame was a form of secular immortality,
a way of transcending the world and death which did not need
the props of religion. Chaucer simply had no idea what this was
all about: his response is sceptical, conservative, respectful of old
pieties. His goddess Fame is not an awe-inspiring figure but a
vulgar coarse-mouthed harridan (see, for example, lines 1776–90)
who shows a marked tendency, as in her shape-shifting (1368–76),
to turn into her much more familiar medieval sister (1547), the
goddess Fortune. In this way, as often, Chaucer 'medievalizes'

what he found in the Italians – not surprisingly, given his literary background.[10]

It is hard to see how *The House of Fame* can be the turning-point in Chaucer's poetic career that it has often been made out to be – the self-conscious assumption, as in Milton's *Lycidas*, of the mantle of the poet, the deliberate turning away from books, dreams and love-poems to the world of experience and reality. The idea is quite laughable, really, though it is easy to see how it appeals to readers who take neo-classical ideas of the poet's vocation for granted. The passage where Chaucer (who takes the unusual liberty of naming himself, 'Geffrey', (729), in his poem) replies to the question as to whether he has come to seek fame has been placed under particularly heavy duress:

> 'I cam noght hyder, graunt mercy,
> For no such cause, by my hed!
> Sufficeth me, as I were ded,
> That no wight have my name in honde.
> I wot myself best how y stonde;
> For what I drye, or what I thynke,
> I wil myselven al hyt drynke,
> Certeyn, for the more part,
> As fer forth as I kan myn art.'   (1874–82)

This has been made to sound like a declaration of poetic intent: the poet will not seek public approbation but will be true to his experience of life and the life of the mind, as far as his artistic power permits, and take the consequences. It is interesting that Pope lifted this passage from its context in the poem, in his imitation of *The House of Fame* called *The Temple of Fame*, and gave his own version of it in order to provide the ending that Chaucer's poem lacks: 'Nor fame I slight, nor for her favours call; / She comes unlooked for, if she comes at all' (513–14).[11] But indeed Chaucer is reticent and enigmatic at best. He seems to be groping for something to say, something that will suggest he is settling down to be a serious poet, less like Milton than Keats (who had trouble with Milton) in *Hyperion*, which was also left unfinished, twice.

The absence of the gravity Pope asks for does not make *The House of Fame* a lesser poem. Like all Chaucer's poems, it has that elasticity of form, that sense of improvization, that makes of reading a perpetually renewing experience. Dante is recurrently present, as in the invocations to Books II and III (there is a touch of comical ostentation in Chaucer's use, for the first time in English, of the classical language of text-division) and the episode of the eagle, but he is held at a distance. The poem is not in any sense a parody of *The Divine Comedy*, more like an embarrassed giggle, that response to grandeur which takes refuge in off-handed irony and levity. There is the same apparent tentativeness in a poem which Chaucer probably wrote at about the same time as *The House of Fame*, the *Complaint to his Lady*, a series of exercises in metrical innovation and conventional love-complaint which includes, quite unexpectedly, eight lines of *terza rima* (15–22). That Chaucer, so many years before Wyatt and Surrey, should have experimented with Dante's peculiarly difficult verse form is astonishing; that he should have abandoned the experiment entirely in character.

The House of Fame begins with a gesture towards the French love-vision poems, which are otherwise of little importance to its conception, in the form of a discussion of dreams, as in the opening of the *Roman de la Rose* or, more fully, in lines 18299–514 of that poem. It is an odd sort of discussion, not proclaiming the value and importance of dreams, as one would expect in a dream-poem, but rambling, diffuse and on the whole uncertain about them. Nevertheless, the poet is hopeful that dreams may turn out to signify something good, especially the dream he is about to recount, which he twice tells us he had on 10 December (63, 111). There has been some notable ingenuity displayed in deciphering the significance of this date. It has been suggested that the comical implication is of a long and deadly boring poem recounting a long and deadly boring dream, all the longer since 10 December was the date of the winter solstice in the fourteenth century, and therefore the occasion of the longest night. Unluckily, the solstice was actually on 12 December. It has been argued that, since 10 December 1379 was the date on which payment was made to the emissary from Milan who brought the news that the marriage with Caterina Visconti was finally off, Chaucer's poem is a deliberately comic piece of non-news, built up as an announcement of tidings of love, but left off, necessarily unfinished, as a rueful joke. It is hard to know how much of a joke this sort of thing was thought to be, but it seems impossible that the poem was originally intended seriously to introduce such an announcement and then adjusted to the changed circumstances. There is a good deal of insistence on the 'love-tydynges' that the dreamer expects to hear (644, 675, 1886, 2025, 2143), but it is clear that the reference is to gossip and tittle-tattle (672–99), and the dreamer's constant harking back to it suggests a certain limitation in him, as in a child who keeps asking where the playground is when told to observe the Niagara Falls.[12]

The date 10 December is given, we might agree, as a touch of 'authenticating realism'. Machaut and Froissart also give exact dates for their dreams, equally arbitrary. The arbitrariness of the date is its mark of authenticity: there is no reason for the poet to give it except that it was the (fictitiously) actual date on which he had his dream.[13]

There is something else about the opening of the poem that needs to be remarked upon, since it suggests a difference of audience as well as of subject-matter. There are a couple of unexpectedly obscene *double entendres* (87, 118), exceptional in the context of Chaucer's poems for public presentation, excluding, that is, *The Canterbury Tales*. It may be old-fashioned to suggest that this indicates an audience of men only, but there are other things about the poem, particularly the pyrotechnic displays of literary and scientific learning and the conventionally cynical allusions to married life, that also argue for a show-off piece before an audience of his male cronies. The idea that it was written to be read out as part of the entertainment before an audience of lawyers at their annual Christmas revels in the Temple is unsupported by external evidence, but it has the right ring.[14]

After his invocation to the god of sleep (exactly the wrong person to ask for poetic inspiration), Chaucer dreams he is in a temple of glass, with tabernacles and pinnacles and a picture of Venus, 'Naked fletynge in a see' (133). There is no need to get too excited about Chaucer's portrayal of Venus here, since it is taken not from Boccaccio but from Pierre Bersuire's commentary on Ovid, which Chaucer had known for a long time. He did not need to go to Italy for it, or for the Gothic decoration of the temple. What follows is definitely more unusual and ambitious, a summary of the story of Virgil's *Aeneid* as it is 'graven' on the walls of the temple (complete with sound effects). Chaucer allows, without comment, the intervention of gods and goddesses in the events of the story, and therefore the idea that events might be thought to be determined by someone other than God – something that he could not let pass without facetious comment in *The Book of the Duchess* – but he can suffer no grandeur. He finds written on a brass tablet the opening lines of the poem:

> 'I wol now synge, yif I kan,
> The armes and also the man

That first cam, thurgh his destinee . . .' (143–5)

The 'yif I kan' has an inimitable idiocy.

The story, as it goes on, is increasingly 'medievalized', particularly in its emphasis upon the love-affair of Dido and Aeneas and its perfunctory treatment of the last six books of Virgil's poem (433–67). Chaucer, like his medieval predecessors, especially the one responsible for the twelfth-century *Roman d'Eneas*, depoliticizes and romanticizes Virgil's story, preferring Ovid's dramatic and emotional presentation of Dido's grief in the *Heroides* to Virgil's mythology of the origins of imperial Rome. Though Chaucer nods towards Virgil's explanation of Aeneas's behaviour towards Dido (427–32), he allows Aeneas to beome the villain of the piece, and he intervenes on Dido's behalf, on the occasions when she is not making her own complaint (300–363), with lamentations on her miserable fortune and accusations against the falsehood of men (265–92, 383–426), a good medieval subject, and a safe one.

There is some subtlety here, both in the suggestion that a story from the past, even one by Virgil, is given meaning by the response of its modern reader (an anticipation of reception theory), and also in the ambiguity created by the conflating of different authorities, Virgil and Ovid (an anticipation of the hermeneutic problems discussed by Gadamer and others). What was authoritative comes to seem indeterminate, a matter for individual response and judgement, which raises the larger epistemological question, How can we be sure that we know what we think we know? Now, we may think that the unknowableness of things is something of a weary platitude, and that a poet is not going to sustain interest for long in talking about something so obvious, but we have to reckon with the immensity of the weight of 'authority' in the Middle Ages and the difficulties, even the dangers, of scepticism. Scepticism is cheap nowadays, but William of Ockham, who at some distance, with the other *moderni*, is Chaucer's philosophical ancestor here, had to pay for it with exile and imprisonment. Chaucer's treatment of the subject, of the ambiguity of our understanding of past or present reality, the possible existence of different kinds or standards of truth, the uncertainty of 'fame', whether as report or reputation, is incomparably skittish and as far from the brave defiance of traditional authority as could be imagined, but it is a theme to which he persistently recurs in *The House of Fame*. There is the questioning of the validity of dreams, the uncertainty created by contrary witnesses to the great events of the past, the conflict between empirical and bookish perspectives on reality in Book II, and the shambles of the House of Fame and the House of Rumour in Book III, where everything that gets to be known gets to be known as an inextricable mixture of truth and falsehood. In other words, there is no such thing as 'truth'.[15]

Chaucer emerges from the temple by a little 'wiket', almost as if he were symbolically leaving the world of the *Roman de la Rose*, of books and love, and finds himself alone in a desert, like that of 'Lybye', (488) alone in some greater world, that is. His prayers to be preserved 'fro fantome and illusion' (493) are answered when he looks up and sees an eagle. Traditionally, the eagle was an image of divinely inspired contemplation and imagination; Chaucer's eagle reminds one specifically, also, of the eagle that carries Dante up into Paradise. A Dantesque invocation begins Book II, and the eagle snatches up Chaucer to take him on his aerial journey.

What follows is one of the best sustained comic passages in English poetry. The eagle has been sent by Jupiter to carry Geoffrey up to the House of Fame, where he is to be treated to some titbits of love-tidings to reward him for his long and dedicated service, as a total ignoramus and complete outsider, to love. The village idiot is to have a day out. The eagle turns out to be a kind of mad scientist, an aerial H. G. Wells desperate to tell other people about his new ideas, who takes advantage of his captive audience (Geoffrey, in the eagle's claws, is too frightened to stir, let alone speak) to pour out the superflux of his learning, on the location of the House of Fame, how all speech reaches there, the nature and properties of sound waves, the inhabitants of the upper air, and much else. It is all solid science, and the eagle is neither garrulous nor pedantic in any ordinary sense: he is simply overwhelmed by the pedagogic opportunity of communicating what he knows to someone who does not know what he knows. He is constantly insistent upon the value of empirical proof, demonstration and experience (707, 727, 737, 787, 814, 826, 839, 854, 878), in a manner that was fashionably up to the minute in the late fourteenth century.

Geoffrey is at first terrified, fearful that this may be his apotheosis –

> 'O God', thoughte I, 'that madest kynde,
> Shal I noon other other weyes dye?
> Wher Joves wol me stellyfye?' (584–6)

– or that Jupiter wants him as another Ganymede, 'the goddys botiller' (592). An audience that knew Chaucer's parentage (his father was the king's deputy butler) and probable sexual preferences would particularly enjoy the allusion. Geoffrey gradually recovers his senses, answering the eagle politely so as not to cause offence but in monosyllables so as to avoid any unnecessary movement. In truth, the eagle asks no more than these monosyllables, nor any more than a sign that his passenger is awake. But Geoffrey manages a touch of irony in agreeing with the eagle on what a persuasive speaker he is, and picking up his reiteration of 'preve' (872–4). By the time the eagle is offering him a personal conducted tour of the constellations, Geoffrey has recovered himself enough to reject it. His mind is elsewhere, on Boethius's lofty imaginings, on the allegorical journeys of the older poets, and he finds the eagle's attachment to reality and its 'thinginess' a little irritating:

> With that this egle gan to crye,
> 'Lat be,' quod he, 'thy fantasye!
> Wilt thou lere of sterres aught?'
> 'Nay, certeynly,' quod y, 'ryght naught.'
> 'And why?' 'For y am now to old'.
> 'Ellis I wolde the have told . . .' (991–6)

The eagle's disappointment is almost palpable.

Playfully, Chaucer is alluding to current debates about authority and experience, about the value of books against empirical observation, about the old learning and the new science. Geoffrey's views are not Chaucer's views: in fact, Chaucer showed himself very receptive to modern science, and was exceptionally knowledgeable in astronomy and alchemy as well as having an intelligent man's smattering of physics. But the pertinence of the debate to the theme that runs through the poem, concerning the relativity of knowledge and perception, and the possible existence of more than one definition of 'truth', is evident.[16]

After the specially Chaucerian delights of Book II, of which Dante, Petrarch and Boccaccio, or all three in conclave, would have understood nothing, Book III is something of a disappointment. After another Dantesque invocation, to Apollo, the allegory of the House of Fame itself, built on its mountain of ice, is a little trite, and the description of the building is overambitiously

extended. The outside of the palace excellently invokes a decorated
Gothic cathedral façade; in fact Chaucer describes the very kind
of building that had the great Vasari exploding with impatience
at Dark Age Gothic and its *maledizione di tabernacolini* ('malediction
of little niches'):[17]

> Babewynnes and pynacles,
> Ymageries and tabernacles
> I say; and ful eke of wyndowes
> As flakes falle in grete snowes.
> And eke in ech of the pynacles
> Weren sondry habitacles.   (1189–94)

In the niches are, not saints and apostles, but minstrels and
musicians, magicians and conjurors, suggestive perhaps of the
more ephemeral kinds of artistic fame (or perhaps hinting, a little
sarcastically, that poets, whose words were but wind in Book II,
are not much more than verbal conjurors). Inside the palace, the
great poets of the past stand upon pillars in rows, perhaps with
some reminiscence of the great hall of the royal palace in Paris,
which Chaucer had seen in 1377, where statues of the forty-seven
kings of France sustained or seemed to sustain the roof.[18] The
honour given to poetry in being placed in such majestic
surroundings comes directly from Chaucer's contact with the
Italian poets and would be unimaginable in any previous writing
in England, at least in English.

The petitions before the goddess Fame, ostensibly the heart of
the poem (1520–1867), are its weakest part. There are those who
seek fame and those who do not, those who deserve fame and
those who do not, and the permutation of their requests with
Fame's more or less arbitrary responses produces a boringly
predictable demonstration of the unpredictability of reputation.
The dreamer, still waiting to hear his love-tidings, is bemused to
know what he is doing here, but the eagle now carries him off to
a sixty-mile-long cage of twigs, full of tidings and the people who
carry them, the place where rumour (*fama*) is manufactured and
disseminated. In modern terms it is like a very large television
news studio, and makes us wonder in the same way who decides
what is news and where it comes from. It is a place of hectic
activity, for which Chaucer drew on both Virgil (*Aeneid*, iv. 182)
and Ovid (*Metamorphoses*, xii. 39), and the verse takes on an

equally hectic insobriety (for instance, 1959–76), threatening nervous breakdown, like some of Skelton's 'Skeltonics'. Character- istically, everything that gets out of the twiggy structure is a mixture of truth and falsehood, though Chaucer is not so radical as to suggest that there was not, once, 'A lesyng and a sad soth sawe' (2089). The noise and bustle and confusion focus momentarily and vividly upon something that is happening in a corner of the hall:

> Atte laste y saugh a man,
> Which that y [nevene] nat ne kan;
> But he semed for to be
> A man of gret auctorite ...   (2155–8)

And that is the last line of the poem, as it survives.

This is such a perfect non-ending for a poem that seemed destined for inconclusiveness that it is tempting to see *The House of Fame* as not accidentally unfinished. It seems appropriate that the questions the poem has raised should be left hanging in the air in this deliberately inconsequential manner. Perhaps, though, Chaucer has said or hinted something about the possible nature of his own poetic gift – that it is for the exploration of that world of meaning which lies somewhere between the 'lesyng' and the 'sad soth sawe', and which chooses deliberately not to declare its own authority and finality.

BOCCACCIO, *ANELIDA AND ARCITE*, AND *THE PARLIAMENT OF FOWLS*

Chaucer brought back with him from his second visit to Italy, in 1378, copies of Boccaccio's two great Italian poems, the the *Filostrato* and the *Teseida*, and probably copies of others of his works too. There is no question in this case that he had physical possession of manuscripts of these two poems, since his work on them, over the next seven or eight years, involved close line-by- line translation as well as paraphrase.

The impact of the Italian writer upon Chaucer was profound, and for a number of years he worked under his stimulus and inspiration. The *Teseida* is used in *Anelida and Arcite*, *The Parliament of Fowls*, *Troilus and Criseyde* and the Knight's Tale, while the

Filostrato provides the matter of *Troilus,* and the *Decameron* at least the suggestion of the *Canterbury Tales.* Dante and Petrarch seem to have existed somewhere nearer the periphery of Chaucer's literary consciousness, and were used for specialized purposes rather than as a general quarry. Boccaccio's work was more congenial to the predominantly secular English poet, and in its reflection of a brilliant and sophisticated urban culture and a wide classical learning it was a revelation to him after the English romances and French love-visions which had hitherto been his principal secular reading-matter in the vernacular. Boccaccio is a spirited and wide-ranging writer, receptive to many influences and open to many points of view, a model of urbanity. As to poetic 'purpose', he is content to write, in the *Teseida* and the *Filostrato,* within the autobiographical convention of the despised and rejected lover, who hopes that his Fiammetta will see from his suffering lovers how much he himself suffers. (He does not expect to be taken too seriously.) To Chaucer it must all have been as refreshing as a Mediterranean holiday, with the further advantage that Boccaccio is not so great a poet as to deter imitation. Chaucer may have been anxious about his relationship with Dante and Petrarch, somewhat overawed by their implacable sense of vocation; Boccaccio was a more congenial soul, happily devoid of the more high-minded forms of poetic dedication and of the high moral principles that went with them. He found it convenient to acquire some later in life, when he turned to the writing of long edifying works in Latin prose, but meanwhile he had something of the wantonness that was, much later, to become a distinguishing mark of the true poet. Chaucer was completely bowled over. It was through Boccaccio, indeed, that he came, somewhat late, to his maturity as a poet: when he discovered Boccaccio, he was already middle-aged, in medieval terms, and all his poetry after *The House of Fame* has a 'middle-aged' quality to it.

Chaucer was drawn especially, in the first place, to the *Teseida,* as the very model of the new kind of English poetry he might write. Boccaccio proclaims that his is the first poem in the vernacular to challenge the classics in portraying the deeds of Mars:

> ma tu, o libro, primo a lor cantare
> di Marte fai gli affanni sostenuti,
> nel volgare lazio più mai non veduti.

> But thou, O book, art the first ever to be seen to bid them [the Muses] sing in the vulgar tongue the deeds undertaken in the service of Mars.

This pride and confidence in the vernacular is what inspired Chaucer to believe that he could extend the range of English poetry and his own poetic ambition in the same way, and truly come into his European inheritance.

Boccaccio's *Teseida delle Nozze d'Emilia* was begun towards the end of his long youthful sojourn in Naples and finished in Florence (1339–41). It is an epic poem in twelve books, with exactly the same number of lines (9896) as the *Aeneid*. It tells of Theseus's conquest of the Amazons and destruction of Thebes, and of the love of Palemone and Arcita for Theseus's sister-in-law Emilia. It ends with the tragic death of Arcita and the marriage of Palemone and Emilia, but not before Boccaccio has shown his command of the epic palette in grand set scenes of battle, much palavering among the Olympian deities, and elaborate descriptions of their temples. Statius is the immediate model, but comparison with Virgil is by no means beyond Boccaccio's aspirations. There is grandeur, colour and spectacle, an uninhibited relish for the display of human emotion, and a readiness to allow narrative an autonomy, a value in its own right, which is only partly compromised by the addition of a moralizing commentary in prose, the *Chiose*.

Chaucer almost certainly did not know this commentary;[19] if he did, he would have had the sense to take no notice of it. In any case he was dazzled by Boccaccio's poem, and for years he could not leave it alone. *Anelida and Arcite* was his first venture at an imitation. It is in two parts, an opening narrative in rhyme royal pentameter which sets the Theban scene for the love of Anelida and Arcite, and a second part, more indebted to Ovid's *Heroides* and French poems of love-complaint, which consists of 'The compleynt of Anelida the quene upon fals Arcite' in elaborately varied stanzas of pentameter mixed with octosyllabics. The frame-narrative resumes briefly, but the poem is left unfinished.

The opening three stanzas of invocation, statement of poetic purpose and citation of authorities are among the grandest pieces of writing in all Chaucer. They catch, and surpass, Boccaccio's evocation of the high epic style, and contain lines of a rare lapidary quality such as Matthew Arnold might have picked out when looking for those 'infallible touchstones for detecting the presence or absence of high poetic quality'. C. S. Lewis, in a similarly appreciative mood, picked out line 18 of *Anelida*, 'Singest with vois memorial in the shade', as one that 'seems to contain within itself the germ of the whole central tradition of high poetical language in England'.[20] Chaucer, as always, makes no reference to Boccaccio, but claims to be following Latin versions of the story by Statius and 'Corynne' (21). It is not quite clear who he thought 'Corynne' was, but the absence of any mention of Boccaccio is remarkable. Chaucer may be taking care to disguise his real debt or, more likely, may not have known that Boccaccio was the author of the *Teseida*: the surviving manuscripts representing the tradition of the manuscript he is presumed to have known do not name Boccaccio as author. He is in any case eager to claim a Latin rather than a vernacular authority for his work: this was a common tactic in an age which had such respect for the authority of Latin.

The opening narrative, after some splendid stanzas of Theban history, takes up the story of Anelida's love and Arcite's falseness with characteristic depth and bitterness of feeling. Anelida devotes her whole being to her lover:

> Ther nas to her no maner lettre sent
> That touched love, from any maner wyght,
> That she ne shewed hit him er hit was brent.   (113–15)

Arcite feigns jealousy in order to exercise more fully the love of power that is in him the substitute for love, and later falls under the sway of another lady who exerts just that same power over him. Chaucer is a connoisseur of the subtle perversions of love and warm in his sympathy for love betrayed, especially the love and lovingness of women: 'Almyghty God, of trouthe sovereyn, / Wher is the trouthe of man? Who hath hit slayn?' (311–12). The *Compleynt* of Anelida proves, however, too formal an instrument for the expression of this feeling, and Chaucer abandons the poem soon afterwards. It is too lacking in variety, too solemn and high-minded in tone, and does not offer the opportunity for shifting the viewpoint and introducing asides that Chaucer needs as a narrator. The second part of the Squire's Tale is a more mature and idiomatic reworking of some of its themes. *Anelida and Arcite* is nevertheless a magnificent fragment, important as an experiment and as an exercise in mastery of the pentameter, and valuable in showing what Chaucer could do in a vein not his own.

In *The Parliament of Fowls* Chaucer returns to the allegorical dream-vision, introducing the dream as in *The Book of the Duchess* with the reading of a book the subject of which is related to the main subject of the poem, and structuring his poem, as in *The House of Fame*, in triptych form: the dream of Scipio, the garden and temple of Venus, and the birds' parliament. The poem is much shorter than the other two, more compact, partly because of its use of the pentameter rhyme royal stanza, fuller and richer in meaning. It is the first poem where we can be sure Chaucer knows what he is doing, even though we may not be sure what it is that he is doing. Like the other poems, it is a seeking and exploring, a questioning and doubting, which begins and seems to end in bewilderment. The effect is to make the reader want to participate with the dreamer in his search for an answer to his question, or at least help him find the right question. Something of significance is at issue, which may be politely described as the place of love in human life or, more bluntly, as the legitimacy of sexuality. The radiancy of *The Book of the Duchess* has grown shadowed; Chaucer has left the 'Chamber of Maiden Thought', to use Keats's phrase, and become acquainted with some of the 'dark passages' of human experience.[21] We are aware of a deeper 'argument' to the poem, even as we enjoy its surface whimsicalities. There is much comedy, whether it is Scipio giving Geoffrey an unceremonious shove (154) when he hesitates at the gate of the garden, or the formal parliament of birds dissolving into raucous and irreverent jeering and squabbling. But the comedy is not the meaning: it is not the parody of the formal and stilted world of allegorical love-vision that many critics want to make of it, in that rush to interpretative judgement that Chaucer has exercised so subtle and curious an imagination to restrain.

Nor is the 'meaning' of the poem to be found in other definitive formulations. The sense of something elusive and baffling, the absence of any exposition of purpose, suggest a meaning embedded in and inextractable from the structure of the poem. When Kane says, 'The *Parlement* . . . is a study of instinct and moral values, a commendation of disinterested public service, a devaluation of self-indulgent physical gratification, and an affirmation of the excellence of socially regulated natural behaviour',[22] he makes us chiefly aware of how much of the poem has been left out, and how much Chaucer encourages us to struggle to avoid saying things like that. Chaucer's poetic techniques are not clever ways of arriving by indirect routes at paraphrasable answers. The techniques of indirection, of non-assertion, *are* the realities. The question is open, and it is necessary that we should be puzzled.

So the reader is engaged in a process of inferring meaning, of picking up allusions and reading between the lines. The structuring of the poem makes of it a series of unexplained juxtapositions rather than a conventionally integrated design. The three slabs of subject-matter, which might also be thought of as representative of the different literary traditions that Chaucer was concerned with – the learned Latin tradition, the French and Italian poetry of secular love and romance, and the as yet embryonic English 'commonwealth of style',[23] eclectic and low-key – are laid side by side, their relationship not made explicit. The effect is not to imply the pre-eminent existence of an externally imposed coherence (in Christian faith and doctrine), which would be the usual explanation of structural incoherence in Gothic painting, but suggestive rather of a painting by Cézanne. There is no 'logical sequence': in fact such poetry and painting questions whether there is, in reality, any such thing, other than the illusion that we acquiesce in order to make tolerable sense of our observation or to serve some ideological purpose. *The Parliament of Fowls* responds to much of the demand that we expect to make of poetry, that it should refuse platitudes and easy answers and try in some way to 'make it strange'.

The opening lines of the poem are certainly strange and enigmatic, as well as announcing a new era in English poetry in their measured command of the pentameter, of the long verse-sentence, and of the rhetorical structures of antithesis and chiasmus. Chaucer writes of a joy that is a terror, an unopposable tyrant whose ways are yet wonderful, giving unforgettable expression to the power of love, of sexuality, to make a plaything of the human will and an irrelevance of the distinction between good and evil. Pondering these matters, Chaucer finds himself, as always, reading an old book, in this case a book that he had referred to airily on three previous occasions (*Romaunt,* 7–10; *Book of the Duchess,* 284–7; *House of Fame,* 916–18), but had now actually got round to reading. It is a medieval favourite, Cicero's *Dream of Scipio* as it was known to the Middle Ages in the commentary of Macrobius. It tells of the blissful life after death of those who work for the 'commune profyt' and the punishment awaiting 'brekers of the lawe' and 'likerous folk' (78–9) before they too come to 'that blysful place' (83). Chaucer is not sure that this is exactly what he wanted to know, nor indeed sure that he knows what he wants to know: 'For

bothe I hadde thyng which that I nolde, / And ek I ne hadde that
thyng that I wolde' (90–1), he says, echoing a conversation
between Boethius and Lady Philosophy (*Boece*, III, pr. 3. 33–6)
on what at first seems a much more serious matter, the knowledge
of the sovereign good.

What Chaucer has found is a Roman moral theorem of the
universe, concerning good and bad action in relation to service to
the state. It is a general statement of rewards and punishments,
almost, as Muscatine says, like the palinode of *Troilus* put at the
beginning (*Chaucer and the French Tradition*, p. 123). It is 'true', but
empty, a moral framework that needs filling out with the body of
lived experience. Scipio's universe is broadly compatible with the
Christian one, but it is very characteristic of Chaucer to refuse the
explicitly Christian answer. He recognizes the necessity of an
admonitory scheme of moral values, but does not want the elimin-
ation of all possibility of manoeuvre in the delicate balancing of
human moral and emotional commitments.

Chaucer falls asleep and dreams, inevitably, of Scipio, who
comes to reward him, as the eagle did in *The House of Fame*, this
time for being such an assiduous student of Macrobius. For his
reward he is taken to a walled garden, the entrance to which has
two inscriptions over the gate, one welcoming the reader to 'that
blysful place / Of hertes hele and dedly woundes cure' (127–8),
the other warning of the deadly sterility of the life within. The
picking up of the earlier phrase describing the heavenly paradise,
and the ominous echo of the inscription over the portal of Hell in
Dante (*Inferno*, iii. 1–9), make the allegory here one of particularly
rich complexity. What is clear is that the reference of both inscriptions is to the same place, in other words to the inextricably
intermingled delights and miseries of love. Chaucer hesitates, but
Scipio assures him that he has nothing to fear, since he no longer
counts in the ranks of lovers and is there only to gather material
for his next book.

The descriptions of the garden of love and the temple of Venus
are Chaucer's homage to Boccaccio, being based principally on
his description of the temple of Venus in the *Teseida*. The splendour
and sensuous luxuriance come from there, the touches of unforced
personal joyousness (171) are Chaucer's alone. The garden, full
of Mediterranean light and colour, is the paradisal garden of
prelapsarian Eden, the place of unfallen sexuality; allegorically, it
is the first experience of being in love, when the world is full of
beauty and the springtime of the heart will last for ever. At line

211 we move abruptly into the shadows: 'Under a tre, besyde a welle, I say / Cupide, oure lord, his arwes forge and file' (211–12). This is the poetry of experience rather than innocence, and images of power and cruelty reassert themselves from the opening lines, as well as images of pain and sorrow, of mercenariness, of disorder, of sterility. Inside the temple, which is made of brass, there are the hot sighs of desire, the stifling air of jealousy, the garlanding of Priapus, and the artificially created allure of Venus. The goddess, dallying with her porter Richesse, lies in a corner of the darkened temple: 'And on a bed of gold she lay to reste, / Til that the hote sonne gan to weste' (265–6). Her golden hair is untressed, save for a golden thread, and the upper part of her body naked, the rest nearly so, as the voyeur-dreamer reports with approval:

> The remenaunt was wel kevered to my pay,
> Ryght with a subtyl coverchef of Valence –
> Ther was no thikkere cloth of no defense.   (271–3)

The temple is full of those given over to sensual passion and its accompanying disasters.

The whole passage has been readily characterized by modern commentators (mostly men) as representing the artifice of 'mere sensuality' (sensuality is always 'mere' in such commentary) and explained as the bad 'courtly' side of love, as opposed to good 'natural' love. There are usually allusions to the atmosphere of dubious nightclubs in the hot late afternoon. The excitement is intense. We should recognize a singular triumph of art here, in the manner in which Chaucer's description, like similar descriptions in Spenser, as of the Bower of Bliss (*Faerie Queene*, II. 12), can simultaneously attract and repel us, deny yet imply a moral evaluation. We can recognize too that Venus is, in the allegorical geography of the poem, the core of sexuality: her temple is *in* the garden. Chaucer has gone beyond the moral dichotomies of the traditional mythologizing of Venus, something for which he is partly indebted to Boccaccio. His Venus is not the Venus of Botticelli who conquered her medieval commentators and took on the aspect of beauty *per se*, but Chaucer suggests at least that there may be a non-moral aspect to beauty.[24]

Nevertheless, the movement back to the garden is something of a relief, like the escape from the anguish of Anna's sexual hothouse to Levin's farm in *Anna Karenina*. It is the same garden as before, but now the goddess Nature is there, sitting under a bower of branches on a hill of flowers, less expensive but certainly more comfortable surroundings than those of Venus. Nature is the noble figure of Alain de Lille (named in line 316), 'the vicaire of the almyghty Lord' (379), the agent of God's will on earth, the personification of natural law and harmony, the one figure in whom occasional writers of the Middle Ages could find some legitimation of sexual pleasure. It was difficult, though, and Jean de Meun was one of those who found it so: postlapsarian sexuality was in itself sinful and only marriage could convert it from a mortal into a venial sin. The role of Nature in all this, however defined, was a little doubtful.

Chaucer, as usual, side-steps the difficult question. His Nature is presiding over a parliament of birds on St Valentine's Day, the day when birds choose their mates (or so Chaucer, who seems to have invented this bit of whimsical folklore, would have us believe).[25] Birds have the allegorical advantage that they may neatly represent the different orders of society (aristocratic birds of prey, 'gentle' seed-fowl, coarse water-fowl like the goose and the duck) and at the same time stand for a 'natural' sexuality in their innocent mating and procreating *en masse*. Their sexual behaviour was admired in the Middle Ages for its 'honesty' and restraint, and certainly it presents fewer practical problems for the allegorist than that of, say, dogs, or horses, or cattle:[26]

> And, Lord, the blisse and joye that they make!
> For ech of hem gan other in wynges take,
> And with here nekkes ech gan other wynde,
> Thankynge alwey the noble goddesse of kynde.   (669–73)

But before this happy end to the day, important business must be settled. There are three tercel eagles, suitors for the hand (or rather foot) of the beautiful formel eagle that Nature holds, and all must make their speeches to her so that she can decide who loves her best. This takes a long time, and the other birds grow impatient. The poem's formality suddenly bursts apart in their lively chatter and exchange of abuse (491–616), rather like the House of Commons now, but strongly suggestive of the atmosphere when an old world of *noblesse oblige* confronts a new world of loud-mouthed upstart ducks and geese (all the speakers are men). Different birds have different answers to the dilemma: the suitors should all remain faithful to the death, says the faithful turtle-dove; they should go and love someone else, says the sharp-thinking goose; they should have a battle, says the falcon; they should all remain celibate, says the cuckoo.

The breakthrough into drama is so breathtakingly Chaucerian that it is tempting to take it as the point of the poem, a criticism of the artificialities of courtly love and the speeches of the three tercel eagles from the point of view of an 'English' comic realism. To do so would be historically naive; it would also be brutally restrictive in terms of the options that Chaucer has opened before us, the wide spectrum of feelings and beliefs about love and sexuality that he has presented with such vivacity. It is not his vocation to argue a case: the problem may not be resolved, but its nature is more fully apprehended. The questionings aroused by the debate are in any case drowned in the noise of the birds rejoicing. The narrator wakes up, having missed the point of everything, as is his wont.

What of the suitors for the formel eagle? Nature prefers the royal tercel, who speaks first, and the falcon, spokesman for the aristocratic birds, clearly implies that the choice is obvious. There is no doubt that the royal eagle makes the best speech: the others are improperly assertive, occasionally specious, and look like born losers. The formel eagle's reply – that she would like to wait a year before making her choice – is nicely assertive of the rights granted to her by Nature (409), and characteristic of poetic love-debates in its postponement of judgement, but it may have a more specific reference. All the circumstances of the debate suggest an allusion to the negotiations for the marriage of Richard II to Anne of Bohemia in 1380.[27] There was a German prince who had been betrothed to her for seven years (see line 453) and the French Dauphin had made a late bid (see line 470). Neither was 'royal' as was the first eagle. The marriage was arranged for the following year. Chaucer's poem stands as a happy inauguration of a brief time of great splendour and brilliance in the English court, in which he was to play a full part. The survival of the *Parliament* in fourteen manuscripts, many more than his previous poems, suggests, especially since they bear witness to a notably complex manuscript tradition and to the existence therefore of numerous early copies, that he was already acquiring a public reputation.

4

Fame:
1380–1386

Chaucer was quite an important person in 1380, as he approached his fortieth year. He had a responsible and well-paid job as a customs official, was in receipt of substantial exchequer annuities as an esquire of the royal household and most probably still in receipt of a further annuity from the Duke of Lancaster, lived in comfortable quarters, rent-free, and was the friend and associate of a large number of well-placed and powerful men. The years until he gave up his job at the customs and vacated the dwelling at Aldgate, almost simultaneously and not coincidentally in 1386, are years of prosperity and of increasing fame as a poet, during which he became well known both at home and abroad and firmly accepted in court circles. He was, during these years, at the height of his public career and, to some extent, at the height of his career as a poet too.

The position that he had won for himself in both worlds, that of the man of affairs and that of the poet, is indicated in a number of ways. On 20 April 1382, for instance, he was appointed controller of the petty custom in the port of London, a post which carried a fixed (but unspecified) wage to add to his income as controller of the wool custom, and involved no necessarily additional responsibilities, since authorization to appoint a deputy was included in the terms of the appointment. (Chaucer had been in theory appointed to the petty custom, which dealt with a miscellaneous range of merchandise, in 1374, but that appointment had been a mere bureaucratic form of words.) The confidence

with which Chaucer now managed his businees affairs is suggested
by the smoothness with which he sought and obtained permission
to appoint a deputy in his principal controllership for the summer
of 1383 (23 June to 1 November), not in order to go about on the
king's business, as before, but for no other reason than that he
found himself occupied doing other things: 'comme pur certeines
ses busoignes il est e serra par temps avenir si grandement occupez
qil ne purra bonement entendre entour son office' (because he is
and will be so greatly occupied in certain of his businesses that he
will not be able properly to attend to his office) (*Life-Records*,
p. 165). It would be pleasant to think that he was 'occupez' with
a particularly tricky part of *Troilus* and needed some time to
concentrate.

Henry Gisors, a man from a similar background to Chaucer's
(his father was a citizen and vintner of London) but one who had
made much less of a mark in the world, was the appointed deputy;
after standing in the wings for a little longer, it was he who took
over the petty custom on 13 December 1386. On 25 November
1384 Chaucer secured permission to have another deputy
appointed, this time for a month, because of urgent business of
his own, 'pro quibusdam urgentibus negociis ipsum tangentibus'
(*Life-Records*, p. 167). It was unusual for a customs controller to
appoint deputies so frequently. One sometimes gets the impression,
from examining the social background of his predecessors and
followers in the office, that the controllership had been something
of a social step down for Chaucer, not all that he (or his wife)
thought he might have achieved after his auspicious beginnings,
and that he may have exercised his relatively high rank to secure
certain unusual advantages for himself in the office. On 17 February 1385 Chaucer obtained permission to have a permanent
deputy at the wool customs, though there is no record of any
deputy being appointed. It looks as though Chaucer was gradually
easing himself out of office. By December 1386 he had given up
both his controllerships.

As to his position at court, Chaucer was still an esquire of the
king's household, though he did not reside at court and the annuity
he received involved no responsibilities other than the readiness
to serve when summoned and to be in attendance on particular
occasions. These occasions were now infrequent, but on 10 September 1385 Chaucer was named among those esquires who
received livery of mourning for the funeral of Joan of Kent, the
king's mother. Many other names occur in this enrolled account

that are familiar in Chaucer's biography, including those of the king's knights, John Clanvowe, Lewis Clifford and Philip de la Vache (*Life-Records*, p. 104).

There is not another syllable in the records or in his poetry to link Chaucer with the Princess Joan, but she has played a large part in his mythical biography, as patroness and muse, probably because she had an interesting life and because there is a natural desire to link Chaucer with such persons. Joan had been a famous beauty, having already contracted at least one marriage when she was sought out by the Black Prince as his bride in 1361, and in later life she had a role as a peacemaker, particularly between her son and his uncles. She also had problems with her two sons by her first husband, Sir Thomas Holland. The elder, Sir Thomas, second Earl of Kent, is said to have been a bad influence upon the king, his half-brother: he was much in favour with him, helped arrange his marriage with Anne, and was in receipt of a large income. His son, the third earl, was one of Richard's henchmen in the years of tyranny, 1397–9, and was put to death soon after Henry IV's accession. Joan's younger son, John, Earl of Huntingdon, killed his cousin Ralph Stafford out of sheer bad temper in a brawl on the way to the Scottish campaign in 1385, and Joan is said to have died of a broken heart because the king would not forgive him. Forgive him he did, though, and Sir John remained faithful, being beheaded in 1400 after joining with his nephew in the conspiracy against the new king.[1]

Chaucer was also beginning, during these years, to win a measure of public recognition as a poet. Some of this recognition is in the form of poetic imitation, as in the French poems of Froissart and the Duc de Berry that have already been mentioned in chapter 2. There is also a very accomplished poem of love-debate, variously called *The Cuckoo and the Nightingale* and *The Book of Cupid, God of Love*, written in the 1380s by Sir John Clanvowe, a knight of the king's chamber, and one of the 'Lollard knights' closely associated with Chaucer. Two lines from the Knight's Tale (I. 1785–6) are directly quoted as the opening two lines of Clanvowe's poem.[2]

There are also, more significantly, references to Chaucer by name. Eustache Deschamps, whose career in France as a busy official person and court hanger-on mirrors that of Chaucer, wrote a poem praising Chaucer as 'grand translateur' (for his translation of the *Roman de la Rose*) and sent it to Chaucer in the early 1380s with some of his own ballades: 'Mais pran en gré les euvres d'escolier / Que par Clifford de moy avoir pourras.'[3] (Kindly accept the schoolboy poems that you will have from me via Clifford). The ballades are contributions to the fashionable courtly debate of the Flower and the Leaf, and may have played a part in encouraging Chaucer to introduce allusion to the cult in the Prologue to *The Legend of Good Women* (F. 189). Deschamps speaks of Philippa, John of Gaunt's eldest daughter, who was to marry King John I of Portugal in 1387, as the patroness of the Flower in England. The Clifford who is referred to by Deschamps as his emissary is Sir Lewis Clifford, knight of the king's chamber, a close associate of John of Gaunt, and one of the most famous of the 'Lollard knights'. He had had a distinguished career, and was well known at the French court, where Deschamps refers to him playfully as an authority on problems of love: 'Demandez ent a l'amoureux Cliffort.'[4] Clifford and Deschamps could have met on many occasions, and Deschamps was at Calais in the spring of 1384 at the same time as Gaunt, when there were negotiations for a peace-treaty. Deschamps was there to inspect fortresses and attend the ambassadors: he was with Oton de Granson, the Savoyard poet already well known to Chaucer, and the two of them nearly got themselves accidentally 'captured' by two overenthusiastic English soldiers:

> L'un me dist 'dogue', l'autre 'ride';
> Lors me devint la couleur bleue:
> 'Goday', fait l'un, l'autre 'Commidre'.[5]

The one said to me 'dog', the other 'ride', whereupon I turned pale; 'Good day', said the one, the other 'come here'.

But Deschamps was generally quite friendly to the English, except when they burnt his house down in 1380.

Other writers who mention Chaucer by name, with reference to his poetry, are Thomas Usk and John Gower. Thomas Usk was secretary to John of Northampton, mayor of London 1381–83, and active in the fierce factional disputes within the city. In 1384 he switched his allegiance to Nicholas Brembre, mayor from 1383 to 1386, and, having become closely identified with the Ricardian interest among the citizenry, was executed by the Lords Appellant in 1388. He was a good deal lower in the social scale than Chaucer. He wrote in the mid-1380s, at a time when he was beginning to be in serious trouble and perhaps already in prison, a long prose allegorical treatise called *The Testament of Love*. The prose has been thought to be somewhat imitative of that of Chaucer's *Boece*, and the treatise as a whole, which contains much veiled and self-exculpatory reference to the intrigues and tribulations of his career, as well as the consolations of Lady Love, is certainly indebted to Boethius. Asked by the author how God's foreknowledge and man's free will are to be reconciled, and more particularly how the foreknowledge of a benevolent God is to be reconciled with the existence of evil, Lady Love replies:

> I shal telle thee, this lesson to lerne. Myne owne trewe servaunt, the noble philosophical poete in Englissh, which evermore him besieth and travayleth right sore my name to encrese (wherfore al that willen me good owe to do him worship and reverence both; trewly, his better ne his pere in scole of my rules coude I never fynde) – he (quod she), in a tretis that he made of my servant Troilus, hath this mater touched, and at the ful this question assoyled. Certeynly, his noble sayinges can I not amende; in goodnes of gentil manliche speche, without any maner of nycete of storiers imaginacioun, in witte and in good reson of sentence he passeth al other makers. In the boke of Troilus, the answere to thy question mayst thou lerne.[6]

The reference is primarily, and rather simplistically, to the pre-destination soliloquy in *Troilus* (iv. 958–1082), which does not address Usk's second question and certainly does not answer his first.

John Gower, who has already appeared as one of Chaucer's attorneys in a document of 1378, and who is one of the co-dedicatees of the *Troilus*, completed about 1386, introduces a passage in praise of Chaucer in the last book of the *Confessio Amantis*, a poem that he began about 1387. The eulogy is put in the mouth of Venus, who claims Chaucer as her disciple and her poet, one who has written much of love. Venus tells Gower that he should advise Chaucer, when he meets him, to reconcile himself to advancing age, as Gower has done in his lover's shrift, and to write 'his testament of love' (VIII. 2955). It was this allusion, incidentally, that led William Thynne, in printing Usk's *Testament* for the first time in 1532, to attribute it to Chaucer, with confusing consequences for the Chaucer biography.

Some recensions of the *Confessio Amantis* omit the praise of Chaucer, not by scribal accident, and this has led to speculations about a quarrel between Gower and Chaucer. Gower may have been upset by some of the kinds of poetry that Chaucer went in for writing after 1387, particularly the fabliaux, thinking that these did not respect the mission to redeem English for serious poetry to which he had appointed Chaucer along with himself; or he may not have responded well to Chaucer's playful allusion to him in the Introduction to the Man of Law's Tale. The Man of Law, at the end of a complaint about how Chaucer has used up all the best stories, mangling them in the process, 'in swich Englissh as he kan' (II. 49), compliments him at least on avoiding filthy stories of incest such as those of Canacee and Apollonius. As it happens, these stories are both told, with considerable feeling and serious-ness of purpose, in the *Confessio Amantis*, and Gower may have thought his efforts were being mocked. If so, he was a little deficient in the kind of self-deprecating humour Chaucer delighted in. The quarrel of Gower and Chaucer makes a good story, but it may well be fiction: the variations in the manuscripts can be readily explained in terms of the mechanics of revision.[7]

Chaucer's general importance as a public man of affairs con-tinues to be demonstrated, also, in actions in which he enrols himself as mainprize or surety for friends or associates who found themselves in difficulties. One such was John Hend, a rich London draper, for whom Chaucer's mainprize was entered on 12 February 1381. Hend later became mayor of London (1391–2, 1404) and in the early fifteenth century, with Mayor Richard Whittington, he was one of the main financial supporters of the Lancastrian kings. In the early 1380s he was in trouble because of his acqui-sition of estates in Essex, the title to which was disputed by the king's escheator, the officer responsible for pressing the royal claim to estates that were deemed to have fallen vacant and thereby reverted to the crown. There was a good deal of legal nicety in such matters, and Chaucer was in no great peril of losing favour when he put himself forward as a guarantor of a rich friend's good behaviour and readiness to keep the peace.

Of his three fellow-guarantors, one is very important. 'Rad-ulphus Strode' (*Life-Records*, p. 282) is without doubt the 'philo-sophical Strode' to whom, with Gower, *Troilus and Criseyde* is dedicated:

> O moral Gower, this book I directe
> To the and to the, philosophical Strode,
> To vouchen sauf, ther nede is, to correcte,
> Of youre benignites and zeles goode.   (v. 1856–9)

Strode was an Oxford logician and philosopher of some repute, a fellow of Merton College, Oxford, in 1359–60, and author of treatises on logic, one of which has survived. He entered upon a friendly academic debate with John Wyclif in 1374, at a time when Wyclif was being cultivated by John of Gaunt and before he became the great heresiarch. Strode makes a very interesting addition to the Chaucer circle, one with whom Chaucer could discuss the questions of predestination and free will, of fortune and destiny, that began to preoccupy him in the 1380s, and with whom he could argue about Lollardy. Strode may have been a poet himself: a late-fifteenth-century addition to a 1422 list of Merton fellows says that 'Strood' wrote a poem called *Phantasma Radulphi* (Ralph's Vision). What is more, there is a 'Radulphus Strode' who was an eminent London lawyer, common sergeant of the city of London, and the occupant of the gatehouse-dwelling at Aldersgate during the same years (1374–86) that Chaucer was in the corresponding dwelling at Aldgate. The presumed shift of the same Ralph Strode from the university to a career offering more opportunity for wealth and public advancement, and perhaps also the opportunity to get married, is many times more plausible than the existence of two Ralph Strodes, more or less exact contemporaries, of equal eminence. If Strode did make the move to secular life in order to get married, it would be interesting to have heard his conversations with Chaucer, who by now may have been thinking that he had missed, through his early marriage, many of the opportunities for living comfortably and writing poetry that would have been available to him if he had taken holy orders.

Chaucer was mainpernor in two other suits in 1386–7 and 1388–89, which will be mentioned in chapter 5, but it is time to return to some generally less creditable associations with the law. At some time in the Michaelmas law term of 1379 (Michaelmas is 29 September), there is a record of Chaucer appointing an attorney to act for him in a plea of contempt and trespass, 'de placito contemptus et transgressionis' (*Life-Records*, p. 340), brought against him by Thomas Stondon. It is not clear which of several possible Thomas Stondons this one was or what act deemed to be unlawful is referred to in the action of contempt and trespass. Since the action was to be brought before the Court of King's Bench, Chaucer thought the matter serious enough to get himself a lawyer, but presumably the dispute was settled out of court, since there is no further record of it.

One should not expect to consider the presence of such records in the Chaucer biography as implying any sort of slur on his character. The law was then commonly, even more than now, an instrument for the pursuit of private purposes and interests having nothing to do with moral justice or equity. However, in the case of Cecily Champain, Chaucer has a bit more explaining to do.

CECILY CHAMPAIN; CHAUCER AND WOMEN; PHILIPPA CHAUCER

On 1 May 1380 there was enrolled in the court of Chancery a formal document in which Cecily Champain ('Cecilia Chaumpaigne') agreed unconditionally to release Geoffrey Chaucer from all actions concerning her rape or anything else, 'omnimodas acciones tam de raptu meo tam [*sic*] de aliqua alia re vel causa' (*Life-Records*, p. 343). Cecily herself came to the court on 4 May to acknowledge the document, which was witnessed by some of Chaucer's most influential friends: Sir William Beauchamp, the chamberlain of the king's household, for whom Chaucer had performed some service in 1378; Sir John Clanvowe and Sir William Nevill, two knights of the king's chamber; John Philipot, collector of customs (1377–83) during Chaucer's controllership; and Richard Morel, a modestly well-off London grocer and member of the Grocers' Company.

Quite commonly in legal documents of the time, *raptus* means 'abduction', the seizing and holding of a young person against his or her will with the purpose of gaining some financial advantage: Chaucer's own father, John Chaucer, was abducted by his aunt in 1324 when she was trying to force the boy into a marriage with her daughter, and Chaucer himself was a member of a commission investigating a similar case in 1387. In both these cases, however, the nature of the offence is made clear by the use of the two words 'rapuerunt et abduxerunt' (*Life-Records*, pp. 3, 375). When *raptus* or forms of the verb *rapere* are used alone, it seems they must mean rape (enforced and completed sexual intercourse), for which no other word is used in law without qualification. Furthermore, 'abduction' would normally refer to the forcible appropriation of the powers of guardianship over a minor; and Cecily would barely qualify as a minor in 1380, her father William, a baker, having died in 1360. The fact that she acknowledges the release in her own recognizance would argue, too, that there was no parent, husband or other legal guardian to do it for her, and that she was a woman of at least 21.[8]

The document has been something of a problem for Chaucer biographers since it was first discovered by Furnivall in 1873. Some have accepted the charge as true and dismissed it in a man-of-the-world way as an escapade; some have found the idea that the charge might be true unimaginable; others are coming to regard the charge as the most important event in the Chaucer biography.[9] It is certainly enigmatic, and nothing is made much clearer by three further documents which are evidently associated with the original release, even though enrolled in the court of the mayor and aldermen of London rather than in Chancery. In the first, dated 28 June 1380, Richard Goodchild, cutler, and John Grove, armourer, both of them citizens of London, release Geoffrey Chaucer from all actions of law they might have against him; in the second, of the same date, Cecily similarly releases Goodchild and Grove; and in the third, 2 July 1380, Grove acknowledges a debt of £10 to Cecily, which was to be paid (and was duly paid) at Michaelmas. The first two documents might possibly be interpreted as the preparation for the third, being legal agreements between the two parties, Chaucer and Cecily, through the agency of a third, confirming that a settlement that has been reached out of court is acknowledged as final. This clears the way for the payment of the sum agreed in settlement, or at least the acknowledgement of the debt; the acknowledgement is made by one of the intermediaries, presumably because Chaucer did not want his name directly associated with the payment. It is not surprising that Grove needed three months to put the £10 together, since it was a large sum of money, the equivalent of well over half of Chaucer's annual salary at the customs. There is some evidence that Chaucer was exerting himself to raise money, principally by gathering in outstanding debts, in the following months: on 28 November 1380, on the same day that he received the half-yearly instalments on his two annuities (£6. 13s. 4d. on each), he was also paid £14 in expenses for the Lombardy visit of 1378 (*Life-Records*, pp. 319–20, 59–60); on 6 March 1381 he obtained £22 as a gift in compensation for his expenses on journeys to France in 1377 and the following years (*Life-Records*, p. 49); and on 19 June 1381 he sold his father's house (*Life-Records*, pp. 1–2). Some of this activity may have been coincidental, but the weight of evidence suggests an attempt to meet an unexpected increase in expenditure, which may have been more considerable than that accounted for by the immediate need to repay Grove for shouldering the payment of the settlement. There may, that is, have been other payments to Cecily.

It has been argued that Chaucer was not the principal in the matter, and it remains possible that he was being released from his responsibilities as surety or *mainpernor* for Goodchild or Grove; but the nature of the four documents argues strongly that he *was* the principal and tried to conceal the fact. It has been argued that the five men he got to witness the release were very respectable people; but their respectability was of course the authority of the witness for the release, not the guarantee of Chaucer's innocence. They secured for him immunity from prosecution, but they did not declare that he had not done what he had been or might be charged with. Their presence is a mark of the importance Chaucer attached to having the charges dropped or not brought. The charges may have been false, and it may have been that Chaucer was being blackmailed by a team of criminals, but it is difficult to understand in that case why he did not allow the action to come to law.

It is not out of the question that *raptus* is a technical term for some offence such as abduction, but the more obvious conclusion seems the more likely one: the charge referred to in the document of release is indeed one of rape. Beyond that, all is speculation. That Chaucer was guilty of *something* is clear from the care he took to secure immunity from prosecution, but it need not have been rape. The charge, after all, was neither brought nor its truth tested. The safest conclusion would be that there is not enough evidence to come to a conclusion, but the temptation to offer an explanation is too strong to resist. The strongest likelihood, in my opinion, is that Cecily threatened to bring a charge of rape in order to force Chaucer into some compensatory settlement and that she then cooperated in the legal release. The actual offence for which she sought compensation is not necessarily the offence named in the charge that she used for leverage and did not press: there are many things that it might more probably have been than violent physical rape, including neglect and the betrayal of promises by the man, or some unilateral decision on his part to terminate an affair that he regarded as over but which the woman, in retrospect, regarded as a physical violation. Some violence of passion is hidden away somewhere behind the legal documents, which reveal only the manipulation of the resources of the law necessary to achieve a settlement. It has often been conjectured that there may be a child hidden away too, and that 'little Lewis', the 10-year-old son to whom Chaucer dedicated the *Treatise on the Astrolabe* in 1391, was the product of the union with Cecily, but the evidence is merely circumstantial.

The incident, though enigmatic and the focus of many questions, provokes some possibly pertinent speculation on Chaucer's attitude to women. He was ever woman's friend, says Gavin Douglas, who, though critical of Chaucer for having misrepresented Virgil – 'My mastir Chauser gretly Virgill offendit' – in speaking ill of Aeneas for abandoning Dido, neverthelesss excuses Chaucer on the grounds of his well-known (and, in Douglas's view, probably excessively indulgent) sympathy for women:

> But sikkyrly of resson me behufis
> Excuss Chauser fra all maner repruffis
> In lovyng of thir ladeis lylly quhite
> He set on Virgill and Eneas this wyte
> For he was evir (God wait) all womanis frend.[10]

Douglas thus joined the band of male comrades always ready to compliment Chaucer on his sympathetic portrayal of women. Chaucer made strenuous efforts to engage this sympathy and did much to deserve the admiration. Yet there are noticeable limitations to his sympathetic understanding of women, limitations imposed by his sex and by the age in which he lived.

What is very clear is that he was preoccupied with women, and with their role in their relationships with men, to a degree quite remarkable in his day, as compared, for instance, with Gower, Langland and the *Gawain*-poet. A particularly insistent question for him is that of women's freedom and independence and their capacity to judge and act on the basis of a fully developed moral consciousness. All these faculties were systematically denied to women in the Middle Ages, and Chaucer is troubled both by the inhuman stupidity of the denial and also by the consequences to men if the rights of women as individuals are allowed. The portrait of Blanche in *The Book of the Duchess* is one of his most successful attempts to blend suggestions of positive and independent moral consciousness into a traditionally male-constructed image of 'the perfect woman'. The success of the portrait, the lack of inner conflict in its representation of the woman, may be that the subject is dead.

Criseyde, Chaucer's most lengthy, loving and pained meditation on the independent 'otherness' of women, is a reminder too of his limitations. The freedom he grants her to be the arbiter of her own destiny, though unprecedented in a literary work, is in the end only a freedom to act in a way that will be pleasing to Troilus; beyond this she has only a freedom to delude herself, and even this is finally stripped from her, as she reverts to the role of the faithless mistress. The Wife of Bath is the beneficiary of a similar imaginative generosity on Chaucer's part: the attempt here is to make a space in fiction not for an independent-minded and attractive woman but for an independent-minded and unattractive one, indeed one who is constructed entirely out of archetypal male hostility and fear. It is hostility and fear, however, that seem to triumph at last over the generous notion that women might be as fully human as men: suggestions of moral consciousness, responsibility and tenderness of feeling in the Wife give way to the more assertive stereotyped images of female termagancy.

Elsewhere, Chaucer responds with a full measure of sympathy to women betrayed, victimized or abandoned. The plight of Dido calls forth some of his most moving writing, and there is something unusually earnest about his sympathy for women, in an age when cynicism towards women, open or covert, was the rule. It is not mere sentimentalization, and he seems implicitly to recognize what Richard Firth Green calls 'the masculine conspiracy to exclude women from the social contract woven into the very fabric of feudalism'.[11]

Yet, though he shows himself thoroughly dissatisfied with images of women in their traditionally submissive roles, as throughout *The Legend of Good Women*, Chaucer is still unhappy about the alternatives. Griselda's freedom of will is powerfully communicated, but it is postulated more as a theological necessity than as the human property of a woman. Sometimes the woman must be eliminated or deliberately reduced to a cipher, as are Emily in the Knight's Tale and Constance in the Man of Law's Tale, so that Chaucer can work out his narrative without the troublesome distraction of woman as 'something other' than the instrument of his purpose. Nothing again was to be as simple as the translation of 'Origenes upon the Maudeleyne' of which he speaks in the Prologue to *The Legend of Good Women* (F. 428) and which is now lost. The famous homily *De Maria Magdalena*, attributed to Origen but actually written in the late twelfth or early thirteenth century, is one of the masterpieces of affective devotion. In dramatic style, the homilist evokes the grief of Mary

Magdalene, the sorrowing, vulnerable yet steadfast woman, inconsolable until Jesus appears to her in the garden. It is a representation of woman that is full of pathos and which yet anticipates,
in its simpler hagiographical style, the image of weakness transfig-
ured in solitary fidelity and tenacity of purpose that was to be so
potent in Chaucer's later heroines. Chaucer's translation, whatever
form it took, was certainly a very suitable witness for Alceste to
call in Chaucer's defence.[12]

As to the representation of women's sexuality, Chaucer, like
other medieval male writers, finds himself both repelled and fascinated. Women must be idealized or deliberately made disgusting:
the terror is of finding that they have sexual desires of their own,
and the answer is constantly to praise restraint, good 'governaunce'
and patience. There is some brave if temporary resistance to these
male stereotypes in Chaucer's portrayal of Criseyde. Her 'coldness'
is shown as a proper and necessary caution, and her yielding to
desire (iii. 1210–11) as a property of her independent womanhood,
not as a symptom of nymphomania. In the Venus of *The Parliament
of Fowls*, however, we see something closer to the archetypal
male fantasies of horror and desire. The goddess is an image of
transparently adorned loveliness which is made the subject of
salacious voyeurism; the recognition of the seductive power of
women's beauty prompts first the desire to vulgarize and diminish
the source of that power and then the search for a means of
condemning morally what threatens male composure and power.
Finally, in the Miller's Tale and the Merchant's Tale, Chaucer
gives a sardonic immediacy to the portrayal of the lecherous old
goat, the *senex amans* of medieval antifeminist writing. Old John
the carpenter is a ludicrous figure, and his lusts are mostly made
present to us in the vulgarly glamorous pin-up portrait of his wife,
but January is something more. In the whole literature of the *senex
amans*, there is no figure in whom the lyricism of male desire and
the associated disgust at the continuing presence of this desire in
an old man are so bitterly evoked. The routine antifeminism of
the Merchant's Prologue leads one to expect an attack on women,
but the fierceness of the hatred is reserved for the old man who
allows himself to become thrall to youthful female beauty. The
association of this loathing with an unexpected kind of sympathy
for January makes one think of him as a psychosexual problem
that is being worked out in the safety of fiction.

Such speculations provide the cue for the last entrance of Chaucer's wife Philippa, who of necessity (because of the lack of documentation) has only a walk-on part in the poet's biography. She may have had only a walk-on part in his life too, as has been suggested. During these years in the early 1380s, her exchequer annuity continued to be drawn regularly every half-year, chiefly by her husband as the assigned payee. The exceptional regularity of payment has to do with Chaucer's knowledge of exchequer practice, and his familiarity with and influence over the officials involved. This is the reason that he was appointed by his wife; the assignation does not indicate that the money went into his own purse nor even that his wife was living with him. On the other hand, it does indicate that they were not estranged. The annuity, we recall, was the pension for Philippa's service as *domicella* in the household of Queen Philippa, who died in 1369. Philippa Chaucer was also in receipt of an annuity from John of Gaunt, originally for her service in the household of Constance, Duchess of Lancaster. In the warrant for payment of the half-yearly instalment due in Michaelmas 1379 (*Life-Records*, p. 87), no mention is made of such service, though this does not mean that it was terminated. The warrant was made upon Gaunt's receiver in Lincolnshire, which, along with the assignation of payment of the Michaelmas 1378 exchequer annuity upon the Sheriff of Lincoln, suggests that Philippa was living in that county. Katherine Swynford, Gaunt's mistress, and probably Philippa's sister, had her own manor at Kettlethorpe in Lincolnshire.

An association with Lincolnshire is further suggested by the memorandum that records Philippa's admission to the fraternity of Lincoln Cathedral on 19 February 1386. Such fraternities or confraternities had become regular institutions in the late fourteenth century (see the Summoner's Tale, III. 2126), providing as they did both for the spiritual benefit of the lay members in the form of prayers said on their behalf and rights of burial, and also for the material benefit of the canons (or monks or friars) in the form of gifts, bequests and the support of rich and influential patrons. The ceremony of 1386 was a grand occasion, principally designed to celebrate the admission of Henry, Earl of Derby, Gaunt's eldest son, now 20 years old. He followed his father and grandfather, both admitted in 1343, and was accompanied on this occasion, his father looking on, by his half-brother John Beaufort, Katherine's eldest son by John of Gaunt, and also by Thomas Swynford, Katherine's legitimate son. It made an interesting group, and it is perhaps the strongest argument of all that she was Katherine's sister that Philippa was there as aunt to this assortment of nephews. Chaucer was clearly not there.

During the early 1380s, Philippa probably shared her life between the household of her husband and that of the Duchess Constance, who spent more time with her husband now that his hopes of a throne in Spain were his main political ambition. Philippa is mentioned in association with 'nostre treschere compaigne' (*Life-Records*, p. 90), that is, the duchess, in a warrant for payment for a New Year's gift on 2 January 1380, and she was clearly at Kenilworth Castle, where Gaunt often celebrated Christmas, at this time. The gift was of a silver 'hanap' or goblet, with an elaborately decorated cover, and was worth 31*s*. 5*d*. Payment for similar New Year's presents to Philippa is recorded on 6 March 1381 and 6 May 1382. There are no records after this, indeed no records of any kind pertaining to Gaunt's household expenses, since the *Register* breaks off in 1383.

Gaunt himself, during these years, was active in government and the king's service, anxious to win support for his plans for a campaign in Spain. He seems to have been a loyal servant of the young king, particularly keen to pursue the king's policy of arriving at peaceful settlements with France and Scotland, the old enemies, and so perhaps to make the way clearer for his own ambitions in Spain. It must have been particularly annoying for him to find himself in 1385 the victim of two successive plots by Robert de Vere, Earl of Oxford, the king's favourite, to discredit him and get rid of him. He behaved well on these occasions, conscious perhaps that good behaviour was in his interests, and, a planned expedition to Spain in 1382 having come to nothing, he finally got his wish in 1386. The king gave his support, Parliament voted a war subsidy, and Gaunt sailed on 9 July 1386. He was out of England, we must remember, during all the stirring events of 1386–9. The Duchess Constance was with him, of course, with her young daughter Catharine, and so most probably, as a junior member of his entourage, was Thomas Chaucer.

Philippa was not of the party. In 1386 she was probably residing more permanently with her sister in Lincolnshire. The last recorded payment of her exchequer annuity was made on 18 June 1387, into her husband's hands, along with the instalments due on his own. There is no mention of Philippa in the record of the payment to Chaucer of his Michaelmas instalments on 7 November 1387, and, from the regularity with which he had up to then been collecting payments for both himself and his wife, it appears that Philippa died some time between 18 June and 7 November 1387.

THE PEASANTS' REVOLT; CHAUCER'S POLITICAL VIEWS

On Wednesday 19 June 1381, a deed was drawn up transferring the title of Chaucer's father's house in the parish of St Martin, Vintry, to Henry Herbury. Just a few days previously, the parish of St Martin, along with the rest of the city of London, had witnessed riot and commotion on a scale and of a violence never known before or since.

The causes of the Peasants' Revolt lie deep in English economic and social history. The loosening of the structures of feudal obligation in the years after the Black Death, with the consequent increase in demesne-leasing and the reduction in villeinage, made people more than usually resentful of government measures such as the Statutes of Labourers, periodically re-enacted from 1351 onwards, designed to restore pre-Black Death wages and conditions of service. The taste of change sharpened the reality of the experience of repression. There was further a loss of morale, and a loss of confidence in the government, as a result of the political scandals of the late 1370s and what was perceived as abject failure in the French wars. More specifically, there was the new poll tax, brought in for the first time in 1377, and reimposed in 1379 and now again in 1380–81. People can bear any amount of oppressive taxation, it seems, but they cannot bear new kinds, and the poll tax was a new kind that pressed particularly heavily on poor people. It was also being collected more efficiently than previous taxes, by an increasingly cold and centralized bureaucracy. It was the return of the tax commissioners to villages where the earlier collection had been deemed to have yielded an inadequate revenue that triggered the first outbreak of violence in Essex.

The violence spread to Kent, and the rebels marched on London, where they joined with a formidably discontented group of London journeymen and low-paid workers. In the sacking and plundering of the city that followed, the revolt was to some extent hijacked, as not infrequently happens on such occasions, by local malcontents and hooligans. The Savoy palace of John of Gaunt was a prime target, and it was burnt down on Thursday 13 June. Gaunt was the rebels' bogyman, because of what was seen as his major part in undoing the work of the 'Good Parliament' of 1376 and in imposing the first poll tax in 1377; he was fortunate to be away on campaign in Scotland. Other targets were tax-gatherers, government officials generally, lawyers, and Flemings. The latter were considered to have taken work away from Londoners and were attacked with particular viciousness: thirty-five took refuge in the church of St Martin's in the Vintry, whence they were dragged out to be beheaded, the headless corpses being then piled outside the church at the corner of Royal Street (La Riole) and Thames Street.[13] On Friday 14 June the rebels made themselves free of the Tower of London, where the king's mother was, and killed his two principal government officers, the chancellor, Simon Sudbury, Archbishop of Canterbury, and the treasurer, Sir Robert Hales. On Saturday they met by arrangement with the king at Smithfield, where the killing of their leader, Wat Tyler, threw them into confusion. Richard seized his moment, and the revolt was over.

It was, in its origins, despite the name that was eventually given to it, a broad-based rising, involving artisans, craftsmen, some clerics and yeomen as well as peasants. Many of them were small capitalists from the prosperous South-East who found the old feudal structures particularly irksome. There was a programme of reform of some kind and a degree of idealism. The attachment of the rebels, in fact, to the person of the king and much of the traditional order that he stood for is remarkable. As E. P. Thompson points out, in his study of the food riots of the eighteenth century, the 'spasmodic' notion of crowd action – that people react violently when some action by the authorities affects their immediate well-being – needs to have set against it the view that such action almost always has some 'legitimizing notion', the belief that informs the men and women in the crowd that they are defending traditional rights and customs and in general that they represent the wider consensus of that community. Those of whom the Sheriff of Gloucestershire wrote in 1766 that they had committed many acts of violence, 'and some of wantonness and excess; and in other instances some acts of courage, prudence, justice and a consistency towards that which they profess to obtain', could be compared with their predecessors in 1381, of whom equally hostile witnesses wrote that that they tried to restrain those who were looting the Savoy, crying out that 'they were lovers of truth and justice, not robbers and thieves'.[14]

It was the admixture with the country-based group of the more volatile population of London, especially the class of lower-paid journeymen who had no prospects of becoming craft-masters, that caused the cataclysmic explosion of violence in the city. Similar outbreaks of disorder in other parts of the country, as at St Albans, Bury St Edmunds, York and Beverley, were much less violent. The vulnerability of the king and his family and his principal officers, the incompetence of the traditional ruling class, and their inability to protect their king or to think up any plan to deal with the crisis, are alike matters for amazement. It was city politicians like William Walworth, mayor of London, and our old friends Brembre and Philipot, who saved the day for them.

Historians disagree on the historical importance of the Peasants' Revolt. It may have contributed to some acceleration in the decline of villeinage, but its chief importance may lie in the lesson it gave to the ruling classes. There were brutal reprisals but no reign of terror; the poll tax was abandoned; rent-increases were restrained and villeinage further relaxed; great lords began to maintain about them armed bodies of liveried retainers; amelioration kept the repressive society stable. Nevertheless, the Revolt, particularly in London, was a brief and horrific experience of ungoverned violence and has remained a potent image of insurrection, whether seen as a promise of liberty or as a relapse into anarchy. The chroniclers of the time unite in devoting to it many pages of their most lurid descriptions and apocalyptic imaginings, and Gower delayed publication of his long Latin poem on the abuses of the time, the *Vox Clamantis*, in order to add to it, as Book I, a vehement allegorical account of the Revolt. He portrays the rebels as domestic animals broken loose from their traditional social restraints and reverting to bestiality; for him the Revolt is a warning of apocalypse.

To this event, catastrophic in itself and in the experience of every Londoner, Chaucer makes one definite and two possible references. One possible reference is in the Knight's Tale, where Saturn claims responsibility, as a planetary influence, for all kinds of malicious and destructive acts:

> Myn is the stranglyng and hangyng by the throte,
> The murmure and the cherles rebellyng,
> The groynynge, and the pryvee empoysonyng.
> (*Canterbury Tales*, I. 2458–60)

The phrase 'cherles rebellyng' is striking, though it is true that references to rebellion and civil strife are customary in accounts of the misfortunes due to Saturn. Less likely, as an allusion to the Revolt, is the description in *Troilus* of the outcry in the Trojan parliament against Hector's refusal of the proposed exchange of Antenor and Criseyde: 'The noyse of peple up stirte thanne at ones, / As breme as blase of straw iset on-fire' (iv. 183–4). The passage expresses Chaucer's characteristic contempt for the 'voice of the people', but it is traditional in its tone and imagery, and the possibility of an allusion to 'Jack Straw' is very slight.[15]

We are left with one certain reference to the revolt, in which Jack Straw, one of the two main leaders of the rebels, is indeed mentioned. The reference occurs in the Nun's Priest's Tale: the fox has seized Chauntecleer to carry him off to the woods, and the whole farmyard has turned out in mock-epic helter-skelter pursuit:

> So hydous was the noyse – a, benedicitee! –
> Certes, he Jakke Straw and his meynee
> Ne made nevere shoutes half so shrille
> Whan that they wolden any Flemyng kille,
> As thilke day was maad upon the fox.
> (*Canterbury Tales*, VII. 3393–7)

Chaucer (though of course it is not Chaucer speaking) alludes here to one of the nastiest episodes of the revolt, but with a nonchalance that suggests that the chief importance of such incidents is to provide poetic images of the mock-heroic.

Chaucer was there in the city, we must presume, and Aldgate, where he had his dwelling, was one of the gates through which the rebels entered London. He is very unlikely to have taken any active part in the week's events; as an esquire of the royal household he might in the past have been expected to, but the household had changed, and Chaucer himself was an example of the process by which the royal household was becoming the civil service and the armed retainer was giving way to the bureaucratic official. As one of the new 'public men' of the age, he had no part in such violent proceedings, and one of the consequences of such changes was that the king was left without his traditional bodyguard.

There is little room for any argument that Chaucer's view of the Revolt was much different from Gower's. He was a member of the upper class and one of the financial officials who might well have been a target for the rebels. His allusion in the Nun's Priest's Tale, facetious and trivial as it is, implies that 'Jakke Straw and his meynee' are to be seen, as Gower saw them, as farmyard animals gone berserk, and the Flemings are not regarded any differently: it is dog-eat-dog. A desperate plea could be entered that Chaucer is parodying Book I of the *Vox Clamantis*, and that he really had other thoughts about the Revolt that he kept to himself. In this way Chaucer can be allowed his greatness as a poet by being made to share, by imputation, the radical or at least more sophisticated opinions of his modern admirers. But it will not do. In fact, Chaucer's allusion to the Revolt is very characteristic of the way he experiences political and social conflict, converting it into material for anecdotal humour, private and personal confrontations, and literary games. Similar deflective and evasive strategies articulate class conflict and the war of the sexes in such scenes of comic confrontation as that of the Knight and the Miller in the Miller's Prologue or that of the Wife of Bath and a series of male religious (Pardoner, Jankyn, Friar) in her Prologue.[16]

We have high opinions of our authors, no less than of ourselves. We wish to applaud their high-mindedness, or the sophistication of their address to questions of political or social concern, or else the ruthlessness with which they strip away the shams of all such high-mindedness and sophistication, conscious that when we do so we are applauding ourselves. Langland and Gower, in the vigour of their response to contemporary problems of class conflict, of poverty and oppression, of the rights of common people, offer plenty of invitations to both applause and derision. Chaucer, by contrast, exhibits scarcely a sign of any direct response to the political and social movements of his day. The many scholarly attempts to make his poems into political *romans à clef*, of which the essays of Leslie Hotson remain prize specimens,[17] are more than usually misguided; one might conjecture that political allusion of this detailed and covert kind, though it may be common in Latin (as in Gower's *Vox Clamantis* or *Cronica Tripertita*, or in the *Prophecies* of John of Bridlington), must be rare in English at this time (*Richard the Redeles* and *Mum and Sothsegger* are exceptions, from very late in the century), since it needs an established, known and knowledgeable audience of initiates to pick up the allusions. Even Langland, though specific on the level of daily life, is notably unspecific on names, dates and identifiable historical events.

As to Chaucer's view of the common people, it is one of routine contempt for them *en masse*, as in the apostrophe against the 'stormy peple, unsad and evere untrewe' of the Clerk's Tale (IV. 995–1001), and routine admiration for them in their individual roles of humble and patient obligation, like the Plowman of the General Prologue, or the poor old widows of the Friar's Tale (III. 1608), the Prioress's Tale (VII. 586) or the Nun's Priest's Tale (VII. 2821). Such are the easiest objects of unexercised social compassion; the contrast with Langland and the gnawing at his conscience of poverty and beggary, in a passage like Passus IX of the C-text of *Piers Plowman*, is very sharp. The description of the 'povre wydwe' of the Nun's Priest's Tale is superbly observed, and an occasion of the most intense delight for its literary ease and allusiveness, its ironies and subtle innuendoes, its geniality of tone, but, with the contrast in one's mind of Langland writing of the suffering and humiliations of the identical class, 'the wo of this wommen that wonyeth in cotes' (C. IX. 83), it may seem insufferably patrician.

Chaucer wrote out of the concerns of his class; if his text requires an opinion on a matter of political or social concern, he responds by articulating the views of that class or by evading the question. Both the conventionality and the evasiveness are encouraged by his perception of himself as a comparative newcomer to the class. So it is with any larger opinions on political matters that find expression in his poetry. Just as Plutarch's and John of Salisbury's image of the 'body politic' served Shakespeare's Menenius as a model of political order in *Coriolanus* (I. i), so Chaucer returns again and again to the idea of 'commune profit', that is, the good of the commonwealth as a whole. The idea is derived from Roman theory of government and appears as the goal of virtuous endeavour in the Dream of Scipio in *The Parliament of Fowls* (47). It is what Boethius claims he has served faithfully (*Boece*, I, pr. 4. 89) as the highest ideal of personal morality and public service, and what Griselda, as the perfect exemplar of true self-government, promotes in her administration of her husband's affairs (Clerk's Tale, IV. 431). The attraction of the idea of 'commune profit', which Chaucer alone of contemporary English writers gives such prominence to, is that it is inherently admirable and at the same time satisfactorily unspecific. The impossibility of any direct application of a Roman theory of the common good to late-fourteenth-century England, given the differences in the two political and social systems, makes of it a mere watchword or catch-phrase; it acts to solidify resolve and deflect attentiveness in much the same way that the medieval political theory of the Three Estates, which bore an increasingly remote relation to the reality of late medieval society, helped to keep in place a comfortable, and enforceable, illusion of those realities.

So it is in other places where Chaucer discusses or seems to be discussing political matters. In the envoy to *Lak of Stedfastnesse*, the king is exhorted to rule well: 'O prince, desyre to be honourable, / Cherish thy folk and hate extorcioun' (22–3). But even a Richard II in the last throes of monomania could hardly have been offended by such bromide advice. Kings in general are enjoined by Alceste in the Prologue to *The Legend of Good Women* to treat rich and poor alike, 'And han of poore folk compassyoun' (F. 390), but the unexceptionable nature of the advice is far less important than the application in the context to the particular 'poor', feeble and defenceless person in question, namely Geoffrey Chaucer.

There is a passage in the Parson's Tale where Chaucer, following his Latin sources, discusses questions directly relevant to the Peasants' Revolt (*Canterbury Tales*, X. 752–76). Tyrannical lordship and associated extortions, he says, are the product of covetousness; they are not justified by the established order of lordship and thraldom. All men are equally thralls to sin, lords as well as churls ('Every synful man is a cherl to synne', X. 763)), and both lords and churls spring from the same seed and have the same chance of salvation. There are echoes here, of course, of the famous motto of insurgency in 1381, 'When Adam delved and Eve span / Who was then the gentleman?' Chaucer seems quite unalive to any such allusion, or to any suggestion of paradox in the existence of two kinds of 'equality', and duly follows his authorities out of the impasse by declaring that, despite the equality of all in the thraldom of sin, nevertheless, 'God ordeyned that som folk sholde be moore heigh in estaat and in degree, and som folk moore lough, and that everich sholde be served in his estaat and in his degree' (X. 771). It is the responsibility of lords to treat churls well, but if they do not it is no one's responsibility to urge or compel them to do so:

> Wherfore I seye that thilke lordes that been lyk wolves, that devouren the possessiouns or the catel of povre folk wrongfully withouten mercy or mesure,/they shul receyven by the same mesure that they han mesured to povre folk the mercy of Jhesu Crist, but if it be amended. (X. 775–6).

The problem is passed on to a higher authority, omnipotent and *not yet*. Chaucer, like his authorities, did not and maybe could not imagine a situation in which political remedies might be found for what everyone recognized to be political injustice and oppression. Langland did try to imagine such a programme of political reform, even though in the end he was obliged to turn his gaze upwards to a higher transcending reality. At least Langland showed an interest and a readiness to be exercised; Chaucer, in the Parson's Tale, hardly seems aware of the moral and intellectual tangle that his authorities have got themselves into, still less interested in trying to find a way out of it.

The theme of *gentillesse*, that true nobility is in virtue not birth, is introduced from time to time by Chaucer, as in his little Boethian poem, *Gentilesse*, or in the old hag's discourse in the Wife of Bath's Tale (*Canterbury Tales*, III. 1109–76). The dramatic context of the latter, in the hag's scheme to convert the knight to an understanding of his own professed values, overwhelms any attempt to extract Chaucer's 'views' on the matter, which in any case are an entirely conventional rendering of views he found in Boethius, Jean de Meun and Dante. However, the context of the passage on *gentillesse* in the Wife of Bath's Tale is one in which Chaucer's imaginative powers are fully engaged, and one in which he may therefore be more fully alive to the political and social implications of a literary-philosophical *topos*. Clearly, the openness of society, the accessibility of high office to those of low birth, which is the practical consequence of ideas about *gentillesse*, was a topic of considerable importance to Chaucer and his friends. Without Chaucer talking about it directly, the hag's monologue offers an opportunity to air the subject in the dramatically transposed context of a domestic fiction, where the issues are apparently those of personal rather than political power, and where, in addition, irony may at any point dissolve the whole process safely into mockery.

This may be the way, too, in which Chaucer achieves a larger resonance for the expression of ideas about *gentillesse* in the Franklin's Tale. The Franklin himself is at a critical pressure-point in changing fourteenth-century society, the point at which old 'freedom' (freedom from servility, that is, as well as freedom of spirit, or nobility), based on gentle birth, meets new 'freedom', based on wealth. His tale ends with a conundrum on *gentillesse* in which it is suggested that it may be difficult to decide whether a clerk or a squire or a knight has been 'the mooste fre' (*Canterbury Tales*,

V. 1622). Traditionally, the nobility of behaviour available to each would have been inscribed in his rank. There is a further possibility, which makes Chaucer's playful and perhaps again ironic interrogation of these social class boundaries still more venturesome, and that is the suggestion that the true hero of *gentillesse* is a heroine, that is, Dorigen.

The presentation and debating of urgent social and political issues in these transposed forms may be a model of the way Chaucer domesticates into literary narrative his response to the events of his day. He is different from Langland, who is like a seismograph in his record of contemporary political and social disturbance, and from Gower, whose earnestness of response issues in direct and strident commentary, especially in his Latin poems. Chaucer's immersion in the events of his day may have been no less complete, but his method of communicating their impact and importance was indirect, whether because of temperament, or the political caution needful to someone of his rank and position, or because of a deliberate choice concerning the materials appropriate to high-literary vernacular poetry. So he will make no direct reference to events like the Peasants' Revolt, but the changes in the social and economic system of which it is a violent symptom will be fully documented in terms of the personal and dramatic conflicts within his fictions. *The Canterbury Tales* will be the fullest record of London life, in its specific historical circumstances and conditions, in the 1380s and 1390s.

'PALAMON AND ARCITE'

In the Prologue to *The Legend of Good Women*, written in 1386–7, the God of Love reproaches Chaucer for having translated the *Roman de la Rose*, 'That is an heresye ayeins my lawe' (F. 330), and for having written of Criseyde in such a way as to make men think that women are not to be trusted. Alceste attempts a defence of Chaucer, arguing that he has in the past written things such as draw people to the service and praise of love:

> He made the book that hight the Hous of Fame,
> And eke the Deeth of Blaunche the Duchesse,
> And the Parlement of Foules, as I gesse,
> And al the love of Palamon and Arcite

Of Thebes, thogh the storye ys knowen lyte.
(F. 417–21)

Chaucer does not list the four works in the exact order in which
he is usually presumed to have written them, but the implication
would be that all four were part of the history of his blameless
poetic career before *Troilus*.

The story of 'the love of Palamon and Arcite' must be what we
now know as the Knight's Tale. It evidently had an existence
before the scheme of *The Canterbury Tales* was devised, and there
is no reason to believe that it was much revised, or adapted to the
'character' of the Knight, in the process of inclusion, except for
the obvious addition of lines 889–92, where the Knight alludes to
the tale-telling competition, and perhaps of the whole paragraph
(875–92). Alceste's acknowledgement in the Prologue to the Legend that 'the storye ys knowen lyte' argues not that it was only
recently written but either that the story, as a story, was not well
known, which was true enough, or that Chaucer's poem had not
reached a wide audience. The latter interpretation seems likely,
given the manner in which Chaucer, at the height of his career
and fame in 1387, might reflect on the comparatively limited
circulation that his early poems had achieved.

He was, of course, about to hit upon an idea for a framework-
narrative in which fugitive earlier writings might be not merely
publicized but incorporated as integral elements in the design.
One function of *The Canterbury Tales* was to provide a secure home
for otherwise unattached compositions, whether to be written or
already written. One was the story of Palamon and Arcite. Alceste
mentions, a little further on in her speech in defence of Chaucer,
works of 'holynesse' that he has written, including *Boece* and 'the
lyf also of Seynt Cecile' (F. 426). The latter duly became the
Second Nun's Tale, again with no apparent attempt to adapt it to
its narrator in *The Canterbury Tales* (see VIII. 62). The Life of St
Cecilia was probably composed in the late 1370s, like the *ABC*,
when Chaucer was working with free translation in some formal
genres as he tried out his first experiments with the pentameter
in stanzas. It is an exercise of more than formal piety, perhaps
the finest poem in the genre of the saint's life in English; some
stanzas from Dante (VIII. 36–56), which Chaucer was to return
to again in the Prioress's Tale, perhaps set the spark to a latent
Marian devotion. Of the fate of the other work that Alceste mentions, 'Origenes upon the Maudeleyne' (F. 428), nothing is known.

It was made, says Alceste, a long time ago, 'goon ys a gret while' (F. 427). No home was found for it in *The Canterbury Tales*.

There is some evidence of allusion in the Knight's Tale to suggest a date in the early 1380s. The description of the return of Theseus and his company from the land of the Amazons, 'And of the tempest at hir hoomcomynge' (I. 884), has been presumed to refer to the sudden rough water that wrecked the boat of Richard's young bride, Anne of Bohemia, just after she stepped ashore in England on 18 December 1381. This would support a date of composition in 1381–82, though it would not work if lines 875–88 were taken to be a later addition. It has also been suggested that the importance attached to 3 May as a day of significance in love-proceedings, not only here in the Knight's Tale (I. 1463, 1850) but also in *Troilus* (ii. 56) and the Nun's Priest's Tale (VII. 3187–90), may be an allusion to the date of betrothal of Richard and Anne, 3 May 1381, the marriage settlement having been signed a day earlier on 2 May. The two were finally wed on 14 January 1382, the bride being at that time not quite 17 and Richard just 16.[18]

The most compelling argument, however, for a date for the Knight's Tale between *The Parliament of Fowls* and *Troilus*, that is, in 1381–2, is the evidence it provides of Chaucer's continuing preoccupation with Boccaccio's *Teseida*. We have already described how this poem swept Chaucer off his feet, and how he had already tried to communicate in English something of its impact upon him, in *Anelida and Arcite* and the *Parliament*. Now he set himself to absorb the poem fully into his own imaginative experience, to test the powers of English as a vehicle for a comparable grandeur and spectacle, and to make the poem make sense in his own terms.

In pursuit of these ambitions, he reduces the *Teseida* to about a quarter of its original length, alluding only briefly to Theseus's battles against the Amazons (*Teseida*, Book I) and Creon (Book II), describing two representative champions, Lygurgus and Emetreus (2128–78) instead of the whole concourse of Greek warriors (Book VI) and presenting the tournament as a comparatively brief general mêlée (2599–651) instead of as a series of individual combats in the epic manner (Book VIII). The traditional heroic and martial content of Boccaccio's epic is thus much reduced, as is the quantity of mythological allusion drawn from Virgil and Statius (the latter's *Thebaid* is Boccaccio's principal source and model). In further attempting to dress his poem in the trappings of antiquity, Boccaccio provided it with an elaborate series of glosses (*Chiose*) and annotations, in which he explains allusions and moralizes the mythological content of the poem, especially the role of the classical deities Mars and Venus, in the manner of a medieval commentator. There is no reason to believe that Chaucer knew the *Chiose* (see above, chapter 3, note 19); it was, in any case, quite contrary to his purposes to allegorize the action in this way, to make of it the base for a conventionally Christian moral physiology of behaviour. On the contrary, the power of his response to Boccaccio's two long Italian poems, the *Teseida* and, later, the *Filostrato*, has much to do with their pagan and classical setting, and the opportunity they give for the exploration of chance, destiny and free will in the affairs of men who live in a world without God. Like Shakespeare in *King Lear*, Chaucer recognized the special urgency brought to this exploration when man was placed naked before the realities of his existence and the forces that seem to control it, and without the consolation of the faith that answers all such questions as 'What is this world? What asketh men to have? (I. 2777) with the assertion of a mystery in which they are transcended.[19]

It was to Boethius that Chaucer turned in his attempt to reshape Boccaccio's poem to a more fully philosophical sense of the human predicament. The *Consolation of Philosophy* of Boethius, which Chaucer translated in full during the period of composition of the Knight's Tale and *Troilus*, may be seen as an attempt to consider man's life within the context of classical beliefs, excluding from the enquiry the consolations of faith. Like Boethius, Chaucer accepts for the occasion the premises of pagan belief, or at least accepts them as far as his characters are concerned. He excises Boccaccio's description of the ascent of Arcite's soul, after death, to the eighth sphere (though he later inserted it in *Troilus*), perhaps uneasy with the blurring of pagan and Christian sentiment, and covers the omission with some brusque remarks concerning the possibility or propriety of predicting the destination of pagan souls (2809–14). Elsewhere, he adds much Boethian material. He gives long and eloquent speeches to Arcite (1223–74), exiled from the sight of Emelye, and to Palamon (1281–1333), left solitary in prison, in which they lament their fate in the manner of the exiled and imprisoned Boethius. It is true, of course, that they show a failure of understanding in not being able to rise to the recognition of the providential order that Lady Philosophy eventually teaches to Boethius. But they are young, have not completed their reading of Boethius or arrived at the exhausted and passionless resignation of Aegeus, Theseus's father, in his response to the world's ills

(2843–50). What Chaucer is interested in is not the statement of reconciliation but the sense of process, of passionate challenge to the order of things, and of the growth of understanding that derives from suffering and blighted hope.

It is appropriate that Theseus should speak with maturer understanding of the lovers' folly (1785–1825), and that he should be associated with the execution of the providential scheme (1663–72). It might seem that his final speech (2987–3069), which is also Chaucer's addition, should close the poem in a declaration of the providential order. It may have been intended to, but it does not: it declines from its grand opening Boethian vision of the work of the 'Firste Moevere' to conventional reiterations of the inevitability of death and even some limp acquiescence in the consolation that death is a fortunate release from the 'foule prisoun of this lyf' (3061). We may take Theseus's speech as a dramatically appropriate political oration, intended to prepare the way for his proposals for a marriage between Palamon and Emelye and an alliance between Thebes and Athens. It is not intended as a solution to the problems of the poem, nor is it Chaucer's way to offer such programmatic solutions. The questions, however, are presented with fierce urgency.[20]

Chaucer deepens the story in another way, by giving to Boccaccio's classical deities their traditional medieval role as planetary influences, and in this way making sense of what an English reader of the time could only have regarded as a classical charade. The influences of the planets were accepted as part of the agency of Providence, as the instrumental causes of certain 'accidents' (like Arcite's death) and of certain dispositions in human beings through which they are induced, though not compelled, to certain acts. The astrological influence of Mars and Saturn is referred to explicitly and in detail (2017–26, 2454–62), and Chaucer makes a point of identifying the propitious planetary hour (2217, 2271, 2367) in which Palamon, Emelye and Arcite attend with prayer their tutelary deities. Their gods figure their destiny, and in some sense too their character. Arcite's prayer reveals a certain bold presumptuousness: he asks for victory, and victory alone (2420), demanding of future events that they be constrained to his will by this victory, through which he will win Emelye. Palamon is more conscious of the greater goal which he seeks, and of the unpredictable means by which it may be achieved: he resigns his fate to Venus (2238–44). He is, in the poem's terms, the more likely postulant; he shows a consciousness, albeit only fitful, of a 'divinity that shapes our ends', where Arcite thinks he alone may 'rough-hew' them.[21]

The distinction in the prayers of the two lovers is part of a consistent pattern of change that Chaucer has wrought in Boccaccio's story. The 'realism' of Chaucer's treatment of the story has often been commented upon, the way in which he represents it in terms of medieval chivalry, with ransoms, heralds, tournaments and much other detail of a vividly realistic kind. In this way the story is drawn within the context of idealized medieval experience. In other ways, though, the events of the story and the behaviour of the characters are made more distant, more remote from everyday experience; above all, the characters are remote from each other, almost like elemental beings propelled by forces beyond themselves. Boccaccio is consistently attentive to the literal circumstances of his narrative, and his characters respond to events and each other in a natural and human way. All this attention to the how and why is passed over by Chaucer, in favour of sudden and unexplained impulse and the operation of chance or destiny on mysteriously momentous days. All trace of the mundane and familiar is removed from the characters. Emelye, who as Emilia plays in Boccaccio a fully personalized role, is systematically depersonalized: she knows nothing, feels nothing, wants nothing, except to remain a virgin, and the only time she is shown speaking is when she makes her prayer to Diana. She exchanges not a single word with either lover, and at Arcite's death simply shrieks in company. Emelye is not a woman with whom Palamon and Arcite fall in love, but the agency through which powerful forces are released and find their way to destruction or resolution.

Palamon and Arcite are depicted with a similar impersonality. In Boccaccio they are clearly differentiated: Arcita is the wholly admirable hero who is unlucky and Palemone the runner-up who gets the prize when the winner is disqualified. In Chaucer it is hard to tell them apart, and neither behaves well: Arcite's sophistry in arguing that he should have precedence over Palamon, or alternatively that there is no such thing as precedence (1152–82), is as deplorable as Palamon's second thoughts about the order in which he would have Theseus slay them (1721–4). As the story moves to its climax, the impression is created, in the prayers in the temples, that the equality of Palamon and Arcite in desert and merit is an impasse which only a trick of fortune will circumvent. It seems that Chaucer has deliberately levelled the two, so that the outcome of the story will appear not nobly tragic but bleakly capricious. Chaucer's additions to the descriptions of the temples of further images of suffering and menace, such as the wolf eating a man at the foot of Mars's statue (2048) or the woman in labour in the temple of Diana (2083), increase the sense of a world in which human beings are at the mercy of cruel and unintelligible powers outside themselves.

This first lengthy interrogation by Chaucer of the world and the providential order makes a cold and powerful poem. It is about love, but no sense of what love is like is communicated, only the cruelty of warring appetites in a chaos ruled by appetency, or the misery of an infatuation that is said to be more like a mania than a malady (1374). That the poem is not as resolutely bleak as it may seem to promise is due to a number of factors. One is the presence of Theseus, whose power as a ruler is recognized to be limited but who at least strives to use it to good purpose. He has the added virtue of being able to change his mind. Another conciliatory move is the change in the story that Chaucer makes by which it is Palamon who sees Emelye first and not Arcite, as in Boccaccio. This gives the working out of the story a certain logic, though it is not altogether reassuring to be made to recognize that the law of destiny is dependent on such fine points. But then, law is nothing but fine points.

More important than these hints of an intelligibility in the order of things is an act that does much to reassert man's power over circumstance and his ability to rise above the claims of his appetite. Arcite, in his dying speech, acknowledges that the fault is in him and that the 'strif and rancour' have been due to his 'jalousye' in love (2784–5). He rehearses, as in a litany, the qualities of the true servant of love and chivalry, attributing them to Palamon but associating himself again with them, after long neglectfulness, through his act of renunciation. He commends his soul to the higher power of Jupiter, not Mars, recognizing in this act the existence of a providential power which lies beyond the immediate instrumentality of passion and circumstance. Finally, he commends Palamon to Emelye: 'Foryet nat Palamon, the gentil man' (2797). Theseus speaks later of the wisdom of making virtue of necessity (3041–2): Arcite here demonstrates the true nature of that virtue in its voluntary and willed activity. There is nothing very comforting about the acquisition of such wisdom in the face of death, but nevertheless the assertion of human free will has a significance quite different from the gift of posthumous vision granted to Boccaccio's Arcita and Chaucer's Troilus. Theseus's long speech, after this, is no more than the chairman's closing remarks.

There is much more in this great though somewhat uneven poem that deserves exposition and comment. Chaucer engages vigorously in the imaginative experience of the story, and, following Boccaccio, gives majestic expression to its ceremonies and pageantry – the heroic chivalry of Theseus setting out for Thebes (975–84), the beauty of Emelye (1033–55), the preparations for the tournament (2483–598), the battle (2599–651). The temples of Venus, Mars and Diana (1918–2088) are done with the greatest magnificence, much detail being added from the *Roman de la Rose*, Ovid and Statius. Certain descriptions, such as those of the statue of Venus (1955–66) and the Thracian setting of the Temple of Mars (1970–94) are done with a lavishness of poetic power that makes the Knight's Tale perhaps Chaucer's *tour de force*.

At the same time there are oddities and unevennesses. There is some instability of tone in serious passages such as the descriptions of Arcite's death (2759–60), of the fate of his soul (2809–16), and of his funeral (2913–66), the last of which is all done, inexplicably, under pretence of refusal to describe (the figure commonly called occupatio). All these features lend themselves to conventional kinds of deconstruction, but if one were thinking in terms of the poet's intention they might be the product of a desire to modulate the poem, as it draws towards its close, from its predominantly minor key. In that case, it might appear that Chaucer has not yet mastered the delicate techniques of narrative control. The apparently salacious aside during the description of the rites in Diana's temple (2284–8) is harder to explain. But it would be pointless, in any of these cases, to suppose that Chaucer is deliberately parodying or subverting the poetic genre, or, more pointless still, exposing the Knight's incompetence as a narrator. All these approaches, though it may seem hard to credit, have been tried.

Readers have also been disturbed by the occasional lapses into colloquialism and apparent facetiousness that seem to mar the decorum of the high style of romance. The use of homely images and proverbs, the gossipy remarks to the audience, the constant chatter of *abbreviatio* and *transitio*, have all been castigated as incompetence, or applauded as subtle irony at the expense of the Knight–narrator's incompetence, or approved, in the postmodern way, as the marks of counter-intentionality and the stimulus to critical self-reflexivity.[22]

More reasonably, one might recognize in this familiar, loose, unbuttoned style of narrative the relics of the form of address Chaucer had cultivated in the dream-poems. Its function had always been to complicate and blur the role of the poet–narrator–performer, to make him less fully suitable to bear the responsibility of being an 'authority', to postpone the determination of intention and interpretation. As the mark of self-deprecation and self-erasure it made the eliciting of meaning seem a particularly readerly privilege. It may be that the informality is somewhat less appropriate in the Knight's Tale (it is certainly strikingly inappropriate to the Knight). We may assume that Chaucer was working towards the mastery of narrative tone and voice that he achieved fully in *Troilus and Criseyde*.

THE TRANSLATION OF BOETHIUS; THE 'BOETHIAN' POEMS

Alceste, in her apology for Chaucer in the Prologue to *The Legend of Good Women*, refers to his prose translation of *Boece* (F. 425), and Chaucer cites it in his 'Retracciouns' at the end of the *Canterbury Tales* as one among the bashfully brief number of writings that do him credit (X. 1088). *Boece*, which was Chaucer's short name for his translation of the *De Consolatione Philosophiae* as well as the regular Middle English form of the philosopher's Latin name, is also mentioned in *Adam Scriveyn*. Chaucer already shows a thorough knowledge of Boethius in *The House of Fame*, for instance in the reference to the soul's ascent on the wings of Philosophy (972), the description of the goddess Fame (1368–76) and the account of 'Domus Daedaly' (1920), and Boethius provides a key transition in *The Parliament of Fowls* (90–1). The story of 'Palamon and Arcite' is deeply impregnated with Boethian philosophizing about destiny, fortune and free will, as is Chaucer's retelling of the story of Boccaccio's *Filostrato* in *Troilus and Criseyde*.

There is, however, a difference between the Boethian influences in the Knight's Tale and earlier poems and those in *Troilus*. Allusion in the Knight's Tale is close and detailed, and Chaucer clearly had a text of Boethius available for consultation; he is already very well acquainted with the work, and picks up phrases and motifs from it with a casual intimacy in addition to making the more obvious large-scale borrowings. The fixing of Theseus's eyes as he begins his 'Firste Moevere' speech (I. 2984) is not only an allusion to the opening lines of Book III, prose 2, of the *Consolation* but can be fully understood only in the context of that passage. The same is true of Arcite's citation of 'the olde clerkes sawe, / That "who shal yeve a lovere any lawe" ' (I. 1163–4), the sophistry of which needs the context in Boethius, where the old proverb is also cited, to be revealed in its full blind obstinacy. It is the story of Orpheus and of the moment of human weakness which deprives him instantly of love and happiness (III, m. 12. 52); Arcite takes the old saw not as a bitter recognition of folly but as a blueprint for future action. Passages like this show how close Chaucer already was to Boethius.

But in *Troilus* there is such a persistent current of Boethian allusion, even in passages where the echoes are not philosophically or in other ways particularly significant, that one must suppose that the translation was just completed or still in progress when *Troilus* was begun. Pandarus's first comforting reassurances to Troilus in Book I, for instance, persistently pick up ideas and motifs from all over the first three books of the *Consolation*, sometimes with wording that seems to suggest that Chaucer was working with his own translation;[23] and it is well known that Troilus's declamation on predestination and free will in Book IV (958–1082) is a verse reworking, sometimes not completely felicitous, of Chaucer's own prose translation of Boethius's speech in *Consolation*, Book V, proses 2 and 3. It is possible that Chaucer's translation of Boethius went on book by book with the writing of *Troilus*. It was finished, as we know from Alceste's reference as well as Usk's use of the work, by 1386–7.

Anicius Manlius Severinus Boethius (*c.* 480–524) was one of the great scholars of late-classical antiquity. He wrote important commentaries on Aristotle and Plato (the latter the only real source for medieval knowledge of Plato), treatises on arithmetic and music (the latter again the standard medieval theoretical text-book on the subject) and treatises on matters of special contemporary dispute in Christian theology such as the doctrine of the Trinity. Boethius was also a distinguished servant of the Roman state under the Ostrogothic emperor Theodosius. He fell out with his master through defending the rights of the senate too strenuously and acting independently in other ways, as he describes in Book I, prose 4, and was put in prison, where he died after being tortured. While in prison he wrote the *De Consolatione Philosophiae*, which was widely read and profoundly influential throughout the Middle Ages and remains one of the noblest productions of the human mind. It was translated by King Alfred and Queen Elizabeth I and has been the solace of many condemned to unmerited suffering. In his prison, lamenting his fate, Boethius meets Lady Philosophy, who teaches him that the goods of this world, being mutable, are worthless, and that true *welefulnesse* is in that self-command which through reason rises to a recognition of the sovereign good and the beneficent ordering of Providence. The work is written in five books, each consisting of varying numbers of alternating *prosae* and *metra*, the former containing the argument, often developed through dialogue, and the latter offering moments of poetic relief (see IV, pr. 6. 372) in which themes relevant to the continuing philosophical discourse are embroidered and elaborated with classical, seasonal and astronomical allusion.

Boethius, though himself a Christian, chose to exclude the consolations of the faith from his enquiry, and to concentrate on those qualities within man's will and reason through which he can choose to ally himself to the sovereign good, rise above the miseries incident to human life, and understand the dispensation of a benevolent providence in which all fortune and misfortune is, to the higher reason, alike good ('Alle fortune is good' (IV, pr. 7. 4–5)). Chaucer was drawn to the work because it asked serious questions about man's life, and about the freedom he has to choose his destiny, and answered those questions without invoking the mysteries of the scheme of salvation. It was not for him, of course, any more than for Boethius, an alternative form of understanding, and there is nothing in the *Consolation* which is contrary or alien to Christian belief; but it was a philosophical system that answered to his own preoccupations as a poet, as we have seen them already articulated in the Knight's Tale, and their predominantly humanist cast.

It was one of the ironies of history that the goddess Fortune, whom Boethius invoked as a personification in order to demonstrate the non-existence, to the higher understanding, of the forces she was presumed to represent, was one of his most enduring legacies to the Middle Ages. Her blind and arbitrary will and the turning wheel which symbolized her power (II, pr. 1. 112, pr. 2. 51) became the stock properties of medieval poetry as a way of talking about the mutability of human life, and they are common enough in Chaucer.

But Chaucer was more deeply concerned with the profounder issue raised by Boethius, that of predestination and free will, and with the very possibility of asserting human free will as anything

other than a theological nicety. The early fourteenth century had
seen a restatement in England, in the writings of theologians like
William of Ockham and Robert Holcot, of the idea, traditionally
characterized as the heresy of Pelagius, that man's good actions,
deriving from his free will, might play some part in winning
for him salvation. Opposition to Pelagianism was theologically
necessary since it involved some abrogation of the free will of
God and of his absolute potency to do whatever he wanted,
unconstrained by what human beings might 'deserve'; St Augus-
tine, in opposing it, had sought to preserve some area of operation
for human free will through his doctrine of prevenient grace, the
power given by God to man to perform those good acts that
might be serviceable to salvation. The neo-Pelagianism of the early
fourteenth century met much fiercer rebuke, especially at the
hands of Thomas Bradwardine, Archbishop of Canterbury
(d. 1349), whom Chaucer mentions in the Nun's Priest's Tale. He
wrote thus in his *De Causa Dei*:

> [The proposition is:] That both the knowledge and the will of God
> are entirely immutable. This has the corollary that God neither
> loves nor hates anew, nor more nor less one time than another,
> and neither prayers or any good works or evil deeds deflect or
> change His divine will in the least, one way or the other. All who
> are to be saved or damned or punished or rewarded in whatever
> degree, He has decided to save or damn or reward or punish in
> the same precise degree from all eternity.[24]

We are not necessarily to suppose that on every street corner of
London questions of free will and predestination were being hotly
debated – though one can imagine that street corners frequented
by William Langland might well have seen some excitement – but
clearly such a ruthless denial, as it must have appeared, of a
natural and necessary property of being human would provoke
and disturb any thinking human being. It is not just a question
of finding a theologically satisfactory answer to a theological question, but of finding the *right* answer, the essential answer, that is,
in the freedom of human beings to choose. All Chaucer's serious
poetry seems to me to be preoccupied with the question of free
will and the manner in which it is possessed by human beings,
and we have already seen how the reshaping of the Knight's Tale
produces a moving demonstration of the activity of free will, even
though Arcite arrives at that freedom only as he is dying. As

Boethius says, 'the laste day of a mannes lif is a maner deth to Fortune' (II, pr. 3. 87–8).

The solution to the problem in the *Consolation* is different. Faced with Boethius's passionate avowal that human free will cannot coexist with God's foreknowledge, and that therefore there is no such thing as virtue or vice and God is the author of evil (V, pr. 3), Philosophy first replies a little wearily: ' "This is", quod sche, "the olde questioun of the purveauance of God" ' (V, pr. 4. 1). It has to do, she says, with different modes of knowing (V, pr. 4. 137–41): God knows all that is to happen, but he knows it all in an eternal present, in which before and after, which are the necessary conditions of the corrupted temporal existence of man, do not exist (V, pr. 6. 109–16, 197–206). His knowledge therefore is not 'fore'-knowledge and does not constrain human free will. The delight with which Chaucer came upon this answer is an informing freedom in all his later poetry. We can take it too that it consoled him for his comparative lack of interest in the welfare of his fellow-creatures, his lack of a Langlandian social and political concern, of which we have already spoken. Philosophy's answer to Boethius's rather pointed question about the lack of reward for merit and the evil tyranny and oppression of those in power (IV, pr. 1) is not that the good should band together to put the wicked out of power but that there is no need for action of any sort, since the good always have true *welefulnesse* and the wicked do not *really* enjoy power or anything else, given that they lack the serenity of virtue. There are a few things wrong with this answer (is there no such thing as 'commune profyt'?) and Langland probably found Boethius rather quietistic (he uses him little), but, broadly speaking, it suited Chaucer.

Chaucer translated the whole work, proses and metres, into prose. In this he followed Jean de Meun, whose French prose translation is a direct source. Chaucer worked closely with both Latin and French, often allowing Jean to do the work for him of translating a synthetic language into an analytic one, unpacking the complex syntax of the Latin into the looser, more 'natural' structures of the vernacular. Chaucer had the Latin beside him too, and often combined Latin and French in doublets (for example 'discussed and chased awey' (I, m. 3. 1–2)); he also used the Latin to check on the accuracy of Jean's translation, and often in the metres, where he thinks Jean may have been inordinately free, he will return to the Latin and translate it with painful literalness, barely managing some of Boethius's more contorted poeticisms (for example III, m. 9. 24–32).

Chaucer also used some version of the Latin commentary on the *Consolation* by the early-fourteenth-century English scholar Nicholas Trivet; it provided him with explanations of allusions and difficult passages, which are occasionally marked in the Chaucer manuscripts as *Glosa*, but commonly not. Modern editions set such passages in italics and in parentheses. Chaucer also incorporates some material from Trivet into his actual translation of the text. There is further material from other earlier commentaries, and it has been very reasonably conjectured that Chaucer had before him a single manuscript which contained a text of Boethius, accompanied by selections from the commentaries of Trivet and others, and the French of Jean de Meun. Such an actual manuscript has not come to light, but Cambridge University Library MS Ii. iii. 21, which contains Boethius's Latin and a variety of commentaries as well as Chaucer's English translation, is an example of the kind of 'Boethius anthology' one might have in mind.[25]

Chaucer worked hard at his translation and does not make many mistakes. Some of the 'mistakes' in understanding Latin that he has been accused of are perfectly accurate translations of misreadings in the Latin text he used, which is a copy of a late-medieval 'vulgate' version of Boethius, adapted to medieval practices and ways of thinking. Sometimes he followed the French in misunderstandings or misreadings of the Latin. Sometimes the misreadings he followed are in the particular manuscript of the French he used and not in the standard text. Occasionally he gets things wrong despite the French, but when one looks at the kinds of Latin manuscript he was using, with their multitudes of abbreviations and contractions, his general accuracy is remarkable.[26]

Chaucer's translation of Boethius is the product of his desire to make the work fully his own, to absorb it, as we have said of the *Teseida*, fully into his imaginative experience. We might think of this activity of translation as contributory to that activity of memory through which a work is rewritten in one's brain: 'A work is not truly read until one has made it part of oneself', until, that is, it has been 'transferred into memory'.[27] This at any rate was one of the things he achieved through his translation, as the deep indebtedness to Boethius of his later poetry bears witness. But the presence of explanatory glosses which are clearly explanations for readers other than himself (for example, I, pr. 3. 31, m. 5. 25) argues that he intended the work to be disseminated and read in the usual way, as does the existence of nine manuscripts, more or less full. There is no evidence whatever that the translation was done for Richard II at the suggestion of his tutor Sir Simon Burley.

In the manuscript of *Boece* which was characterized above as a 'Boethian anthology', Cambridge University Library MS Ii. iii. 21, there is a poem of eight eight-line ballade stanzas, without refrain or envoy, which has come to be called *The Former Age*. It is ascribed to Chaucer and written into the manuscript, as an integral part of it and in the main scribe's hand, immediately after the prose translation of Book II, metre 5, the theme of which it treats in a much-amplified poetic manner. It is one of a series of poems expatiating on Boethian themes that Chaucer seems to have been prompted to write by or during his work on the Boethius translation. *The Former Age* is a recital of the benefits of the fabled golden age of Saturn, when there was no cultivation, no cooking, no mining, no brewing, no trade, no war, no self-indulgent luxury:* how very different from today is the predictable conclusion. *The Former Age* is interesting as the poetic reworking of a classical *topos* (theme for poetic reworking) but, like some of the other poems in this group, it is remarkable for its blandness and lack of reflexivity. There is no thinking going on about the criminality of the real present (attempts to relate the poem to events of 1398–9 are unconvincing), or about the function of other-worldly fantasy in displacing discontent, nor is there any indication, even in the poetic imagery, of what might be missed from civilization in this catalogue of absences. The theme needs its context in Boethius to make proper sense. The poem is an example of the inertness of Chaucer's mind and imagination when there is no narrative to stimulate them.[28]

Also in the Cambridge manuscript, immediately following *The Former Age*, there is a copy of another Boethian poem, *Fortune*, a triple ballade (three poems each of three eight-line stanzas with refrain) with envoy in rhyme royal. By contrast with *The Former Age*, which appears in only one other manuscript, *Fortune* found its way also into nine of the standard fifteenth-century anthologies of Chaucer and Chauceriana. It is a dialogue between 'Le Pleintif countre Fortune' and Fortune herself, generally indebted to Book

---

* Chaucer, in a manner that tells us something about medieval diet, misses Boethius's point about vegetarianism, as did Jean de Meun, and has people sleeping on 'gras or leves' (44) instead of eating them.

II of the *Consolation*. The Pleintif declares his defiance of Fortune, despite having fallen into disfavour through her mutability, and contents himself with the sufficiency of his self-command; Fortune, who is gratified to find her existence confirmed by this act of defiance, suggests that the Pleintif, having solved the problem of misfortune, might nevertheless be looking a gift horse in the mouth if he did not actively seek good fortune; she concludes by praying to 'Princes . . . three of you or tweyne' (73, 76) to help this man out or ask 'his beste frend' (also mentioned in the refrain to the second ballade) to do so, if only to stop him complaining to her. Chaucer makes a witty little dramatic narrative out of a quite serious matter, perhaps as the prelude to a genuine request for help from his 'beste frend', that is, the king, through the 'princes', that is, the dukes of Lancaster, York and Gloucester, two or three of whom, by an ordinance of 1390, had to authorize royal gifts. Richard would not object to some mild fun being made of this arrangement, and of course a witty and amusing begging-poem always has a better chance of success than a dull and sincere one. Chaucer, as we shall see, was not too happy with his office as clerk of the king's works in 1390, and, as a half-serious plea for rescue, the complaint against Fortune would be quite timely.[29]

There are three other 'Boethian' poems, shorter (three rhyme royal stanzas with refrain and also, in two cases, envoy) and in a more serious vein. All appear frequently and sometimes together in the standard fifteenth-century Chaucerian anthologies, and all are examples of the power of eloquence: intellectually commonplace as they are, they generate considerable moving power through their command of the rhetorical discourse of gnomic generalization and exhortation. *Truth* is generally but unmistakably Boethian in tone. It exhorts the reader to give up striving for things in this world, which is not our true home anyway (17; compare *Boece*, I, pr. 5. 9–20): be true to your own higher self, 'And trouthe thee shal delivere, it is no drede'. Consisting mostly of single-line aphoristic statements and commands, with strongly marked parallelism and antithesis, *Truth* is a poem of remarkably sustained nobility. It bears a striking resemblance, in theme and phrasing, to some lines from the *Confessio Amantis* (v. 7735–42), and perhaps a common debt to a Senecan apophthegm and the general Roman tradition of curial satire.[30]

One of the twenty-three manuscripts of *Truth*, the one that contains the best copy of the poem, has an envoy addressed to 'Vache', exhorting him to follow the advice of the poem. This envoy has often been thought to be an afterthought, but it picks up so neatly the apostrophe within the poem, 'Forth, pilgrim, forth! Forth, beste, out of thy stal!' (18), that it may well be taken to be integral with the original composition. There is no reason at all to question the identification of 'Vache' with Sir Philip (de) la Vache (*c.*1346–1408), a knight of the chamber from 1377 and a very well-off Home Counties gentleman, whose career had touched Chaucer's at many points, whose wife was the daughter of his good friend Sir Lewis Clifford, and whose name appears frequently in records beside names that appear in the Chaucer life-records. In 1386 Vache was forced to resign his lucrative office as keeper of the royal manor and park at Woodstock, whether because of mismanagement or because he had fallen out with Gloucester, the man of the moment: Chaucer's poem addresses Sir Philip's situation very aptly, and gains added eloquence and feeling from the poet's recognition of how close he may be himself to needing a similar consolation.[31]

Gentilesse, of which some mention has already been made (p. 150 above), is a poem on a familiar medieval theme. It is based on Boethius, Book III, prose 6, metre 6, though the spark may have come from some strikingly similar reflections on the same theme in Boccaccio's *Filostrato* (vii. 94). Chaucer is here in his most unreflexive mood. He disposes the argument, concerning the relation between virtue and noble birth, in the simplest possible way: he denies that there is any relation, ignoring Boethius's very sensible qualification that men of birth may be constrained to behave well by some desire not to betray their noble ancestry (pr. 6. 45–51). *Gentilesse* has a peculiar literary interest in that some of the manuscripts in which it appears are manuscripts of Henry Scogan's *Moral Balade*. Henry Scogan (*c.*1360–1407) was tutor to the four sons of Henry IV during their childhood, and towards 1407, when they were in their teens and he had long given up tutoring them, he wrote a poem and sent it to them at a feast they were having in the Vintry at the house of Lewis John.[32] He urges them to begin early in virtuous behaviour, knowing that there is no virtue inherent in birth nor lordship. He quotes lines from Chaucer's Wife of Bath's Tale (III. 1121, 1131–2) – 'My mayster Chaucer, god his soule have! / That in his langage was so curious' (*Moral Balade*, 65–6) – in support of his point (at lines 67–9, 97–9), and at lines 105–25 he quotes the whole of the poem *Gentilesse*, adding:

Lo here, this noble poete of Breteyne

> How hyely he, in vertuous sentence,
> The losse in youthe of vertue can compleyne.   (126–8)

Later in the poem he alludes further to the Wife of Bath's Tale
and also to the Monk's Tale. Scogan is thus entitled to join that
important group of early Chaucer readers and admirers of whom
we shall speak in the next chapter.

Lak of Stedfastnesse, the last of these five poems, is only very
generally indebted to Boethius. It laments the mutability and
variableness of the world, very much in the manner of the genre
of poems on the evils or abuses of the age, and very much too in
the gnomic one-line style that was to become almost an obsession
in Lydgate's poems of moral reflection:

> Trouthe is put doun, resoun is holden fable,
> Vertue hath now no dominacioun;
> Pitee exyled, no man is merciable.
> Through covetyse is blent discrecioun.   (15–18)

The copy of *Stedfastnesse* in Trinity College, Cambridge, MS
R. 3. 20, a John Shirley manuscript, has an 'Envoy to King Richard', which exhorts the king, in the most general and unexceptionable terms, to rule well and prevent wrongdoing. As always,
Shirley's heading may be the product of guesswork (he had a genius
for inventing plausible occasions and provenances for poems), but
it seems entirely likely that Chaucer might address Richard in this
inoffensive way around 1386, before the king's behaviour became
so bad that any exhortation might be construed as rebuke. Gower
was being similarly polite to Richard at this time, though he was
later to become very impatient.[33]

TROILUS AND CRISEYDE

The composition of *Troilus and Criseyde* dates from 1381–86,
when Chaucer was at the height of his career and public fame
as a poet. The suggestion that he was already at work on the
poem in 1382, and made then the complimentary allusion to
Queen Anne (i. 171), has been mentioned above in the discussion of the Knight's Tale, and the poem was clearly finished
by 1386, when it is referred to in the Prologue to *The Legend of*

Good Women and by Thomas Usk. That the Knight's Tale preceded *Troilus* has already been argued; *Boece* was probably still under way when *Troilus* was begun but it was finished before Chaucer began work on Troilus's predestination speech in Book IV. The use without gloss of the word *future* (v. 748), which, as a neologism in English, Chaucer felt he had to explain in *Boece* (V, pr. 6. 19), argues similarly for the prior completion of *Boece*. That Chaucer was working on Book III VTF *Troilus* in 1384 or 1385 is confirmed by the reference (iii. 624) to a most portentous astrological conjunction which appeared in 1385 for the first time since AD 769. Those interested in astrology, as Chaucer was, would have been keenly aware of this great wheeling of the planets and its foreboding significance, and the comically reductive nature of Chaucer's reference (it causes the rain which obliges Criseyde to stay overnight at Pandarus's house) was probably no less appreciated. It seems to me that the reference would have given greater pleasure and had more point before rather than after the conjunction actually occurred, but either is possible.

The story of Troilus and Criseyde was well known in fourteenth-century England. It had been invented by Benoit de Sainte-Maure, who intercalated the sad story of the lovers' parting and subsequent fortunes into the middle third of his *Roman de Troie* (*c.* 1160), a reworking in French verse of the whole classical story of Troy as it came down from late-antique redactors. Benoit's work was given an even wider circulation in the Latin prose version that was made of it by Guido delle Colonne, the *Historia Destructionis Troiae* (completed 1287). Chaucer knew and used both these works, the former quite extensively, but his direct and principal source is Boccaccio's *Filostrato* (1338). Boccaccio extracted the story of the lovers from the general matter of Trojan history, balanced the account of the departure of Criseida from Troy and her subsequent infidelity with a warm and detailed description of the passionate beginnings of the love-affair, and gave to the whole an urbane, sophisticated and lascivious colouring such as would appeal to the Neapolitan society in which he had recently lived. To Chaucer it was a revelation of what a 'modern' story of love might be – unrestrained in its depiction of sexual love, with a frank acceptance of the woman's sensuality and of the role of the go-between, Pandaro (whom Boccaccio invented); thoroughly contemporary in tone, with a Troy of familiar streets, houses, palaces and town gardens; and devoid of moral principle or attitudinizing. It must have seemed to him not only thoroughly modern but thoroughly wicked, like the 'new French novels' which scandalized and delighted successive generations of nineteenth-century English readers. Whatever adjustments Chaucer made to the tone of the *Filostrato*, his story remains, as was Boccaccio's, pre-eminently a story of the urgencies, glories, pains and absurdities of sexual love. It was surely the talk of the court in the 1380s, and was perhaps regarded as something of a 'problem' romance, like those of Chrétien de Troyes, provocative of exciting discussion, especially when men and women were together.

Chaucer lavished more care on the *Troilus* than on any other of his poems. It is, quite self-consciously and deliberately, his masterpiece, and the *The Canterbury Tales* seems by contrast (though it is not) a work of careless ease and relaxation. The opening lines are sententious in the high epic style, with the characteristic syntactical inversion of the epic exordium (i. 1–5) and the ominous invocation of Tisiphone (i. 6–11). In the closing lines (v. 1828–69) Chaucer turns, with unprecedented solemnity, to a Christian view of the story he has told, in which its delights and unprofitable pains are alike transcended, and ends with Dante's prayer to the Trinity. He asks his poem to take its place modestly among the great writers of antiquity (v. 1792), and makes an earnest plea that its language and metre shall not be misrepresented by later scribes (v. 1793–8), as indeed they were, very badly.

He seems to have taken particular care in preparing his poem for 'publication', and he mentions it in *Adam Scriveyn* as one of the works he has had to proof-read very meticulously after getting it back from the scribe. There are signs of quite extensive revision, particularly in the addition at some stage in the compositional process of slabs of serious philosophical material – Troilus's hymn to love (iii. 1744–71) and predestination speech (iv. 958–1082), both from Boethius, and the ascent of Troilus's soul to the eighth sphere (v. 1807–27), taken from the *Teseida* (Chaucer did not use this passage in the Knight's Tale). There has been some debate about whether this is revision of a work previously deemed to be completed or revision as part of a single compositional process, but there was certainly some kind of revising activity, its traces almost removed in the extant manuscripts (the contrast with the state of the *Canterbury Tales* manuscripts is striking).[34]

The poem also demonstrates Chaucer's now complete mastery of the rhyme royal stanza, and his power of exploiting it for every variety of poetic narrative and expression. The stanza where he

moves from his elaborately self-abnegating prologue to the matter
of Troy is an example of one kind, and an unexpected kind, of
command:

> Yt is wel wist how that the Grekes stronge
> In armes with a thousand shippes wente
> To Troiewardes, and the cite longe
> Assegeden, neigh ten yer er they stente,
> And in diverse wise and oon entente,
> The ravysshyng to wreken of Eleyne,
> By Paris don, they wroughten al hir peyne.   (i. 57–63)

The majestic surge of the first four lines, with their striking enjamb-
ment, and the winding delays, inversions and enclosures of the
last three almost embody in themselves the essence of the heroic
story.

Chaucer's changes to Boccaccio are considerable, though the
story, of the growth, flourishing and coming to an end of a love-
affair, remains essentially the same. He adds much to the serious-
ness and grandeur of the story by his renewed attention to the
epic and classical background, which had been almost erased in
Boccaccio, and by the frequency of his allusion to the destinal
patterning of events. He gives his poem a greater literary elevation
by the addition of elaborate proems to each book (except the fifth)
and of a wealth of literary and classical allusion, especially drawn
from Statius and Dante. The whole poem is expanded through
the systematic use of those processes of amplification (such as
description, apostrophe, *exclamatio, sententia*) which were standard
for the treatment of given material in the medieval arts of poetry,
and also through the embedding in the narrative of numbers of
songs, complaints, epistles and soliloquys. All this gives the poem
its characteristic leisureliness and luxurious expansiveness, evidenced for instance in the description of Troilus falling in love
(i. 204–315). Chaucer has also much modified the sensuality of
Boccaccio's poem, giving to Criseyde a role much more like that
of the courtly mistress of French tradition. Where Boccaccio's
Criseida falls in eagerly with the plan to take a lover, Chaucer's
Criseyde is infinitely hesitant, and all the characters in *Troilus*,
even Pandarus, engage in the expression of refined and idealized
sentiments concerning love which would have rung very hollow in
Boccaccio. This is what C. S. Lewis meant when he spoke of
Chaucer having 'medievalized' the *Filostrato*.[35]

Chaucer, while adding much new material, follows the general lines of Boccaccio's narrative quite closely in Books I, IV and V, but in Books II and III he departs from Boccaccio completely for very long stretches. These are the books where Chaucer is developing with infinite and loving care that characterization of Criseyde which all readers recognize to be the irresistible core of attraction of the poem. From being more or less colourless in Book I (102, 132, 281) and not much more than an instrument (i. 56) in a story which has Troilus as its hero (i. 1), she takes over the poem, as Chaucer first responds to and then engages fully with the barely imaginable possibility of a fully realized female subjectivity, a woman with the self-awareness, the moral and emotional self-consciousness, the elusive and enigmatic self-communing, that it was orthodox to deny to women as a sex. The influence of Pandarus, as a being without responsibility except to provoke action in others, in releasing both Criseyde and Chaucer to this process of dramatic self-revelation is very important. Long tracts of Books II and III in which Pandarus is present (for example ii. 78–595, 1352–1750) consist entirely of uninterrupted dialogue and unmediated narrative link, building up that depth of engagement with the evolving drama that one associates with unbroken camera sequences in cinema.

Chaucer works hard to protect Criseyde from being either easily accepted or condemned or in any way pigeon-holed. He suggests a painful recognition of the real vulnerability of her situation in Troy (ii. 708) at the same time that he gives her a shrewd practical and managerial power (for example, iii. 641) that takes the sentimentality out of our sympathy. The gentleness, pliability and warm seductiveness that she displays with Troilus contrast sharply with the occasional coarseness of her manner when she is with Pandarus (iii. 1565). Throughout, Chaucer represents for us the cruelties and absurdities of sexual love as well as its splendours. Troilus's readiness to tell lies at Pandarus's instigation and the raw quality of his unslaked desire after his first night with Criseyde (iii. 1531, 1539, 1546, 1650), as well as the many absurdities that accompany that night's business (though perhaps the earlier scene where Pandarus imagines he hears all the town bells ring as the lovers kiss for the first time (iii. 189) takes the prize), go with much that is tender and touching in the description of the love-affair. One of the most beautiful examples of the ambiguity with which the poem is so charged is the description of Troilus's love-making:

Hire armes smale, hire streghte bak and softe,
Hire sydes longe, flesshly, smothe, and white
He gan to stroke, and good thrift bad ful ofte
Hire snowissh throte, hire brestes rounde and lite.
(iii.1247–50)

Delicious as it is, there is nothing more delicious here than the suggestion of Troilus offering a kind of greeting to various parts of Criseyde's body as he goes his rounds, like a gardener.

Chaucer complicates the conduct of the narrative even further, and also distances it from any centre of authority, by pushing himself forward busily as narrator. He frequently suggests the presence of a listening audience and thus gives himself the role of performer within the narrative, as he did in the dream-poems. His denial of any knowledge of love or of any power over the story or responsibility for it makes him almost the unwitting participant in the poem's action, able to act only as Chorus. He assumes no role but that of priestly servant of love (i. 15, iii. 41), in which he is all enthusiasm. He is constantly currying favour with the reader on love's behalf or on Criseyde's, vaunting the power of love, encouraging the love-affair forward, reprimanding those who say Criseyde gave herself to love too quickly. The movement towards the climax of the story is accompanied by busy invocations to God, which the narrator shares with Pandarus, to allow the course of true love to run smooth. When Pandarus finally settles to sleep, and the narrator is left alone with the lovers, his embarrassment is discharged in volleys of exhortations, celebrations, confessions of incompetence, execrations on those who are niggards of love.[36]

The embarrassment, one should add, is real enough. The narrator is not separate from Chaucer, someone other than Chaucer whose responses are engineered for the purposes of delivering sets of messages that can be received and decoded and dismissed as non-authoritative. The narrator, in the most literal sense, is Chaucer, authoring, performing, experiencing. We have spoken about this before, in relation to the dream-narrator of *The Book of the Duchess*, but the point needs to be made again concerning the narrator of *Troilus*. The role of the poet in this age of residual orality (when the conventions of oral delivery continue still to be dominant) is not that of the old performer-minstrel, but that of a new kind of performer-participant, part of the group, not a mere entertainer. He is closer to his audience, more used to irony and obliqueness and the manipulation and variation of the narrative voice, like a comedian in a club rather than one on television.

Modern convention assumes that first-person narrative is fallible and the voice of the narrator, when it is heard, false. This cannot be assumed in the Middle Ages, and the reason has essentially to do with oral delivery and the implied real presence of the poet as performer. The audience does not believe that the things he says about the story are actually his own views, but they certainly do not believe they are someone else's. The poet as performing self does not articulate the views of a known group, with known ideas, not even those of the group he purports to be addressing. He is to some extent a 'personality', an eccentric, and his presence contributes to an undoing of systematic or predetermined interpretations, especially those associated with a dominant cultural or ideological group. He keeps us guessing, and contributes importantly to that element in the literature of recreation that Chaucer's court education had taught him was so vital: its discussibility.

From the end of Book III onwards, the tone of the narrative changes. References to the power of Fortune begin to shadow the story and the narrator, acknowledging his helplessness, can only attempt to pluck some temporary comfort from Criseyde's good intentions. In Book V his voice takes on a prophetic, regretful, occasionally sardonic tone, echoing, as often, the response of Pandarus.[37]

These complexities of narrative have their power and purpose in giving depth to Chaucer's portrayal of Criseyde, of her relationships with her lover and her uncle, and of her role as a woman in a city at war and dominated by male warriors. In a particular way, too, they contribute to the exploration that Chaucer is here engaged in of the complexities of the human will. Free will is the theme of the poem, as it is thrown aside by Pandarus, won and lost by Criseyde, and found (perhaps) by Troilus. Pandarus quite blithely ties himself to the wheel of circumstance, comforting himself and others with the thought that if things are bad they cannot help getting better. Criseyde chooses a different way: in a whole series of reported self-questionings and self-communings (for example, ii. 449–55, iii. 918–24), Chaucer uncovers for us the process by which the will, seeking its own ends but unwilling to accept the charge of responsibility for the actions that bring about those ends, disguises the process of decision-making in a multitude of external and irresistible causes. Criseyde thus confines her will, as

a woman must, to a sphere of small and manageable operations
from which the least discomfort and inconvenience will arise.
She tries to live a small life and to survive. The analysis of these
processes of mind is one of the great achievements of Chaucer's
poem, as he imagines into existence a notion of the will as a
market-place or theatre, a place of mysteriously complex transactions and actings-out, rather than as a judiciary, with counsel
for the pro and counsel for the con presenting matters in rational
order to the triumphal judgement of the will. Criseyde recognizes
the larger and more generous operation of her freewill when she
responds to Troilus's conventional claims to have 'caught' her,
and demands that she 'yield', thus: ' "Ne hadde I er now, my
swete herte deere, / Ben yolde, ywis, I were now nought heere!"'
(iii. 1210–11). As has been said, this is the speech that we most
like Criseyde for having made, not because it shows her to be a
really nice person, but because it confirms, in the most particular
way, the belief that human beings are free to choose, even if the
freedom confirmed is, as here, the freedom to choose one's own
constraints.[38]

Chaucer's attention to human will and consciousness is given
an added dimension of complexity, as he well knew, by the pagan
setting. The absence in the characters of a fully defined sense of
what free will consists in, as illustrated in Troilus's incapacity to
press his Boethian arguments about predestination to their Boethian conclusion, means that the investigation is conducted with a
more than usually painful honesty. A particular contribution to
the debate is made by the use of Christian religious terms (grace,
mercy, contrition, penitence, etc.) in reference to sexual love. This
is usually no more than a conventional conceit in medieval poetry,
but it comes to have a special point in a poem like this in reminding
us of a world of which the characters of the poem must perforce
remain in ignorance. The result is not to make a joke of religion
(though Pandarus comes close at times) or to substitute a religious
understanding for a poetic one, but to give a greater keenness to
the awareness of free will and its limitations.[39]

At the end of the poem, Criseyde wraps around herself again,
in a subtler manner than before, the protective folds of acquiescence, denying, as usual with the assistance of the narrator's
tumbling earnestness, her power to do any more than accept
what must be:

Retornyng in hire soule ay up and down

> The wordes of this sodeyn Diomede,
> His grete estat, and perel of the town,
> And that she was allone and hadde nede
> Of frendes helpe; and thus bygan to brede
> The cause whi, the sothe for to telle,
> That she took fully purpos for to dwelle.   (v. 1023–9)

She gives up her power to be fully human in her determination to be safe and to survive, and slips back into the plane of the poem as she acknowledges that her future existence will be merely textual. She thinks of 'thise bokes' in which she will be defamed (v. 1060), takes her leave with a stagy tearfulness (v. 1085), and appears again only in the form of her letter (v. 1590), where she has manifestly given up her will and power of words to Diomede. Thus Chaucer takes refuge in the end in the stereotyped image of woman's pliability. His betrayal of his creation was not overtly what he was apologizing for in the Prologue to *The Legend of Good Women*, but it should have been.

Troilus too has the sense that his life might be made into a story (v. 585), but he is puzzled at the process by which it has been brought to such sudden closure. Though his desire is the engine of the narrative, Troilus seems to have little of the self-awareness that makes Criseyde so winning and so richly interesting. His own free will seems to be swallowed up in the fierceness of his desire to an extent that makes him seem the creation of circumstance and Pandarus. Unexpectedly, his reaction to the loss of Criseyde is not to call down upon her the thunderbolts of the gods, as does Boccaccio's Troilo, but to acknowledge that the unwaveringness of his love for Criseyde is indeed the very ground of his being:

> 'Thorugh which I se that clene out of youre mynde
> Ye han me cast – and I ne kan ne may,
> For al this world, withinne myn herte fynde
> To unloven yow a quarter of a day!'
>
> (v. 1695–9)

The search in his heart for an alternative course of action makes him aware that his will is indeed the will to love. To the extent that he 'does what is in him' as a virtuous pagan, to recur to the language of late-medieval nominalism, he earns a place in the story and in the eighth sphere.

Chaucer's story is unlikely to have been a warning to England of the consequences of immorality.[40] Its freedom in the treatment of the historical story – a freedom that Chaucer explicitly asks for at the beginning of Book II – is an imaginative freedom as much as anything, designed to give Chaucer the room he needs to explore, particularly, female will and consciousness. The brilliance and joyousness of Books II and III of the poem may have to do with a time when Richard and Anne's court was, in the early 1380s, specially a place of youth and festival, and the old idea of London as 'the New Troy' could have a momentary flourishing.

5

Reversals, New Beginnings:
1386–1391

Chaucer's early poems do not seem, for the most part, to have circulated very widely. During the mid-1380s, however, Chaucer became famous, so that by 1386, or soon thereafter, when he wrote the Prologue to *The Legend of Good Women*, he was able to have Alceste confidently command that the completed martyrology of Cupid's saints should be delivered to Queen Anne: 'And whan this book ys maad, yive it the quene, / On my byhalf, at Eltham or at Sheene' (F. 496–7). That the *Troilus* was the means through which Chaucer finally established his reputation as a poet can be deduced from the reference made to it, almost immediately after its completion, by Thomas Usk; from the part it played in the courtly fictions of *The Legend of Good Women*; and from the supposition that Chaucer would not have embarked on such a large enterprise and lavished such care on it had he not been secure of encouragement and praise. The distance travelled from the tentative hints of poetic ambition in *The House of Fame* (1873–82) to the modestly presumptuous claim to a place in the poetic hall of fame in *Troilus* (v. 1786–92) is very considerable.

The change is not so much a matter of the receiving of patronage as of the acquisition by Chaucer of an audience, a listening and reading public, whose tastes and responses both acted as an encouragement in the task of writing and also had an influence in shaping the manner in which that task was carried out. Chaucer's references to his audience in *Troilus*, present and listening 'in the place', are not necessarily to be taken literally, but they do figure an importantly imagined reality. We can pay attention, therefore, to the reality and importance of a historical audience, and to the way in which an author both creates and is created by the tastes of that audience, at the same time that we recognize the truism that the audience invoked within the fiction is always a serviceable fiction.[1]

In trying to arrive at some understanding of the nature of Chaucer's historical audience, as it developed in the 1380s, it is necessary first to ask some questions about the nature of his relationship with the royal court. Was he, in the simplest sense, 'a poet of the court'? The affirmative answer to this question has traditionally been rooted in the interpretation of a famous picture that forms the frontispiece to a fine manuscript of *Troilus*, Corpus Christi College, Cambridge, MS 61, done about 1420. The picture shows Chaucer, in a kind of outdoor pulpit, addressing a richly costumed court audience, in which a king is clearly recognizable; further scenes of ceremonial procession and meeting are shown in the background of the picture. It is, coming as it does in the manuscript, a picture that is strongly suggestive of an original occasion when *Troilus and Criseyde* was presented before an assembled court audience. This suggestion has been enthusiastically followed up by modern scholars, some of whom, swayed by the familiar title given to the picture, 'Chaucer Reading to the Court of Richard II', have forgotten to notice that there is no book in front of the poet. I have argued elsewhere that the *Troilus* frontispiece, though it has proved a remarkably successful publisher's 'blurb' for the poem, is not an authentic reconstruction of a historically real occasion, as it was intended to be taken, but a pictorial metaphor, suggested by the audience implied within the poem, which uses the well-established iconographic model of the 'preaching picture' as the basis of its composition.[2]

The traditional interpretation of the picture has depended much on a desire to associate Chaucer with the king and with the highest levels of court patronage, as if the sophistication of his poetry could have derived only from such an association. Any intimacy of association, it should be clearly understood, is extremely unlikely. The king was the fount of patronage, and Chaucer would not have received the favour he did if he had been disagreeable to the king, but the kinds of favours he received were the routines of an increasingly bureaucratic administration, and they rewarded

Chaucer for equally routine kinds of service. There is no suggestion that his annuities and gifts and offices were the reward for his poetry; indeed the job at the customs, with its stipulation that Chaucer must keep the records in his own hand, might well have stopped a lesser man from writing poetry altogether. If Edward III or Richard II actually knew Chaucer it was with but a fleeting recognition. The compliments to Queen Anne in *Troilus* and *The Legend of Good Women* are such as are proper to pay but require no more than the recognition on the part of the audience that the compliment has been paid. The same is true of the exhortation to the king in *Lak of Stedfastnesse*. Mention of royal personages does not imply the existence of patronage or even close acquaintance. There is a well-known shortage of personal records for Richard's reign, which historians often bemoan, including the accounts of his own chamber, and it may be that personal references to Chaucer are lost, but the total absence in the Chaucer poems and manuscripts of dedications to the king or presentation-pictures, such as medieval poets are only too eager to supply on the slightest of pretexts, argues very strongly against direct royal patronage.[3]

It has often been argued that Chaucer in any case stood to gain little from Richard as a literary patron, since the king showed comparatively little interest in books. He lived in a different world from that of the French kings Charles V and VI, who had their own library in the Louvre of over a thousand volumes, with its own royal librarian, who regularly commissioned and bought books, as did the royal dukes of Berry and Burgundy. Richard, indeed, showed less interest in books than his supposedly philistine successor. Gower's story, in the *Confessio Amantis* (Prologue, 51–3, first recension copies only), of Richard suggesting to him the subject ('love') of his new poem when they met on the Thames one day, is no doubt true, but again it was to Henry that Gower eventually dedicated the *Confessio Amantis*. But if by 'patronage' we mean the creation of an environment in which literature and the arts are encouraged to flourish, and if by that we mean, principally, the release from the royal coffers of the necessary funds, then the climate of Richard's reign was far more congenial than that of Henry, who was chronically short of money.[4]

However, we shall find no real nourishment for a poet in Richard, or in Anne, whose English was in any case likely to have been primitive. Gaunt must have made some gracious acknowledgement of *The Book of the Duchess*, but he is not known to have had any great interest in books or poetry, and was in any case preoccupied

with other things. So was Thomas of Woodstock, Duke of Gloucester: the long list of his books that was inventoried when he was
declared a traitor (by a legal accident, the only major book-
inventories of the period, those of Sir Simon Burley, Thomas of
Gloucester and Henry, Lord Scrope of Masham, are all of the
books of declared traitors) is difficult to assess in terms of his
literary interests. None of the books is in English, except for
three Bible-translations, and there is no evidence of an active
involvement on Gloucester's part in the English literary culture of
his day. He did write a short military treatise in French, and
probably adhered to that older French-dominated court culture
which welcomed, as late as the early 1380s, the *Life of the Black
Prince* in French verse by the Chandos herald. As for the aristocracy
in general, though they are not to be thought of as 'growling and
factious backwoodsmen', evidence of their literary tastes is hard
to come by. Edward, second Duke of York (the vacillating Aumerle
of Shakespeare's *Richard II*), quotes two lines, somewhat garbled,
from the Prologue to *The Legend of Good Women* (F. 25–6) in his
preface to the translation of a French hunting-book that he made
while he was in prison (1406–13). But of those who stayed out of
trouble or out of prison, little is known.[5]

THE 'CHAUCER CIRCLE'

For Chaucer's real sources of nourishment, his real audience, we
might do well to look beyond the immediate entourage of the king
and his nobility to the multitudes of household knights and
officials, diplomats and civil servants, who constituted the 'court'
in its wider sense, that is, the national administration and its
metropolitan milieu. It is here that we find men whose known
interests and known association with Chaucer make them apt
candidates for a 'Chaucer circle'. The group of 'Lollard knights',
with whom Chaucer's name is often linked in the records, includes
knights of the chamber whose literary interests and acquaintance
are the very stuff of Chaucer's poetry.[6]

Sir Lewis Clifford was a close friend of Deschamps and brought
back from France Deschamps's poem in praise of Chaucer; he was
also a friend of Oton de Granson, the Savoyard poet three of
whose ballades are translated by Chaucer in *The Complaint of Venus*.
Sir Richard Stury was a friend of Froissart and possessed a fine

copy of the French *Roman de la Rose*, now British Library MS Royal 19. B. xiii. Sir John Montagu wrote poetry (presumably in French) that earned the praise of Christine de Pizan and later, as Earl of Salisbury and one of Richard's latest adherents, commissioned a French *Metrical History of the Deposition and Death of Richard II*. Sir John Clanvowe, the most important, in this connection, of all these Lollard knights, was the author of the first 'Chaucerian' poem, *The Book of Cupid*, and also of a religious treatise, *The Two Ways*.

This last shows some sympathy with Lollardy, but it is most important for the evidence it gives of individual secular men tackling for themselves the problematic 'ways' of letter and spirit. Some of Chaucer's writing, in its association with such a man, serious-minded yet not a religious, seems to fall into place, especially in its grappling with questions of free will and moral responsibility, and it is entirely reasonable to see in a group of friends like this, with common intellectual and literary interests, common political and foreign associations, and perhaps a more than common danger in their lives and allegiances, the real life of a poet. They all lived, furthermore, at a time when what later became known as Lollardy was passing through its first and less sectarian phase, a broad left movement of markedly idealistic tendencies, offering accommodation to a wide range of criticism of the established church as well as opportunities for a more personal non-sacerdotal kind of piety. Anne Hudson, while properly sceptical of the older view that Chaucer had Wycliffite sympathies, speaks of 'the indications given by Chaucer's allusions of the contemporary interest in the ideas that Wyclif had advanced' and of 'the way in which "Wycliffite" concerns coincided with the intellectual interests of the time'. Later, because its radical energies could not be absorbed within an increasingly rigorously institutionalized church, it was to be found seditious and heretical, and persecuted in ways that shrivelled the intellectual life of the fifteenth century, but in the mean time, in the late 1370s and early 1380s, there was a time of questioning and scepticism that was of great importance to Chaucer's as to Langland's poetry.[7]

Of course, we know that we are unlikely to get any explicit comments on Lollardy from Chaucer: he will be his usual cautious and evasive self, and make a joke of what might be very important to him or dangerous. Even the cheap joke that he has the Host make, about the Parson being a 'Lollere' because of his opposition to swearing (Man of Law's Epilogue, II. 1173), was removed, for one reason or another, in later revisions of *The Canterbury Tales*. The possible further suggestion of a Wycliffite tendency in the Parson, in his vehement condemnation of fables (Parson's Prologue, X. 30–6), was allowed to stand, as being more ambiguous in its reference to the practice of Lollard preachers.[8] Yet the whole portrait of the Parson in the General Prologue, though nothing in it can be labelled strictly Wycliffite, has the spirit of a radical and reforming movement, and the sharpness and special energy of Chaucer's anticlericalism in general suggest that he once knew something of the fervour that sent Clanvowe off to die on pilgrimage to the Holy Land. Being Chaucer, he converted this fervour into a framed portrait of rural virtue, distant, admired, somehow of the past.

The Chaucer circle can be expanded to include other known associates of Chaucer, men with whom he is connected in the records or in other ways. Sir Philip de la Vache was one such, a man close enough to Chaucer, as we have seen, to be the beneficiary of some well-phrased advice and exhortation in *Truth*. Sir Simon Burley, whose life touched Chaucer's at many points, was tutor to the young Richard II and had a library the inventory of which, compiled after his execution in 1388, is one of the few that records a book in English, 'i livre de Englys del Forster et del Senglier'.[9]

Henry Scogan, whom we have already come across as the author of a poem that embedded Chaucer's *Gentilesse*, was the recipient of one of Chaucer's wittiest occasional poems and one of the most delightful begging-letters it can ever have been anyone's privilege to receive. *The Envoy to Scogan* warns Scogan of the terrible vengeance that Cupid may visit upon him for having announced that he has given up his disdainful mistress, and expresses too Chaucer's fears that the vengeance may extend to 'alle hem that ben hoor and rounde of shap' (31), including himself. As he says, though, he himself gave up all that kind of thing long ago, and his 'muse', that he exercised when young, now rusts away quietly in its sheath. What he needs, forgotten as he is 'in solytarie wildernesse', is some share in the stream of grace (the Thames) at whose spring-head (Windsor) Scogan kneels and which has run dry by the time it gets to him (in London). Probably written in the 1390s, when Chaucer liked to pretend that he was short of money and out of favour, the poem is a living witness to the kind of sophistication and nimbleness of response, to irony, shifts of tone, *double entendre* and contrariety, that Chaucer could expect from members of his circle, and we can perhaps imagine something of the delight it created when it was read out at some convivial gathering.[10]

Only comparatively less delightful, perhaps on a similar occasion, was another epistolary poem, also written in the 1390s, *The Envoy to Bukton*. This is addressed to Sir Peter Bukton, who like Chaucer had served on campaign with Gaunt and given testimony at the Scrope–Grosvenor trial. Having himself 'reysed' in Prussia, he would have been one to appreciate the list of the Knight's campaigns in the General Prologue, and his offical responsibility for dykes and ditches in Holderness, in Yorkshire, would make a nice coterie allusion out of the otherwise perfectly meaningless and very specific geographical location of the Summoner's Tale. *The Envoy to Bukton* is not too genial, and its advice to Bukton to avoid the prison of marriage has a bitter edge: it would have given pleasure in an all-male company. The suggestion that Bukton should take warning by reading the Wife of Bath on the subject is the kind of self-simplifying reference that Chaucer habitually makes to his own poetry.[11]

On a slightly lower level, but still part of 'the court' in its wider sense, there were government and city officials who were part of the Chaucer circle. Thomas Hoccleve, clerk in the office of the Privy Seal, knew Chaucer in the 1390s, and had his picture set in manuscripts of *The Regement of Princes* in memory of his beloved master. He imitated Chaucer in many ways, in his colloquial manner and autobiographical vein, and tried to keep up Chaucer's practice of working with contemporary European poetry by doing a version of Christine de Pizan's *Epistre au Dieu d'Amours* (1399) in his *Letter of Cupid* (1402) which would have driven Christine berserk if she had seen it. Another literary disciple was Thomas Usk, whose *Testament of Love* and praise of Chaucer have already been spoken of. The dedication of *Troilus* to John Gower and Ralph Strode, Oxford logician and London lawyer and fellow-member of the Brembre faction, reminds us of the larger London milieu in which Chaucer lived and wrote and was read, and some place must be reserved too for William Langland, with whom he must have crossed paths in the city for many years and of whose works he shows at least some knowledge.[12]

We do not know enough about the Chaucer circle to identify changes in its composition, but it seems very likely that its epi-centre drifted away, during the late 1380s and 1390s, from the more central of the concentric circles that made up 'the court'. It changed partly because of the simple passage of time, being a group that came together by chance and contingent circumstance at a particular historical moment, and which passed away when its members died or otherwise removed; but the change coincided with the gathering around himself by Chaucer of a more privy group of friends and disciples with whom he could share *The Canterbury Tales*, a definitely 'non-court' poem. Strohm, in his essay on 'Chaucer's Fifteenth-Century Audience' (see n. 1), argues that the failure of the early fifteenth century to draw in full upon the Chaucer legacy was due in part to the dispersal of his audience. While accepting this, I would think of the initial erosion of his 1380s audience as having taken place in the early 1390s, at the latest, and point further to Chaucer's increasing isolation in these later years from the court, elements of which had always previously been important in his audience.

PUBLICATION

There was, with this, a change of emphasis in the manner in which Chaucer's work was 'published'. The early poems, we may presume, were composed primarily to be read aloud to congenial groups on suitable occasions, or to be circulated on a very limited basis in written copies. Chaucer himself would be the first 'publisher', reading his work to small groups or perhaps to an individual patron, and having a small number of copies made, or making them himself, for circulation to a close circle of friends and associates. There is no concrete evidence that this is what he did, but contemporary models for such practices are readily available.

The story that Froissart tells in *Le Dit dou Florin*, of reading his poem of *Meliador* in·instalments to Gaston, Count of Foix, on successive evenings after dinner throughout the winter months of 1388–9, provides a good example of the poet's role in the traditional entertainment of an aristocratic household. Another form of evidence takes the form of author-pictures, as of Machaut, in manuscripts directly associated with the poet himself, reading to a small group of aristocratic listeners, the book of his poems standing open upon a lectern in front of him.[13]

There are many such author-illustrations, and the general practice of reading aloud in intimate groups, where the reading is undertaken by someone other than the author, is also well evidenced. Criseyde's paved parlour (*Troilus*, ii. 82) is the scene of what we must regard as a typical form of polite entertainment. Even quite modest households had at least one compendious volume, with romances, songs, histories, saints' lives and pious tales, from which the most literate members of the family would read to the rest. The Auchinleck manuscript (National Library of Scotland, Advocates' MS 19. 2. 1) was one such volume, and Advocates' MS 19. 3. 1 was likewise itself a 'library *in parvo*'.[14] The practice of 'romanz-reding on the bok' is referred to as one of the entertainments at Havelok's coronation in Denmark (*Havelok*, 2332), and interestingly distinguished from the more noisy and general performance recital of 'gestes' by professional minstrels and *disours*: 'Ther mouhte men here the gestes singe, / The gleumen on the tabour dinge' (2333–4).[15] This is a reminder that professional recitation, with some improvization and some form of musical accompaniment, remained common practice in great households, though it surely came to be regarded as rather raucous and vulgar by the late fourteenth century. Apart from its presence as a relic in the conventional formula 'read and sing' in *Troilus*, 'And red wherso thow be or elles songe' (v. 1797), it has no relevance to consideration of Chaucerian publication.

In addition to reading their works aloud, authors also published their writings in written copies. There is very full evidence for such publication, both informal and formal, in records pertaining to Petrarch and Boccaccio. Informal publication involved the circulation of written copies to a group of friends, with conventional requests that they should tolerate imperfections and offer advice for improvements. Formal publication, which Petrarch found more difficult to bring himself to than did Boccaccio, was the delivery of a fair copy to a promised or potential patron, with the request that he should allow the work to come forth or be published (*emittas in publicum*) under his auspices and with his name to give authority and protection. This is as near to formal 'publication' in the modern sense as is possible in a manuscript culture. Machaut, Froissart and Deschamps brought out similarly authorized 'collected editions' of their poems, with or without the support of named patrons, and Christine de Pizan comes close to being a professional 'publisher' of her own work, bringing out poems in multiple copies for royal and other readers and making a living from their patronage.[16]

Poems circulated thus in written copies would always be available for reading privately as well as for reading aloud, and there is clearly a considerable growth in private reading in the late fourteenth and fifteenth centuries. However, the literary genres, structures and styles appropriate to oral delivery, whether delivery by recitation or by reading aloud, persist long into the era of silent reading. Stereotyped beginnings and endings, direct address to the audience, episodic narrative structure, exposed transitions, formulaic, rhetoricated and diffuse style, and other characteristic marks of the poetry intended for oral delivery, remain, even though the actual realities of publication and reception have substantially changed. Nor will this be remarked upon as inappropriate or anachronistic, since poetry naturally maintains an illusion of direct or even intimate address to a listening audience. On the other hand, references to the physical form of the written text in the hands of the reader, or to the pages that the reader may turn over to refer back to some earlier episode or to skip forward to some more acceptable material ('Turne over the leef and chese another tale' (Miller's Prologue, I. 3177)), seem to be appropriate only to private reading. Such references would draw attention to their own impropriety in oral delivery.[17]

All Chaucer's poems up to *The Canterbury Tales* are appropriate for and may be assumed to have been primarily intended for oral delivery. Written copies were made for circulation, but not many. They may have been made by professional scribes. By the 1380s, Chaucer was certainly using a professional copyist, as he describes in his poem to *Adam Scriveyn*:

> Adam scriveyn, if ever it thee bifalle,
> Boece or Troylus for to wryten newe,
> Under thy long lokkes thou most have the scalle,
> But after my makyng thou wryte more trewe;
> So ofte adaye I mot thy werk renewe,
> It to correcte and eke to rubbe and scrape,
> And al is thorugh thy negligence and rape.

It may be that he needed more copies than he could well make himself now that his work was becoming more and more widely known (he refers to the possibility that Adam may copy the two works again on another occasion); Hoccleve, it is true, made autograph copies of his own writings, even for presentation purposes, but he was a scribe by profession, and fairly obscure, and Chaucer was not. The two works that Chaucer mentions are also much longer than anything he had attempted previously, and professionally made fair copies, whether for his own use or for further copying and circulation, were clearly desirable.

Chaucer expresses himself very dissatisfied with Adam's standard of accuracy as a copyist, and complains bitterly about the amount of time he has had to spend correcting the copy he received back from Adam. There were no doubt good grounds for dissatisfaction (see also *Troilus*, v. 1796–7) but one should also recognize the conventional nature of such complaints, and the manner in which Chaucer implicitly sets himself beside great writers of the past, such as Petrarch, who had offered similarly magisterial rebukes to the technicians of the trade. If asked, the scribe Adam could probably have entered a few remarks of his own about the quality of the copy he was supposed to work with. Chaucer perhaps used wax tablets for his first drafts, but even after he had started to copy on to parchment there would have been second and third thoughts, additions and excisions, and exemplars most probably came to the scribe in a fairly dishevelled state.[18]

Chaucer's practice of having copies of a text professionally made and then correcting those copies when they were returned meant that from the inception of the process of publication there was the possibility of more than one 'authorized' text. It is next to impossible to imagine that the correction of the copy did not involve some further minor or even major revision on Chaucer's part: the manner in which Langland, revising the B version of *Piers Plowman* in his C version, was drawn away from the specific targets of his discontent into more general tinkering in surrounding areas of the text is an example of the temptations and opportunities constantly offered to the medieval author (as opposed to the modern author) to revise his work.[19]

Indeed, in any stage of composition that precedes formal 'publication', which as we have seen is a far less systematic or normal practice in the days of manuscript than in those of print, the text remains in a somewhat fluid state. So, with a poem like *Troilus*, there exists from a very early stage at least a first draft, from which Adam the scribe may well have pirated a further copy or even been paid in part with permission to make such a copy for his own use, and a second draft, both with the potential for extensive circulation. It happens that the textual tradition of *Troilus*, a poem that many must have wished to lay their hands upon, fits well with such a hypothesis of composition and recomposition. A significant number of manuscripts have readings that are clearly authorial, as for instance in being closer to Boccaccio's Italian, but which have equally clearly been superseded in authorial revision, as witnessed in another group of manuscripts. It would be difficult to talk about such 'first shots' and *ad hoc* revisions in terms of the practice of later writers, preparing their work for printing. There is no 'first edition', released for publication by the author, followed after a due interval by a 'second edition' containing his revisions. The process of composition and recomposition may well be continuous, with versions of the text at any stage 'leaking' into circulation. This is as true of Langland and Gower as it is of Chaucer. It does not make the work of the editor of such texts any easier, but he might well acknowledge that what he is presenting, and has to present, that is, a fixed text that claims unique authority, is a convenient and artificial creation of the editorial process.[20]

Chaucer's first three dream-vision poems were not formally 'published'. Even *The Book of the Duchess* contains no explicit acknowledgement of John of Gaunt's role in approving it, such as would have been usual. *Troilus*, by contrast, is almost formally released for publication, though the dedicatees are Chaucer's friends, Gower and Strode, and not any aristocratic or other patrons. *The Legend of Good Women* is to be given to Queen Anne when it is finished, though it never was finished, and it is doubtful that it was ever presented to her. Gower, Hoccleve and Lydgate, like the French poets, are by contrast profuse in their invocations of royal and aristocratic patrons, real and hoped for, and Chaucer can hardly have been more remote than they were from such sources of patronage.

There has already been some discussion of Chaucer's preference for an audience of his own choosing. It seems to have been a consistent preference. He was circumspect to the point of evasiveness in his references to the historical events and persons of his day, but he drew the line at the obsequiousness that went with the acknowledgement of patronage. Something of the tone of subservience that was required can be seen in Christine de Pizan's address to Philip of Burgundy when asked by him to write a history of his brother Charles V:

Having arrived in his presence, after the appropriate greeting, I told him the reason I had come and the wish I had to serve his highness and to please him, as far as I was worthy, provided that I might be informed by him of the nature of the treatise on which it pleased him I should work. Then he, after condescending to thank me more fully than my unworthiness deserved, graciously told and declared to me the approach and the subject it pleased him I should adopt; and, after many fine proposals received from his grace, I took my leave with this pleasant commission.[21]

Chaucer knew that his poetry existed in a larger world than this of 'princepleasers'.

Chaucer's impatience with the role of 'poet of the court' that he acquired, in however marginal a capacity, through the writing of *Troilus and Criseyde* can be deduced from the lamely unconcluded *Legend of Good Women*. The world in which he had achieved such a position was in any case disappearing. In *The Canterbury Tales* he abandoned the role, and committed himself to a work in which the author as performer was laughingly self-erased. The fiction of *The Canterbury Tales* is one of oral reportage: it is, on the face of it, the most oral of all Chaucer's poems, with all the tales purporting to be narrated *viva voce* to a listening audience. But this fiction is entirely enclosed within a frame-narrative which is explicitly addressed to the private reader, as we have seen in the Miller's Prologue, and private reading is the natural medium of *The Canterbury Tales*. Chaucer may have read portions of individual tales to selected friends, but the full quality of his narrative and dramatic artistry in the *Tales* is best appreciated in private reading, as those who have listened to dramatic readings or, worse, dramatic adaptations will readily testify.

Chaucer had no copy of *The Canterbury Tales* made, and did not prepare the work for publication. Parts of it circulated in written copies, but it was not until after his death that the work began to be copied as a whole. When it began to be so copied, the demand for it was such that it contributed, along with other major pieces of late-fourteenth-century vernacular writing such as Gower's *Confessio Amantis*, to a revolution in book-production. Certainly, the turn of the century marks a point at which vernacular book-production shifted decisively from the provinces to London, with copies being made on a more repetitive and less individual basis, and with spelling beginning to be systematized on metropolitan models. Long before printing was introduced in 1476, the needs it satisfied, and the commercial organization of book-production it gave a new dimension to, were already in existence.[22]

The Legend of Good Women

The Legend of Good Women is the least noticed of Chaucer's longer poems. It was written after he had completed *Troilus and Criseyde*, Chaucer offering it as a penance, at the demand of the God of Love, for having written of Criseyde in such a way as to encourage men to think women untrustworthy (Prologue, F. 333). Some of the legends may have been written before this time, but there is no evidence for this, and the argument for an early date based on poetic quality is a poor one. Since the weaknesses of the *Legend* as a story collection are the very weaknesses that Chaucer attended to in *The Canterbury Tales*, it is extremely unlikely that he went on writing legends after the plan of *The Canterbury Tales* had begun to form in his mind in 1387. Nor does he mention the *Tales* in the list of his writings that is given in the Prologue (F. 327–34, 412–30).

We may take it that the *Legend* was written 1386–7, at the height of Chaucer's career as a 'poet of the court'. He makes easy allusion to fashionable court games and observances, such as the worship of the daisy and the division of courtiers into amorous orders of the Flower and the Leaf, and has Alceste promise the completed work to Queen Anne (F. 496–7). The importance of this allusion, in relation to the audience Chaucer is appealing to, is not in the literal truth of the matter (that Anne either commissioned or received the work is very doubtful) but in the confidence that such a statement of expectation will be recognized as proper. The pretext for the writing of the poem is itself a court game of a kind that Machaut had provided a precedent for in his *Jugement dou Roy de Navarre*: there too the poet is accused of defaming women, is arraigned before a lord sympathetic to ladies, offers his defence, submits to his literary penance. None of this actually happened, of course, to either poet, and Chaucer knew well enough that, if apology for his literary treatment of Criseyde were needed, the apology he makes could hardly be more laughably wide of the mark; but it made a good game, and a good occasion for a court poem.

So it seemed: but the court audience that was to delight in the wit and ingenuity and scandalous whimsicality of Chaucer's fiction was about to be rudely scattered; and Chaucer was himself to find that the tone of address expected in a committedly 'court' poem was not one that he could happily sustain. The intimacy and casualness of manner leads, amid much brilliantly inventive writing in the Prologue and some passages of genuine emotional power in the legends, to some unfortunate self-indulgence and a fatal lowering of the imaginative temperature. As the impetus to continue the work slackened, Chaucer lost interest. He attempted to play the card he had played with such success in *The House of Fame*, and to make a virtue of inconclusiveness by ending with the tantalizing promise of a conclusion: 'This tale is seyd for this conclusioun' (2723). This is the last line of the legend of Hypermnestra, and the last line of the *Legend* (the ten manuscripts that have the poem more or less complete, of the total of twelve, all have the legends in the same order). But what had been a smart move once now appears limp and self-indulgent

Some of the claustrophobically 'court' quality of the Prologue can be illustrated from comparison with the later revision (Prologue G) that Chaucer did after the death of Queen Anne in 1394. Chaucer omits the lines referring to the Queen, but her death was not the occasion of the revision. Prologue G demonstrates clear dissatisfaction with the looseness of structure of the original Prologue F and eliminates some of its more extravagant poetic posturing.* (There is resemblance, in motive and method, to Langland's handling of his B version in his C revision of *Piers Plowman*.) So, early on, G omits the overheated expression of passion for the daisy (F. 50–60) and dedication to its service (F. 84–96, 103–110: the former of these passages was taken from the opening lines of the *Filostrato*, which in 1386 was very fresh in Chaucer's mind), as well as suggestions of *double entendre* in his descriptions of the daisy and the mating of the birds (F. 117, 152). G omits the direct address to 'Ye lovers that kan make of sentement' (F. 69) and the request for their help, and puts the subsequent eulogy of those who have written of the daisy (the French poets, but also, by association, 'you lovers here') in the third person. Later, Chaucer

---

* Prologue G is named after the unique manuscript in which it appears, Cambridge University Library MS Gg. iv. 27, and Prologue F after the best of the other manuscripts, Bodleian Library MS Fairfax 16. There was a time when G, which contains the best text of the *Legend* as a whole, was thought to be the original version, and was called Text A (the version contained in the other manuscripts being called Text B), but J. L. Lowes, in a series of famous articles (see ch. 4, n. 3), demonstrated the priority of F and established the dates of the two versions.

distances himself more from the action by having the nineteen ladies of Alceste's retinue sing the beautiful *balade* in praise of Alceste, instead of singing it himself, as in F. 247–69. The change is a great improvement, and the naming of Alceste at G. 179 is not inconsistent with the dreamer's later failure, kept from F, to recognize her (G. 450): in the earlier reference, he speaks explicitly as the poet who, now awakened from his dream, knows how it ended. G also cuts out the very personal tone of the references to Alceste (the daisy), who is called 'my lady' three times in F (271, 273, 275). Meanwhile, in G only, the God of Love makes some sharp comments on the jaundiced view of love that old folks like Chaucer acquire as their spirit declines (G. 259–63), and even the kindly Alceste wonders whether Chaucer, once in his youth a servant of love, is now in his old age a 'renegat' (G. 401).

Structural improvements include the clarification of the transition at F. 97–102: G makes explicit the reason that the poet spoke earlier of old books (to authorize his later use of them in the legends) where F is lazily non-committal. Chaucer also tidies up and conflates the two references to the debate of the Flower and the Leaf in F (72, 188–96; cf. G.71–80) and begins the dream earlier (G. 89–104) so that the poet does not have to go out in the country, do his worship of the daisy, go home, go to bed, and dream of going out in the country again to do his worship of the daisy, as he does in F. He also remembers to have the dreamer wake up (G. 545–6).

The later part of the Prologue is less extensively revised, though there is a major addition (G. 267–312) where the God of Love lists all the sources that Chaucer might have looked in, if he had been so inclined, to find stories of good women. Chaucer mentions here some of the books he is known to have worked with during the years 1387–94, such as the treatises of Jerome and others he used for the Wife of Bath (G. 280–1) and the encyclopaedic *Speculum Historiale* of Vincent of Beauvais (G. 307). But it is not simply a matter of dragging in allusion to some of his recent reading. The God of Love also draws attention to an important element in the legends, or at least an element that Chaucer came to recognize as important. They are stories of good women, but, being drawn exclusively from classical sources (Virgil, Ovid and others), they are all stories of women whose goodness did not derive from Christian faith:

For alle keped they here maydenhede,
Or elles wedlok, or here widewehede.
And this thyng was nat kept for holynesse,
But al for verray vertu and clennesse.   (G. 294–7)

They are love's martyrs, but not Christian martyrs. In this way, Chaucer, though he acknowledges still the exemplary function of narrative, makes also a qualified assertion of the autonomy of narrative, an autonomy at least in respect of those demands made upon the Christian author that his writings should serve the faith. The value to Chaucer of such an assertion was to be more richly demonstrated in *The Canterbury Tales*.

Beneath the play and paraphernalia of the court 'occasion', the Prologue is, like *The House of Fame*, another poetic apologia and prospectus. At crucial times in his career, Chaucer, like Langland, Milton, Wordsworth and Keats, seems to have needed to examine his poetic achievements and ambitions, and particularly to debate questions of the 'matter' of poetry. The playful approach, as always, is a mask for deep and abiding concerns. The opening lines launch smoothly into a deceptively light and graceful defence of books as the witness to a truth that lies beyond what we perceive. The hidden agenda, of course, is that there is, strictly speaking, only one book that is truly a witness to super-real truth, and that is the Bible; and Jesus there makes it very clear to Thomas that the alternative to seeing is not reading but believing. But any daring suggestion of an alternative form of 'truth' is quickly dissolved into Chaucer's admission that he just loves reading. The one thing that gets him away from his 'devocioun' to his books is his reverence for the daisy. The movement seems to be from books to reality (nature, experience), but it becomes clear that the worship of the daisy (the personal experience of love and life) is truly communicated and understood only through what has been written of it. The rhetoric of poetry is the heart of experience. Alceste, the truth of experience (the daisy) transformed into a book-derived mythical figure, now becomes, in the dream, a fact of experience.

Later in the Prologue, Chaucer embarks on further commentary on the art of poetry and the role of the poet. The accusations against him produce a kind of critical bibliography of his works to date, and an analysis of some of the difficulties under which he has written, and some excuses: the accusations are not all fair, and he has at least always tried to do his best, but may have been swayed by the inertia of convention or the demands made by patrons, or may simply have followed what his authorities said (G. 340–52). The argument being pursued behind this smoke-screen of playfulness has to do with the nature and function of poetry, given the inadequacy of the adjustment of language to truth, the illusions of perception, and the difficulty of the movement from the defective intention to the defective act of 'making'. Behind this further lies some notion of a truth in poetry that may be distinct from morality. Chaucer is moving from the notion of 'good' and 'bad' as moral absolutes to a notion of good and bad as values in relation to the poetic service of love. Fidelity and truth in love and in writing of love are commensurate with Christian faith and moral truth, but not the same. In moving thus beyond the epilogue to *Troilus*, Chaucer is also bidding some kind of farewell to the poetry of the court: he actually shows that poetry in the process of transformation.

The legends that follow do not bear out the promise of the Prologue, and some have wished to find in this a joke at the expense of women (Chaucer tells only ten of the nineteen he promised, a sign that he ran out of good women or found their lives boring) or cunning satire. It has been said to be satire on a conventionally minded court for missing the point about Criseyde; or on the God of Love and the narrator for their typically male view of 'good' women as those who characteristically display patience, love, fidelity and submissiveness; or on the kind of story that fulfils a simple exemplary function. But these are costly forms of rescue, and I think we can take it as axiomatic that Chaucer does not write 'badly' so as to illustrate or dramatize a point. *Thopas* is not an exception to this rule: it is brilliantly bad.[23]

The problems that he had with the legends are real problems. If he created the fictional framework because he was keen to try his hand at shorter narrative poems within a frame, he soon realized he had chosen the wrong kind of frame and the wrong kinds of narrative. The systematic nature of the externally imposed theme, a martyrology of Cupid's saints, imposes a rigidity on the kind of story he has to tell and also on the way he has to tell it. It is at times as if he were performing a *real* penance. It was a valuable lesson to him – to avoid the kind of frame-narrative that rests on an external organizing principle (like the *Legenda Aurea* or, to some extent, Gower's *Confessio Amantis*, which was begun at the same time and maybe in some spirit of friendly emulation) and to look for one that had some internal dynamism and potential for organic growth, as in the *Decameron*. We should remember too that, within the legends, Chaucer was tackling some difficult stories, stories such as that of Philomena that defied humane treatment in their primitive and violent tenor, and tackling also some difficult technical problems. Much of the time, he was converting into narrative form poems by Ovid (the *Heroides*, letters of distressed heroines) that consist largely of lyrical and dramatic monologue, and throughout he was fighting against the instinct towards ampli-fication – the enriching of the story with exclamation, apostrophe, digression and all the other forms of rhetorical dilation – that was so deeply ingrained in medieval writers and so characteristic a technique in the *Troilus*. Chaucer may have been learning the craft of short fiction, but it seems that at times he watched himself with some amusement at the task.

The faults of the legends are obvious, and no reader, however conversant with the rhetorical techniques of *abbreviatio* and *occupatio*, can long tolerate the constant chatter of brevity-formulas: 'It would be a waste of time to tell of Dido's earlier career (996–7); it would take too long to follow Virgil word for word (1002–3); I have neither the time nor the patience to rehearse the villainy of Jason (1552–8) or Tereus (2257–8) or Demophon (2491); I am in a hurry to finish the *Legend*, so I will press on quickly (2454–8).' Some of the tales , such as that of Philomena, are told so cursorily and dismissively as to make one wonder why Chaucer took them up. The stories of Dido and Ariadne are the two longest and are generally better told than the others – one has the sense of a cold motor sputtering fitfully into life at times – but in the former the attempt at a rapid narration of the sack of Troy (930–45) is a disaster. There are also curious moments of inattention that create a grotesquely comic effect, as when Thisbe finds Pyramus mortally wounded, 'Betynge with his heles on the grounde' (863), or Lucrece reacts with apparent nonchalance as Tarquin jumps into her bed: ' "What beste is that", quod she,"that weyeth thus ?" ' (1788). What can Chaucer possibly have had in mind? One is tempted at times by the astute piece of explication offered by Carolyn Dinshaw (*Chaucer's Sexual Poetics*, p. 86). Chaucer, serving the needs of those who ask for unproblematic tales of properly submissive suffering women, adopts in the end the peculiarly masculine strategy of discovering such stories to be boring: women are kept in their place and then blamed for being boring by being in it.

If he was in playful competition with Gower, and the rules were those of conventional story-telling, Chaucer lost almost every time.

But there are effective moments in the narratives, such as the superb *tour de force* of the naval battle of Actium in the legend of Cleopatra, and moments of real pathos in the stories of Dido and Ariadne. There are also some important kinds of experimentation with the narrative voice. He offers to share the experience of the narrative directly with the audience, with address to men in the audience (665–8), apostrophe to Pyramus and Thisbe as 'ye loveres two' (743–4), rhetorical question (869), apostrophe to the 'sely wemen, ful of of innocence', who trust men (1254), indignant apostrophe to Theseus (1952), virulent denunciation of Tereus (2228), constant authorial commentary and imprecation (799–80, 1166, 1874, 2177, 2180, 2227). Sometimes the tone is very intimate, as Chaucer slips perhaps too easily into the cosiness of coterie address. He hopes that our heads will never ache before we find a man as true as Cleopatra (705) and says that it is hard to speak in full of the extent of Jason's falsehood: 'But in this hous if any fals lovere be, / Ryght as hymself now doth, ryght so dide he' (1554–5). There is also the remark Chaucer makes at the end of the legend of Phyllis:

> Be war, ye wemen, of youre subtyl fo,
> Syn yit this day men may ensaumple se;
> And trusteth, as in love, no man but me. (2559–61)

There is a jocular allusion here to Ovid's claim to be the preceptor of Love (*praeceptor Amoris*), but one must admit that it falls rather flat.

With these techniques of involvement, which are also of course to some extent distancing devices, since they draw attention to the relationship of author and audience, there are also reminders of the textuality of the discourse. Chaucer refers to his sources (1228), directs the reader to Ovid for fuller treatment of the stories of Dido (1367) or Medea (1678–9), commonly, in the brevity-formulas, treats the story as a *thing* to be lopped and pruned and filleted. Most striking of all, and strongly suggestive of both immediacy and staginess, is the image of the author as a kind of pillory-master, bringing forth his characters to suffer deserved public opprobrium: 'Have at thee, Jason! Now thyn horn is blowe!' (1383). With Minos, it sounds like a bear-baiting arena: 'Juge infernal, Mynos, of Crete kyng, / Now cometh thy lot, now comestow on the ryng' (1886–7). The vitality here is undeniable. This paradoxical sense of distance and closeness, of alienation and involvement, of apparent objectivity and myopically close focus, is one of the experiments in a technique that Chaucer was to develop to full perfection in *The Canterbury Tales*.

EVENTS IN ENGLAND, 1386–1391

Court life in the early 1380s was spoken of earlier, no doubt with some exaggeration, as a golden age, a personal and political honeymoon for the young king. Richard gradually assumed *de facto* personal power during these years, in default of any formal arrangement for transfer of power from the Council that had conducted government business during the early years of his reign, and he showed a precocious sense of his kingliness in confronting the rebels in June 1381. His instincts were autocratic, and during the years that followed he built up a 'court party', a loyal personal following entirely dependent upon his patronage for their high position in government. The principal among these were Robert de Vere, Earl of Oxford, and Michael de la Pole, Earl of Suffolk, the latter of whom was made Chancellor of England in 1383; others were Thomas Mowbray, Earl of Nottingham, Earl Marshal of England from 1384 (whose allegiances were sometimes a little ambiguous), and Sir Simon Burley, Richard's former tutor. There was also a great increase in the number of chamber knights, from three in 1377 to seventeen in 1388; they formed a new and powerful group of household retainers, their loyalty explicitly to the person of the king.[24]

As part of this deliberate extension of his personal power, Richard also began to bypass the traditional bureaucracy of government. He sequestered more and more revenues to the chamber, and developed the use of the signet, the king's personal and secret seal on executive documents, thus avoiding the tiresome constraints of the offices of the Exchequer and of the Great and Privy Seal, whose processes were at least nominally under the supervision of Parliament. He also extended the practice by which the king, instead of asking Parliament, raised money by striking private deals with London merchants like Brembre.

All of this was much to the annoyance of the great magnates, who found themselves eased out of the positions of power as the king's principal advisers that had traditionally been theirs. It was not that they wished for power for themselves, or for the king to be weak; they certainly had no desire for constitutional reform, and their interests were even more remote from those of the Commons and the commonwealth at large than were the king's. They were very content for the king to rule, and to manipulate 'the law' as cynically as they did themselves, provided that he did not thereby threaten their vested interests.

This he was beginning to do in a number of ways. He ignored their traditional prerogatives as members of the Great Council; he struck at their traditional status by ennobling commoners like de la Pole and giving de Vere in 1385 the vainglorious title of Duke of Ireland; and he showed no appropriate largesse in the distribution of lands and properties to the great men of the realm, treating them as if they belonged in their rank by virtue of his patronage. This last was a particular cause of discontent to Thomas of Woodstock, an irascible man at the best of times and a great nurser of grievances. As the youngest son, by far, of the old king, he found himself continually at the end of the queue in the receiving of the honours and the wealth appropriate to his station. Passed over when his 11-year-old nephew Henry, Gaunt's son, was preferred before him to the Garter in 1377; foiled of his expectations of inheriting the whole of the vast Bohun estates through his wife Eleanor de Bohun when her sister Mary, who he had hoped would become a nun, married the same Henry in 1380; fobbed off by the king with annuities and customs grants instead of lands when he was created Duke of Gloucester in 1385 – he was an explosion waiting to happen. Sometimes the resentment of the magnates was directed against Richard because of actions that might seem like sensible managerial policy: the Earl of Northumberland, for instance, became the king's inveterate enemy when the king started to interfere with the earl's monopoly of the profits of the wardenship of the Northern Marches.

Nothing about Richard's behaviour annoyed the nobles more than his reluctance to go to war, which was consistent with his own firm refusal to fight in tournaments. His quest for peace with France and his muted response to Scottish provocation, which might seem the basis of a quite far-sighted foreign policy, deprived them of the profits of war (for war was often temporarily profitable to the nobles, even though it did not contribute to long-term economic wealth) and deprived them too of the opportunity of doing the one thing that they were supposed to be good at. Richard did eventually mount an expedition to Ireland in 1395, which was so successful that he was encouraged to repeat the experiment in

1399, but fighting in Ireland was neither profitable in the usual sense nor much of an opportunity for glorious feats of arms. The latter was more important than we might expect: this English nobility still hankered after the great days of Edwardian chivalry, and when no fighting of the usual kind was available they became irritable.

One solution was to go off fighting on 'crusades', wars against Muslims and other non-Christians on the borders of Europe which could claim to be righteous wars and which gave the chance of military exercise and martial glory. Prussia was the resort of many in search of such exercise: there was always fighting to be done there, against plausibly non-Christian opposition, and the countryside was very suitable for cavalry warfare. Sir Thomas Holland, Earl of Kent, the king's half-brother, took himself there, and so did Sir John Montagu, Earl of Salisbury, Sir Thomas Percy in 1391 and his nephew Hotspur in 1383. Henry of Bolingbroke made two trips there, in 1390 and 1392, and came back with his military (and therefore political) reputation much enhanced. The no doubt mixed motives with which knights went out on such campaigns included neither the desire for loot and ransoms nor the hope of easy success, for there was precious little of either of these commodities in 'Pruce' and 'Lettow'.

Chaucer's Knight, who had also been to these places, was perhaps more nostalgic than most in his adherence to some old belief in crusading idealism, but there is nothing cynical in Chaucer's portrait. In fact, crusading was an ideal to which English knighthood paid more than lip-service in the late fourteenth century. Chaucer's view of the matter is more likely to have been shaped by his experience at the Scrope–Grosvenor trial of 1386 than modern cynicism about crusading chivalry will readily understand. Many of his fellow-witnesses mention having been on crusade as examples of their chivalric and military experience, and the portrait of the Knight is not much more than could have been constructed from the collective experience of the Scropes themselves.[25]

Richard II, in neglecting these among the other desires and prerogatives of his baronage, was storing up resentment against himself. His behaviour in other respects also was construed as wilful and devious. He seems to have been suspicious of Gaunt and to have framed at least one plot to get rid of him. But Gaunt was generally loyal, and was in any case busily engaged in getting rid of himself: his departure for Spain in 1386 on his long-anticipated mission to reclaim his wife's kingdom of Castile removed a stabilizing influence and left the field clear for opposition to the king to emerge in the open under the leadership of his angry young brother.

At the 'Wonderful Parliament' of October 1386 (the one in which Chaucer sat as MP for Kent), the opposition faction demanded control of the king's choice of advisers and handling of revenue, and in particular the removal of the unpopular chancellor. Richard II acquiesced with an ill grace and spent the following months evading the commission of government set up by Parliament to oversee his household. The hated de Vere remained close to the king. Eventually, in November 1387, Gloucester and his followers lost patience and brought appeals of treason against de la Pole, de Vere and others such as the lawyer Sir Robert Tresilian and the London merchant Sir Nicholas Brembre. Richard tried to delay by referring the appeals to Parliament, and meanwhile de Vere scrambled together an army which was summarily routed by a force led by Bolingbroke in a skirmish at Radcot Bridge, on the Thames, on 20 December 1387. Richard, with what was left of his household, withdrew to the Tower of London, where he was confronted by Gloucester with hints of abdication and reminders of what had happened to his great-grandfather, Edward II. At the 'Merciless Parliament' of February 1388, with the king under their thumb, the Appellants got what they wanted – the condemnation for treason of de la Pole, de Vere, Archbishop Neville, Tresilian and Brembre, with the addition of some other of the king's party such as Sir Simon Burley and Thomas Usk. The first three fled into exile, the last four were executed.

The opposition party thereupon began to lose momentum. Divisions between the five Appellants began to appear, particularly between the more extreme, Gloucester, Richard, Earl of Arundel, and Thomas Beauchamp, Earl of Warwick, and the more moderate, Bolingbroke and Mowbray. The limited extent of their support became apparent, and they began to fall out with the Commons, as over the question of liveried retainers (that is, in effect, the keeping of private armies). Gloucester himself had had some of his reasons for discontent removed, having acquired the lands he coveted from the forfeited properties of the 'traitors'. As for fighting, the Appellants' resumption of war against France proved disastrous, and their response to the Scottish invasion of 1388 was quite inadequate. Soon Richard was in a position to assert again the royal prerogative, always an instrument of immense if intangible potency, and he found his position now strengthened by the removal of his 'favourites'. As usual, they made excellent scapegoats. By 3 May 1389 he felt confident enough to dismiss Gloucester and Arundel from the 'committee of protection' set up over him, and resume, at the age of 22, his regality. In November 1389 Gaunt, who had renounced his claim to the throne of Castile in return for a large money payment, was recalled from Bordeaux, where he had been serving as the king's lieutenant; his renewed presence in England, as a firm upholder of the royal prerogative, marked the end of this period of turmoil.

Richard, in the next few years, which were a time of comparative stability in English political life, kept broadly to the terms laid down by the 1386 commission with regard to the financing of the chamber, the use of the signet and the acceptance of conciliar supervision. He asked Parliament less often for money and made an effort to restrain the growth of 'livery and maintenance' among the magnates. But the magnates thwarted him in the latter and turned his thoughts to ways in which he too might create a new kind of power-base of his own, an armed retinue instead of a circle of court adherents. The livery of the White Hart was introduced in 1390 and the recruiting of the Cheshire archers began soon afterwards. The truce of 1389–93 was uneasy, and masked deep disagreement.

Chaucer's Life, 1386–1389

Chaucer's deposition in the court of chivalry in the Scrope–Grosvenor trial on 15 October 1386 has already been alluded to as part of the evidence for establishing the poet's date of birth. It may also be taken, in a symbolic way, as the high point of his career as a public man. A man of no birth and little fortune, he was here associated with some of the most distinguished men of the realm, many of them friends amd members of his circle, in the determination of a fine point of chivalric privilege. Not only that: Chaucer was at the same time also, as MP for Kent, a member of the Parliament that sat at Westminster from 1 October to 28 November 1386. As this busy and successful man passed through the cloisters of Westminster Abbey on his way from the refectory, where the trial was held, to the chapter-house, where the parliamentary Commons met, he could think himself, for a moment, at the centre of his country's affairs.

The writ for election had gone out to the Sheriff of Kent on 8 August, and the election had taken place at some date subsequently, though in truth it was less a matter of being 'elected' than of being nominated by the sheriff. Chaucer was elected as one of the two knights of the shire and not as one of the four burgesses, as a modern observer might think more appropriate. It was sometimes difficult to persuade knights to act as 'knights of the shire', just as many who were eligible to be knighted paid to avoid the burdensome privileges that knighthood carried with it. Consequently many lesser gentlemen and esquires found themselves asked to serve. Chaucer's Franklin was one such (General Prologue, 356) and Chaucer another. For such men, a place in the Commons as a parliamentary knight was a great honour, and highly prized.

Chaucer received 4s. per day (the same rate that knights received on active duty overseas) for the fifty-nine days that Parliament was in session, plus some small amount for travelling expenses. The total was £12.4s. 6d., a substantial but not a temptingly large sum for work that was time-consuming and potentially risky. There is a possibility that Chaucer was 'elected' as a reliable king's man in anticipation of some difficult passages in the October Parliament. Tout puts it more strongly: 'I have no doubt that Chaucer's presence in Parliament was part of a policy which Edward III and Richard II handed on to later generations. I mean the policy of securing the complacency of the Commons by the infusion of a liberal sprinkling of courtiers and placemen among their ranks' ('Literature and Learning', p. 385). It was certainly a little unusual, though not unprecedented, for a knight of the shire to hold the seat, as Chaucer did, for one session only.

As it turned out, the Parliament of 1386 saw some particularly stormy sessions. Suffolk's opening speech was answered by Gloucester and his followers with the demand that Suffolk and others of the king's household be removed; the king threatened to dissolve Parliament, retired to Eltham in high dudgeon, returned, and found himself obliged to acquiesce in the sacking and planned impeachment of Suffolk and in the imposition upon himself of a parliamentary commission of government. All this was to have serious consequences in the next two years. One of the minor petitions presented by the Commons among the formal opening business of Parliament was unexpectedly relevant to Chaucer: part of the routine and general attempt to loosen the king's personal hold on the government bureaucracy, it was a request that controllers of customs appointed for life should be removed from office, on suspicion (*ex officio*, so to speak) of financial malpractice, and no such life appointments be made in the future. A polite and temporizing answer was returned by the crown, with no promise of positive action, and the matter was probably forgotten in the more exciting proceedings that followed.

Chaucer can hardly have been unmoved by such a petition, being himself one of the very controllers singled out, whether justly or not, for criticism, but he does not seem to have been stirred to any precipitate action. He gave testimony at the Scrope–Grosvenor hearing on 15 October, was in person at the exchequer to receive the Michaelmas instalments on his own and his wife's annuities on 20 October, and was in person in the Court of Common Pleas on 13 November to give mainprize for the appearance of Simon Manning of Kent on 27 January following to answer an action of debt. The background to this case is in a long history of litigation and actions of debt brought against Manning and his co-defendant, Robert Atwood, by William Newport, a fishmonger and probably a moneylender. Most of the people involved came from Kent, which suggests that Chaucer was now living there (the lease of the Aldgate dwelling was granted to Richard Forster on 5 October 1386). The only other point of interest in the case, apart from the evidence it gives of Chaucer's life maintaining its even tenor, is the appearance of Simon's wife Katherine in one of the documents. The Kent Visitation of 1619 has a Manning pedigree which identifies this Katherine as Chaucer's sister, 'Catherina soror Galfridi Chawcer militis celeberimi poetae Anglicani' (*Life-Records*, p. 289). Heraldic documents of this kind are not always unreliable, but there is no other evidence for such a sister and she remains a shadow.*

On 28 November, the day of the dissolution of Parliament, payment was assigned of Chaucer's fee as controller, along with that of the collectors. Less than a week later, on 4 December,

---

* Chaucer has also had daughters rather arbitrarily assigned to him: an Elizabeth 'Chausier' and an Agnes Chaucer appear in late-fourteenth-century records (*Life-Records*, pp. 545–6), but the supposition that they are Chaucer's daughters, made for instance by Howard (*Chaucer and the Medieval World*, p. 93), rests on no more than the coincidence of the common surname.

letters patent were enrolled appointing Adam Yardley as Chaucer's successor as controller of the wool custom and subsidy in the port of London, and shortly after, on 14 December, Henry Gisors succeeded him as controller of the petty custom. It is very tempting to see a direct connection between the parliamentary petition and Chaucer's resignation from the two controllerships, but it would probably be a mistake. Chaucer had been relinquishing more and more of his duties at the quay to deputies, and had already moved out of the Aldgate residence, probably in the summer. The changes were planned and deliberate. There is no evidence that there was any witch-hunt of customs officials in the aftermath of the October Parliament, or that Chaucer was the victim of one. It is possible that Chaucer anticipated trouble and arranged in advance to remove himself from the scene of it. He could see that the customs controllerships were likely to come under attack as one of the obvious targets of a more vocal opposition, and he knew too that the mayor and aldermen of London were becoming uneasy, in the unsettled state of the time (there were distinct threats of a French invasion in the summer of 1386), about the leasing of gatehouse dwellings to private persons. So Chaucer quietly decamped to Kent. He was probably only too glad to give up an arduous and thankless job that he had held for an unusually long time, and to look for some quieter place to live, especially now that his wife was such an infrequent visitor.

That Chaucer's life was not thrown into sudden crisis by the political developments of 1386 is further evidenced in the continuation of his appointment as a member of the commission of the peace for Kent. First made on 12 October 1385, the appointment was renewed on 28 June 1386, and Chaucer stayed on the commission until, at the latest, 15 July 1389. He is not named on the commission of the peace for Kent issued on that date, perhaps because three days before he had been appointed clerk of the king's works.

Chaucer's appointment as a justice with the commission of the peace for the county of Kent was a definite advance up the social and political ladder. It was made most probably at the instigation of Sir Simon Burley, an old friend, who as constable of Dover and warden of the Cinque Ports was the senior member of the commission. The office of justice was to share in the work of a group of magistrates responsible for dealing with a range of minor offences, including common assault, breaches of the laws relating to the sale of victuals (such as profiteering and giving false measure) and offences against the labour laws (such as seeking or paying excessively high wages). The commission was also responsible for conducting preliminary hearings of more serious cases, with a view to presenting an indictment before a higher court. The sessions of the peace were held four times a year, each session lasting about three days; they could be held in any one of a number of towns, but the most obvious place was Canterbury. If Chaucer was much called upon (only a minority of the men commissioned as justices were likely to serve on any particular occasion), he would have got to know the journey to Canterbury quite well during this period. The pay was, in theory, 4s. a day for a maximum of twelve days a year, but membership of the commission gave so many opportunities for winning friends and making money that the official pay was probably of little importance.

On the commission, Chaucer was associated with members of the three groups, magnates, lawyers and gentry, of which it was traditionally composed. Among the magnates were some very distinguished men indeed, not only Burley, who was one of the most influential men around Richard II, but also the Lords Cobham and Devereux. The lawyers, who would have provided many models for Chaucer's Sergeant-at-Law, included Sir Robert Tresilian, chief justice of the King's Bench. One can see how close Chaucer was to some of those who later incurred the wrath of the Appellants. Among the gentlemen, most of them knights, who served on the commission during Chaucer's term of office were several who had previous associations with Chaucer, as for instance at the customs (Hugh Fastolf) or at the Scrope–Grosvenor trial (Sir James Peckham). It was not absolutely necessary to be a resident of Kent to hold office on the commission, but it was usual, and Chaucer's acceptance of the appointment suggests strongly that he had plans as early as 1385 to move away from London.

Chaucer held this office throughout the years of the troubles, serving under Lord Devereux after Burley had been executed on 5 May 1388. Though he was clearly, in a very real sense, a 'king's man', he was not regarded as a troublesome one. But he may have taken some precautions. On 5 July 1387 he received letters of protection (his 'passport') to go to Calais on the king's business in the company of William Beauchamp, captain of Calais. Many others, knights, esquires and merchants, received letters at the same time, but not all made the journey. Beauchamp was an old associate of Chaucer's. It may be that these advance arrangements were made, by Chaucer or by his friends, in case he needed to be kept out of harm's way until things in England had settled down.

Other activities during the period, however, suggest that his life was following a not abnormal routine. On 1 August 1387 Chaucer was sitting on a commission of enquiry in Dartford (Kent) to hear testimony in a case of abduction. John Lording and two others were accused of abducting ('rapuerunt et abduxerunt' (*Life-Records*, p. 375)) Isabella, daughter and heiress of William Hall, from the custody of Thomas Carshill at Chislehurst (Kent) on 20 March 1387. Lording, a wealthy London mercer, was Isabella's husband, and he subsequently brought an action of trespass against Carshill and others charging that they had abducted Isabella from the London house of one of his friends in October 1386. The commission on which Chaucer sat found the Chislehurst abduction charge proved, but the business ground on for many years until Lording was pardoned in 1398. A small point of interest, in relation to earlier discussion of the Cecily Champain case, is that 'rapuerunt et abduxerunt' is used throughout these records where there can be no question of rape.

Later during this period, in the Michaelmas law term of 1388, Chaucer was mainpernor for Matilda Nemeg, acting as surety for her appearance in the Court of Common Pleas on 20 January 1389 to answer the charge of her employer, Maria Alconbury, that she had left her employer's service before the end of her agreed term. In previous instances where Chaucer's mainprize had been taken, some association is known or can be deduced, for instance service to a social superior (Beauchamp, Romsey) or rich merchant (Hend), or local Kentish connections (Manning). But nothing is known of his relationship with Matilda.

It is interesting to note that in this very same term, in this same court, while Chaucer was offering his mainprize, he was himself the subject of writs being brought against him for his own appearance in court to answer Henry Atwood in an action of debt. Atwood was an innkeeper, which may suggest the nature of the debt (£7. 13*s*. 4*d*.). Chaucer was summoned to appear in court on 20 January 1389, and then, with warnings of more and more severe consequences if he did not do so, on five successive dates thereafter up to 20 January 1390. He never answered the summons, as commonly happened, and the whole affair fizzled out, probably with an out-of-court settlement.

This was not the first time Chaucer had been summoned for debt. On 16 April 1388 John Churchman had initiated an exchequer action against Chaucer for the recovery of a debt of £3. 6s. 8d. The writ was later transferred to the Sheriff of Kent, where Chaucer was living. Churchman, whom we have already met as the man who rebuilt the customs quay, was collector of the petty subsidy in the port of London, a wealthy grocer and merchant, and probably a moneylender, who on this same date entered writs against a dozen other persons, from all over England, some of them for debts running into hundreds of pounds. Evidently Chaucer was one of the very minor victims of Churchman's campaign to collect on his bad debts. Chaucer had probably taken advantage of his professional acquaintance with Churchman to run up debts with him, whether for goods or not. The debts are a sign that he was adapting slowly to living under slightly more straitened circumstances, but not a sign of financial crisis. Chaucer still had his annuities and, even though he was borrowing against them with rather greater frequency than in the past, he was not in financial distress. On the whole, it was not poor men who got into debt.

However, the political storms continued to blow, and on 1 May 1388 Chaucer resigned both of his exchequer annuities (the original annuity and also the later annuity commuted from the wine-grant) to John Scalby. There may have been some need to raise money (annuity rights were sometimes sold in this way), but it is probably of more significance that the 'Merciless Parliament', which sat from 3 February to 4 June 1388, had begun to prosecute its campaign against the king's household, and the growth of that household attributable to his personal patronage, by attacking the practice of granting life annuities. Particular attention was paid to those who had been granted annuities in the time of Edward III and who had subsequently received further grants. Chaucer was in this situation, and knew enough to realize that it would be prudent to give up his annuities. There was no general rush on the part of others to do the same, but Chaucer as always was circumspect, and removed himself well in advance from any possible firing-line. Chaucer's tactics have been shrewdly compared by Strohm with those of Usk, who embraced the politics of faction completely, perhaps because being a man of lower estate he had less choice, and paid the penalty in 1388.[26]

It is clear that the years 1386–9 saw a radical change in Chaucer's life, a change that accelerated as the political crisis deepened and as Chaucer realized what the situation might require. He resigned his job, left his house and gave up his annuities, all of them actions that he took in anticipation of disagreeable moves on the part of the opposition party to purge the king's household and withdraw privileges from those who had enjoyed his personal patronage. There was no 'king's party' in the strict sense of the word, since all who were in government were the recipients of royal patronage in some measure. But insofar as there was one, Chaucer was of it. There were some who became particularly closely identified with the king, and probably took advantage of their position to gain inordinate wealth and power: we have seen what happened to some of them, such as Burley, Brembre and Tresilian, all of them close to Chaucer in some way. And there were others who distanced themselves shrewdly from the king in the years 1386–8, including chamber knights like Clifford; these managed to survive successfully into the 1390s. Chaucer was one such, though admittedly in reduced circumstances.

It was at this point, one might say, that he reaped the reward for having kept his poetry free from overt political commitment and out of the arena of warring political factions. Whatever he had done with his public career, he had sacrificed nothing in his poetry to the demands of court patronage. He had remained polite and non-committal about everything in public and political life, affirmed no special allegiance to king or any affinity, and avoided anything that might be construed as an allusion.

It is very possible that during the early or mid-1380s he wrote the prose translation of the *Livre de Melibee* of Renaud de Louens which later became incorporated in *The Canterbury Tales* as Chaucer's second tale, *The Tale of Melibee*. It is a treatise, imperfectly disguised under a very thin allegorical narrative, advocating the settling of disputes by taking counsel and by negotiation, but Chaucer does nothing to make it into the anti-war tract that some might have expected him to write in support of Richard's policy of peace with France. Nor can the work be construed in any but the most general terms as the kind of advice to the king on taking counsel and choosing counsellors that Richard was so evidently in need of. All Chaucer does, in deference presumably to the king's youth, is quietly omit (at VII. 1199) a reference to the woe that befalls a land that has a child as its lord (Ecclesiastes 10: 16).[27]

CLERK OF THE KING'S WORKS, 1389–1391

On 12 July 1389, Chaucer was appointed clerk of the king's works (*Life-Records*, p. 402). The warrant for this appointment received the royal seal, therefore, just over two months after Richard resumed his regality on 3 May, and it is difficult not to see some connection between the two events. The restoration to public office of a valued royal servant would be one of the government's early priorities, though it does not appear that Roger Elmham, Chaucer's predecessor in the post, had his departure in any way hastened. Chaucer was no doubt pleased to have his regular income back at its accustomed level: since the sale of his exchequer annuities (on which he may still have drawn a small income), he had been living on the annuity of £10 per annum long ago granted by Gaunt and presumably still being paid (the records are lost), and had found himself occasionally somewhat embarrassed. Now he was in receipt of a regular 2*s*. a day, which amounted to an annual income of £36. 10*s*.

But the job was in no sense a sinecure, and we should put out of our minds any idea that it was a reward for a favoured poet. On the contrary, if any appointment could have been contrived to ensure a writer's silence, this was it. It was an arduous post, involving heavier and more direct responsibilities, especially in the handling of money, than the office of controller of customs. The job had traditionally been done by a member of the professional clerical bureaucracy; Chaucer was only the second layman (Roger Elmham had been the first) to hold the office.

The office of the King's Works, based in the Palace of Westminster, administered the building and repair programme of properties belonging to the king, and Chaucer as clerk was the head of the clerical staff in charge of operations. His principal job was the payment of wages and the provision of materials and workmen, and he probably also had some responsibility to see that the construction plans for which finance had been agreed upon were properly implemented. He worked with a controller, William Hannay, a senior clerical officer who had earlier himself been clerk of the works and who had the same responsibility to Chaucer that Chaucer had had as controller to the collectors of customs – with the difference that Chaucer paid Hannay his wages. As clerk, Chaucer was also responsible for purveyors or local deputies at the major establishments, and had a permanent clerk to act as his administrative assistant (none of the records is in Chaucer's own hand, even though they originate with him). He worked with (and paid) the chief mason, the chief carpenter, the chief joiner, the chief plumber, the chief glazier, the chief smith, and various subordinate clerks. He was thus often dealing with men much senior to himself such as Richard Swift, master-carpenter since 1378, and Henry Yevele, the king's chief mason (*capitalis cementarius* (*Life-Records*, p. 420)) and the master-builder of his age. Yevele had been employed by Edward III as early as 1360, had designed the alabaster tomb of the Duchess Blanche, supervised Gaunt's improvements at the Savoy, and was now working, under Chaucer's administrative jurisdiction, on the new nave in Westminster Abbey. His great work on Westminster Hall, with its magnificent hammerbeam roof designed by Hugh Herland, was still to come, after Chaucer's term of office.

At a lower level, in addition to consultation with such distinguished persons, there would be much hiring and payment of workers, keeping of books, travelling, chasing after and disciplining workmen who broke their contracts, and arranging for the protection of property and building supplies from theft. The initial taking over of the inventory of 'dead stock' (*mortui stauri* (*Life-Records*, p. 406)) must have been a job in itself, judging from the odd bits of junk, old iron and broken machinery faithfully recorded in the indenture of the Tower of London, for instance (*Life-Records*, p. 407). There was also the business of making arrangements for the collection of the money assigned to pay for the works, which as usual was upon various royal debtors – the collectors of the wool customs and subsidy, above all, but also sheriffs, the 'farmers' of royal estates, earls and abbots, and the keeper of the royal mint.

The properties placed under the control of the clerk of works varied with each appointment, and occasionally other clerks would be appointed to handle specific properties. Chaucer was charged with responsibility for Westminster Palace, the Tower of London, the royal manors at Eltham, Sheen and King's Langley, and half a dozen other places. It sounds as if Chaucer was constantly on the move, but in fact the bulk of his work was at the Tower, where the building of a new wharf accounted for over half the total expenditure (£654 out of £1,130) during his term of office.

On the anniversary of his first appointment, on 12 July 1390, he had St George's Chapel, Windsor added to his list of responsibilities, 'la quele chapelle est en poynt du ruyne et de cheier a la terre si ele ne soit le plustost faite et emendee' (which chapel is on the point of falling to the ground in ruin if it is not quickly restored) (*Life-Records*, p. 408). Chaucer did not have a great deal of success with the chapel. Though he spent £100. 17*s*. 4*d*. on the purchase of stone for rebuilding, no work was actually done, and the stone, after being stored in the great hall of the lower bailey for over a year, was disposed of by his successors for work elsewhere. No repairs were done until 1396 to the chapel, which fell down some twenty-five years later and was completely rebuilt by Edward IV.[28]

Among the other business that Chaucer had to attend to during his term of office was the supervision of the building of the lists at Smithfield for the tournament of 1390 (Froissart says it began on the Sunday after Michaelmas). This jousting, the first to be held in London for a number of years, was the prelude to Richard's campaign to establish peace with France: the idea was to show that fighting was respectable and could still be fun even though it was controlled and legitimized. The tournament may have seemed tame to soldiers like Bolingbroke, especially in comparison with the great jousts held at St Inglevert, near Calais, in March and April of the same year, where Bolingbroke had been acclaimed the best of those who challenged the redoubtable Marshal Boucicaut.

Chaucer's responsibility for the Smithfield tournament recalls that other tournament he had described in the Knight's Tale, some years before. If he now did any retouching of the description of the magnificent Athenian lists – an open theatre walled with stone, with tiered seats rising on the outside to a height of sixty feet, the whole thing a mile in circumference (I.1885–92) – it was with a wry sense of the difference between 'the cheap magnificence of fiction' and the hard facts of reality. The lists at Smithfield consisted of rickety wooden scaffolds (they had collapsed before now) and the circuit, if Chaucer was using the material he took over from Elmham, was but 'xxxii perticatas' (*Life-Records*, p. 473), or thirty-two perches (exactly one-tenth of a mile).[29]

Another task that fell to Chaucer as appertaining to his office, as also to his residence in Kent, was to sit on a commission to oversee repairs to banks and drainage ditches along the Thames between Greenwich and Woolwich after a disastrous storm on 5 March 1390, which had also blown down a hundred oaks on the Eltham estate. The commission had to decide what needed doing, order repairs, and determine responsibility for payment. There

were four lay members, including Chaucer, in the six-man commission, in addition to two lawyers, and they all, like Chaucer,
had strong Kentish connections. They included Sir Richard Stury,
an old associate of Chaucer's, who had been captured and ransomed in the same campaign in 1359–60 and in attendance with
Chaucer at the peace-negotiations at Montreuil in 1377.

These were burdensome and time-consuming duties enough, but
they were not all Chaucer had to put up with. On 3 September
1390 he was robbed of £20. 6s. 8d. of the king's money, as well
as his own horse and other property, at a place called 'le fowle ok'
(*Life-Records*, p. 478), at Hatcham, in Kent (just west of what is
now New Cross), doubtless as he was on his way to Eltham to
pay the workmen's wages. On 6 September he was robbed again,
of £10, in Westminster, and later on that same day of a further
£9. 43d. at Hatcham, again. This bizarre sequence of events looks
like something more than bad luck, but there may be some confusion in the records. A commission was appointed to look into
the matter of the first robbery, some of its members drawn from
the commission of the peace for Kent on which Chaucer himself
had sat quite recently, but seems not to have come up with any
indictment. Chaucer was discharged on 6 January 1391 from
repaying the money stolen in this first robbery, of which no
further mention is made in the records. Meanwhile, a well-known
highwayman, Richard Brierley, had confessed to the second robbery and implicated others of his gang in his confession to the
third. They were all variously jailed or hanged in the next few
years, some for other offences.

On 17 June 1391, Chaucer was instructed to give up the office
of clerk of works to John Gedney, and on 8 July to take no further
part in the restoration of St George's Chapel. He had been called
on 18 February to an audit on 3 April, at which he was to present
the accounts for his period of office up to that date. It was a little
unusual to be called for an audit so soon (the procedures were
actually set in motion in the previous November), but Chaucer's
term of office was not in the event particularly short in comparison
with that of his nine predecessors and successors in the post during
the reign of Richard II (see *Life-Records*, p. 411). The audit revealed
that there had been an overspending of £20. 19s. 2 d. (*Life-Records*,
p. 457) on allowed expenditure. Chaucer himself had borne this
extra charge, and the consequent debt owed to him by the crown
was paid in a series of quarterly instalments, the last on 13
July 1392 (*Life-Records*, pp. 468–9). There was also a debt of

£66. 13*s*. 4*d*. owed by Sir William Thorpe which was uncollected when he died in April 1391, and which Chaucer had recorded as paid, in order to balance the books, by entering it in the accounts as a fictitious loan by himself to the government. This was common practice. The debt was assigned to him to collect from Thorpe's estate, but was eventually paid by the exchequer on 22 May 1393.

It would be possible to leap to a large number of conclusions concerning the significance of these records and what they tell us of the manner in which Chaucer vacated his post. Perhaps Chaucer was being sacked for dilatoriness or inefficiency, or perhaps he had simply had enough of being beaten up and robbed, in addition to all the other encumbrances of office. It would certainly be understandable if he wished now, after due time, to give up the office, though it would have been more pleasant to have had the opportunity of resigning. His readiness to stand down may have coincided very satisfactorily with the crown's desire to replace him. John Gedney was much more of a practised professional civil servant, and was clearly the man to take on the increased burden of administration as Richard's building plans became more ambitious. Annual expenditure during his term of office, which lasted until 1396, was more than twice that during Chaucer's (*Life-Records*, p. 474). Even if the reduction in income was painful, Chaucer must have been readily persuaded that he had had enough. He appears to have been living in Kent during his period of office (*Life-Records*, pp. 448, 492), when he could find any time to be there in the midst of his constant journeying, and to Kent he now retired.

New Beginnings

During this time of change, upheaval and increased busyness, Chaucer was more rather than less active in writing. His loss of interest in *The Legend of Good Women*, and the disintegration of the audience that had sustained him in his poetry of courtly address, left him with the ambition still unfulfilled of creating a framework for a collection of stories in which he could experiment freely with what he now recognized to be his genius for narrative poetry. Though it is difficult to determine any definite dates for any part of *The Canterbury Tales*, and difficult even to decide for certain when he started work on them, it seems extremely probable that the idea came to him immediately in the wake of his abortive experiment with the *Legend*. The new framework, with pilgrims to Canterbury telling stories as they rode along the way, had every advantage that the framework of the *Legend* had so manifestly lacked: the tales could be infinitely various, and could represent every possible genre of narrative; since they were told by different pilgrims, there was the possibility of exploring variation in voice and dramatic appropriateness; there was no external scheme imposing a rigid set of rules on theme and manner of treatment; the framework was capable of organic development and expansion, as the pilgrimage progressed and the members of it interacted with one another; and, though there was a fixed end to the framing narrative, it was one that could be indefinitely deferred.

There was something more too – a further opportunity to assert the autonomy and intrinsic value of narrative. We have seen already how Boccaccio led the way in seeking some independence for narrative, even though the most he could make of it was recreational or pastiche, and we have also seen tentative steps on Chaucer's part in the Prologue to *The Legend of Good Women* towards the idea that truth in narrative, like truth in behaviour, is not a Christian monopoly. *The Canterbury Tales*, in their way, press these claims further, persistently defying attempts to reduce them to a grand design. The scribe who insisted on sacramentalizing the *Tales* as a 'Book' in his final rubric ('Heere is ended the book of the tales of Caunterbury, compiled by Geffrey Chaucer, of whos soule Jhesu Crist have mercy') missed the point, as have others.[30]

Discussion of *The Canterbury Tales* as a whole, since dating of individual tales and even of the General Prologue is so difficult, must be reserved for the next chapter, though some reference to them has been introduced here, since they were a major preoccupation of Chaucer during the years 1387–91.

As to other forms of writing, there seems to have been little activity. The lost translation of Pope Innocent III's *De miseria condicionis humane* (also known as the *De contemptu mundi*) to which he refers in the revised Prologue to *The Legend of Good Women* ('Of the Wreched Engendrynge of Mankynde' (G. 414)) must have been done between 1387 and 1394. Translating such a gloomy and repugnant treatise was a grim task, which Chaucer undertook presumably as part of his long-term practice, evidenced in his other prose translations, of absorbing major works of the European intellectual tradition into his imaginative repertoire by translating them. The use that he subsequently made of this translation is evident in the Pardoner's Tale and in the Man of Law's Prologue, though it is unlikely that the translation as a whole is the prose tale which the Man of Law so mysteriously proposes to tell (II. 96).

There was also the *Treatise on the Astrolabe*, extant in part or whole in thirty-one manuscripts, many of which include added material ('Supplementary Propositions') not by Chaucer. The prologue to the treatise (Chaucer's only piece of original English prose, apart from the Retraction) opens with an address to 'Lyte Lowys my sone', and Chaucer goes on to speak of little Lewis's ability and eagerness to learn, of how he has given him an astrolabe, constructed for the latitude of Oxford, and is now providing these instructions to show him how to use it. It is not a complete set of instructions, for various reasons, one of which is that 'Somme of hem ben to harde to thy tendir age of ten yeer to conceyve' (23–4). The treatise will be simplified, and written 'under full light reules and naked wordes in Englissh, for Latyn canst thou yit but small, my litel sone' (26–8). But there is no loss, since what is taught in different languages may lead to the same conclusion, 'right as diverse pathes leden diverse folk the righte way to Rome' (39–40, cf. *Troilus*, ii. 36–7, Prologue to *Melibee*, VII. 940–64). Chaucer turns aside from Lewis for a moment to apologize to others, who may read the treatise, for its simple style and repetitiveness, explaining that 'curious endityng and hard sentence is ful hevy at onys for such a child to lerne' (45–6) and that he thinks it 'better to writen unto a child twyes a god sentence, than he forgete it onys' (48–9). He then returns to Lewis, expresses the hope that the 'lighte Englissh' of the treatise will convey all that Latin could, bids him 'preie God save the king, that is lord of this langage' (56–7), and finally acknowledges, in a characteristic vein, that the work is not his own invention: 'I n'am but a lewd compilator of the labour of olde astrologiens, and have it translatid in myn Englissh oonly for thy doctrine' (61–4). Chaucer does indeed make extensive use of the *Compositio et operatio astrolabii* of Messahala, especially in Part II of his treatise, but much is his own.

The treatise uses the year 1391 (II. 1, II.3) for its specimen calculations, and there is no reason not to assume that this was the year in which it was written. If this was the year in which Lewis was 10 years old, he was either a late bloom of Chaucer's marriage or his son by Cecily Champain. Embarrassed by the latter possibility, scholars have tried to demonstrate that the address is to Chaucer's presumed godson, the son of Sir Lewis

Clifford, or even that the form of address is conventional, a way of presenting a simplified work of instruction in the vernacular as something intended for a child.[31]

But the discovery of a Welsh record of 1403 in which Thomas Chaucer and 'Ludowicus Chaucer' appear in a list of men-at arms who formed part of the garrison at Carmarthen Castle (*Life-Records*, pp. 544–5), and in which 'Thomas Chaucer' is certainly the poet's son, has strengthened the natural supposition that Chaucer was indeed addressing his own 10-year-old son in the prologue to the *Astrolabe*. 'Forget not thys, litel Lowys', he says, in paragraph 6 of Part I, and maintains a fairly constant sense of his son's presence in his use of vocatives and imperatives, and passing remarks like, 'Take than thin Astrelabie with bothe hondes sadly and slighly ... '(II. 29.16–18). In speaking of the equator (I. 17. 19–20) he describes how the 'cercle equinoxiall' turns from east to west, 'as I have shewed the in the speer solide', which must refer to earlier, more elementary work that Chaucer had done with his son on the use of the globe. Chaucer took care to have pictures provided in the copy of the treatise he had made, and these are neatly copied in some of the early manuscripts. The best of these, Cambridge University Library MS Dd. 3. 53, has a fifteenth-century colophon saying that Lewis was a student of Strode at Oxford, but the author seems to have been one of those enthusiasts who, knowing two facts, think they must be related. Strode, resident in London since 1383, died in 1387. Little Lewis was clearly, however, living in Oxford, and it is very natural to suppose that he had been put to school there.

The *Treatise on the Astrolabe* is interesting for a number of reasons. It is evidence, first of all, of Chaucer's keen interest in and sound knowledge of astronomy, a passion that he shared with Gower, with members of the 'Merton school' of scientists at Oxford, and with several people at court. Richard II himself seems to have been more interested in pseudo-scientific works of prognostication such as the *Libellus Geomancie* that appears, dated 1391, in a collection of such texts in Bodleian Library MS Bodley 581. But it was for Princess Joan of Kent that John Somer composed his *Kalendarium* in 1380 and Nicholas of Lynn dedicated his *Kalendarium* to John of Gaunt in 1386. Chaucer refers to both these astronomers in his prologue to the *Astrolabe* (85–7), and made particular use of the latter in two elaborate passages in *The Canterbury Tales* that tell the time by the length of a man's shadow (Introduction to the Man of Law's Tale, II. 1–14; Parson's Prologue, X. 1–11). Nicholas of Lynn's shadow-tables take up a great deal of space in his calendar and were clearly a fashionable hit with the scientifically minded amateurs of the time. They have an element of the absurdly theoretical which no doubt appealed to some: thus the calculation for the length of a man's shadow when the sun is 0°1′ above the horizon on 19 May is 20636′54″ (nearly four miles). Nicholas, in the Miller's Tale, was surely named after his illustrious predecessor in the science of the stars.[32]

As one reads through the *Astrolabe*, too, even though only two of the five parts announced in the prologue were completed, one can see the germs of many significant astronomical allusions in Chaucer's poetry. The magnificent poetic apostrophe on the precession of the equinoxes in the Man of Law's Tale (II. 295–308) is there in embryo in Part I (17. 35–40), while Part II includes the calculations that provide the proper planetary hours for the temple visits in the Knight's Tale (I. 2217, 2271, 2367). There is even a fascinated hesitancy expressed about judicial astrology (telling fortunes by the stars), as if Chaucer were not sure whether he should meddle with it or not – 'Natheles these ben observaunces of judicial matere and rytes of payens in whiche my spirit hath no feith' (II. 4. 57–9). He was to turn this hesitancy to very effective dramatic use in the Franklin's expostulations about 'magyk natureel' in the Franklin's Tale (V. 1131–4, cf. 1265–6, 1291–3).

It is also a matter of some remark that Chaucer should even have attempted at this date a translation of a technical scientific Latin work into English prose. There are precedents in Old English, but the only Middle English precursor seems to be a compilation of Latin urinaries into English, the *Liber Uricrisiarum*, done by a Dominican friar, Henry Daniel, in 1376. There is a possibility also that the anonymous English translation of the *Exafrenon Pronosticacionum Temporum*, a weather-forecasting treatise by Richard of Wallingford (d. 1336), was written as early as the late 1380s, and by the early fifteenth century treatises on astronomy, astrology and other scientific subjects were beginning to appear in English translations and compilations in some numbers. But Chaucer, as usual, without making much fuss about it, and in a manner workmanlike rather than supremely accomplished, seems to have come close to inventing English scientific prose, just as he had invented the pentameter, the pentameter couplet and rhyme royal, and done the first English prose translation since Anglo-Saxon times of a major Latin philosophical work, in his *Boece*.[33]

It is possible that Chaucer, not content with the elementary *Treatise on the Astrolabe*, also wrote a much more advanced treatise, *The Equatorie of the Planetis*, which shows how to make and use an instrument for computing geometrically the positions of the seven planets. The treatise was discovered by Derek J. Price in 1951 in the library of Peterhouse, Cambridge (MS 75. I, now in the Cambridge University Library), and edited by him in 1955, with an introduction claiming that the work was not only by Chaucer but that the manuscript was a Chaucer draft holograph. There has been less discussion of this startling claim than might have been expected, perhaps because the matter of the treatise is so alarmingly technical, but a flurry of activity in the last few years has made up for past neglect. The strongest argument for Chaucer's authorship, to the layman, seems to be the inscription 'radix Chaucer' written in beside some calculations based upon the fixed date (radix) December 1392, but this, since the 'author' of a radix is simply the person who chose or who had chosen for him a particular date as the basis for calculations, seems to prove no more than that Chaucer was known to the person who wrote the treatise. The argument from handwriting, based on a comparison between the 'Chaucer' of the inscription and a signature supposed to be Chaucer's in the 1378 records of the controller, is persuasive but inconclusive. Vocabulary, syntax and spelling are all in dispute. Yet the contents of the treatise are not so very different from what Chaucer promised in his prologue to the *Astrolabe* as Parts III, IV and V of the treatise. Perhaps the most significant conclusion one can draw at the moment is that Chaucer belonged to the group that was interested in and could appreciate such scientific writing and, if he did not write the *Equatorie* himself, he could have done, and knew who did.[34]

There is a last enigmatic example, to be mentioned here, of the passion for astronomy that so occupied Chaucer during these years, that he shared with his court audience, and that so informed all his writing. *The Complaint of Mars* takes the story of Mars and Venus surprised in their love-making by Vulcan, and retells it as an astronomical drama, with the role of Vulcan as discoverer played by Phebus. The lovers' journeys, meetings and partings, and their enforced separation and sadness after being discovered, are figured in the varying pace and orbit of the planets through the heavens and their progressive weakening and flight in face of the sun. Most surprising is the 'Compleynt of Mars' which concludes the poem (155–298) and gives it its name. It is written in a difficult nine-line stanza (aabaabbcc), has no astronomical reference, and is a bitter and quite serious complaint (in its ridiculous context) against the cruelty and injustice of a world in which true love can go unrewarded and so bereft. It has reminiscences of the Knight's Tale and *Troilus*, as the structure of the whole poem has reminiscences of *Anelida and Arcite*.

The enigmatic nature of the poem has led to several attempts to interpret it as a *roman à clef*, but, if it was one, the key has not been found. One might argue that the very success of such a poem with its excited circle of initiates would depend upon the key not being found. It is surely a court poem, intended for a court entertainment, subtle enough to cause some interestingly knitted brows, but not so abstruse as to scare away those who were not experts in astronomy. The date projected by the astronomical detail is 1385, which seems about right.

6

Renewal:
The 1390s

CHAUCER'S LIFE IN THE 1390s

After he left the office of the king's works in 1391, Chaucer had no regular income, except for the annuity of £10 which was presumably still being paid to him from the exchequer of the duchy of Lancaster. None of the documents survive in which the continuation of payment after 1380 would for certain have been recorded, but Chaucer's omission of any effort to secure the annuity when the Lancastrian estates were confiscated to the crown after the death of Gaunt on 3 February 1399 does not argue that he had not been receiving it up till then. It may suggest only that he was more circumspect than his son Thomas, who did secure just such a confirmation of his own annuity (*Life-Records*, p. 274). The grant of an additional annuity to Chaucer by Henry IV after his accession in 1399, in addition to the confirmation of the annuity from Richard II, would suggest that Henry was simply continuing his father's bounty.

But, though living under reduced circumstances, Chaucer was not embarrassed for money. He was continuing, up to 13 July 1392, to receive reimbursement for unbudgeted expenditure at the king's works that he had paid for out of his own pocket, and some time in early 1392 he also received a gift of £10 from the crown for unspecified 'bono servicio' (*Life-Records*, p. 120). The likely explanation of this gratuity is that Chaucer had persuaded the authorities that he deserved some interim recognition for the heavy debt he continued to bear on the crown's behalf in respect of the Thorpe estate. This large sum, £66. 13s. 4d., was eventually paid to him on 22 May 1393 (*Life-Records*, p. 469).

Oddly enough, just two weeks after receiving the third and final instalment that settled the earlier debt, a sum of £13. 6*s*. 8*d*., Chaucer is recorded, on 28 July 1392, as having borrowed 26*s*. 8*d*. from Gilbert Mawfield. The loan was for one week and was repaid promptly. Exactly why Chaucer should have needed this money is not clear, unless he was perpetually up to his ears in debt and any incomings were promptly claimed by his creditors. It is much more likely that we are witnesses to the routines of day-to-day financial management: borrowing and being in debt are not a sign that one is short of money in this newly commercialized society. Chaucer was in very good company, furthermore, in arranging a loan with Mawfield. A prosperous London merchant and money-lender, Mawfield had on his books, which by chance survive, not only Henry Scogan, Henry Yevele and John Gower, but also the dukes of Lancaster, York and Gloucester, the Earl of Derby and five bishops. There are dozens of others who appear in Mawfield's accounts and also, coincidentally, in some sort of association with Chaucer in the Chaucer life-records, an indication, it has been remarked, of the comparatively small world that constituted Chaucer's London society.[1]

One would be similarly inclined to be doubtful that the several actions against Chaucer for debt during the 1390s are signs that he was in financial distress. A month or so after receiving payment on the Thorpe estate account, a very large sum indeed, he was being pursued for a debt of £3. 6*s*. 8*d*. by William Venour, a London grocer and moneylender. After persistent failures to appear in court to answer the debt (Chaucer had what might be called a 'professional' attitude towards being in debt), Chaucer eventually settled out of court towards the end of the year. In the autumn of 1394 he was again being dunned, this time by John Layer, a grocer, for a debt of £2. 4*s*. This was a debt for goods purchased, and since grocers commonly dealt in a variety of wares aside from foodstuffs, it may well be that Chaucer had run up an account for paper, parchment and books. Chaucer followed his usual practice of procrastination: the last date on which he was summoned to appear in court, 25 June 1395, and the date therefore on or immediately after which he must have settled out of court, was as it happens the exact day on which he drew an advance instalment on his renewed exchequer annuity. In June 1398, when Chaucer was certainly very well off again, he was being pursued by the widow of Walter Buckholt for a debt of £14. 1*s*. 11*d*., probably incurred in the purchase of timber when Chaucer was clerk of works. This was serious money, and Chaucer engaged an attorney and also took out a guarantee against arrest. The suit was settled or dropped within a few months.

Well before this, Chaucer was again in possession of a regular and substantial income. On 28 February 1394, 'dilectus armiger noster Galfridus Chaucer' (*Life-Records*, p. 514) was granted an exchequer annuity of £20 for life, which in some sense replaced the two annuities of 20 marks each (£26. 13s. 4d. in total) he had surrendered to John Scalby in 1388. The annuity may be regarded as in effect a pension, in somewhat belated recognition of his service as clerk of the king's works. Payment continued regularly if not always promptly until the end of the reign. Chaucer seems to have found more occasion now than in the past to ask for advances of small sums in anticipation of the regular dates for payment, especially in the year 1398 (when he may have been moving house).

Money and presents continued to shower upon Chaucer, in this late revival of his fortunes. During the year 1395–6, the fur trimming for a rich scarlet gown for Chaucer was paid for from the great wardrobe of Henry, Earl of Derby. No particular service is specified, and there probably was none: Chaucer was quite a well-known figure, we should remember, and Henry knew it would do him no harm at all to throw a little largesse in the poet's direction. Then, on 1 December 1397, there was a grant by Richard of a tun of wine yearly in the port of London. Such grants were a regular way of rewarding royal servants (they cost a good deal less than money): Chaucer had received an earlier grant of a pitcher of wine daily from Edward III in 1374, a grant that he had had commuted for an extra annuity of 20 marks in 1378. An annual tun (252 gallons) was not as much as a daily pitcher, or gallon, but it was quite enough, we may think. There was some delay with the paperwork on this occasion, and the first tun, due on 1 December 1397, was not delivered until 16 October 1398, by which time the second was almost on its way.

Some time during the 1390s, Chaucer found himself appointed as deputy forester for the forest of North Petherton in Somerset. The date and other circumstances of the appointment are obscure, the only record being that of an eighteenth-century antiquarian. There is the possibility of two appointments, one in the early 1390s and the other in the late 1390s, but nothing is clear. Chaucer's son Thomas held the same post from 1405 until his death in 1434, but he did not succeed his father. The forest belonged to the Mortimers, one of the greatest landowning families in England, but had been farmed out to Sir Peter Courtenay during the minority of the heir, Roger, fourth Earl of March. Roger reached his majority in 1395, the year in which he also became heir presumptive to the throne (his death in 1398 left his 7-year-old son Edmund with little prospect of entering upon the inheritance which was technically his). The best that can be conjectured of Chaucer's role is that he was acting in some capacity in a dispute between the owner and the farmer of the estate, much as he did in connection with Sir William Beauchamp in 1378. He probably received a fee. The job was quasi-legal and very boring, and we are not to imagine him traversing the woodland rides of Somerset, or living or probably even visiting there.

Almost equally obscure is the occasion for which Chaucer received royal warrant of protection on 4 May 1398 for going about England on the king's urgent business. The document covers two years from the date of issue, and includes a specially worded statement to protect the recipient from lawsuits. It is evidently a very different document from the letters of protection or 'passport' that he had been accustomed to receive for his trips overseas. One would guess that the formal wording of the document ('ad quamplura ardua et urgencia negocia nostra . . . in diversis part-ibus infra regnum nostrum Anglie' (*Life-Records*, pp. 62–3)) was simply taken over from a *pro forma* exemplar by the clerk respon-sible for drawing it up, and that its primary purpose is general legal protection and nothing to do with travel to remote parts of the country. Chaucer, always circumspect, may have asked for it as a special precaution against any unpleasantness arising from the Buckholt suit about to come to court.

All this time Chaucer was living in something like semi-retirement in Kent. On Sunday, 4 May 1393, he was one of the witnesses, probably at the door of Woolwich parish church, to a deal involving the transfer of property from John Horn, a London fishmonger, to Sir Nicholas Sarnesfield, the king's standard-bearer and a well-known figure at court. John Horn later complained that he had been coerced into agreement, which, given the very different social rank and access to power of the two parties, may be only too likely. Chaucer no doubt received a small fee for his services. Somewhat later, on 21 February 1395, he was one of the witnesses to another transfer, this time of the manor of Spittlecombe and adjacent estates in the area of Greenwich and Deptford from the Archbishop of York to the Archbishop of

Canterbury and others, including Chaucer's old friend Sir Philip de la Vache. In the following year, on 5 March 1396, he was one of the witnesses to the re-enfeoffment of York in the properties, and then again on 6 April to the conveyance of the same properties to Gregory Ballard, one of the king's butlers. Chaucer acted throughout with the same group of witnesses. On the same day, Ballard appointed him as one of his attorneys to assist in the conveyancing process. One did not have to have legal training to act thus as an attorney or representative in legal and business matters: Gower had acted as Chaucer's attorney in 1378. It might be done out of friendship or for a fee.

These documents, along with many other evidences that have been cited along the way (summarized in *Life-Records*, pp. 512–13), make it clear that Chaucer had been living in Kent throughout the 1390s, and probably since 1385. Kent of course is not a place of exile ('But here I am in Kent and Christendom / Among the muses where I read and rhyme', says Wyatt, cheerily), and Greenwich, which is where Chaucer is likely to have been living ('Lo Grenewych, ther many a shrewe is inne!' (I. 3907)), is no more than five or six miles from London Bridge. A horse of almost any kind would have made the round trip easily possible in a day. But it was nevertheless very different from living in the city and gave Chaucer a point of vantage from which he could survey 'the great wen' as he settled down to *The Canterbury Tales*.

There is evidence that Chaucer moved back to London in 1398. There was a debt of £1 that he had incurred in 1389 as a result of his failure to repay a 'prest' or advance on his annuity in 1387, and the record of the debt had been drifting through the exchequer accounts ever since. In 1398 responsibility for collecting the debt was transferred from the Sheriff of Kent to the Sheriff of London, which suggests that Chaucer was back in the capital a year at least before he took the lease of the house in Westminster on 24 December 1399. The debt, incidentally, was never collected, and was declared 'desperate' (that is, uncollectable) in 1399.

During the last decade of his life, Chaucer was almost entirely occupied, as a writer, with *The Canterbury Tales*. It was, indeed, and was intended to be, a plan that could accommodate almost anything a writer might desire to do. He took time off to write the *Treatise on the Astrolabe* in 1391, and to revise the Prologue to *The Legend of Good Women* in 1394–5; *The Envoy to Bukton* and *The Envoy to Scogan* both come from the 1390s, addressed to members of the band of grizzled veterans ('Lo, olde Grisel lyst to ryme and playe!'

(*Scogan*, 35)) which is what his audience had dwindled to. It is tempting to think that some of his more sardonic and sceptical little poems about love, such as *To Rosemounde, Against Women Unconstant* and *Merciles Beaute* (the last two unattributed in the manuscripts, but generally accepted as Chaucer's), date from this period, but one has to be wary of those romantically simple-minded assumptions that associate poems celebrating love with youth and poems satirizing love with old age. It may be just the other way round, and in any case poets love to inhabit the imagined bodies of others. Evidence of date from other sources, where it is available, is much more convincing. Unfortunately, it is not often available.

THE CANTERBURY TALES

Chronology

A biographer of Chaucer might properly wish to relate the develop-ment of the plan of *The Canterbury Tales* and the chronology of the composition of individual tales to the events of Chaucer's life and the larger history of the times through which he lived during the last decade of the fourteenth century. Unfortunately, this is impossible. On the one hand, Chaucer's life did not have many events in it that we know about and he refrained, as usual, from direct allusion to public events; on the other, the evidence for chronology is based upon such a fragile network of interdependent and unprovable hypotheses, as will soon be only too clearly demon-strated, that any deductions about specific connections between life, works and times would be quite unsafe. Speculation on such matters is valueless. Howard has some sharp and pertinent remarks about the preference of scholars for remaining non-com-mittal about the evolving plan of *The Canterbury Tales*: 'There is, however, a long-standing preference among some Chaucer scholars for the chaotic and inexplicable. It is easier to say 'we know nothing, there is no evidence' than to follow the arduous process of hypothesizing and reasoning.'[2] But 'the arduous process of hypothesizing and reasoning' produces only the spider's web of chronology that I have alluded to, and in Howard's case it gives way very soon to forms of reasoning a good deal less than arduous: for instance, 'In his last years he seemed to turn to somberer topics' (p. 438). There is no evidence at all for this, however well it may fit the novelettish shapes of popular biography, and I shall be inclined to suggest, later on, that the work of Chaucer's last years, or even his last months, was the 'knitting-up' of Fragment I and the writing of the Miller's Tale and Reeve's Tale. But nothing will be allowed to rest upon such speculation, and, after discussion of what is and can be known of the circumstances of the work's production, I shall discuss the *Tales* in terms of their general embodiment of Chaucer's maturer reflections upon the life of men and women in society and in the Christian faith.

The beginning of Chaucer's work on *The Canterbury Tales*, and the inception of the plan, are usually assigned to the year 1387, but the chief basis for this date is that it is the first year when he is not known to have been engaged on another major work. However, the *Tales* certainly followed *Troilus*, where they may be fore-shadowed in the reference to further making 'in som comedye' (v. 1788), and certainly followed *The Legend of Good Women*. The *Tales* go unmentioned in the list of Chaucer's works in the Prologue to the *Legend*, except for the two already written that were sub-sequently incorporated, 'Palamon and Arcite' and 'the lyf ... of Seynt Cecile' (Prologue, F. 420, 426), and it seems obvious that the conceiving of the idea of the framing narrative of *The Canterbury Tales* is what brought work on the *Legend* to a timely end.

   Although it may be assumed, then, that Chaucer started work on *The Canterbury Tales* around 1387, when he was living away from London in enforced idleness, it is difficult to be certain of much else. With very little topical allusion that might help with dating, and no pre-1400 manuscripts that might give precise indications of stages of composition, the chronology of the *Tales*, where any can be established, is no more than a pattern of infer-ences. One thing we should be quite clear about is that the order of composition was not the order of the *Tales* as they customarily stand in modern editions. We should be clear enough about this to prefer any amount of chaos and inexplicability to the pretence that arguments can be put forward on the basis that it was. It is by no means, even, a necessary assumption that Chaucer began by writing the General Prologue, though he clearly intended it to stand first, or that the General Prologue as it stands in the manu-scripts is what Chaucer originally wrote. Plausible arguments have been put forward, for instance, that the final group of pilgrims (see lines 542–4) is a late addition, and that the portrait of the

Wife of Bath did not take its present form until after her Prologue was substantially in existence. Likewise, the Parson's Tale, however well it may suit the trite image of Chaucer as an old man declining into orthodox piety as death approached, is not particularly likely to have been written last or even late. This is true too of the Retraction that follows it and is closely integrated with it. Moods of piety may come upon a man at any time.[3]

Within the general flux, there are a few certainties and a few reasonable deductions. It is certain that the Knight's Tale and the Second Nun's Tale were written before the _Tales_ were begun, since they are referred to in the Prologue to _The Legend of Good Women_; they bear so clearly the marks of their pre-_Canterbury Tales_ origin (for example, I. 1201, VIII. 78) that they are unlikely to have been much revised for inclusion in the _Tales_, except in obvious and superficial ways. The fact that they are left with their original titles in the revised version of the Prologue to the _Legend_ in 1394–5 does not necessarily mean that at that point they had not yet been incorporated into the _Tales_.

The scheme of _The Canterbury Tales_, among many other creative opportunities, evidently had a practical usefulness for Chaucer in providing a secure and easily assigned home for earlier pieces which might otherwise be given little attention (as has happened with _Anelida and Arcite_) or even lost from the canon. There may be more in this category than the two for which there is definite evidence, though the tendency of scholars to treat tales they despise as pre-_Canterbury Tales_ work, making the _Tales_ into 'a kind of foundling asylum for the waifs and strays of [Chaucer's] earlier begetting',[4] has made speculation on the subject a little suspect. Two religious tales in rhyme royal stanzas (the Clerk's Tale and the Man of Law's Tale) and one in eight-line stanzas (the Monk's Tale) have commonly been spoken of as early work, one of the assumptions being that the stanzaic form, as in the Second Nun's Tale, is a mark of earlier composition. But this is not so: Chaucer uses rhyme royal consistently in the _Tales_ for purposes of stylistic decorum, associating it with a form of the 'high style' suitable for religious narratives with a strong emotional content. The Man of Law's Tale, moreover, draws directly on the _De Miseria condicionis humane_ of Innocent III, a translation of which, or part of which, Chaucer adds to the list of his writings in the revised Prologue to the _Legend_ (G. 414) and which he must presumably therefore have been working on between 1387 and 1394.[5]

As for the Monk's Tale, it does seem difficult to conceive of

Chaucer meddling seriously with such a jejune notion of 'tragedy' after he had revivified the form in the Knight's Tale and *Troilus*. Yet the Monk's Tale is one of the few which contain an allusion securely datable from external evidence, namely, to the death of Bernabò Visconti (VII. 2405), which took place on 19 December 1385. Chaucer had good reason to take an interest in the much-feared lord of Milan, 'God of delit and scourge of Lumbardye' (VII. 2400), whom he had met and had dealings with in 1378. Against the supposition that the Monk's Tale must therefore have been composed after 1385 and most probably during the *Canterbury Tales* period it is commonly argued, and with good sense, that the Bernabò stanza, along with the other 'Modern Instances' (Pedro of Castile, Peter of Cyprus, and Ugolino of Pisa (VII. 2375–457)), was added at a later date to liven up a rather tired compilation of 'falls of princes'.

Beyond these indications of early or relatively early date, there is little to go on, though there has been a good deal of speculation based on more or less likely accounts of the development of the plan of *The Canterbury Tales*. The hypothesis that the Shipman's Tale was originally designed to be told by a woman, based on the fact that in the opening remarks about husbands, and their need to be generous to their wives, the narrator speaks of wives as 'we' (VII. 12–19), seems obvious enough. It exposes an earlier stratum in the development of the design of the *Tales*, and suggests that Chaucer had little inclination or opportunity to tidy away the evidences of such stratification. It makes sense too of the cancelled Epilogue of the Man of Law's Tale (it appears in a group of manuscripts of lesser but good authority), in which a 'joly body' (II. 1185), surely to be identified with the Wife of Bath at some stage in her gestation, proposes to tell a tale. This epilogue was dropped, but not lost, when the following tale was reassigned. Alternative explanations of the feminine pronouns at the beginning of the Shipman's Tale are rather forced, and betray some nervous resistance to the 'workroom theory', the idea that the manuscripts of *The Canterbury Tales* give evidence of a work that was both continuously evolving and unfinished. Critics dislike the interpretative complexities of such a situation (just as editors dislike the practical problems it causes), preferring instead to create their own.[6]

If the Shipman's Tale was originally designed to be told by the Wife of Bath, then the reallocation of the tale to the Shipman indicates that Chaucer later conceived a larger role for the Wife.

The larger role is certainly there, in her Prologue and Tale, and the impact of the Wife of Bath on the maturing development of the *Tales* as a whole is clearly evident in the references to her and her ideas elsewhere. In the Merchant's Tale she is alluded to by name in the discourse of a character within the story (IV. 1685–7), a brilliant stroke of ultra-dramatic realism. At the end of the Clerk's Tale she is named (IV. 1170) in the concluding stanzas (IV. 1163–76) which, with the ironical Envoy (IV. 1177–1212), are evidently a later replacement for the original single concluding stanza, written pre-Wife of Bath, which Chaucer intended to cancel. In the Franklin's Tale, the references to *soveraynetee* in marriage (V. 751) and to the joy of marriage (V. 804–6) – the latter lines, in their turn, echoing some mordantly ironic lines in the Merchant's Tale (IV. 1337–41) – awaken reminiscences of the Wife's manifesto concerning women's right to *maistrye* in marriage and her pronouncements on the 'wo that is in mariage' (III. 3). There is even external evidence that the Wife of Bath had become something of a talking-point in London literary circles in the 1390s. In *The Envoy to Bukton*, written perhaps about 1396, Chaucer remarks, with acid playfulness, that if his friend is seriously contemplating marriage he should read what the Wife of Bath has to say about it first: 'The Wyf of Bathe I pray yow that ye rede / Of this matere that we have on honde' (29–30). Chaucer may further have responded to the interest created by the Wife of Bath by adding some lines to her Prologue which tend to make her even more outrageous and provocative.[7]

There are other signs of stratification which are capable of interpretation in relation to the relative date of individual parts of *The Canterbury Tales*. The cancellation of the Nun's Priest's Epilogue (VII. 3447–62), for instance, and the reuse of some of its material in the Host's words to the Monk (for instance, VII. 1945), suggest that the development and integration of Fragment VII was undertaken during the mature phase of composition of the *Tales*. The rewriting of the Nun's Priest's Prologue so as to accommodate a new interruption of the Monk's Tale by the Knight (VII. 3961–80) and avoid having the Host interrupt this tale as well as *Thopas* (VII. 919) belongs to the same period. The use of particular sources can also sometimes provide evidence of date. Chaucer's work some time during the period 1387–94 on the *De Miseria* has already been mentioned as indicating a date somewhat late in that period for the Man of Law's Introduction and Tale (as also for the Pardoner's Tale, which makes extensive use of Innocent III's treatise). Another work that figures large in the revised Prologue to the *Legend* but not at all in the earlier version is the treatise of 'Jerome agayns Jovynyan' (G. 281), where Chaucer is told he can find plenty of stories of good women. He presumably mentions St Jerome's *Epistola adversus Jovinianum* now, and not before, because he had been reading it recently. The use of Jerome in the Wife of Bath's Prologue and the Franklin's Tale again suggests a date for these pieces later rather than earlier in the composition period of the *Tales*.

These of course are all relative dates, indicative of sequence of composition rather than absolute dates. The evidence for the latter is almost non-existent, and the attempts to be specific, for instance in arguments for topical or astronomical allusion, have generally persuaded none but their proponents.

Publication

There are eighty-two manuscripts of *The Canterbury Tales*, ranging in date from the very early to the very late fifteenth century, and including fifty-five complete or near-complete copies, seven fragmentary copies which may be presumed to represent once-complete manuscripts, and twenty manuscripts containing excerpts deliberately selected for inclusion in an anthology or other compilation. The number of surviving manuscripts is very large for a vernacular work in English, and in fact only *The Prick of Conscience* survives in more copies, a comparison somewhat misleading in terms of actual popularity since the latter poem had the advantage, for copying and preservation, of an exclusively dogmatic religious subject-matter. It is hard to know how many manuscripts of *The Canterbury Tales* once existed, and are represented by those that survive, but the work was certainly popular and widely known from the time it began to be circulated.

No manuscripts of any part of *The Canterbury Tales* survive from before 1400, and Chaucer did little to prepare the work for publication. Individual tales were read to or circulated among his friends, as we hear in *The Envoy to Bukton*, and perhaps there was some limited general circulation of portions of the work. No specific audience is addressed, or implied in the manner of address, and there is little sense of the listening group, except for the fictitious listening group that is constituted by the pilgrims. Questions of audience, and the author's relation to his audience, which had

produced some intricate manoeuvring in earlier poems, are here
playfully side-stepped by having the audience planted in the
poem (see the discussion above, pp. 185–90). The author meanwhile masquerades as a mere reporter, bound only to represent
accurately what he heard, with all its broad language and coarse
subject-matter (General Prologue, I. 725–42; Miller's Prologue,
I. 3171–86). The show of care to avoid offending members of
his audience is itself a mark of the change of that audience,
from a known and particular group, however 'imaginary', whose
capacity for taking offence would be well known, to an unknown
and general mass of anonymous readers, including ourselves.

When Chaucer addresses his audience directly, it is a reading
audience that he addresses (Miller's Prologue, I. 3177). Only a
reading audience can assimilate readily the impropriety of the
references to reading that are made in the course of a tale supposedly told by a pilgrim (Knight's Tale, I. 1201; Second Nun's Tale,
VIII. 78). The tone is quite different from that of earlier poems,
where it was generally possible for the reader to call into imagined
existence the mixed group of 'gentils', men and women, that
constituted the primary audience, imagined or real. When that
term 'gentils' is used in *The Canterbury Tales*, as in identifying those
who object to the 'ribaudye' they anticipate from the Pardoner
(VI. 323–4), it is a joke, having the character of the modern 'ladies
and gentlemen', used in public address at a boxing-match or a
pub outing.

Yet the differences in tone in *The Canterbury Tales*, and the success
of Chaucer's self-concealing and evasive strategies, do not prevent
us from thinking that we can detect an implied audience. It is, in
imagination, a miscellaneous company, of lettered London men, to
be appropriately scandalized and delighted by the Wife of Bath
and the fabliaux, flattered by the invitation to share in a gentleman
scholar's easily carried burden of learning (so much more easily
carried now, as well as heavier, than in *The Book of the Duchess*),
and intrigued by the novel exposé of London low life in the Cook's
Tale. The inclusion amongst the dramatis personae of real London
people in the persons of Roger of Ware, the Cook, and Herry
Bailly, the Host (I. 4336, 4358), might also suggest to members
of the audience the possibility of further allusions to merchants,
lawyers and shipmen that they knew.[8] Above all, in imagining the
audience, one finds it to be, perhaps exclusively, an audience of
men.

Chaucer continued throughout the 1390s with revisions and developments of the plan of *The Canterbury Tales*, circulated portions of it piecemeal, and died leaving the work unfinished. He made no attempt to bring the work into any final shape, even though, having told twenty-three of a possible thirty tales, he had come close to completing a one-tale-per-pilgrim plan (the only pilgrims who do not tell tales are the Plowman, the Yeoman and the five Guildsmen). The usual explanation of the failure to carry forward the four-tale two-way plan proposed by the Host in the General Prologue (I. 792–4) is that Chaucer, or the Host, gradually acquiesced in its impossibility. The Host tells the Franklin that everyone 'moot tellen atte leste / A tale or two, or breken his biheste' (V. 697–8), and he says to the Parson. 'For every man, save thou, hath toold his tale' (X. 25). A much better explanation of the discrepancy is that the four-tale plan was a late addition to the General Prologue, designed to extend the tale-telling possibilities of *The Canterbury Tales* almost indefinitely, meanwhile postponing the bringing to an end of a project that had become coterminous for Chaucer with life itself. The 'ending' of *The Canterbury Tales*, with the Parson's ringing words comparing the pilgrimage, as the pilgrims prepare to enter Canterbury, with the pilgrimage of every man's life to 'Jerusalem celestial' (X. 51), thus becomes the conclusion of a plan that had been superseded. Chaucer's characteristic aversion to closure could hardly be more neatly expressed.

What Chaucer left behind him when he died was a mass of papers, in which the tales he had written formed a series of fragments, some consisting of one tale only, with prologue and possibly also ending material, and others consisting of anything from two to six tales, fully integrated internally with dramatic links. These fragments, in which the dramatic potential of the Canterbury pilgrimage frame-narrative had been fully and vigorously exploited, themselves remained, however, without beginning or ending links to preceding or following matter. The General Prologue, with Fragment I, was obviously enough to be placed at the beginning, and the Parson's Tale, with the Retraction, at the end. The rest was a matter for the judgement of Chaucer's editors, since Chaucer had made no final decisions.[9]

There was some eagerness to bring out a complete text of the work that London had been talking about and having glimpses of for the past decade, but the first attempt to do so was attended by some confusion. The Hengwrt manuscript (Aberystwyth, National Library of Wales, MS Peniarth 392D), made within three or four years of Chaucer's death, contains an excellent text of *The Canter-bury Tales* but the arrangement is somewhat jumbled. Some of the links are missing, and some other links are used, with the names of the pilgrims changed, to arrange the tales in a manner that is only superficially plausible. The Canon's Yeoman's Prologue and Tale are completely missing. The collection was evidently put together in a great hurry, and the changes of ink, the spaces left for matter known to exist but not immediately available, the fudging of the lay-out to hide errors in such calculations, all indicate that the copyist was working with exemplars that were arriving on his desk in fragmentary form and unpredictable sequence. The hustle and bustle of the writing-shop, as Chaucer's editors tried to put together as a matter of urgency the first copy of the whole text of the long-awaited masterpiece, could hardly be more vividly conveyed.[10]

A few years later, before 1410, the same copyist, whether or not under the instructions of the same editor or editors, produced the famous Ellesmere manuscript (San Marino, California, Hunt-ington Library MS EL. 26. C. 9). There was time now for a more leisured scrutiny of the papers, and a more reasoned ordering of them, and opportunity to incorporate extra material, or fuller texts of existing material, that had subsequently come to light, whether from Chaucer's own shelves and cupboards or from friends close to him who had been favoured with copies of portions of the *Tales* prior to his death. The Ellesmere editor, with all the texts before him, was now able to work out an order that made the best sense of what was available, to embark on the careful editing of his copy, and to prepare the work for de luxe presentation. Carefully written and put together, beautifully produced, with miniatures of the pilgrims painted in the margin at the head of their tales, and containing an excellent text, the Ellesmere manuscript has held sway in editions of the *Tales* for a century, ever since Skeat used it in his great edition of Chaucer in 1894. To the extent that Robinson's editions of 1933 and 1957 were based on Skeat, and that the new *Riverside Chaucer* is based on Robinson, the Ellesmere text *is The Canterbury Tales*, since Robinson and now the *Riverside* have been and are the editions most extensively used for citation in critical books and articles.[11]

There is a danger in this. It does not have to do with the text: whatever the relative merits of Hengwrt and Ellesmere, they are singly or together outstandingly good witnesses to what Chaucer may be presumed to have written. It has to do with the ordering of the *Tales*. Even though there is no Chaucerian order for the fragments, the editor, whether the original editor of Ellesmere or a modern editor, has still to put the *Tales* in some order. The Ellesmere is no doubt the best that could be arrived at, and modern editors are sensible to follow it. But the inevitable consequence is that the presentation of Chaucer's unordered fragments as 'the book of the tales of Caunterbury' (as the editorial rubric at the end of the Retraction in Ellesmere has it) gives a spurious authority to a pragmatic editorial decision. It becomes a widely accepted belief, enforced by the hypostatizing nature of 'the book', that *The Canterbury Tales* as they are presented in the modern edition are the *Tales* in the order in which Chaucer intended them to be read (and even in which he composed them), and it is not uncommon to find the unfinished state of the work, and its existence as a series of fragments, treated as a mere hiccough in the author's communication of his text to his readers.

One of the earliest examples of this attempt to turn the unordered fragments of the *Tales* into the 'whole book' of *The Canterbury Tales* was the reordering suggested by Henry Bradshaw to Frederick J. Furnivall which has come to be called the 'Bradshaw shift'. Assuming that Chaucer intended to put the references to places on the way to Canterbury in the correct geographical sequence, and finding Rochester (VII. 1926) coming incorrectly after Sittingbourne (III. 847) in the Ellesmere sequence, Bradshaw proposed moving Fragment VII to follow Fragment II, the two together forming Fragment B in a new ordering system and putting the places in the 'right' order. In the interests of a kind of consistency that Chaucer might be presumed to have observed (he knew the way to Canterbury well enough, after all), an ordering was thus established that made deliberate use of a link (the Epilogue of the Man of Law's Tale) between the 'tale of Constance' and the 'tale of the hundred franks' that Chaucer had equally deliberately discarded at an earlier stage when he reassigned the 'tale of the hundred franks' to the Shipman. Only one manuscript, and that a late and very bad one (Bodleian Library, MS Selden Arch. B. 14), links Fragments II and VII in this way; meanwhile, the four-tale two-way plan, which ought presumably to have figured large in any literalist reading of the frame-narrative of *The Canterbury Tales*, was quite forgotten.[12]

More recently, the very good books of Alfred David and Donald Howard are examples of studies of the *Tales* that are flawed because of their assumption that editorial arrangement in the edition they happen to be using corresponds with authorial design and that the *Tales* are intended by the author to be read in the order in which they there appear and may even have been composed in that order. In a more casual way, some very recent writers, Lee Patterson and Carolyn Dinshaw, use the sequence Man of Law's Tale/Wife of Bath's Prologue as an integral part of their speculations about special effects of design created by juxtaposition and sequence.[13]

To argue that *The Canterbury Tales* should be presented as a set of fragments in folders, with the information as to their placement in the manuscripts fully displayed, would no doubt be counted a little extreme. But the idea of presenting them in such a way at least acts as a reminder of the proper context of understanding in which discussion of the structure and design of the *Tales* needs to be entered into.

Plan and Materials

Something has already been said about the development of Chaucer's plan for *The Canterbury Tales*, especially the apparent change of mind about the number of tales to be told, and the increasing prominence of the role of the Wife of Bath. Little more can be safely deduced, except that the *Tales* were unfinished at his death and that the surviving manuscripts bear witness to different stages in the work's evolution. Some emphasis has been placed on the good sense of keeping in mind the provisional and incomplete status of the work, and of evolving only those theories of integrity and grand design that take account of this fact of its existence. This means evolving no theories at all. Indeed, one could claim that the unfinished state of the work is one of its most significant achievements, enabling Chaucer to resist the closure that his own age and his modern admirers would wish to impose upon him, and to preserve that openness, that lack of certainty, which is so much the special character of his writing.

Further, the 'carelessness' of consistency, the difficulties that Chaucer places in the way of those who wish to think of the pilgrimage in a thoroughgoing naturalistic manner, may be the absence of a kind of care which would have prepared the *Tales* for an inappropriate kind of attention. The vagueness and inconsistency of geographical reference and the absence of attention to the circumstances of the journey inhibit precisely the kind of literal-

mindedness that would swiftly have revealed the intrinsic absurdity
of the pilgrimage frame-narrative and collapsed the whole delightful illusion completely. It is interesting to look at two fifteenth-
century poems that are attached, quite self-consciously, to the
Canterbury Tales frame, Lydgate's *Siege of Thebes* and the anonymous
Tale of Beryn, and to see how attentive both are to the literal
circumstances of the journey. The former, purportedly a tale told
by Lydgate to the pilgrims, makes several references to the passing
of pilgrimage-time during the telling of the tale, something that
Chaucer never does except at the very opening of the Knight's
Tale (I. 889–92), while the latter has a lively account of the arrival
of the pilgrims at Canterbury, and of their adventures as a group,
quite unlike anything in Chaucer. We may safely assume that
Chaucer, in eschewing this kind of amusing but trivializing natu-
ralism, knew what he was doing.[14]

Yet the pilgrimage frame-narrative of *The Canterbury Tales* was
clearly important to Chaucer, and provided him with many advantages and opportunities. It gave him the chance to experiment
with short verse narratives of a much more varied and stimulating
kind than those that had had him dragging his feet in *The Legend
of Good Women,* and in particular it gave him the reason, indeed a
veritable obligation, to follow his 'cherles' in telling stories of low
sexual intrigue (fabliaux), as well as scurrilous anecdotes such as
the Summoner's Tale. These tales, including the Miller's, Reeve's,
Merchant's and Shipman's Tales among the fabliaux, are among
Chaucer's most striking and characteristic achievements. There is
nothing like them in Middle English and nothing quite like them
anywhere in English literature. Creating a space for them within
the English literary tradition was not so easy a task as it may
seem in retrospect, and Chaucer's apologies for having to tell them,
in the General Prologue (I. 725–42) and the Miller's Prologue
(I. 3171–86), are only partly humorous. For a poet who had
been praised by Gower, acclaimed by Thomas Usk as 'the noble
philosophical poete in Englissh', had his hour of glory as a court
poet, and shared some of the poetic ambitions of Dante and
Petrarch, it was a little difficult to explain how he came to be
writing such stuff. He knew, but it was difficult to explain.

The sleight of hand by which he does so is deft, and it takes
some time to realize that the attribution of the fabliaux to the
'cherles', which seems, like *The Canterbury Tales* as a whole, so
'natural' a representation of observed reality, is in fact a highly
original dramatic innovation. In social reality, fabliaux in French,

Italian and Latin were traditionally the entertainment of upper-class and clerical audiences. Chaucer, in associating the fabliaux with the churls, finds a place for them in English poetry by making the familiar equation between social class and moral behaviour and also by refusing responsibility either for the equation or for the portrayal of the bad behaviour.[15]

Chaucer's apology, of course, refers specifically to the tales that follow, those of the Miller, Reeve and Cook. The Shipman's Tale seems to need little apology, so polite is its representation of misbehaviour, and the Merchant's Tale, a story with a fabliau-ending told by a non-churl, offers its own apology for bad language (IV. 2350–1) at the coarse climax of the story, on the same basis as Chaucer's, though with a vile prurience all its own. Chaucer's awareness of the delicacy of the English poet's role is more subtly present in the Manciple's pretended apology for using the low word 'lemman' (IX. 205). In his desire to transgress the usual courtesies of language and at the same time to acknowledge formally that they exist, the Manciple is a greasy middleman for some of Chaucer's own concerns.[16]

Those concerns have to do with the establishing for English poetry of the propriety of impropriety, and with the winning for English of areas of literary activity that, unlike French, Italian and Latin, it had not traditionally had a part in. The frame-narrative, with the attributions of tales that it made possible, gave Chaucer freedoms that he valued, including the freedom to experiment with all kinds of tale, to unburden himself of certain kinds of authorial responsibility, not least that of being an *auctor*, and to take that oblique and indirect slant on his material that stimulated the curiosity of his imagination. It would perhaps not do to put the matter quite as bluntly as Alfred David, in *The Strumpet Muse*: 'Through the invention of the frame story, Chaucer is able to escape his moral obligations as a poet' (p. 75). There are different ways of construing a poet's 'moral obligations', and some obligations, such as exploring and reflecting upon the moral life of people in society, might be thought more valuable as well as more interesting than others, such as pronouncing upon it. No doubt those who took it upon themselves to advise medieval poets on how they should conduct their business, including the alter egos of the poets themselves, placed a value on such pronouncements, but Chaucer was fortunately able to evade their administration. However he won his freedom, the use that he put it to was astonishing: one can see him securing the right of an English poet to tell new kinds of tale, but nothing could prepare one for the Miller's Tale. To see such a poem, familiar as it has become, anew in the context of late-fourteenth-century English literary culture is to recognize a miracle.

Another poem that might equally be regarded as a celebration by Chaucer of the liberating possibilities of the *Tales* is the Nun's Priest's Tale. The tale takes as its moral the well-known Pauline dictum that 'al that writen is, / To oure doctrine it is ywrite, ywis' (VII. 3441–2), and advises its listeners: 'Taketh the fruyt, and lat the chaf be stille' (3443). This unexceptionably medieval conclusion seems to prepare the tale for a characteristically medieval form of exegetical reading ('fruit' and 'chaff' are standard metaphors for the meanings selected and discarded in such reading), and the bait has been readily swallowed. In fact, Chaucer's manner of telling the story constantly and hilariously frustrates the conventional desire to read it as an exemplum, and the temptingly suggestive allegory of the Fall inexorably self-destructs. There is something audacious about the undoing of the procedures of exemplification, the principal means of assigning moral and theological meaning to secular narrative in the Middle Ages, and it seems likely that it was the framework of the *Tales* that gave licence to such audacity.

These are advantages and freedoms that Chaucer won for the telling of particular tales and kinds of tales. He was also keenly responsive to the dramatic potential of the pilgrimage frame-narrative itself. This had a capacity for organic and dynamic development denied to collections of tales like *The Legend of Good Women*, framed according to some externally imposed principle of organization. From the time the Miller breaks in upon the Host's plan for the Monk to tell the next story after the Knight, events seem to unfold with an unplanned naturalness. The development of the longer fragments (I and VII) is particularly rich. Quarrels provoke two sets of paired tales (Miller/Reeve, Friar/Summoner), and the role of the Host was exuberantly expanded in successive revisions.

The sense of dramatic vitality is so strong that there is a temptation to read the tales as principally an expression of the characters of their tellers. There are occasions when this is evidently appropriate, especially where the pilgrim has a quasi-autobiographical introductory monologue, as in the cases of the Wife of Bath, Pardoner and Canon's Yeoman. The tales of these three are inseparably and significantly connected with the programmes of

self-revelation and self-advertisement that they have put before us.
There are other tales where our memory of the General Prologue
portrait, whether or not reinforced by introductory matter to the
tale, gives us a more limited yet still potent consciousness of the
pilgrim–narrator. The tales of the Reeve, Franklin, Prioress and
Manciple are examples. Other tales are allocated with a no more
than general sense of appropriateness, and others still with none
at all (Man of Law, Physician, Shipman). There are dangers in
looking too hard for subtle revelations of character in the performance of individual pilgrims. If it is made into a consistent practice,
it returns Chaucer to the straitjacket of narrative interpretation he
had struggled so hard to escape. 'Dramatic' reading routinely
detects 'inadequacies' in the narrator's performance which are then
used as the basis for fanciful speculations about the narrator's
character; these processes of 'ironization' are often the result of
simple misreading of the kind of story being told, and distract
attention from the tales as tales and the important literary contexts
in which they are better to be understood.[17]

The pilgrimage itself is also important in *The Canterbury Tales*.
Chaucer chose it for many reasons: for its naturalistic plausibility
as a way of bringing a variety of people together; for its mixture
of pious purpose and holiday spirit; for the potential it had finally
to 'knit up all the feast'. If he had any idea that it was to provide
a recurrent figure for the journey of man's life through the world,
he soon abandoned it, for there are remarkably few references,
between the General Prologue and the Parson's Prologue, to the
journey as a pilgrimage. In fact, it might be argued that in planning
to bring the pilgrims back to Southwark, and in making the point
of their journey the completion of the tale-telling competition and
the awarding of the prize to the winner, Chaucer has relegated
the religious pilgrimage to a secondary role. This would be mis-
chievous, but the revision of the tale-telling plan can certainly be
read in that way.

As to the materials from which *The Canterbury Tales* were constructed, one's impression of originality is both perfectly accurate
and also somewhat misleading. The frame at least is completely
original. There had been many story collections before, and some
with a narrative frame, but the only one that decisively influenced
Chaucer was Boccaccio's *Decameron*. In his conclusion, Boccaccio
makes the same disingenuous excuses as Chaucer for the coarseness
of some of his matter, claims immunity from censure on the basis
that he is a mere reporter, and suggests that anyone who wants

can read the tales they like and leave those they dislike. Boccaccio also provides models if not sources for all four of Chaucer's fabliaux as well as for the Franklin's Tale, and the original Italian of the story of Griselda that Chaucer took from Petrarch for the Clerk's Tale. But Chaucer had long completed his apprenticeship to Boccaccio, and whatever ideas he took now from the *Decameron* he transformed almost beyond recognition. His pilgrims are infinitely various where Boccaccio's are all from the same class, and his development of the frame narrative is full of surprises where Boccaccio's is planned and predictable.[18]

The tales themselves, however, are almost always from known sources or have well-established analogues, as one would expect with a medieval author. Only the Cook's Tale, the Squire's Tale and *Sir Thopas* seem to be more or less original, an indication perhaps of the kind of value Chaucer placed on 'originality', in the sphere of story-invention at least. The Cook's Tale is too scabrous to be continued and is left deliberately and tantalizingly unfinished; the Squire's Tale, begun with the best of intentions, draws attention more and more to its own tendency to stray from the point (V. 401–8) and to ramify uncontrollably (V. 651–70); while *Thopas* is open parody, a comprehensive anthology of themes and motifs from popular romance which contains, it has been said, 'everything that the chivalric romance ought to have – except sense'.[19]

For the rest, Chaucer draws mostly upon materials familiar to his medieval readers.* The Wife of Bath and the Pardoner are constructed from hints in the *Roman de la Rose* and from the miscellaneous detritus of antifeminist and homiletic writing. The *Roman de la Rose* is also the direct and probably the only source of the Physician's Tale (Livy is cited (VI. 1) as a Latin *auctoritas*, but not used) and the initial inspiration of the Monk's Tale, though there supplemented from Boccaccio's Latin prose *De Casibus Virorum Illustrium*. The Manciple's Tale derives from the French *Ovide moralisé* rather than from Ovid, the Clerk's Tale from a French translation of Petrarch's Latin, and *Melibee* from a French translation of the Latin *Liber Consolationis et Consilii* of Albertanus of Brescia. Chaucer's preference for vernacular sources, where he could get them, is clear. Only the Parson's Tale and the Prioress's

---

* The Knight's Tale and the Second Nun's Tale, written earlier, are excluded from the following discussion.

Tale are entirely from Latin sources, the former a conflation of two penitential treatises which survive in many manuscripts, the latter from some collection of Miracles of the Virgin such as provides the closest analogues. Several tales are taken over, as far as their bare plots are concerned, from popular anecdote (Friar's Tale, Summoner's Tale, Canon's Yeoman's Tale), and the basic trick-plots of the four fabliaux and the Nun's Priest's Tale are probably from the same source, though there are close French and Italian analogues. The Franklin's Tale is from Boccaccio, though much changed.

There is some innovativeness in Chaucer's use of the writings of the Italians, but the only tale that draws upon a quite unexpected source is the Man of Law's Tale, which derives directly from the Anglo-Norman Chronicle of Nicholas Trivet. So surprising is it to find Chaucer working with an isolated episode from a long and fairly undistinguished work in a language he was accustomed to scorn (Chaucer shows little knowledge of the extensive Anglo-Norman literature of the thirteenth and fourteenth centuries) that some credence must be given to a recent hypothesis that Chaucer got his knowledge and perhaps his copy of the text directly from his friend John Gower, who did his own version of the Constance story in the *Confessio Amantis*. The serendipity of Chaucer's use of source-materials, the magpie-like nature of his raids on scholarly texts, may be the product, more than we know, not of his own indefatigable reading but of his conversations with more learned friends.[20]

The striking omissions revealed in this survey of materials are of course the fourteenth-century French and Italian poets who had provided the principal impetus for Chaucer's writing in the 1370s and 1380s. It is partly that they were now in Chaucer's bones and untraceable, partly that he does not now wish to work, as he did in the Knight's Tale, *Troilus* and *The Legend of Good Women*, with already existing literary works. He no longer needed the prompting they gave, but was prepared to work more independently, coursing more freely through his rich and varied store of reading and reminiscence.

Itemizing the sources of each tale does in fact give a misleading impression, since it misses that great body of writing in Latin anthologies, miscellanies, compendia and encyclopaedias, which is what gives the 'many-storied' quality to Chaucer's writing in *The Canterbury Tales*. Antifeminist writings such as Jerome's *Adversus Jovinianum*, the *Epistola Valerii ad Rufinum* and the *Lamentationes* of

Matheolus, whether or not through French intermediaries such as
the translation of the *Lamentationes* or Deschamps's *Miroir de Mariage*
(or through some lost 'book of wikked wyves' such as the Wife of
Bath refers to (III. 685)), inform not only the Wife of Bath's
Prologue but also the Merchant's Tale and the Franklin's Tale.
The influence of Innocent III's *De Miseria*, which Chaucer translated, has been mentioned earlier. Echoes of sermons and sermon
literature are everywhere, and of course the Bible and the liturgy
are plundered for some of Chaucer's most dazzling literary effects,
like the allusions to the Song of Songs in the Miller's Tale
(I. 3698–703) and the Merchant's Tale (IV. 2138–48). Robert
Holcot's commentary on the Book of Sapience, one of the most
widely known intellectual rag-bags of the fourteenth century, is
the direct source for passages on dreams in the Nun's Priest's Tale,
and the vast encyclopaedia of Vincent of Beauvais, the three-part
Speculum Maius, is used for Pertelote's advice on laxatives.

The *Speculum* is a new kind of book, the kind that one could
look things up in, and mention of another book like it can conclude
this survey. The *Communiloquium* of the Franciscan John of Wales
(late thirteenth century) is a manual of writings useful for both
preachers and laymen, including illustrative sayings and stories,
in the form of a vast anthology of several thousand quotations
from the Bible and from classical, patristic and medieval authors.
It is the kind of volume, if not the very one, that supplied the poet
with what Pratt calls 'the raw materials for some of his brilliant
passages of characterization, drama, and satire'. In it he found
useful sayings and stories neatly arranged and collected under
headings and easy to locate. There is extensive use made of it in
the Wife of Bath's Prologue and Tale, the Summoner's Tale,
Pardoner's Tale and Nun's Priest's Tale, and a variety of parallels
elsewhere, suggesting that Chaucer was 'steeped in it', though he
never mentions the work. Latin glosses, such as often appear in
the best early manuscripts of *The Canterbury Tales*, are written
in the margins of Ellesmere beside passages borrowed from the
Communiloquium; the glosses, which must derive from Chaucer's
autograph manuscript, refer to John of Wales's authorities, such
as Valerius, Seneca, Juvenal and John of Salisbury, in just the
form and order in which John of Wales cites them, and quote from
them in his version of their words. The relevant passages in
Chaucer are likewise incontrovertibly derived from John of Wales
and not from the authorities Chaucer cites (for instance, in Wife
of Bath's Tale, III. 1165, 1168, 1184, 1192; Summoner's Tale,

III. 2018). Many books Chaucer is presumed to have known can thus be removed from the shelves of his putative library.[21]

Most impudent of all, Chaucer habitually uses preaching materials from John of Wales to give vivid illustration to the doubtful practices of his own 'false preachers', the Wife of Bath, the Pardoner and the friar of the Summoner's Tale. We can recognize here a characteristic technique; the traditional materials are taken over, and their direction reversed by the dramatic context, thus creating that rich and often hilarious confluence of meanings that so taxes the single-minded reader. The antifeminist writings employed by the Wife of Bath similarly find themselves going back up the one-way street they came down, and Innocent III's remarks about poverty in the *De Miseria* are comically misapplied in the Introduction to the Man of Law's Tale.

Society

There are various ways in which a biographer might organize a discussion of *The Canterbury Tales*, once it is recognized that there is no possibility of organizing the discussion chronologically, in order of composition of tales, and no use in organizing it sequentially, in order of editorial arrangement. One choice is to relate the tales to the formal genres that they belong to in literary tradition and so see them within their 'horizons of expectation'; another is to seek thematic linkings and juxtapositions; another is to invent an organizing principle and use it as a kind of searchlight to throw on the tales. But in a biography it seems appropriate to think in terms of what, in life and experience, is represented, and this, crudely, is the matter of what follows.[22]

Some comments have already been made (see chapter 4 above) on Chaucer's generally conservative and conventional expressions of opinion on politics and social questions, or, more frequently, the absence of any expression of opinion at all. Examples were given that included passages from *The Canterbury Tales*, and they seemed to confirm the generally structural and aesthetic function of references to government and kingship, the organization of society, social class, social conflict and the poor. These are not Chaucer's 'subject', as they are Langland's. However, no writer can withdraw himself from the social and cultural practices in which his existence as an individual and the language that he uses are embedded, and there are ways of tracing the presence of these practices that produce a different result from looking for evidence of Chaucer's 'political views'.[23]

Chaucer's own position, now in his late maturity as a writer, should be remembered, and it is well described by Brewer:

> He was the new man, the literate layman who was not a clerk, the courtier who was not a knight; he was not poor (like Langland) but not rich; a salaried man, not landed gentry (like Gower); he was not even a merchant like his father and grandfather.[24]

Such a man had a special slant on the English society of his day: it was a somewhat ambiguous position, poised somewhere between the court (in the widest sense of that term) and the city and shifting in relation to those two poles, and it may be thought to have contributed to a certain ambivalence as well as a sharper awareness of social structure and class.[25] Chaucer was particularly aware of the increased social mobility of the later fourteenth century, which had London merchants rising to the rank of knighthood or even higher, and members of the nobility cultivating their rich friends in the city and joining their guilds and confraternities. Much of the increased mobility was due to the great demographic disasters of the early part of the century (the famine of 1315–17, the pestilence of 1349) and the shaking up they had administered to the rigid hierarchies of society. New attempts to control what was perceived as a socially undesirable violation of established hierarchies, such as the sumptuary laws, which attempted to lay down what different classes might or might not wear, show a hankering after social definitions which are increasingly archaic. New tax laws, meanwhile, were making assessments of the relative wealth and taxability of aldermen and barons, burghers and *bachilers*, which put traditionally distinct social groupings in the same tax bracket.

Langland viewed these changes with alarm, but Chaucer seems remarkably undisturbed by as well as vividly alert to them. We can see this alertness to some extent in his mixing of styles, as Muscatine long ago pointed out, in his discussion of the bourgeois and courtly elements in Chaucer's style. The Duke of Athens, speaking of the excesses of young lovers (Knight's Tale, I. 1806–14), talks like a middle-aged bourgeois husband, while the students of the next two tales have all the pretensions if not the skills of courtly lovers. We can see it too in the subtle way Chaucer uses dress and array as a site of social conflict and change.

Alysoun, in the Miller's Tale, dressed to kill, anticipates the vulgarization of glamorous high fashion, while the Reeve, in his 'long surcote of pers' (I. 617), apes the grand sobriety of dress of men much his traditional superior in rank. In another context, we can see how the Knight of the General Prologue has in some measure exchanged clothes with the Monk, laying claim, in his rust-stained tunic of 'fustian' (I. 75), to the humility that the Monk, in his fur-trimmed gown and 'bootes souple' (I. 203), has so ostentatiously laid aside.

One should recognize, however, the partial and tactical nature of these transgressions. The closing lines of the description of Alysoun make it clear that there are some traditional distinctions of social class that remain very sharp indeed:

> She was a prymerole, a piggesnye,
> For any lord to leggen in his bedde,
> Or yet for any good yeman to wedde.
> (Miller's Tale, I. 3268–70)

The old world of the *pastourelle*, evoked again at the beginning of the Wife of Bath's Tale, in the scene of casual upper-class rape, is clearly alive and strong.

The Franklin's Tale is one of the tales where Chaucer explores some of the consequences of social change and mobility. The Franklin himself is at an important bridging-point in the new society, where land, wealth and power have achieved or almost achieved the transition to 'gentle' status. His precise social status is ambiguous, partly because Chaucer has made him so unrepresentative of the historical 'class' of franklins, who would not have expected to rise to the rank of sheriff or MP for their county. His sensitivity on the question of *gentillesse* suggests nevertheless that he has those 'pretensions of the upwardly mobile' that were attracting comment in his day.[26] He shows a certain self-consciousness about his position, and his remarks about the Squire and his own son reveal both the monetary calculations he is accustomed to make as well as the desire to be seen to be above making such calculations in the interests of the higher *gentillesse*:

> I have a sone, and by the Trinitee,
> I hadde levere than twenty pound worth lond,
> Though it right now were fallen in myn hond,
> He were a man of swich discrecioun

As that ye been! Fy on possessioun,
But if a man be vertuous withal! (V. 682–7)

The Host is, we may think, unnecessarily short with him, but the
Host generally has the roughness towards those he sees as his
equals (after all, Herry Bailly was a Member of Parliament too)
that goes with genuine obsequiousness to rank, as evidenced in
his words to the Knight, the Squire and the Prioress.

In his tale, the Franklin pursues the question of *gentillesse*, suggesting that it is not restricted to one class only, though leaving
any conclusion to that effect to be drawn by the reader ('Which
was the mooste fre, as thynketh yow?' (V. 1622)). The negotiation
of the marriage relationship is also itself made more delicate by
the insistence on the distinction between the rank of Arviragus,
who is a mere knight, and that of Dorigen, who is of 'so heigh
kynrede' (V. 735) as to be far above him. The concept of mutual
respect that is built into their marriage has in this way a real point
in relation to class mobility, and it is spoken of with unexpected
earnestness (V. 761–90). The tale might be said to be a new way
of thinking about social relationships, in which conflict and
impasse can be resolved by mutual forbearance, not just between
men and women, but between social classes.

Certainly, its mood of harmonious reconciliation – 'On every
wrong a man may nat be wreken' (V. 784) – is markedly different
from that other spirit of legalized and vindictive malice that motiv-
ates the Reeve (I. 3913–20), and the students in his tale
(I. 4179–82), or the Friar and the Summoner, and the Manciple
and the Cook, in their spiteful outbreaks of professional hostility.
There is more quarrelling in *The Canterbury Tales*, more shuffling
away of nastiness in superficial reconciliations, as also at the end
of the Pardoner's Tale, than fits well with the image of Chaucer as
a the genial observer of the social scene or even as the sophisticated
promoter of 'a commonwealth of style'.*

Chaucer's handling of social conflict and relationship may be

---

* This is Strohm's term (*Social Chaucer*, ch. 6) and conveys something of the
generosity with which he views Chaucer's social and political self-positioning. In
this he has much in common with Anne Middleton (see ch. 3, n. 6), who sees
Chaucer as involved in the establishment of a new and responsible role for the
poet as a 'public' commentator on matters of public concern. In the present
study, I have to see Chaucer as much more alienated from his society than this,
much more pessimistic, much less 'responsible'.

none the less observant for that. If the gentleness of the Franklin's
Tale may be viewed as self-consciously nostalgic – it is one of the
lays told by 'thise olde gentil Britouns in hir dayes' (V. 709) –
then there is likewise given to Dorigen's promise an old-fashioned
sanctity: 'Trouthe is the hyeste thyng that man may kepe'
(V. 1479). Griselda's strict observance of her marriage-promises
to Walter is similarly located in a distant past: 'It were ful hard
to fynde now-a-dayes / In al a toun Grisildis thre or two' (Clerk's
Tale, IV. 1164–5). But there is much in *The Canterbury Tales* that
speaks of that contemporary movement in society, deriving from
increased literacy as well as from the increased fluidity of social
structures, that replaces oaths and promises with negotiated contracts and is suspicious of what cannot be assigned a value.
Chaucer, in *Lak of Stedfastnesse*, speaks regretfully of a time long
ago when 'mannes word was obligacioun' (2), but in the world
that he describes a man's word was subjected to a much more
sceptical scrutiny. The unwritten allegiances of feudal society were
being written as indentures, in this new age of 'bastard feudalism',
and the fixed hierarchies of the past, based on land-tenure and
service, were giving way to 'a complex network of marketable
privileges and duties'.[27]

In law, too, the increasing use of litigation and the increasing
sophistication of legal procedure had also had the effect of 'weakening and straining the bonds of affection existing in feudal lordship
and kindred loyalties'. The law, which had once functioned and
been thought of as a last resort when all means of reconciling
disputes had failed, was now becoming a first resort. *Pactum legem
vincit et amor iudicium* ('Agreement prevails over law and love over
judgment') still meant something in the twelfth century, and records show disputes settled by *amor* (out of court, as at 'love-days')
rather than by *lex*, but by Chaucer's time love-days had a bad
name (General Prologue, I. 258) and *Amor vincit omnia*, as inscribed
in the Prioress's brooch, is no more than an invitation to frivolous
thoughts.[28]

In *The Canterbury Tales* generally, vows and promises are made
to be broken, once the exchange rate has changed. 'Sworn brotherhood', one of the oldest and closest of personal ties, is tossed aside
by Palamon and Arcite (with some ironical reminders from the
narrator, I. 1652)), and entered into by the summoner and 'yeoman' of the Friar's Tale with the simple intention of mutual profit
(III. 1527–30). In the Shipman's Tale, what seems to be a form
of sworn brotherhood entered into by the merchant and Daun

John (VII. 40–2) is quickly disclaimed by the monk when he sees that doing so may be to his advantage. The claim of 'cosynage', he says, was solely for the purpose of 'cozenage' and getting to know his friend's wife better. The institution of lay confraternity (Chaucer's wife Philippa entered one at Lincoln, we recall) is sourly viewed in the Summoner's Tale as an exchange of money for dubious spiritual benefits (III. 2124–30). The Cook's delight in the 'argument of herbergage' which he finds in the Reeve's Tale (I. 4329) is in part his enjoyment of a practical and cynical piece of wisdom, relevant to both the Miller's Tale and the Reeve's Tale, 'Ne bryng nat every man into thyn hous' (I. 4331), that seems to cock a snook at the old shibboleth of a sacred contract between host and guest. Guests have become lodgers in this new world.

The General Prologue is Chaucer's most explicit account of his society. It is not comprehensive, as has often been remarked, and the omissions are interesting. There is no one of higher rank than the Knight, and the absence of the aristocracy, though naturalistically plausible, serves as a reminder of the comparative absence of that class from *The Canterbury Tales* as a whole. There are no doubt good practical reasons for this, in terms of Chaucer's own delicate social position, but something more is needed to explain the comparable absence of admired authority-figures or heroes, whether kings, knights or fathers. The Knight is the person of rank on the pilgrimage, but his interventions (to reconcile the Pardoner and the Host, and to silence the Monk) are comically ludic representations of authority, and the one occasion when his authority might have been traditionally employed (in restraining the Miller) is conspicuously denied it. For the rest, the Host makes whatever decisions are to be made, a not too serious suggestion of the role of the new bourgeoisie. Elsewhere there are very few authority-figures and none who are granted ungrudging respect (except Theseus, and some deny it even to him). There is none of the traditional respect for age, and Chaucer's fathers, such as those in the Man of Law's Tale and the Physician's Tale, have a very odd idea of their parental responsibilities. All this could be given a Freudian reading, very easily, but the significant conclusion to be drawn has to do with Chaucer's scepticism concerning the nature and role of authority, which is an essential part of his position as a writer. Women, as we shall see, frequently occupy the positions vacated by powerful men.[29]

The General Prologue gives even less representation to the lower classes of society, again partly for good practical and naturalistic reasons. The Plowman is the only representative of the rural peasantry, and he is presented as a spiritual rather than a social reality; there is a similarly deodorized quality to the peasant widows of the Friar's Tale and the Nun's Priest's Tale. Even the Plowman could be seen as belonging to the upper ranks of the peasantry, since he was to some extent a specialized worker, one who hired himself and his plough to the poorer peasants, and therefore generally more prosperous. The Miller and the Reeve, though 'cherles', belong to this same class of better-off and even socially aspiring peasants. There are no representatives in Chaucer of the 'real' peasantry or of the urban underclass that figures so prominently in Langland, though there are some, such as the Summoner and the Pardoner, who might nevertheless be regarded as the scum of the earth.

Into the narrow social spectrum that is left, Chaucer has squeezed, so it appears, all England, though the sense of comprehensiveness is illusory. The model that he uses is estates satire, which provides him with the principal coordinates for his discussion of society, namely work and money, though he turns the model inside-out in consistently denying its claim to morally evaluative power. His pilgrims have all the 'faults' of the traditional victims of estates satire, but they are not openly castigated for them; the faults seem to be part of the pattern of behaviour appropriate to their professions and to their relation to the money economy. Rank is not disregarded (the ordering of the groups of pilgrims is generally hierarchical), and there are idealized representations of each of the three estates, in the portraits of the Knight, Parson and Plowman, but what Chaucer mostly gives us is a society in which all relationships have become negotiable and in which money can buy anything, including health, husbands and salvation.

Chaucer views this world, of exchanges and equivalences, the London that he knew, with a remarkable acuteness and an equally remarkable lack of outrage. His description of commercial practice and his use of commercial metaphor are not necessarily loaded with moral implication, and the construction of a naive 'Chaucer the pilgrim' who always misses the point of what he describes is a perhaps intrusive technique for reinstalling traditional moral commentary. On the contrary, Chaucer seems hardly to raise an eyebrow at economic practices which still incurred widespread ecclesiastical censure and public condemnation. 'Real' production and consumption were the arbiters of economic effort in this traditional view, and the making of profits through moneylending, currency speculation or even large-scale wholesale and retail trading was still frowned upon. Buying cheap to sell dear, or 'forestalling' – a practice so embedded in capitalist economies that it seems 'natural' to us – is something that Langland still fulminates against in *Piers Plowman* (C. III. 82, IV. 59).[30]

The uninflected mode of representation is characteristic not only of the General Prologue but of some of the tales. In the Canon's Yeoman's Tale there is a striking difference between the futile idealism of the attempt to produce gold in *Prima Pars* and the non-productive but completely successful cheating of *Pars Secunda*. In the first part, nothing works; in the second part, everything works beautifully. It has been argued that Chaucer is representing here, somewhat ridiculously, and in a satirically and obliquely personalized manner that we have come to recognize as characteristic, the difference between productive and emergent non-productive capitalism.[31]

One of the reasons for obliqueness might be that the ruling merchant oligarchy of London, with which Chaucer had close connections, belonged to the emergent group, as did Chaucer's Merchant and the merchant of the Shipman's Tale, while the faction headed by John of Northampton, often spoken of as representing the non-victualling guilds, might be said to represent the lower-ranking trading artisans engaged in production. Chaucer says very little about this London group. Even among his out-of-town characters, the most vivid, the Reeve, is the one who is most fully engaged in non-productive financial manipulation and malpractice.

Donaldson, who invented 'Chaucer the Pilgrim', has this summary of the Shipman's Tale:

> The story demonstrates that the vision of life as a purely mercantile arrangement sterilizes those who hold it so that all human values disappear, including that of human awareness. Within the tale neither the cheating nor the cheated perceive any significance in their actions beyond the immediate financial gain or loss that is incurred, and since there is no real financial loss, the events cause hardly a ripple on the surface of their lives. Sensitivity to other values besides cash has been submitted to appraisal and, having been found nonconvertible, has been thrown away.[32]

This is memorably said, but the tale itself does little to require such a reading. Indeed, the merchant, and the capitalist values for which he stands, are given an unprecedentedly measured and sympathetic treatment, as he explains to his wife and later to the monk the nature of the business he is in. He is friendly without being obsequious, generous without being foolishly indulgent, careful without being mean. The only thing he has which a traditional 'hero' might not have had is a care in the construction of his self-image which would have been unnecessary to the already constructed hero of the past. His greatest concern, in all the tale, is that he might have given Daun John the impression that he had arranged to meet him in Paris in order to ask him for the return of the money (VII. 338, 383–94). There is some recognition here, on Chaucer's part, of the greater role 'self-fashioning' must play in the more open world of negotiated settlements and arrangements, and of the way in which some of this self-fashioning will involve the appropriation to mercantilism of the ideals of courtly society: so when the merchant speaks of the 'name' that those who 'creaunce' must strive to preserve (VII. 289), there is an echo of that other kind of 'name' that Arviragus for instance was concerned about (Franklin's Tale, V. 751).

Chaucer is not only responsive to the new mercantilism: he is also unusually alert to the increasing participation of women in the economy, a participation which was partly due to post-Black Death labour shortages, and his portrayal of the Wife of Bath as an independent and successful businesswoman is not the grotesque fantasy it has sometimes been imagined to be. Women could be members of trade guilds, and a married woman could have the status of a *femme sole*, that is, one who would be allowed to trade as if she were single and to make contracts in her own name. Such women were particularly active in the cloth industry.[33]

With all this awareness of changing social and economic realities, Chaucer's refusal of social and moral commitment remains profound. This, as I have suggested, can be seen as a considerable achievement, in the face of a medieval orthodoxy that required either assent or jest ('ernest' or 'game') but could not tolerate the two together. It is also, in a way, a human weakness, and Chaucer's positioning of himself in relation to the political and social matter of his writing, a positioning which we might characterize as one of habitual irony, is defensive and self-protective as well as innovative and daring. The London of Chaucer's day, in which and of which he writes, was a turbulent and dangerous place, in which commitment could lead to real consequences, as with Usk. Chaucer was not so disposed, and his poetry, though vivid in its picture of a world of fraudulent and other new kinds of exchange, leaves some gaps. There is nothing of the agrarian discontents that fuelled the Peasants' Revolt, of which he may be presumed to have known little, but likewise nothing of the political infighting that characterized the London that he knew extremely well. There are, among the pilgrims of the General Prologue, none of the artisan class and journeymen who constituted such a significantly volatile part of the city's population, and only a brief glimpse of that part of society elsewhere in the tales, in the Cook's Tale. Even the portrait of the Guildsmen is of a group of members of those guilds who were uninvolved in the major power struggles of the London merchant oligarchy, reference to whom might have been construed as a form of alignment or criticism. The Guildsmen's ambitions to be aldermen are sufficiently ridiculous, given the insignificance of the guilds they belong to, and they are therefore safe to refer to. These ambitions are also principally attributed to the aspirations of their wives. In this way, characteristically, Chaucer shifts the politics of power to the arena of domestic satire.[34]

Marriage

Marriage figures large in *The Canterbury Tales*, both as a social reality and as a way of talking about the distribution of power in social relationships. It appears as a significant part of the subject-matter in at least fifteen of the twenty-four tales, and it is prominent as a theme in its own right in five or six. Kittredge was right, in a famous article (see n. 7), to recognize its importance as a theme in *The Canterbury Tales*, though his attempts to find in the so-called 'Marriage Group' (Fragments III–V, principally the Wife of Bath's Prologue and Tale, Clerk's Tale, Merchant's Tale and Franklin's Tale) the statement, development and solution of a problem concerning woman's sovereignty in marriage was both overrestrictive and oversanguine. The importance of the Wife of Bath in stimulating questions about marriage and power is nevertheless not to be underestimated, and has already been mentioned as a vigorous part of the life of *The Canterbury Tales* in the 1390s.

Sometimes marriage is employed in primarily religious tales as a traditional symbol of divinely sanctioned relationships. As a divinely sanctioned relationship in itself, and as a figure of the marriage between Christ and Holy Church, it is carefully analysed in the Parson's Tale (X. 915–43), with particular attention to the regulation of sexual conduct within marriage. The simplest and most desirable form of regulation was of course total sexual abstinence, and this is what makes the marriage of Cecilia and Valerian in the Second Nun's Tale such a perfect figure for the relationship of Christ and the church as well as for spiritual procreation, the multiplying of the faithful through preaching and martyrdom. In *Melibee* the traditional functioning of marriage and of the role of man and woman in marriage as an image of the hierarchical relationship of God and man, of the higher and lower faculties, is interestingly reversed in the marital relationship of Melibee and Prudence. Melibee not only accedes to his wife's advice but acknowledges formally her right to give it and to govern his conduct, for which she argues in measured and reasonable terms (VII. 1064–110). The reversal, however, is traditional and only apparent. Prudence points out that the acceptance of her advice by her husband is not a relinquishing of 'maistrie' on his part (VII. 1081–3) but a demonstration of superior lordship (like Theseus's acquiescence in the ladies' pleas for mercy in the Knight's Tale, (I. 1760–81)), and in any case her allegorical name and role, like that of similar personifications in Prudentius and Alain of Lille, make her indivisibly part of the nature of the protagonist, his 'resoun' as opposed to his 'ire' (VII. 1765–6).

These are conventional tales, and they represent marriage in a fairly conventional way. The distance travelled to the Man of Law's Tale and the Clerk's Tale, two religious tales in which marriage likewise plays a significant part, is immense. Constance's marriages, like Cecilia's, are both essentially acts of conversion, the cause in the case of the Sultan (II. 240), the result in the case of King Alla (II. 686–91), and her whole life is one of preaching, conversion and martyrdom. But it is a life that lacks the simplicity of Cecilia's, since Constance must submit to the sexual attentions of at least her second husband:

> They goon to bedde, as it was skile and right;
> For thogh that wyves be ful hooly thynges,
> They moste take in pacience at nyght
> Swiche manere necessaries as been plesynges

To folk that han ywedded hem with rynges,
And leye a lite hir hoolynesse aside,
As for the tyme – it may no bet bitide.
(II. 708–14)

The euphemisms and circumlocutions here are uncomfortable and embarrassing, and the impression they create, of the distasteful ordeal by sex through which Constance must fulfil her earthly destiny, is not to be explained away in terms of the narrator's prurience. Jarring effects in Chaucer's narratives are too often smoothed out in this way. Like Emelye in the Knight's Tale, who insists on her desire to remain single, 'And noght to ben a wyf and be with childe' (I. 2310), Constance gets married because she has to. The narrative moves without further ceremony to the getting and bearing of a child (II. 715, 722).

If marriage is for Cecilia a danger that can be thwarted, and for Emelye and Constance an ordeal that must be borne, it is for Griselda a martyrdom. Petrarch had attempted to allegorize the marriage as an exemplum of the relationship between God and his creatures, and Chaucer pays faithful lip-service to the Latin writer's anaesthetic interpretation of the story. But even as he does so (IV. 1142–8), he reinstates the awful humanness of Griselda and her experience:

> For sith a womman was so pacient
> Unto a mortal man, wel moore us oghte
> Receyven al in gree that God us sent.
> (IV. 1149–51)

Marriage is not, in the Clerk's Tale, a convenient analogy for the comfortable relationship of a loving God and a grateful subject; it is a literally and uniquely accurate way of representing truthfully the exercise of absolute power over a powerless subject. The medieval institution of marriage does not have to be much strained to provide an apt context for Walter's tyranny, especially when its hegemonies are reinforced by the great disparity of rank between the marquis and his bride and by her own special marriage vows (IV. 351–64).

Chaucer, furthermore, makes a point of insisting on the human reality of the situation, giving to Griselda some bitter reflections on her experience of motherhood (IV. 650–1) and an outburst of sad regret when she remembers the past:

O goode God! How gentil and how kynde
Ye semed by youre speche and youre visage
The day that maked was oure mariage!
(IV. 852–4)

How touchingly her reference to 'the day that maked was oure mariage' echoes Walter's use of the same words (IV. 497) when he reminded her of the same day and her promise of obedience. Behind Griselda's quizzical and slightly sardonic awareness of the realities of her situation there is a voluntariness of submission which is not powerless, but this does little to mitigate the horror of her experience of wedlock.

Elsewhere, marriage is a prison (truly, wedlock), much as it was described in *The Envoy to Bukton*. The gibes against marriage are familiar and, coming as they do from the celibate fraternity, predictable, but Chaucer gives them a memorable vividness in his stories. The husbands of the Miller's Tale and the Manciple's Tale think they have their wives tamed and in cages. Old John the carpenter has a newly wed 18-year-old wife: 'Jalous he was, and heeld hire narwe in cage' (I. 3224). Phoebus in the Manciple's Tale tries to take the same precautions against being made a cuckold: 'Jalous he was, and wolde have kept hire fayn' (IX. 144). The narrative warns, however, that keeping wives away from sexual contact with others is like keeping a bird in a cage (IX. 163–74): even if the cage is made of gold, the bird will still want to get out. In fact it is John and Phoebus who are in prison, in thrall to their obsessive uxoriousness, and it is their wives who are free and make free with themselves.

The prison of marriage is of course a stock property of the fabliaux: there could be no fun in the intrigue, which nearly always involves the seduction of a not too unwilling wife, if there were no restraints to be overcome. In that sense, marriage performs a structural function, but Chaucer's way with narrative is always to load it, or overload it, with representational value and significance, and these hilarious comic tales are full of cruelly revealing marital moments.

One of the oddities of Chaucer's fabliaux, in fact, properly commended as they are for their gusto and carnivalesque spirit, is the reductive contempt that they display not only for marriage, which is usual, but for the sexual urges which drive the coupling participants. The Reeve's Tale is the most obvious example. The story has been deliberately emptied of that movement of affection, that tingling of sexual desire, that is present in the closest analogue, the French story of 'Le meunier et les ii clers'.[35] There, one of the students conceives a pressing attachment to the miller's daughter while they eat together at dinner, and arranges to come to her at night. The other, left without solace in his lonely bed, observes the miller's wife tripping out to the privy, all naked, and it is this sight that prompts him to move the cradle. In the Reeve's Tale, by contrast, there is no movement either of affection or of lust but only the desire for revenge and 'esement' (I. 4186) and not to be thought 'a daf, a cokenay' (I. 4208). The coupling is that of animals. Cruelly, the only touch of affection comes from the daughter Malyne, who 'almoost . . . gan to wepe' (I. 4248). But only 'almoost', one notices: there is a meanness even here. A similar perfunctoriness attends the description of the climactic sexual act in the Miller's Tale and in the Shipman's Tale, with the result that those who look in Chaucer for the titillation that Boccaccio and the French fabliaux supply are mostly disappointed.

The Merchant's Tale is so salacious that it may seem an exception, but the bitterness of its portrayal of marriage and sexuality is so profound that January's own excitement communicates itself only as ridiculous, while the arboreal coming together of May and Damyan is described with a prurience so gross (IV. 2348–53) that it is impossible to share it. The systematically and sardonically destructive account of marriage in the Merchant's Tale is what Chaucer has added to the old pear-tree story, and it is specifically the laying bare, the pathology, of a man's view of marriage, and not just an old man's either. The sarcastically exposed inanities of the opening encomium on marriage, the blind self-delusion of January as he declares his opinions on marriage, his conviction even at the end that he can exchange his wealth for his wife's sexual favours, all have to do with that version of control and power that marriage is supposed to give to men:

> Al that hire housbonde lust, hire liketh weel;
> She seith nat ones 'nay', whan he seith 'ye'.
> 'Do this', seith he; 'Al redy, sire', seith she.
>
> (IV. 1344–6)

May is the product of this system, the image that is produced in its mirror (IV. 1582), and she turns out of course to be everything that men do *not* want: 'as stille as stoon' when she is brought to bed (IV. 1818), cold in her appraisal of January's performance

(IV. 1854) as in her reception of his later attentions (IV. 1961), coldly lustful towards Damyan ('She taketh hym by the hand and harde hym twiste . . . ' (IV. 2005)), and coldly unfaithful even as she protests her fidelity:

> And with that word she saugh wher Damyan
> Sat in the bussh, and coughen she bigan,
> And with her fynger signes made she.　　　　　　(IV. 2207–9)

The description of the Christian marriage ceremony drips with contempt for the priestly rituals that make everything that a man wants so conveniently, swiftly and licitly available:

> Forth comth the preest, with stole aboute his nekke,
> And bad hire be lyk Sarra and Rebekke
> In wysdom and in trouthe of mariage;
> And seyde his orisons, as is usage,
> And croucheth hem, and bad God sholde hem blesse,
> And made al siker ynogh with hoolynesse.
> 　　　　　　　　　　　　　　　(IV. 1703–8)

Blaming all this on the narrator, even though it is what Chaucer tempts us to do, as a persuasively easy way out, will not, in the end, do.

Some refuge from this unblinkingly hostile analysis of marriage might be found, though not immediately apparent, in the Wife of Bath's Prologue and Tale. At first it might seem that what we are to get is the old arguments against women, and particularly against getting married to them, reduced to risibility by being placed in the mouth of a woman. After all, it is about the 'wo that is in mariage' (III. 3) that she proposes to speak, and the sorrow that she refers to, it is clear, is what she causes her husbands, not what she suffers herself. Yet her exposition of the case for marriage (as against virginity) is so challenging and energetic, her rhetoric so wickedly persuasive, her down-to-earth practicality so obviously 'right', in a way, that we are drawn to think of her Prologue as something more than a *tour de force* of paradoxically recycled antifeminist commonplaces.

It begins to seem, indeed, that she speaks from a woman's experience and with a woman's voice. The torment to which she subjects her first three husbands, and the purgatory that she makes of the earthly life of the fourth (III. 489), are no more than the visiting upon them of the powers she has learnt and wrested from men. She shows what men, and antifeminism in particular, have done to women. David Aers puts it in this way:

> While Chaucer presents her rebellion as real, he simultaneously discloses the complexities involved in opposing dominant social and ideological forms. He dramatizes the affirmation of the established culture in her negation of it, creating an aesthetic representation of the way subordinate groups or individuals may so internalize the assumptions and practices of their oppressors that not only their daily strategies of survival but their very acts of rebellion may perpetuate the outlook against which they rebel.[36]

This is cogently put; yet we might be tempted to resist the Foucauldian model of subversion and containment that is suggested here. We might point to some unexpected ruptures in the familiar pattern; to the satisfactions that the Wife of Bath offers to her old husbands, not only in the enjoyment of her person but, perhaps more important, in the flattering suggestion she makes to them that she is jealous of their attentions to other women (393–9). We might point to the flood of nostalgic reminiscence of past joys which seems at times genuinely to take her by surprise (469–80, 585–6); to the half-suppressed consciousness of a morally regulated 'normal' world to which she would wish to belong ('Allas, allas! That evere love was synne!' (614)) and which she elsewhere professes to despise ('I ne loved nevere by no discrecioun' (622)); to the confession of weakness she makes in acknowledging that she took her fifth husband 'for love, and no richesse' (526).

The stage seems set for the emergence of a new woman, one who seeks power only in order to love truly, from a position of independence, one who is not afraid to be weak. Unfortunately, the stage collapses, or at least Chaucer allows it to deconstruct. The marital harmony that she achieves at the end of the Prologue is not the harmony of reciprocal trust and mutual self-surrender: though she is 'kynde' (823) and 'trewe' (825) to her newly cowed husband, the kindness and truth is exclusively on her own terms, not part of some mutually agreed new dispensation.*

---

* To the question, why is he cowed? the answer is not that he is physically overcome, but that he is made to recognize the sovereignty of his wife's nature. Her will to be sovereign is more powerful than his, and the exercise of it controls

Chaucer's subtle changes in the traditional story of transformation that the wife proceeds to tell seem to make renewed gestures
towards an ideal of marital harmony. Men's exercise of power
over women is represented as rape; they have to be educated to
understand that this is not what women want and not really what
men want either. In order that he may learn this lesson, the knight
is reduced to physical powerlessness, his life in the hands of women,
and then instructed in the ideals of his own profession by his
bride. He undergoes a course of education which enables him to
understand what is good for him. He is a reformed man. Yet,
stubbornly, as the tale has it, it is *his* transformation that makes
possible *her* transformation. The suggestion must be that, though
the old hag (who is also the Wife of Bath) speaks the language of
sovereignty, what she really seeks is the recognition by the man
of the individuality, the inward reality of her existence as a person,
separated from the trappings of youth, beauty, breeding and riches
which act as the conventional communication of her desirability
as a woman. When that recognition has been made – and it seems
to be a mere token, a formal, quasi-legal statement (III. 1236–8),
that is required – then the fullness of her own love is released and
she is 'transformed'.

The marriage ideal is thus one of trust, the mutual surrender
of power which we find called 'pacience' in the Franklin's Tale
(V. 773). The tentative hints which could be discerned at the end
of the Wife of Bath's Prologue of a more generous notion of
marriage relationships than that of unilateral exercise of power are
in the Wife of Bath's Tale advanced more confidently, perhaps
because story-telling itself encourages a kind of generosity of the
imagination. It is not, however, Chaucer's way to allow such
satisfactions to remain unalloyed, and the happy ending is put in
jeopardy by the Wife's own concluding remarks, which are a
return to the comically monstrous aggressiveness which is her
performative role as a woman.

One might look to the Franklin's Tale for the resolution of these
ambiguities, and indeed a case can be made that the marriage
relationship of Arviragus and Dorigen is set before us as an ideal.
Arviragus swears to take upon himself no 'maistrie' (V. 747),

---

him in ways that he cannot emulate. As he bends over her, concerned that he
may really have hurt her, there is a momentary relaxation of the will to dominate,
and his wife seizes upon it. Jankyn has no hope after this.

Dorigen promises to be his 'humble trewe wyf' (758), and Chaucer adds a long paragraph of reflection on the necessity of such generous relinquishing of power to successful human relationships. The terms he uses are 'pacience' (773) and 'suffrance' (788), not because he wishes to enforce the traditional moral connotations of such words, but because it was difficult to find a vocabulary to talk about a truly loving mutuality of human relationship that was not moral: perhaps the language of emotional maturity is inevitably moral. At any rate, we can see that he is groping towards a language that will express the notion of a willing forbearance, a voluntary acceptance of constraint upon or diminution of the demands of the self. 'Pacience' and 'suffrance' are his way of talking about mutual tolerance, a positive and willing embrace of the will of another as a means to the strengthening of the bond of love.[37]

Generous and attractive as it is, the ideal is deeply compromised in being transferred from discussion of *amicitia* or spiritual friendship to the discussion of marriage. Marriage is a social institution, and power is vested in it and inseparable from it. Arviragus's own lack of power to relinquish his power as a husband and a lord is eloquently spoken in the subterfuge to which he must resort. He will obey his wife in all things, as a lover should his lady, 'Save that the name of soveraynetee, / That wolde he have for shame of his degree' (V. 751–2). As the story unfolds, it becomes clear that the husband's power is merely suspended, not yielded, and that the relationship of a husband and wife cannot be isolated from the society which sanctions it and supplies its terms of reference. Arviragus has his reasons for making Dorigen keep her promise to Aurelius, but they are the reasons appropriate to a male society dominated by notions of honour and shame. Dorigen is not expected to understand them, only to do what she is told. Arviragus and Dorigen live happily ever after, we are told, rather perfunctorily ('Of thise two folk ye gete of me namoore' (1556)), but things are not the same, and the embarrassments of the story's denouement are only temporarily forgotten in the amiable courtesies of the tale's ending. The three official competitors in this contest of *gentillesse* are, it should be observed, men only.

An odd conclusion might be drawn concerning Chaucer's representation of marriage in *The Canterbury Tales*. Just as the most moving evocation of true love in the *Tales* is that of the falcon for the faithless tercelet in the Squire's Tale, so the fullest, most humanly realized, and on the whole happiest picture of marriage is that of Chauntecleer and Pertelote in the Nun's Priest's Tale.

It all speaks less of Chaucer's affection for birds (which, like Swift's for horses, was probably restrained) than of his disaffection for human beings.

Religion

Chaucer has been spoken of, in these pages, on the evidence of writings such as the *ABC* and the Life of St Cecilia, as a man of somewhat more than formal piety. This estimate, uninformative as it is, can be considerably added to and elaborated upon in respect of *The Canterbury Tales*.

There is, in the first place, an extraordinarily large quantity of reference in the *Tales* to religion and religious practice. Apart from the half-dozen or so tales that have as their ostensible motive the demonstration and promotion of the Christian faith, there are a large number of others which have officers of the church as their tellers or principal characters, or which are otherwise full of religious allusion. Furthermore, six of the longest and most detailed portraits in the General Prologue are devoted to ecclesiastics (Prioress, Monk, Friar, Parson, Summoner, Pardoner), in the proportion of five bad (one not so bad) to one good, so that the principal memory of reading the General Prologue is of the detailed and minute revelation of ecclesiastical malpractice. This is a mark of the suitability of such malpractice to satirical observation, and not necessarily an indication that Chaucer had an opinion of the church lower than that of most of his contemporaries (this would still make it pretty low), but it does serve also as a measure of the extent to which fourteenth-century life was saturated in the influence of the church, its practices, regulations, writings and daily and seasonal rhythms.

There is hardly a tale, in fact, in which these influences are absent. Chaucer takes us deep into the practice of religion among the common people, and the parasitic life, for the most part, of its practitioners upon them. To be the victims of clerical rogues often seems to be the principal role of the common people in Chaucer's poetry. In the Pardoner's Prologue it is their desire for prosperity, domestic comfort and spiritual security that makes them ready to be gulled by his clever talk. They are hopelessly outclassed. In the Friar's Tale the old widow's conversation with the summoner has the ring of absolute authenticity: this is how these tricksters worked, and the widow is fortunate that there is another devil there, with other plans for her kitchen pan (III. 1635). The following tale, the Summoner's Tale, immerses us in the minute particulars of the begging and preaching practice of the friars, reminding us of the range of their powers and the persuasiveness of their skills. Again, the victim displays, on this occasion, an admirable unwillingness to be tricked. Like the other tales told by ecclesiastics, including the Nun's Priest's Tale, the Summoner's Tale is packed with religious and biblical allusion, including the grotesque parody of the Pentecostal visitation in the final plans for the divided fart.

Even in tales that seem to have nothing to do with religion, that are even irreligious, the church is everywhere, like the ubiquitous friars at the beginning of the Wife of Bath's Tale, 'As thikke as motes in the sonne-beem' (III. 868). The Wife is outrageous, but her discourse is entirely framed in terms of her questioning and qualification of the views of the church, just as her life is organized according to its observances and festivals:

> Therfore I made my visitaciouns
> To vigilies and to processiouns,
> To prechyng eek, and to thise pilgrimages,
> To pleyes of myracles, and to mariages.   (III. 555–8)

January, in the Merchant's Tale, is concerned above all to be on the right side of the church and its strictures concerning marriage, and the full tide of his lust cannot be loosed until he has assured himself that there can be no sin in his sexual acts with his wife, whatever he does (IV. 1838), now that he has a proper church marriage. Much of the delight of the Shipman's Tale would be lost if the merchant's friend were not a monk, able to take 'confession' from the merchant's wife and proffer his 'portehors' so daintily for her to swear upon (VII. 135). One of the funniest moments of the Reeve's Tale is the joke about the parson's care that his (illegitimate) daughter should make a good marriage: 'For hooly chirches good moot been despended / On hooly chirches blood, that is descended' (I.3983–4). The Miller's Tale, meanwhile, is more loaded with allusions to church activities than any other of the comic tales, sometimes at the most affecting moments:

> And thus lith Alison and Nicholas,
> In bisynesse of myrthe and of solas,

Til that the belle of laudes gan to rynge,
And freres in the chauncel gonne synge.   (I. 3653–6)

The whole organization of the narrative is in the interstices of a
world of ecclesiastical needs and routines – friars getting up to
sing lauds, John the carpenter working out at Osney Abbey,
Absolon censing the parish ladies, or playing Herod 'upon a
scaffold hye' (I. 3384).

The ubiquity of the Christian faith and its practices in these
tales is not a sign that they are to be interpreted allegorically as
witnesses to the higher law of charity.[38] There would otherwise
be no tales 'that sownen into synne' for Chaucer to retract at the
end of *The Canterbury Tales* (X. 1086). But religion is nevertheless
important: the fun and audacity of these tales, the delighted
outrage of the reader, would be the less if we *really* thought that
religion were as irrelevant to the important business of life as the
characters seem to think it is.

As for the two serious 'romances', the Knight's Tale and the
Franklin's Tale, it is significant that they are both deliberately set
in pre-Christian or pagan times, as if Chaucer, in his confrontation
with questions of life, *trouthe* and destiny, felt an obligation to resist
the importunacy of the message of Christian consolation. Our
consciousness, nevertheless, of what is absent, of the immanence
of the Christian view of man and the world as we read of men
and worlds supposedly benighted, is a very present part of our
experience of these poems.

There is, however, a group of religious tales which do not imply
or allude to the Christian faith but are predicated explicitly upon
it, and specifically upon the assumption that the significance of
human life is in the transcending of its secular limitation through
that faith. The Second Nun's Tale is the purest example of the
form, but the Man of Law's Tale and the Prioress's Tale rest
equally upon the same assumption of transcendence, as does the
Clerk's Tale implicitly through its allegorical sense. The 'narrative
of faith', as this type of story might be called, implies as a necessity
the existence of another world which gives meaning to, or, better,
fulfils the meaning of, the struggles and sufferings of this world.
The Parson's Tale is the exposition of the framework of doctrine
within which the narrative of faith exists. The Monk's Tale, if it
can be said successfully to demonstrate anything, demonstrates
the meaninglessness of life when that narrative of faith is absent
or denied. The Physician's Tale is a tale which has been unsuccess-

fully abstracted from its history: deprived of its political significance in the story of the Roman state, it is surrounded with the
narrative and stylistic observances of a religious tale but not given
any alternative or allegorical point. Virginia has all the attributes
of a Christian virgin-martyr except a good reason, in Christian
faith, for dying.[39]

There is a great range of religious writing here, and the Prologue
to the Prioress's Tale alone would be sufficient to demonstrate
Chaucer's command of the more exalted strain of affective devotion. Worked up, like lines 36–56 of the Prologue to the Second
Nun's Tale, from the address to the Virgin which Dante gives to
St Bernard in Canto 33 of the *Paradiso*, it is in a semi-liturgical
high style full of echoes of the divine office. It nevertheless conveys
a deeply personalized sense of its speaker, directed by the speaker's
humble consciousness of presumption in telling a tale in praise of
the Virgin and by her desire to identify herself with the innocence
and sweetness of childish piety. It is a woman speaking of a
woman, and of children: one of the freedoms that *The Canterbury
Tales* gave to Chaucer was the freedom to speak in voices and to
explore modes of feeling that he need not acknowledge as his own.

The passage serves to draw attention too to a striking characteristic of these Chaucerian narratives of faith: two of them may be
told by women, but all of them are about women or, in this one
case, a small child. The heroines are Constance, Griselda, Cecilia
and Virginia, and we might remember Prudence too. There are
no heroic male saints, no celebration of the fortitude of a man
such as the saint towards whose shrine the Canterbury pilgrimage
itself is directed. Religious women traditionally played their part
in the stories of martyrdom that bore witness to the faith, but not
usually thus, to the exclusion of men. The markedness of their
absence in Chaucer's poetry is of a piece with the general absence
of male authority-figures that was commented upon earlier. It has
indeed been well argued, by David Benson, that women are so
dominant in Chaucer's religious tales that 'men are viewed with
approval only when they begin to act like women'. The examples
of Melibee, of Valerian and his brother in the Second Nun's Tale
and of King Alla in the Man of Law's Tale come readily to mind.[40]

Why are women allocated such an exceptionally prominent role
in Chaucer's religious tales? One answer is that their relative lack
of power in the social and domestic real world makes them apt
representatives of a spirituality which goes out of its way to
embrace powerlessness. They are the very image of that meekness

and humility that are spoken of in the beatitudes as specifically blessed. Through women, the meaning of power and weakness, as they relate to the world of the spirit, can be redefined. Chaucer gives memorable expression, as does Shakespeare in some of his female heroines, to the identification of the Christ-like with the womanly, of the mystery of faith and humility with the mystery of 'the other', of woman:

> Men speke of Job, and moost for his humblesse,
> As clerkes, whan hem list, konne wel endite,
> Namely of men, but as in soothfastnesse,
> Though clerkes preise wommen but a lite,
> Ther kan no man in humblesse hym acquite
> As womman kan, ne kan been half so trewe
> As wommen been, but it be falle of newe.
> (Clerk's Tale, IV.932–8)

Chaucer comes close in these tales to that revelation of compassionate understanding to which Langland, with 'this wommen that wonyeth in cotes' (*Piers Plowman*, C. IX. 83), and Gower, with his Canacee (*Confessio Amantis*, III. 143–336), seem generally so much more open.

Yet Chaucer, amid all the moving and pathetic circumstance of these tales – Griselda and Constance speaking to their children, Virginia seeking 'a litel space' to lament her death, the 'litel clergeon' of the Prioress's Tale learning the song to the Virgin even though he will be beaten for it – remains aloof and uncommitted.[41] This indeed is the whole character and point of *The Canterbury Tales*. The stanza about Job from the Clerk's Tale, quoted above, is impersonally phrased and admits a sly allusion, 'whan hem list', and at the end a limp qualification – 'but it be falle of newe' – which allow the assertion to be construed as an ironical aside. The recognition of the special spiritual witness afforded by women is not protected from the further recognition of the special satisfaction that men may take in granting them such a role. To identify the narrative of faith with the narrative of women's lives marginalizes faith in the measure that women are already marginalized. It is just very good to know that someone else is taking care of these important matters.

Hence the unease that most readers feel about Chaucer's religious tales, interesting and enjoyable as that unease may be. One suspects, in a word, his sincerity. There always seems to be a space left for scepticism, for a superior otherness of viewpoint which will see pathos as sentimentality and religion as religiosity. The voicing of the Prioress's Tale both adds to its moving power and also 'contains' that moving power by relegating it to the activity of female affectation and self-indulgence. The rhetoric of God's grace in the Man of Law's Tale is at times magnificent but it cannot but be felt as intrusive upon the absorption of the reader in the experience of the story, part of that constant barrage of imprecation, apostrophe and ironic foreshadowing that is the ostentatious narrative mannerism of the tale. The discussion of different versions of the story with which Chaucer interrupts the drama of the denouement ('Som men wolde seyn . . . ' (II. 1009, 1086)) may carry some allusion to Gower but its effect is to distance the reader still further. The distance created between reader and subject by the mode of narration is sufficient to allow a critical consciousness to continue to operate, not so much upon the events and characters of the story as upon the nature of such stories, and the simplicities of religious feeling upon which they rest.

Even in the Clerk's Tale, there is something of this effect of distancing. Chaucer makes much more than Petrarch of the swoon into which Griselda falls when her children are restored to her, and adds detail of a kind of *rigor mortis* in which she holds her children in that swoon (IV. 1100–3). The purpose of this swoon, from which she awakes as 'from hire traunce' (1108), is to make a break with the narrative of her impossibly patient fidelity, to seal it off like a tomb from which she now returns to life. Even in this greatest of his religious tales, Chaucer thus keeps open the ironical option.

It might well be said, of the Clerk's Tale and Man of Law's Tale particularly, that Chaucer is less interested in faith and the sentiment of piety than in questions of free will and determinism that had always preoccupied him. Religion manifests itself most seriously in terms of questions of conduct, and of the relation between acts and their consequences. These are for Chaucer matters of intense interest which allow nevertheless for detachment as well as sympathy: 'A moral indifferentism in principle appears to accompany sympathetic observation and acceptance of the consequences of human action.'[42] So the question of free will, of the capacity of human beings to decide what happens to them, which is the driving force behind the Knight's Tale, the translation of Boethius, *Troilus and Criseyde* and the Franklin's Tale, is dominant still in these religious tales. The abiding memory of the Pardoner's

Prologue and Tale, for instance, is of the corrupted will of the
Pardoner, a will totally atrophied in lying and hypocrisy, leaving
the Pardoner capable only of automatic self-rehearsal and narcotic
repetition of his 'entente' (VI. 423–34). Constance's by contrast is
a will equally totally resigned to God. Constance inexplicably
refuses to tell her rescuers who she is or where she comes from
(II. 524, 972), when to do so would make things a lot easier
for her. She has abandoned any effort at self-assertion or self-
preservation that might constitute an infringement of God's sole
power to determine the life of his creatures. She is one of nature's
anti-Pelagians.

Griselda is quite different, and much more interesting. Seeming to have given up all her free will to Walter with her marriage
vows – 'as ye wole youreself, right so wol I' (IV. 361) – she
finds herself in a more difficult situation than Constance. No
rescue is at hand when Walter makes his outrageous demands
upon her, and what she decides to do is to reiterate, repeatedly,
her promise:

> 'I have', quod she, 'seyd thus and evere shal:
> I wol no thyng, ne nyl no thyng, certayn,
> But as yow list.'
>
> (IV. 645–7)

Chaucer also makes her much more vividly aware of the trials
she is put to, and gives her a certain sharp and quizzical insight
into Walter's behaviour. The voluntary nature of Griselda's
actions, performed as they are in the full knowledge of the
unjustness of the circumstances in which they are required,
becomes a uniquely eloquent testimony to the power of love and
obedience. It is a power not only in itself but in its capacity to
change others, since there is more than a suggestion that the
influence of Griselda's submissiveness upon Walter is not so
much to convince him that his plan to test her has worked as
to persuade him to a change of heart: 'This sturdy markys
gan his herte dresse / To rewen upon hire wyfly stedfastnesse'
(IV.1049–50). The freely willed embrace of undeserved suffering,
offered out of determination to set no bounds to love and obedience
towards a higher will, in the end reforms that higher will to the
love which is its true being. So, in the theological terms which
constantly press for recognition in the Clerk's Tale, absolute
potency, postulated as a theological necessity, is subdued to and
constrained by love, the Father by the Son.

The ending of the narrative of the Clerk's Tale is the high point of Chaucer's religious poetry. It is a moment soon dissipated in gestures of withdrawal, concessions, high clowning, as Chaucer characteristically encloses the tale in a network of ambiguities and interpretative paradoxes. Only in the Parson's Tale can he be said to speak unequivocally from and of the truth of faith, and it is significant that the Parson's Tale is not a tale at all, but a general penitential treatise with a lengthy account of the Seven Deadly Sins and their remedies. It is the ground-plan of salvation.

The Parson's Tale is a work of considerable care and skill, much the best piece of writing of its kind in English, and it is the expression of a deep and orthodox piety; or, at least, it accepts the necessity of contracting in to the comprehensive, all-pervading, non-negotiable system of belief which is called the Christian faith. There is no escaping back into *The Canterbury Tales*, no possibility of containing the Parson's Tale within any framework of irony or dramatic voicing. The manner of the treatise, and its demonstration of the abstract, systematic, all-inclusive and definitive nature of its statement of all that is to be known, is not merely something to set beside the various kinds of fictionality that have gone before, but a denial of the validity of fiction.

Finally, Chaucer acquiesces completely in this, and moves at the end of the tale not back into the uncompleted fiction of the pilgrimage but directly into the realm of action in relation to his own life. The Retraction, in which he begs forgiveness for and formally revokes all his 'translacions and enditynges of worldly vanitees', is Chaucer's own historical response to the call for penitence, and penitence *now*, which is the imperative logic of the closing paragraphs of the Parson's treatise. The Retraction grows inevitably out of the Parson's Tale, and confirms the passing of artistic into historical consciousness. It is Chaucer's own act of satisfaction. The Parson had spoken of the pilgrimage to Canterbury as a symbol of man's spiritual journey to a celestial Canterbury, but proceeded to turn that symbol into reality, the only ultimate reality. What was allegory has become plain fact.

The only relic of Chaucer the poet we can find in the Retraction, apart from the mischievously perfect line of pentameter ('and many a song and many a leccherous lay', X. 1087)) embedded in the reference to all the songs of love he wishes he hadn't composed, is in the opening he leaves for a play of interpretation upon his statement of 'entente'. He comments thus on Paul's dictum (2 Timothy 3: 16):

For oure book seith, 'Al that is writen is writen for oure doctrine',
and that is myn entente. / Wherfore I biseke yow mekely, for the
mercy of God, that ye preye for me that Crist have mercy on me
and foryeve me my giltes; / and namely of my translacions and
enditynges of worldly vanitees, the which I revoke in my retracciouns.

(X.1082–4)

The sense of 'Wherfore' is characteristically oblique. Having
declared that it is his purpose to confirm the statement that
everything that is written is written for our doctrine, Chaucer then
goes on to say that for that reason he is revoking all his secular
poetry. What this seems to mean is that, since all that is written
is written for our doctrine, that which does not serve that purpose
must by definition be unwritten. Hence the revoking, or unwriting,
of the Chaucer texts. The truth of Christian doctrine is demonstrated and best served by their non-being. The other possible
interpretation is that it is the act of revocation itself which is the
significant serving of the doctrinal purpose. The Chaucer texts
remain: they become doctrine by being revoked, in the same way
that a bad life may become spiritually edifying through a final act
of spectacular penitence.

The final self-assertion of the poet, though, is in the fact that
this was not by any means, as I believe, a final act. It was an act
appropriate to the occasion of completing the Parson's Tale ('this
litel tretys') and to an ending for *The Canterbury Tales* which was
subsequently superseded.

Epilogue

Richard II's disagreements with his magnates were too deep to remain hidden for long after the uneasy truce of 1389. Richard had no premeditated schemes of revenge, but by 1397 baronial opposition to his authority, as he perceived it, had grown so obstinate that he needed to make a pre-emptive strike.

Gaunt was no longer the threat he had formerly been thought to be. Having returned from Spain in 1389 without the crown he coveted, Gaunt lost interest in his Spanish wife, whom he relegated to a melancholy little court at Leicester while he lived openly with Katherine Swynford. After Constance's death on 25 March 1394, he married Katherine in January 1396 and soon afterwards secured the legitimation of his Beaufort children, which was probably the sum of his remaining ambitions. He supported the king staunchly throughout the 1390s, even in the royal policy of peace with France and Scotland, which was a major cause of discontent to other magnates such as Gloucester, Arundel and the Percys and also to a large section of public opinion. The Irish campaign of 1394–5 was a tactical success for Richard, but the settlement did not last, and anyway war with the Irish was not considered very serious. Returning home, he cemented the Anglo-French peace with his marriage to the French king's daughter Isabella in March 1396.

Richard was all this time consolidating his power-base in the royal domain of Cheshire, where he had the beginnings of a private army, and also following his former practice of establishing an inner circle of favourites, this time including members of the traditional nobility such as the earls of Rutland (Albemarle) and Nottingham (Mowbray) as well as upstarts like William LeScrope, Earl of Wiltshire. None of this was much to the taste of the Duke of Gloucester, who remained the leader of the opposition, but a Commons complaint in January 1397 about the extravagance of the king's household was peremptorily dealt with.

Richard saw now his chance to silence his chief opponents, and he had Gloucester, Warwick and the Arundel brothers suddenly arrested in August 1397. Gloucester was sent to Calais, where Mowbray was captain, and probably murdered there. Richard meanwhile packed London with his Cheshire archers for the opening of Parliament in September 1397, where he had Arundel condemned to execution and Warwick and Archbishop Arundel exiled. Gaunt was loyal throughout. The procedure was modelled, with a nice sense of theatre, on that of the Appellants in 1388.

Richard moved on quickly. He made the Shrewsbury Parliament of January 1398 grant him the income for life from the customs in return for 'pardon' for treasonous activities during 1386–8. Whole counties were forced to seek pardon in this way. There were also obligatory 'loans' to the crown, fiercely resisted by the Percys, with whom the king was now extremely unpopular. Richard may have seen these as moves to secure his safety and financial independence, but they looked like the beginnings of tyranny. The Council was now packed with his creatures, including Rutland, LeScrope and the Earl of Huntingdon, the king's half-brother. The only problems remaining were Roger Mortimer, Earl of March, a great landowner and heir presumptive to the the throne, who was conveniently killed in Ireland on 20 July 1398; and the dukes of Norfolk (Mowbray) and Hereford (Bolingbroke). The former knew too much about events in Calais, the latter had always been aloof, and both had been among the original Appellants. Fortunately, the two of them became tangled in mutual accusations of treason, which enabled Richard, after the grand theatre of the aborted trial by combat on 16 September 1398, to have them both exiled.

It is often argued that Richard, deeply grieved by the death of Queen Anne on 7 June 1394, lost touch with reality in these later years and behaved in an irrational manner. Yet his actions were skilfully and successfully directed to the securing for himself of a remarkable degree of autocratic power, and even theatrical extravagances such as the assault on Arundel when he showed lack of proper respect at Anne's funeral in 1394, or the performance beside de Vere's coffin in 1395, can be seen as the deliberate cultivation of a kind of 'magnificence' of behaviour which is itself an enforcement of power.[1]

The event that precipitated Richard's downfall was the death of John of Gaunt on 3 February 1399. Richard had earlier agreed to allow Henry livery of his inheritance if his father died while he was in exile. Now he revoked this, changed the six years' exile to perpetual banishment, and on 18 March appropriated the Lancastrian estates to the crown. He then, at the end of May 1399, left for Ireland again. This was a disastrous series of misjudgements, arguing that what he had lost touch with was not reality but public opinion, since, having packed his councils with yes-men, there was no one to tell him that such action was insupportable. Henry landed in the north of England at the end of June, having obtained the unexpected support of the Duke of Orleans (something Richard could be excused for not anticipating), and the discontented, especially the powerful Northern barons, quickly rallied to him. Richard returned from Ireland in July to find that his English army had been dispersed and that he had no alternative but to accept the promises of Henry, conveyed to him at Conway Castle by the Earl of Northumberland, that he came but to seek his Lancastrian inheritance. The promises were or turned out to be false, and Richard was forced to abdicate on 30 September. Henry was crowned on 13 October and Richard died not long afterwards at Pontefract Castle.[2]

CHAUCER'S LAST MONTHS

Chaucer's life was affected, like everyone else's, by the removal of the king. In particular, he had, as once before, to secure the confirmation of his annuities and grants from the new king. It has often been assumed that this matter went on quite briskly, but in fact it proved a great deal simpler to obtain confirmation than to obtain payment. On 30 September 1399 Henry was proclaimed king; on 13 October, the day of his coronation, letters patent were issued confirming Chaucer's annuity of £20 and making him a further grant of 40 marks per year. But this is not quite what it seems. On 18 October Chaucer swore out a statement that he had lost his copies of the documents that showed he was entitled to the £20 annuity and a tun of wine, and on 21 October new

documents were issued. Why was this necessary if confirmation
had already been granted on 13 October? The answer is that
the dating of the letters patent is entirely theoretical. The king's
coronation day was an obviously appropriate and totally unlikely
date for the issue of such documents. The letters patent were
actually issued around 16 February 1400, as is shown by their
position in the physical sequence of relevant documents, and only
then was the warrant made for payment.[3]

Meanwhile Chaucer had, on 24 December, taken out a lease on
a tenement in Westminster. He had not expected to stand specially
high in Henry's esteem, but he had anticipated that, if he went
through the routine channels, he would get the money he was due.
Now he was possibly in real financial difficulties, and the new
house was not cheap. So in January or early February, it may be
presumed, he wrote or unearthed from his files *The Complaint of
Chaucer to his Purse* and sent it to the king with an 'Envoy' in which
he managed to congratulate Henry not only on having secured the
crown but also on having a threefold title to it (as indeed Henry
had argued in his official claim to the throne):

> O conquerour of Brutes Albyon,
> Which that by lyne and free eleccion
> Been verray kyng, this song to yow I sende . . .

The astuteness and tactfulness of the compliment is hardly less
skilful than the witty punning of the *Complaint* itself, which, with
its image of the purse as his lady, and its play on *lyght* (empty,
fickle), *hevy* (full, pregnant) and *dye* ('Beth hevy ageyn, or elles mot
I dye' is the refrain), is suggestive enough to give pleasure without
being so obscene as to give offence.

Whether he received the poem or not, Henry swiftly made
amends for what was probably an oversight. On 21 February
Chaucer received £10 as a gift from the king, to pay the arrears
of the half-yearly instalment of his annuity due on 29 September
1399, payment of which had been authorized on 9 November
1399 but not made. Mandates were issued on 11 May and 14
May for payment of the arrears since the beginning of the reign
on the new annuity of 40 marks and the confirmed annuity of
£20, and part payment of 100*s.* on the latter was made on 5
June. At some time during Henry's first regnal year Chaucer also
received his tun of wine. There are no further records of payment;
Chaucer never received anything on the new annuity.

Neither the payment of 21 February nor that of 5 June was made to Geoffrey Chaucer in person. This was not an unusual practice in itself, but it was a little unusual for Chaucer, who had regularly in the past turned up in person to collect the instalments on his annuity. He may have been ailing. The tenement that he took on a 53-year lease (an unexpectedly long lease for a man nearly 60) on 24 December 1399, at a quarterly rent of 53s. 4d., was in the garden of the Lady Chapel of Westminster Abbey, and it may have been decided on by Chaucer as the equivalent of 'sheltered accommodation'. Royal servants were often pensioned off as corrodars to live at the state's expense in guest quarters in designated monasteries; what Chaucer got was the next best thing. Chaucer's predecessor and successor in the house were both persons who had been in the royal service; in 1411, after a break in the records of some years, it was being leased by Chaucer's son Thomas.

The property lay within the sanctuary which was attached to the abbey, and Chaucer had to promise, like other lessees, not to receive without permission persons seeking protection. There are no grounds whatever for the notion that he was seeking sanctuary for himself, to escape pursuit for actions of debt. He was most probably in failing health, though I should like to believe he was in these months engaged in expanding the plan of *The Canterbury Tales* and adding the non-finishing touches to the Cook's Tale rather than sinking into the penitential gloom that preceded the deathbed repentance that Thomas Gascoigne so predictably attributes to him:

> Chawcerus ante mortem suam sepe clamavit ve michi ve michi quia revocare nec destruere jam potero illa que male scripsi de malo et turpissimo amore hominum ad mulieres et jam de homine ad hominem continuabuntur. Velim. Nolim. Et sic plangens mortuus. (*Life-Records*, p. 547)

> Chaucer before his death often cried out, 'Woe is me! Woe is me! For I shall not now be able to revoke or destroy those things that I have wickedly written concerning the wicked and filthy love of men for women and which will now be passed down for ever from man to man, whether I wish it or not'. And so complaining he died.

Gascoigne (1403–58), who was at various times Chancellor of Oxford University and who wrote his *Dictionarium Theologicum* between 1434 and 1457, could readily have constructed this very appropriate scenario out of Chaucer's own Retraction, and his credibility as a witness is in any case seriously impugned by the story he made up about the condition of John of Gaunt's mortal remains, a story so discreditable to its author and so disgusting in itself that Armitage-Smith chose not only to leave it in Latin but to put his own account of it into Latin too.[4]

No further payments on his annuities were made to Chaucer after 5 June 1400, and the tenancy of his house at Westminster passed to one Master Paul between 28 September 1400 and 28 September 1401. Though 'there is no record of a will, the traditional date of Chaucer's death, 25 October 1400, is most probably accurate. He was buried in the abbey at the entrance to St Benedict's chapel, the most south-westerly of all the chapels, a humble place in the church beginning to be used for the graves of monastic officials. His remains were moved in 1556 to a new tomb set against the east wall of the south transept, a part of the abbey which has since become known as 'Poets' Corner' (plate 1). It is the inscription on this tomb, reported in 1606 but now illegible, that provides the date of his death (plate 14). 'Bones which were exposed', write the authors of the *Life-Records*, 'when Robert Browning was buried in the east aisle of the transept in 1889 were measured by the coroner, who estimated that they had belonged to a man about five feet six inches in height' (p. 549).

Chaucer's Descendants

Chaucer's wife Philippa had died long ago. If the speculations concerning two possible daughters are dismissed, he was survived by two sons, Lewis, of whom the little that is known has been told, and Thomas, of whom a great deal is known (see table 4). Born probably about 1367, he was retained for life in John of Gaunt's service at Bayonne in 1389, having served with him on the Spanish campaign of 1386–9, and in 1395 Gaunt paid £100 for the marriage of Maud, daughter and co-heiress of Sir John Burghersh of Ewelme, to his young follower. This was favour on a grand scale, perhaps partly to be attributed to the memory of Thomas's mother, the sister of Gaunt's long-time mistress and the faithful servant of his recently deceased second wife. Through the marriage, Thomas came into large estates in Surrey and elsewhere, and the Lancastrian usurpation further improved his prospects.

Plate 1. The Chaucer Tomb in Westminster Abbey. Photograph by courtesy of the Dean and Chapter of Westminster.

On 16 October 1399, three days after the coronation, he was appointed constable of Wallingford Castle for life, thus increasing his interests in Oxfordshire, where he became sheriff in 1400 and knight of the shire for the first time in 1401. He was to represent Oxfordshire in fourteen other Parliaments before his death in 1434, and was elected Speaker on five occasions, in 1407, 1410, 1411, 1414 and 1421. At the time of his death, though he had refused knighthood, there can have been few knights richer than he.[5]

In the political dissensions of Henry IV's reign, when he was at the height of his career, Thomas showed himself a true son of his father:

It was a situation which called for some adroit trimming on Chaucer's part if he was to remain throughout the reign's difficult closing

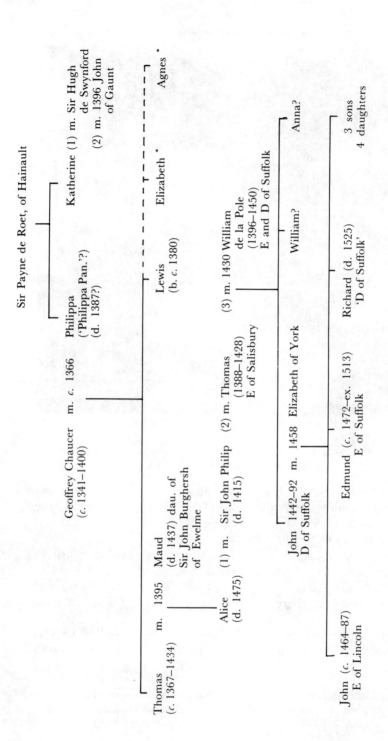

Sir Payne de Roet, of Hainault

Geoffrey Chaucer   m. c. 1366   Philippa   Katherine (1) m. Sir Hugh
(c. 1341–1400)   ('Philippa Pan.'?)   de Swynford
                                  (d. 1387?)   (2) m. 1396 John
                                                                of Gaunt

Thomas   m.   1395   Maud   Lewis   Elizabeth *   Agnes *
(c. 1367–1434)   (d. 1437) dau. of (b. c. 1380)
                        Sir John Burghersh
                        of Ewelme

Alice   (1) m. Sir John Philip   (2) m. Thomas   (3) m. 1430 William
(d. 1475)   (d. 1415)   (1388–1428)   de la Pole
                                     E of Salisbury   (1396–1450)
                                                             E and D of Suffolk

John 1442–92   m. 1458   Elizabeth of York   William?   Anna?
D of Suffolk

Edmund (c. 1472–ex. 1513)   Richard (d. 1525)   3 sons
E of Suffolk   'D of Suffolk'   4 daughters

John (c. 1464–87)
E of Lincoln

* See chapter 5, p. 204.

Table 4. The Chaucer family tree (2)

years the pensioner simultaneously of the king, of the prince of
Wales, and of the bishop of Winchester. But he succeeded brilliantly
. . . It says much for his political skill that he did not forfeit a single
office for his part as Speaker in the two succeeding parliaments, at
one of which at least demands were voiced for the king's abdication;
and that he retained the confidence of both sides in what at one
time threatened to become a civil war.[6]

During the reign of Henry V he was a trusted servant in some
delicate diplomatic negotiations, and he was thought worthy of a
place, even as a commoner, in the largely aristocratic minority
council of Henry VI. McFarlane, summarizing his career, speaks
of him as 'a self-made man of great wealth, acquisitive yet circumspect, politic and *affairé*, well versed in all branches of administration and diplomacy, a practised chairman and envoy, influential
and respected' (p. 337). Whatever ambitions the father may have
entertained in his own public life were indeed amply fulfilled in
the career of his son.

The exceptional favour granted by Gaunt to Thomas Chaucer
as a young man brings back to mind the hypothesis that he was
actually Gaunt's son by Philippa, Geoffrey's wife, and that the
poet, for a consideration, agreed to have him brought up as his
own son (see chapter 2, note 4). The chief evidence for this
hypothesis is the tomb of Thomas Chaucer, which has, among its
display of coats of arms, the arms of Roet (his mother) quartering
those of Burghersh (his wife), but not the quartering that might
have been expected of Chaucer and Roet, that is, of his ostensible
father and mother (plates 2 and 3).[7]

It is not easy to explain this. It might be argued that Geoffrey
Chaucer was never granted a coat of arms, that, though frequently
called *armiger* (an esquire), he was not armigerous. But a seal used
by Thomas Chaucer in 1409 may have been inherited from his
father, the inscription upon it, though indistinct, possibly reading
'Ghofrai [?] Chavcier' (*Life-Records*, p. 542); it has on its obverse
a shield with the arms *parti per pale a bend over all*, which is a
version of the coat commonly ascribed to the Chaucer family in
the fifteenth and sixteenth centuries and blazoned *parti per pale
argent and gules, a bend counterchanged*. A second possibility is that
the arms of Geoffrey Chaucer were omitted in the collection of
armorial quarterings on his son's tomb as being insufficiently
distinguished: what Thomas Chaucer had planned for his tomb
was an armorial roll-call of the great families of England with

Plate 2. The tomb of Thomas Chaucer in Ewelme Church, Oxfordshire. Photograph: Robert Erbe, by courtesy of the Rector, Ewelme Church, Oxfordshire.

which he had associations, and in such company there was no room for his father. The question of Thomas's ancestry cannot be regarded as completely resolved, but, as McFarlane observes, 'to disprove [Thomas] Chaucer's legitimacy is a far cry from proving Gaunt his father' (p. 333). If he were Gaunt's son, then the favour shown to him was not exceptional but paltry; and in any case, the whole scenario of subterfuge and concealment is more appropriate to the nineteenth century than the fourteenth.

Of Thomas's interest in his father's writings there is no evidence, though the reasonable opinion has been put forward (see chapter 6, note 9) that he had a part in bringing out an early edition of *The Canterbury Tales.* John Bowers, in a recent paper, puts forward the more controversial suggestion that Thomas's lease of the Westminster house his father had lived in was not as a *pied-à-terre* for attendance at Westminster Parliaments but as a way of organizing and controlling the 'Chaucer archive', his father's library and the manuscripts of his writings. Bowers proposes further that Thomas, who had close contacts with John Lydgate, was participating in the formation of 'an official poetic that was

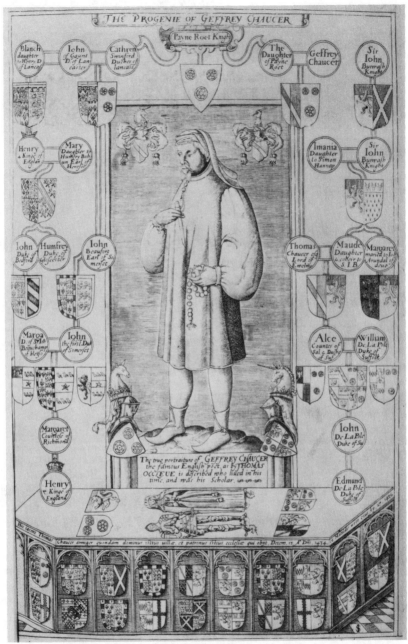

Plate 3. The 'Progenie' page, engraved by John Speed for Thomas Speght's edition of the *Workes* of Chaucer (1598). Photograph by kind permission of the Librarian of the Houghton Library, Harvard University. Copy call-number fSTC 5078(A)

282 *Epilogue*

Plate 4. The tomb of Alice, Duchess of Suffolk (Chaucer's granddaughter) in Ewelme Church, Oxfordshire. Photograph: Robert Erbe, by courtesy of the Rector, Ewelme Church, Oxfordshire.

Lancastrian in its social commitment and Chaucerian in style and subject-matter'.[8]

Thomas died on 18 November 1434, his widow Maud on 4 May 1437, and their daughter Alice was left as sole heiress. She had been married and widowed twice, without bearing any children, and was now married to William de la Pole, Earl of Suffolk, later (in 1448) Duke of Suffolk, and for a time the most powerful man in England. Alice fell into disfavour after the disgrace of her husband and his murder on 2 May 1450, and a splendid marriage to Margaret Beaufort (granddaughter of Thomas Chaucer's cousin-german, John Beaufort, first Duke of Somerset, and later Countess of Richmond, mother of Henry VII) planned for her eldest son John de la Pole, born in 1442, fell through. Alice, like a good Chaucer, saw the wisdom now of forging some connections with the Yorkist party, and she had her son married to Elizabeth, second daughter of Richard, Duke of York, in 1458. John joined the Yorkist side in 1461, temporized during the Lancastrian readeption of 1470–1, but soon regained Edward IV's trust. He seems to have inherited from his mother (who died 20 May 1475, and

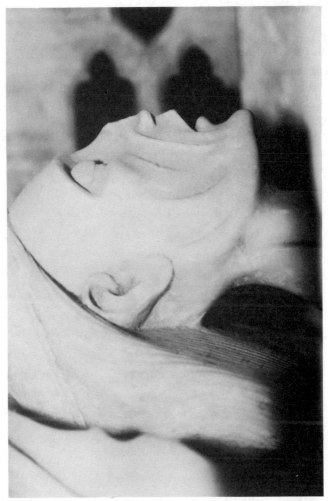

Plate 5. The tomb of Alice (detail). Photograph: Robert Erbe, by courtesy of the Rector, Ewelme Church, Oxfordshire.

was magnificently buried in a double-decker cadaver tomb at Ewelme (plates 4 and 5)) the Chaucerian family skill in manoeuvre, and he died still in favour, now with Henry VII, in 1492.

He was the last of the family to have such success. His eldest son, John, was created Earl of Lincoln in 1467, was declared heir presumptive to the throne, in the right of his mother, on the death of Richard III's son in 1484, and died at the battle of Stoke in 1487 fighting for the cause of the pretender Lambert Simnel. The second son Edmund succeeded to the dukedom on the death of his father in 1492, but was in and out of trouble until Henry VIII had him beheaded in 1513. His younger brother, Richard, himself attainted in 1504, now styled himself Duke of Suffolk, served with Louis XII of France, claimed the crown of England, and died fighting for Francis I at Pavia in 1525. There were other sons, but around 1539 the male line of the de la Poles became extinct, and with it Geoffrey Chaucer's descendants. Chaucer's collected *Workes*, on the other hand, had just come out, in 1532.

Appendix I The Chaucer Portraits

There is a tradition of Chaucer portraiture remarkable both for the early date at which it became established and for the exceptional attention that is paid to lifelikeness of representation.[1]

Probably the first picture of the poet is the pilgrim portrait in the Ellesmere manuscript (San Marino, California, Huntington Library MS EL 26. C. 9), made soon after he died.[2] In this manuscript, all the pilgrims who tell tales are shown on horseback in the margin of the text beside the beginning of the tale that they tell; Chaucer is shown beside the beginning of the text of *Melibee*, a sensible choice, given that the alternative was *Sir Thopas*. Three illustrators worked on the pilgrim portraits in Ellesmere,[3] and the Chaucer portrait is the only one done by the best of the three (plate 6). It is a most expressive portrait, and has a quality of particularity in the facial features absent from the other pilgrim portraits, vivid as some of them are. The odd disproportion of Chaucer's body, and of his body in relation to his horse, is the result of a technical problem which will be discussed in a moment.

The next portrait, in terms of probable date, is the one in British Library MS Harley 4866 (plate 7), a manuscript of Thomas Hoccleve's *Regement of Princes*, written in 1411–12.[4] The manuscript was made in the early 1410s, possibly as a presentation copy for Henry, Prince of Wales, who had commissioned the poem. Towards the end of the work, Hoccleve finds occasion, not for the first time, to offer a tribute of praise to his master Chaucer. The tone is one of warm remembrance, as of a much revered teacher, and is quite different from the tone of John Lydgate's many eulogies of Chaucer, which are more formal and fulsome as well as much longer. As he speaks of Chaucer, it comes upon Hoccleve that

Plate 6. San Marino,
California, The Henry E.
Huntington Library, MS
EL 26. C. 9. *The
Canterbury Tales*. f. 153v.
By permission of the
Librarian of the
Huntington Library.

Plate 7. British Library, MS Harley
4866. Hoccleve, *The Regement of Princes*.
f. 88r. Photograph by permission of
the British Library.

many of those whom he addresses will not have known the poet personally. So he will have a likeness of him painted in the manuscript:

> Al thogh his lyfe be queynt, the resemblaunce
> Of him hath in me so fressh lyflynesse
> That, to putte othir men in remembrauce
> Of his persone, I have heere his lyknesse
> Do make, to this ende, in sothfastnesse,
> That thei that have of him lest thought and mynde
> By this peynture may ageyn him fynde.
>
> (*Regement*, 4992–8, text from MS Harley 4866)

Hoccleve goes on, in the following two stanzas (4999–5012), to suggest that the portrait of Chaucer will be like a religious image in creating remembrance of the poet, taking the opportunity meanwhile to castigate those (the Lollards, that is) who opposed such images.[5]

This 'iconization' of Chaucer is audacious enough, but the innovativeness of Hoccleve's general proceeding is also itself quite extraordinary. The point of the picture is that it is to be an actual likeness of Chaucer, not an idealized portrait, and it must be emphasized what an early date this is for a portrait to be and to be claimed as an accurate likeness. We ourselves cannot know that the portrait is a lifelike one, but Hoccleve's claim that it is an authentic likeness is one that could have been readily tested by many people still alive in the 1410s, including Henry, and Hoccleve would have been a fool to make so specific a claim unless it were demonstrably true.

Such a tradition of individualized portraiture, including portraiture of authors, was known in imperial Rome, but it was generally alien to the Christian Middle Ages. There had been sensitive and expressive human portraits, of course, showing apostles, saints, kings, martyrs and patriarchs in a profoundly 'realistic' way. But there could be no authentic particularity in such pictures, nor was any sought, and even when portraits or sculptures were of living people, where they could have been done from life, there was no great interest in or desire for such particularity, or at least for any more than a highly idealized version of it. Subsequently, there was a change, and the movement towards individualized portraiture can be traced through the fourteenth century in Italy and France, especially in manuscript illustration. There is, for instance, an early tradition of representationally accurate Dante portraiture, and the French king and the French royal dukes are customarily portrayed in manuscript presentation pictures of the late fourteenth century in a consistently idiomatic way that suggests real-life representation.[6]

In England there had been little or nothing even of this, though Jeanne Krochalis points out (in the article cited in note 4) that the famous picture of Lord Lovell and the artist John Siferwas in the Lovell Lectionary (British Library MS Harley 7026, f. 4v), painted before 1408, has very strikingly the character of real-life portraiture; she points out too that memorial sculpture was becoming increasingly accurate in its record of facial features, especially through the use of death-masks. Hoccleve seems nevertheless to have 'invented' English portraiture, and invented it for the purpose of imprinting upon his readers an image of Chaucer the man. Hoccleve responded vividly in his poetry to Chaucer's 'autobiographical' mode of writing, and in his praise of Chaucer he responds just as vividly to the reality of Chaucer the person, who is such a living presence to every reader of his poetry. The picture that Hoccleve caused to be painted in his manuscript of the *Regement* is in a way an enactment and affirmation of the value of biography, as well as an icon.

It is, as it appears in Harley 4866, a marvellously expressive portrait, and it has a definite kinship with the Ellesmere picture. The facial features are similar, as are various details of array, including the pen-case, or 'penner', around the neck as an 'attribute' (like the Ellesmere Physician's urine-bottle) to signal the profession of the subject.[7] The hands are disposed in a very similar way, and the adaptation by which the hand holding the horse's reins in the one picture becomes the hand holding the rosary in the other (or vice-versa) is a skilful piece of improvisation. The allusion to Chaucer's piety would be entirely understandable as a deduction from the Retractions to *The Canterbury Tales*, as would the subject's grave sobriety of demeanour. The other hand, meanwhile, can point with equal appropriateness to 'his lyknesse' (or 'in sothfastnesse') or to the beginning of Chaucer's *Tale of Melibee*, or maybe indicate in the more generally traditional way the speaker's demand for attention. The physical reversal of the image, so that the one is a mirror-image of the other, is characteristic of copies made by tracing.

The Ellesmere manuscript is usually presumed to be somewhat earlier than the Harley, but the odd proportions of the Ellesmere picture surely derive from the attempt to adapt a three-quarter-length portrait, such as that in Harley, as a full-length equestrian portrait. The reason for portraying the pilgrims on horseback is obvious, though the further suggestion has been made that the particular mode of representation, especially the little 'platform' of grass on which some of the horses (including Chaucer's) stand, may imitate the pilgrim badges sold at Canterbury.[8] If the Ellesmere picture is not based directly on the Harley picture, then it would presumably derive from a common exemplar, and the best supposition would be that Hoccleve had such an exemplar in his possession before or soon after Chaucer's death (whether or not borrowed from Geoffrey's son Thomas) and made it available to the editor of Ellesmere (if indeed he was not himself the editor).

Since there are over forty manuscripts of *The Regement of Princes*, it might be anticipated that there would follow now a long catalogue of Chaucer portraits. This is not so. In fact, very few manuscripts contain the picture, despite the clear statement in the text that it is needed: this may be because, since the picture was in the margin and did not therefore have to be part of the planning of the lay-out of the book, no tradition of providing illustration became established; or it may be because most customers for the *Regement* did not want to go to the extra expense. Traces of the portrait are still visible in British Library MS Harley 4826, but the picture itself, which seems to have been of a full-length figure, was cut out by 'summe ffuryous ffoole' who is roundly reprimanded in verses added at the bottom of the page in the sixteenth century:

> Off worthy Chawcer/here the pickture stood
> That much did wryght/and all to doo us good
> Summe ffuryous ffoole/have Cutt the Same in twayne
> His deed doo shewe/He bare a barren Brayne.
> (Text from MS Harley 4826)

In British Library MS Arundel 38, another manuscript possibly prepared as a presentation copy for Prince Henry around 1412, the whole page containing the Chaucer stanzas and presumably also the portrait has been cut out. Judging by the quality of the presentation picture that survives (f. 37r), it was a finely executed picture, perhaps from the same *atelier* as the Harley portrait.

The two manuscripts of the *Regement* in which the portrait actually survives are, as a consequence, the more disappointing. The picture in British Library MS Royal 17. D. vi, for instance, is somewhat clumsily executed (plate 8). It is a free copy of the

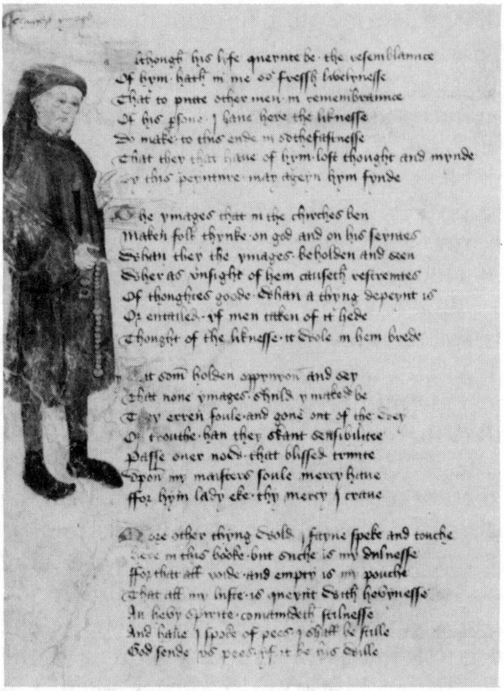

Plate 8. British Library,
MS Royal 17. D. vi.
Hoccleve, *The Regement of
Princes*. f. 93v. Photograph
by permission of the
British Library.

Plate 9. Philadelphia, The Rosenbach
Museum and Library, MS 1083/10.
Hoccleve, *The Regement of Princes*. f.
72v. Photograph by permission.

Harley portrait, with the addition of awkward legs and feet to make it into a full-length portrait, and the facial features are much coarsened. In the copy of the *Regement* in the Rosenbach Library in Philadelphia, MS Rosenbach 1083/10, there is an exact and rather pleasant water-colour copy of the Harley portrait (plate 9), inserted at almost the right point in the text, but it is probably of the eighteenth century.

These are the only manuscripts of the *Regement* that have or are known to have had the Chaucer portrait, though in some others there is, at the appropriate place in the margin of the text, a verbal allusion ('The figure of Chaucer', or 'Chaucers ymage') to the absent picture.

There is a very interesting relation between the Harley portrait tradition and the picture of Chaucer in one of the most famous English paintings of the early fifteenth century, the frontispiece to the copy of *Troilus and Criseyde* in Corpus Christi College, Cambridge, MS 61. In this painting (plate 10), which is an idealized representation of Chaucer reciting his poem to a court audience, Chaucer is shown half length, standing in a pulpit. He is more fashionably arrayed than in the Harley picture, younger, with less expressive features (perhaps inevitably, given the size of the portrait), but in other respects he is portrayed in a manner definitely reminiscent of the near-contemporary Harley portrait.[9]

Miniatures of Chaucer as author occur in the historiated initial *W* on the first leaf of three copies of *The Canterbury Tales*, British Library MS Lansdowne 851 (plate 11), Bodleian Library MS Bodley 686 (plate 12) and the Devonshire manuscript. The miniatures are of good quality, but the portraits are highly stylized, and have little if any connection with the tradition that is being described here as 'authentic'. They are the product of the long-established tradition of portraying the author in some stylized form in the initial miniature. In the last two, Chaucer is pictured as beardless and youthful, and in the Devonshire, most unusually, as seated outdoors on a bank of flowers, presumably in allusion to Chaucer's representation of himself in the Prologue to *The Legend of Good Women*.[10]

At some point in the sixteenth century, when Chaucer's reputation was growing rapidly as a result of the successive printings of his work by Caxton, Pynson, Wynkyn de Worde and Thynne, a grander tradition of Chaucer portraiture was established. These portraits are certainly derived from the Harley tradition, whether by adaptation from Harley 4866 or possibly more directly from

Plate 10. Cambridge, Corpus Christi College, MS 61. Chaucer, *Troilus and Criseyde.* f. 1v. By permission of the Master and Fellows of Corpus Christi College, Cambridge.

Plate 11. British Library, MS Lansdowne 851. *The Canterbury Tales.* f. 2r. Photograph by permission of the British Library.

Plate 12. Oxford, Bodleian Library, MS Bodley 686. *The Canterbury Tales.* f. 1r. Photograph by permission of the Bodleian Library, Oxford.

the full-length pictures that once existed in Harley 4826 and in a
non-*Regement* manuscript of great importance, destroyed in the
Cotton fire of 1731, British Library MS Cotton Otho A. XVIII.
Dating portraits belonging to such a closely imitative tradition is
difficult, but one of the earliest seems to be the mid- to late
sixteenth-century full-length full-page portrait in British Library
MS Additional 5141 (plate 13).[11] Chaucer has already, it will be
seen, begun to acquire an added *gravitas* suitable to the father of
English poetry, and the insertion of a coat of arms and a wholly
improbable date is designed to reinforce the impression of grandeur, antiquity and authenticity. (The rather carefully drawn daisy

Plate 13. British
Library, MS
Additional 5141.
Photograph by
permission of the
British Library.

meanwhile alludes to the poet's dedication to that flower as it is expressed in the Prologue to *The Legend of Good Women*.) In this tradition of portraiture, though the left hand still holds the rosary, the right hand is turned inward to finger the pen-case, both because this is a gesture conventionally employed to draw attention to professional status in Renaissance portraits, and also because the pointing hand (whether pointing in the old preacherly tradition or pointing to the text) was now irrelevant. A more pompous version of this portrait, with coat of arms and the date 1400, and again characterized by the rotundity of figure thought appropriate in Renaissance portraits (though perhaps with some allusion to the Host's playful remarks about Chaucer's corpulence), appears as a full-page illustration in the Delamere manuscript of *The Canterbury Tales*, probably inserted in the late sixteenth century.

An unknown part in the establishment of this sixteenth-century tradition of portraiture was played, as has been hinted already, by the full-length portrait of Chaucer on a single leaf pasted into Cotton Otho A. XVIII. This manuscript was destroyed in the Cotton fire of 1731, but had been seen and used in the early eighteenth century by the engraver George Vertue, who dated it about 1400 and thought it to be the original of the Westminster Abbey tomb portrait (1556) and of John Speed's engraving for Thomas Speght's *Workes* of Chaucer (1598) (plate 3).[12] There are some resemblances between the lost portrait, as Vertue describes it and as it appears in his engraving (plate 21), and the portrait that survives in Additional 5141, suggesting that the latter may possibly also be a copy of the Cottonian miniature. Since Additional 5141 itself consists of a single vellum leaf, and the size and (reported) nature of the two pictures are compatible, it seems entirely possible that it is the very leaf that Vertue found pasted in as a singleton in Cotton Otho A. XVIII, and which was somehow removed before the fire.

The portrait on Chaucer's tomb in Westminster Abbey may itself have played an important part in disseminating the renewed tradition of Chaucer portraiture. In 1556, a marble canopy with four arches was erected over the tomb in the east aisle of the south transept by Nicholas Brigham, perhaps as part of a move to reclaim Chaucer, with his rosary, for the temporarily restored Catholic ascendancy. Within the arches he placed an inscription, now illegible, and on the left of the inscription a painted portrait of the poet, now scarcely visible (plate 1). In his *Theatrum Chemicum Britannicum* of 1652 (where Chaucer appears because of his repu-

Plate 14. Elias Ashmole, *Theatrum Chemicum Britannicum* (1652), p. 226. Engraving of Chaucer's tomb in Westminster Abbey. Photograph: David Whiteley.

tation, deduced from the Canon's Yeoman's Prologue and Tale, as an alchemist), Elias Ashmole published a copper engraving of the monument (plate 14), but because the portrait was, as Ashmole says 'somewhat decay'd' the engraver had it restored after the original 'left to Posterity by his worthy Schollar Tho. Occleve'. The wording here suggests that it was Thomas Speght's 'Progenie' picture of 1598 or 1602 (plate 3) that was used for the retouching. Speght's picture itself of course derived from the tradition of which the original tomb portrait may have been an important early ancestor.

Whatever the direct origin of the sixteenth-century tradition, it is principally exemplified in the new kind of panel portrait or 'library portrait' and in the 'Progenie' pages of printed collections of Chaucer's poetry.

'Library portraits', some of which may actually have been intended for the libraries of the stately homes that sprang up after the Dissolution, are more interested in grandeur than authenticity. Chaucer must look like the founding father of English poetry. Such portraits are increasingly at the whim of fashion, and the original lineaments of the Harley portrait are eventually completely lost. There are many of these portraits, mostly of later date than their owners claim, though some may go back to the sixteenth century.

The full-length 'Sloane' portrait in the National Portrait Gallery (plate 15) clearly belongs to the tradition of Additional 5141, though Chaucer is made to look slightly more alert. Like many of the library portraits, it is quite small, the figure of Chaucer being no more than 10 inches from crown to toe. (The rather ill-drawn feet have led to speculation that Chaucer had some congenital deformity or else very short legs.) The picture in the Bodleian Library (plate 16) is one of a series in which Chaucer is shown from the waist up (slightly less than three-quarter length) and with features increasingly patriarchal. Others in the series include the rather handsome portrait now in the Houghton Library of Harvard University (plate 17) and the one more recently installed in the English Reading Room of the University of California at Los Angeles (plate 18). The former belonged to the Stokes family of Stanshawes Court in Gloucestershire until 1803, and was said by the family to have been in their possession for three hundred years.[13] This looks to be an overenthusiastic estimate. The UCLA portrait, which is a twin of the Harvard portrait, was bought by Professor Lawrence Clarke Powell from the premises of Stevens and Browne in Duke Street, London, in 1959, and has been the subject of investigation by Professor Edward I. Condren, of the Department of English at UCLA. His findings, which he has kindly communicated to me, include a carbon dating of *c.* 1400 for the oak panel on which the portrait is painted, and a pigment dating of c.1400–1600. I am not inclined, however, to a date for the painting much earlier than the the mid- to late sixteenth century.

Portraits of Chaucer continued to be commissioned for the galleries of stately homes. The large three-quarter-length picture of Chaucer painted on canvas (126 × 101 cm) that once hung in Bothwell Castle was probably commissioned by the first Earl of Clarendon (1609–74). Though it has the latest in landscape backgrounds, the portrait still shows quite clearly the influence of the Harley tradition. Not so the Rawlinson pastel portrait in the Bodleian Library, bequeathed by Dr Richard Rawlinson in 1755, in which Chaucer has been dandified beyond recognition (plate 19). Other library portraits of Chaucer are to be seen at Knole in Kent (plate 20), at Longleat House in Wiltshire, in the Plimpton

Plate 15. London, National Portrait Gallery, no. 532. The 'Sloane' portrait. Photograph by permission.

Plate 16. Oxford, Bodleian Library. Chaucer panel portrait. Photograph by permission of the Bodleian Library, Oxford.

Plate 17. Harvard
University, Houghton
Library. Chaucer panel
portrait. Photograph by
kind permission of the
Librarian of the
Houghton Library.

Plate 18. Los Angeles,
University of California,
English Department Reading
Room. Chaucer panel
portrait. Photograph: Tim
Strawn.

Plate 19. Oxford, Bodleian Library. The Rawlinson pastel portrait. Photograph
by permission of the Bodleian Library, Oxford.

Library at Columbia University,[14] and elsewhere, but none, except
perhaps the Knole portrait, can plausibly be dated before 1600.

The other function of the new tradition of portraiture was to
provide models for the handsome 'Progenie' pages of collected
editions of Chaucer's works. The first is the one in Thomas
Speght's 1598 edition of the *Workes*, where the full-length picture
of Chaucer, engraved for the edition by John Speed, is set like an
altar retable above the tomb of his son and between the family
trees of John of Gaunt and of Chaucer himself (plate 3). Speght
has a label at the bottom of the picture with the inscription: 'The
true portraiture of GEFFREY CHAUCER / the famous English poet,
as by THOMAS / OCCLEUE is described who lived in his / time, and
was his Scholar.' In the 'Life' of Chaucer that Speght introduced
into this edition, there is further information, in the section on
'His Bookes' (sig. c. i), about the origin of the Chaucer portrait:

Plate 20. Knole, Kent. Chaucer panel portrait. Photograph: Courtauld Institute of Art. Reproduction by permission of Hugh Sackville West, Esq., of Knole.

The which Occleue for the loue he bare to his Master, caused his / picture to be truly drawen in his booke *De Regimine Principis*, dedicated to / Henry the fift: the which I haue seene, and according to the which this in / the beginning of this booke was done by John Spede, who hath annexed / thereto all such cotes of Armes, as any way concerne the Chaucers, as he / found them (trauailing for that purpose) at Ewhelme and at Wickham.

Speght obtained much biographical and other information from the bibliophile and antiquary John Stow, and it is quite possible

Plate 21. George Vertue's engraving (1717) which forms the frontispiece to John Urry's edition of Chaucer (1721). From the copy in the Houghton Library, Harvard University, call-number fEC C3932 C721w. Photograph by kind permission of the Librarian of the Houghton Library.

that Stow brought to Speght's notice a manuscript such as he describes. If so, it would be easy to conclude that the later tradition of Chaucer portraiture begins here, in 1598, and all the library portraits are later copies of this widely disseminated image. But the Hoccleve portrait tradition was quite well known, and Speght was aware of the advantage of claiming a fresh and authentic source. If he is not telling the complete truth, then the hypothesis of an early- or mid-sixteenth-century origin for the later portrait tradition would stand.

The 'Progenie' page was reprinted in Speght's second edition of 1602 and in the publishers' 'third' edition of 1687, and pictures of Chaucer continued afterward to be newly engraved to act as frontispieces for editions of his works or for other purposes. George Vertue, for instance, made an engraving in 1717 which became widely known as the frontispiece to Urry's edition of 1721 (plate 21); he said it was based on the miniature in Cotton Otho A. XVIII, later destroyed in the Cotton fire. J. Houbraken did another engraving in 1741, based on the Sloane portrait, for a series of 'Heads of Illustrious Persons'. But we are a long way now from Chaucer.

List of Portraits (pre-1700)*

Manuscript Portraits

Cambridge, Corpus Christi College, MS 61. Chaucer, *Troilus and Criseyde. c.* 1410–20. Chaucer addressing a court audience, f. 1v (picture space 21 × 12 cm).

London, British Library, MS Additional 5141. A single vellum leaf, with a full-length full-page framed portrait on the recto (picture space 23 × 14.5 cm) and a brief and fanciful life of Chaucer on the verso. Mid to late 16th c. (the 'life' must be post-1598).

[London, British Library, MS Arundel 38. Hoccleve, *The Regement of Princes. c.* 1412. Whole leaf, presumably with Chaucer portrait, cut out between ff. 90 and 91.]

[London, British Library, MS Cotton Otho A. XVIII (destroyed in the Cotton fire of 1731). Miscellaneous compilation, with a vellum leaf pasted in at the end, containing a portrait of Chaucer, shown full length, 6–7 in. in height, right hand holding the 'penner'. So described by the engraver George Vertue in the early 18th c. and dated by him *c.* 1400.]

London, British Library, MS Harley 4826. Hoccleve, *The Regement of Princes. c.* 1450. Traces of a full length portrait cut out from margin of f. 139r.

---

* This is a list of portraits pre-1700 known to me. There are certainly more. The ones in brackets are those that do not survive or are not certainly known to exist.

London, British Library, MS Harley 4866. Hoccleve, *The Regement of Princes. c.* 1412. Three-quarter-length portrait at f. 88r.

London, British Library, MS Lansdowne 851. Chaucer, *The Canterbury Tales. c.* 1425. Author-portrait in initial miniature, f. 2r.

London, British Library, MS Royal 17. D. vi. Hoccleve, *The Regement of Princes. c.* 1430–40. Chaucer portrait, full length, f. 93v.

Oxford, Bodleian Library, MS Bodley 686. Chaucer, *The Canterbury Tales. c.* 1435. Author-portrait in initial miniature, f. 1r.

Oxford, Bodleian Library, MS Rawlinson poet. 223. Chaucer, *The Canterbury Tales. c.* 1450. The seated figure in the historiated initial at the beginning of *Melibee*, f. 183, is presumably intended for a portrait of Chaucer, and not Melibeus.

Philadelphia, Rosenbach Museum and Library, MS 1083/10 (*olim* Phillipps 1099). Hoccleve, *The Regement of Princes.* c. 1440–50. Late copy (18th c.?) of the Harley 4866 portrait, f. 72v.

San Marino, California, Henry E. Huntington Library, MS EL 26. C. 9. Chaucer, *The Canterbury Tales.* c. 1410. Equestrian portrait at f. 153v.

Tokyo, private collection of T. Takamiya (MS 32), the former Delamere MS (*olim* Boies Penrose 10). Chaucer, *The Canterbury Tales.* c.1450–70. Full length full-page portrait inserted, probably mid to late 16th c.

Tokyo, private collection of T. Takamiya (MS 24), the former Devonshire MS from Chatsworth House. Chaucer, *The Canterbury Tales.* c. 1450–60. Author-portrait in initial miniature, f. 1r.

Panel Portraits and Oil Paintings

[Bothwell Castle, Lanarkshire (former residence of the earls of Home). Oil on canvas, three-quarter length, 126 × 101 cm. Late 17th c. Now thought to be at The Hirsel, Coldstream, the present residence of the Home family.]

Cambridge, Massachusetts, Harvard University, Houghton Library (formerly known as the Seddon or Fairfax Murray portrait). Panel painting on oak, waist up, 46.5 × 36.5 cm. Mid to late 16th c.

Knole, Sevenoaks, Kent (residence of Lord Sackville, and of the former earls of Dorset). Panel painting, 33.3 × 28 cm. Late 16th c.?

London, National Portrait Gallery, no. 532, the 'Sloane' portrait (no. 320 in the Sir Hans Sloane collection, transferred from the British Museum in 1879). Full length, oil on oak panel, 30.5 × 27.3 cm. Late 16th c.

London, University of London, Sterling Library (formerly Chester-field House collection). Oil on canvas, 76 × 63 cm. Perhaps made for the 1st Earl of Halifax (d. 1695).

London, Westminster Abbey. Portrait painted in arch of canopy over Chaucer's tomb in south-east transept. 1556. Now scarcely visible; engraved, with some retouching, in Elias Ashmole, *Theatrum Chemicum Britannicum* (1652), p. 226.

Longleat House, Wiltshire (residence of the Marquess of Bath). Oil on canvas, 76 × 63.5 cm. One of a set of copy portraits commissioned by the first Viscount Weymouth (d. 1714) to furnish his new library in the late 17th c.

Los Angeles, University of California, English Department Reading Room. Panel painting on oak, waist up, 46.5 × 36.5 cm. Mid to late 16th c.

New York, Columbia University, Plimpton Library (acquired by George Plimpton in 1922 from the estate of Baroness Burdett-Coutts of London). Oil on wood panel, bust, facing right, 39 × 32 cm. 16th/17th c.

[Oxford, All Souls College (formerly in Wroxton Abbey, the residence of Lord North). An exact duplicate, but in tempera, of the Bodleian portrait. Believed to have passed into the private collection of John G. Adams, Esq., of Henley-in-Arden, Warwickshire, son of a former Warden of All Souls.]

Oxford, Bodleian Library. Panel portrait, waist up, 35.5 × 26.5 cm. Late 16th c.

Oxford, Bodleian Library. Pastel portrait, bust, bequeathed by Dr Richard Rawlinson in 1755. Late 17th c.?

[Oxford, St John's College. Oil on canvas, three-quarter length.]

York, private collection of Mr Daniel McDowell (from the Chaucer Head bookshop in Stratford-upon-Avon, part of the collection of the late Miss Dorothy Withey, from a Warwickshire country house sale in the early 19th c.). Oil on oak panel, 19 × 16 cm. Late 17th c.

Portraits in Printed Books

[London: first printing]. Thomas Speght (ed.), *The Workes of our Antient and Learned English Poet, Geffrey Chaucer*. 1598. Full length portrait, 26 × 23 cm, on the page headed 'The Progenie of Geffrey Chaucer'. Reprinted in Speght's second edition, 1602, and in the 'third' edition, 1687.

Appendix II Chronological Table

Chronological Table

In the following table, the significant historical and literary events of the time are inset into the main events of Chaucer's life.

1327–77 REIGN OF KING EDWARD III	
1338	Boccaccio completes *Il Filostrato*.
c. 1340	Completion of copying of National Library of Scotland, Edinburgh, MS Advocates' MS 19. 2. 1 (the Auchinleck MS), a large compilation of English romances and other poems, perhaps known to Chaucer.
1341	Boccaccio completes his *Teseida delle Nozze d'Emilia*.
Early 1340s	Born in London, (only?) son of John Chaucer, a prosperous wine-merchant, and his wife Agnes

1346	English victory at the battle of Crecy.
1347–9	John Chaucer holds office as king's deputy butler in the port of Southampton.
1348–9	The Black Death reaches England.
1349	Deaths of Richard Rolle, English mystic, and the scholars and theologians Robert Holcot, William of Ockham and Thomas Bradwardine.
1350s	Beginnings of the reflourishing of alliterative poetry in the West and North-West.
1351	The first Statutes of Labourers, attempts to fix wages and control movement of labour.
1356	English victory at the battle of Poitiers; King John of France captured, and lives at the English court 1357–60, in luxurious captivity, with much of the French royal household.
1357	In service as a young 'page' in the household of the Countess of Ulster, wife of Lionel, second surviving son of Edward III.
1359–60	In service as a *valettus* or yeoman in the retinue of Prince Lionel in France; captured at the siege of Reims, and ransomed.
1360	Treaty of Bretigny begins period of uneasy peace with France.
1361	Severe revisitation of plague.
1361–7	Jean Froissart, French poet and chronicler, in the household of Queen Philippa as 'clerc de la chambre'.
1364	John Chaucer stands surety that Richard Lyons will cause no harm to Alice Perrers (later the king's mistress).

1364 8 Apr.	Death of King John of France, at the Savoy; accession of Charles V.
Mid-1360s	William Langland begins *Piers Plowman*, A-text.
1365/6	Marries Philippa, eldest daughter of Paon de Roet (of the household of Queen Philippa) and sister of Katherine, subsequently mistress (*c.* 1370) and third wife (1396) of John of Gaunt, Duke of Lancaster.
1366	Death of Chaucer's father; his mother remarries.
1366 Feb.–May	In Spain (Navarre) on a diplomatic mission connected with English intervention in Castile.
1367 6 Jan.	Birth of Richard of Bordeaux (later Richard II), second and only surviving son of the Black Prince.
1367 3 Apr.	Battle of Najera, the Black Prince's temporarily successful intervention in the restoration of Pedro of Castile.
1367 20 June	Granted an annuity of 20 marks as an esquire of the royal household, in which he had probably served for some years.
c. 1367	Birth of a son Thomas, who was to be a retainer of the house of Lancaster and an important public figure in the early 15th century.
Late 1360s	Translation of (part of) *Roman de la Rose*, THE ROMAUNT OF THE ROSE; perhaps also writing poetry in French.
1368	Oton de Granson, the poet of Savoy, settles at the English court.
1368 July–Sept.	Abroad (in France?) on the king's service.
1368 12 Sept.	Death of Blanche, Duchess of Lancaster, John of Gaunt's first wife. THE BOOK OF THE DUCHESS written not long after.
1369 23 Mar.	Murder of Pedro of Castile.

1369	15 Aug.	Death of Queen Philippa.
1369	Sept.	In France with John of Gaunt's expeditionary force.
1370		The sack of Limoges, the Black Prince's last and most brutal foray into French territory.
1370	June–Sept.	In France again, on the annual campaign.
1371	Sept.	John of Gaunt marries Costanza (Constance) of Castile, Pedro's daughter.
1372	30 Aug.	Philippa Chaucer granted an annuity by John of Gaunt for service in the household of the Duchess Constance.
1372	1 Dec.–1373 23 May	In Italy (Genoa and Florence), as a member of a trading and diplomatic mission; first contact with the poetry of Dante, Petrarch and Boccaccio.
1373		John of Gaunt's unsuccessful *chevauchée* through France.
1374		Death of Petrarch.
1374		Granted a pitcher of wine a day for life by the king (23 Apr.); granted lease for life of rent-free dwelling over Aldgate (10 May); appointed controller of the customs of hides, skins and wools in the port of London (8 June); receives an annuity of £10 from John of Gaunt (13 June).
1375		Death of Boccaccio.
1375		John Barbour's Scots poem of *The Bruce* completed.
c. 1375		Gower begins his Anglo-Norman *Mirour de l'Omme*.
1376	8 June	Death of Edward the Black Prince.
1376		The 'Good Parliament': the Commons attempts to purge the royal household and assert control over the king's choice of advisers.

1376–7	In France on several occasions, deputed from the customs to serve on commissions negotiating for peace and the marriage of the young king.
1377	Death of Guillaume de Machaut, French poet.
1377 21 June	Death of Edward III; accession of Richard II.
1377–99	REIGN OF KING RICHARD II
Late 1370s	Langland revising *Piers Plowman*, B-text.
Late 1370s	ANELIDA AND ARCITE.
1378	Beginning of the Great Schism; popes in Avignon and in Rome.
1378	First record of York cycle of Mystery Plays.
1378 May–Sept.	In Italy (Lombardy), on diplomatic business to Bernabò Visconti, lord of Milan. THE HOUSE OF FAME probably complete by this time.
1380 4 May	Released by Cecilia Champain from any legal action relating to her *raptus* (rape).
1380	Year of birth of Lewis, Chaucer's only other known child, who was 11 years old when Chaucer wrote the *Treatise on the Astrolabe* for him in 1391.
c. 1380	THE PARLIAMENT OF FOWLS written, probably with some allusion to the negotiations that ended with Richard II's marriage to Anne of Bohemia on 3 May 1381.
c. 1380–1	'PALAMON AND ARCITE' (THE KNIGHT'S TALE).
1381	Death of Chaucer's mother.
1381 June	The Peasants' Revolt.
Early 1380s	Langland at work on *Piers Plowman*, C-text; Gower completes his Latin poem *Vox Clamantis*.

c. 1381–6	TROILUS AND CRISEYDE; probably simultaneously with the BOECE, the prose translation of the De Consolatione Philosophiae of Boethius.
	1382 Official condemnation of the heretical opinions of John Wyclif.
	1385 Robert de Vere, Earl of Oxford, the king's favourite, made Duke of Ireland.
	1385 The French poet Eustache Deschamps sends a poem of praise to Chaucer.
1385 10 Sept.	Receives livery of mourning as an esquire of the king's household on the death of the king's mother, Princess Joan of Kent.
1385 12 Oct.	Appointed as a member of the commission of the peace in Kent; occasional service until 1389; now probably resident in Kent.
	c. 1385–7 Thomas Usk writes his Testament of Love, in which he praises Chaucer.
	Mid-1380s Sir John Clanvowe writes The Book of Cupid, with quotation from 'Palamon and Arcite'.
	1386 9 July Gaunt sails for Spain; away until Nov. 1389.
1386 By 5 Oct.	Lease given up on Aldgate dwelling.
1386 Oct.–Nov.	Member of Parliament for Kent at one session, the 'Wonderful Parliament', where the opposition began its attempt to curb the king's power.
1386 15 Oct.	Gives testimony at the Scrope – Grosvenor hearing.
1386 4 Dec.	Resigns from the customs.

c. 1386–7	THE LEGEND OF GOOD WOMEN.
1387	Death of Philippa Chaucer.
1387	John Gower begins his *Confessio Amantis*, containing Venus's praise of Chaucer.
1387	John Trevisa writing his English prose translation of Higden's universal history, the *Polychronicon*.
1387 20 Dec.	Battle of Radcot Bridge; de Vere routed.
c. 1387	Begins THE CANTERBURY TALES.
1388	The 'Merciless Parliament': the Lords Appellant secure the removal of some of the king's closest advisers, and the execution of other adherents, including Thomas Usk.
1388 1 May	Transfers his annuities to John Scalby.
1389	Christine de Pizan begins her writing career at the French court.
1389 3 May	Richard resumes his regality.
1389 12 July	Appointed clerk of the king's works.
Late 14th cent.	Copying of British Library MS Cotton Nero A. x, containing *Sir Gawain and the Green Knight*, *Pearl*, *Patience*, and *Cleanness*. Copying of Bodleian Library MS Eng. poet. a. 1 (the Vernon MS), a massive compilation of English religious and didactic writing in prose and verse.
1390 Sept.	Robbed on the highway of the king's money.
1391	A TREATISE ON THE ASTROLABE; continuing work on THE CANTERBURY TALES.
1391 17 June	Resigns as clerk of the king's works.

1392	THE EQUATORIE OF THE PLANETIS, attributed by some to Chaucer.
1394	Death of Queen Anne.
1394	Granted royal annuity of £20.
1394–5	Revises Prologue to THE LEGEND OF GOOD WOMEN.
c. 1395	Second version of the Wycliffite Bible in English.
1395/6	Receives a fine gown of scarlet from Henry, Earl of Derby (the future Henry IV).
1396	Death of Walter Hilton, canon of Thurgarton, author of *The Scale of Perfection*.
1396?	ENVOY TO BUKTON; mentions Wife of Bath.
1397	Richard takes his revenge upon the Appellants; Duke of Gloucester murdered at Calais.
1397 1 Dec.	Royal grant of a tun of wine per year.
Late 1390s	Thomas Hoccleve a poetic disciple of Chaucer.
1398	Shrewsbury Parliament; beginning of Richard's 'tyranny'.
1399 3 Feb.	Death of John of Gaunt.
1399 30 Sept.	Deposition of Richard II; accession of Henry IV.
1399–1413	REIGN OF KING HENRY IV
1399 24 Dec.	Takes lease on house in precincts of Westminster Abbey.
1400 Feb.	THE COMPLAINT OF CHAUCER TO HIS PURSE; Henry IV renews payment on Chaucer's annuities.
1400 25 Oct.	Chaucer's death; buried in Westminster Abbey; later moved to the east aisle of the south transept, first tenant of 'Poets' Corner'.

Notes

Introduction

1 Crow and Olson, *Chaucer Life-Records* (1966). See appendix, pp. 550–96. (Subsequent references to this volume will be incorporated into the text, as *Life-Records*.)

2 *The Riverside Chaucer*, ed. Benson (1987), is used for all references to and quotations from Chaucer's works.

3 Donald R. Howard, *Chaucer: His Life, his Works, his World* (1987).

4 The allusion is to the idea put about by some modern writers on Renaissance drama, such as Jonathan Dollimore and Catherine Belsey, as previously by D. W. Robertson, that individual subjectivity, or interiorized self-recognition, or 'personality', somehow did not exist in the Middle Ages, or at least went unrecognized in literary texts. On this bizarre conjunction of old 'historical criticism' and new 'new historicism' (and 'cultural materialism'), see David Aers, 'A Whisper in the Ear of Early Modernists; or, Reflections on Literary Critics Writing the "History of the Subject"', in *Culture and History 1350–1600: Essays on English Communities, Identities and Writing*, ed. David Aers (Harvester Wheatsheaf, London, 1992), pp. 177–202.

5 I adapt the words of Peter Conrad, in a review of Jean Canavaggio's biography of Cervantes in the London *Observer*, 8 July 1990 (p. 55).

6 An example of the looseness of speculation into which biographical scholars may be drawn, and the increasing irritation of more careful scholars in having to undo all their bad work, is in the exchange of Haldeen Braddy and John Matthews Manly in *RES* 11 (1935), pp. 204–13, in connection with the former's theory concerning the occasion of *The Parliament of Fowls*.

7 Roland Barthes, 'The Death of the Author' (1968), tr. Stephen Heath, *Image, Music, Text* (Hill & Wang, New York, 1977), pp. 142–8 (p. 146). The term 'author-function' is from Michel Foucault, 'What is an Author?' (1969), in *Textual Strategies: Perspectives in Post-Structuralist Criticism*, ed. and tr. Josué V. Harari (Cornell University Press, Ithaca, NY, 1979), pp. 141–60 (p. 160).

8 See esp. A. J. Minnis, *Medieval Theory of Authorship: Scholastic Literary Attitudes in the Later Middle Ages* (Scolar Press, London, 1984). I have also profited greatly from the paper by John Plummer, 'Is Chawcer Dead?', given at the International Congress of the New Chaucer Society at Canterbury in August 1990. I am very grateful to Professor Plummer for sending me a copy of his paper.

9 John Gardner, *The Life and Times of Chaucer* (Knopf, Random House, New York, 1977).

10 The desire to find Chaucer, and to mark his place in the development of the increasing sense of identity that medieval poets convey (a development that is partly due to the growth in private reading), is well described and evoked in the excellent essay of Donald R. Howard, 'Chaucer the Man', *PMLA* 80 (1965), pp. 337–43.

11 On these 'networks and processes', see the introduction to the adventurous new book by Peter Brown and Andrew Butcher, *The Age of Saturn: Literature and History in the Canterbury Tales* (Basil Blackwell, Oxford, 1991), pp. 2–3. For the earlier style of biographical scholarship, see above, n. 6. Other examples are legion. Some of the classics of the genre are the book by George Williams, *A New View of Chaucer* (Duke University Press, Durham, NC, 1965), and essays by J. Leslie Hotson such as 'The *Tale of Melibeus* and John of Gaunt', *SP* 18 (1921), pp. 429–52, and 'Colfox *vs.* Chauntecleer', *PMLA* 39 (1924), pp. 762–81. See also Mary Giffin, *Studies on Chaucer and his Audience* (Editions L'Eclair, Hull, Quebec, 1956).

12 See John Harvey, *Henry Yevele* (Batsford, London, 1944), pp. 42–3.

13 Thomas Speght, 'Chaucer's Life' (1598); William Godwin, *The Life of Geoffrey Chaucer* (1803); J. R. Hulbert, *Chaucer's Official Life* (1912), esp. pp. 77–84; J. M. Manly, 'Three Recent Chaucer Studies' (1934), p. 264.

1 Beginnings (*c.* 1340–1360)

1 It was Richard Firth Green who first drew my attention to the legal formula 'etatis x1 annorum et amplius' as it appears in an inquisition *post mortem* in 1353; see L. C. Hector, *Palaeography and Forgery*, Borthwick Institute of Historical Research, St Anthony's Hall Publications, 15 (St Anthony's Press, London and York, 1959), p. 17. Dr David Smith, the Director of the Borthwick Institute, has since generously drawn up for me a long list of witnesses' ages as given in the records of the York Archiepiscopal Court, 1380–5, and the formula appears frequently, alongside exact ages for other witnesses. For the Scrope–Grosvenor inquisition, see *The Controversy between Sir Richard Scrope and Sir Robert Grosvenor in the Court of Chivalry*, ed. Sir N. Harris Nicolas (2 vols, London, 1832). The editor works hard, in his commentary (II. 404), to make Chaucer about 55 years old at the time of the deposition, aware of the then commonly accepted date of birth of 1328.

2 Lister M. Matheson, 'Chaucer's Ancestry: Historical and Philological Reassessments', *ChauR* 25 (1991), pp. 171–89 (pp. 179–81). I am grateful to

Professor Matheson and to the publishers of the *Chaucer Review* (Pennsylvania State University Press) for allowing me to make use of the Chaucer family tree on p. 173 of his essay.

3 For a detailed study of this side of Chaucer's family, see Vincent B. Redstone and Lilian J. Redstone, 'The Heyrons of London: A Study in the Social Origins of Geoffrey Chaucer', *Speculum*, 12 (1937), pp. 182–95.

4 There is much on the movement between classes in medieval London in the indispensable study of Sylvia L. Thrupp, *The Merchant Class of Medieval London* (1948), ch. 6, 'Trade and Gentility', pp. 234–87. The best recent study of the English upper class in the period is Chris Given-Wilson, *The English Nobility in the Late Middle Ages* (1987).

5 Thrupp, *Merchant Class of Medieval London*, p. 162. Thrupp has an invaluable account of elementary education in London (pp. 155–63), as well as much on the houses and furnishings and style of life of the merchant class (pp. 130–54). For London as an educational and intellectual centre, see William J. Courtenay, 'The London *Studia* in the Fourteenth Century', *M&H*, ns 12 (1985), pp. 127–41, repr. with some changes in Courtenay, *Schools and Scholars* (1987), pp. 91–106; D. W. Robertson, *Chaucer's London* (1968), ch. 5, 'London as an Intellectual Center', pp. 179–222.

6 For Scogan and Picard, see the notes to the edn of the *Moral Balade* in *Chaucerian and Other Pieces*, ed. Skeat (1897), p. 237; John Stow, *Survey of London* (1603), ed. C. L. Kingsford (2 vols, Clarendon Press, Oxford, 1908), I. 239–41. See also below, ch. 4, n. 32. For Lydgate, see Pearsall, *John Lydgate* (1970), pp. 184–7.

7 The suggestion that Gower wrote his *Cinkante Balades* for the London *puy* was made by Fisher, *John Gower* (1964), pp. 75–83, and the suggestion concerning Chaucer's *Complaint* by Howard, *Chaucer and the Medieval World*, p. 267. Martin Stevens, 'The Royal Stanza in Early English Literature', *PMLA* 94 (1979), pp. 62–76, argues that the *puy* may have been where the rhyme royal stanza originated, since the purpose of the *puy* was the crowning of a *chauncon reale*. None of this speculation, it must be said, is very convincing. On the *puy* in general, see further Nigel Wilkins, 'Music and Poetry at Court: England and France in the Later Middle Ages', in *English Court Culture in the Later Middle Ages*, ed. Scattergood and Sherborne (1983), pp. 183–204 (pp. 185–6).

8 Philip Ziegler, *The Black Death* (Collins, London, 1969), p. 160.

9 Millard Meiss, *Painting in Florence and Siena after the Black Death* (Princeton University Press, Princeton, NJ, 1951); Joseph Polzer, 'Aspects of the Four-teenth-Century Iconography of Death and the Plague', in *The Black Death: The Impact of the Fourteenth-Century Plague: Papers of the Eleventh Annual Conference of the Center for Medieval and Early Renaissance Studies*, ed. Daniel Williman, Medieval and Renaissance Texts and Studies, 13 (Center for Medieval and Early Renaissance Studies, Binghamton, NY, 1982), pp. 107–30. Other essays in this volume, including those by Robert E. Lerner, 'The Black Death and Western European Eschatological Mentalities' (pp. 77–106), and

Siegfried Wenzel, 'Pestilence and Middle English Literature: Friar John Grimestone's Poems on Death' (pp. 131–59), confirm the view that the impact of and reaction to the plague was less dramatic than has been supposed.

10 Alan Macfarlane, *The Origins of English Individualism: The Family, Property and Social Transition* (Basil Blackwell, Oxford, 1978).

11 See e.g. Christopher Dyer, *Standards of Living in the Later Middle Ages: Social Change in England, c. 1200–1520* (Cambridge University Press, Cambridge, 1989), pp. 207, 216.

12 F. R. H. Du Boulay, 'The Historical Chaucer' (1974), p. 35.

13 For the earlier argument that Chaucer was educated at the Inns of Court, see Edith Rickert, 'Was Chaucer a Student at the Inner Temple?' *The Manly Anniversary Studies in Language and Literature* (University of Chicago Press, Chicago, 1923), pp. 20–31; John Matthews Manly, *Some New Light on Chaucer* (1926), pp. 7–14. For a reappraisal of the evidence, see D. S. Bland, 'Chaucer and the Inns of Court, a Re-examination', *ES* 33 (1952), pp. 145–55, and, more recently, Joseph A. Hornsby, 'Was Chaucer Educated at the Inns of Court?' *ChauR* 22 (1988), pp. 255–68. Hornsby argues conclusively against the Rickert hypothesis.

14 The argument for Chaucer's attendance at St Paul's School was first put forward by Edith Rickert, 'Chaucer at School', *MP* 29 (1932), pp. 257–74.

15 Thrupp, *Merchant Class of Medieval London*, p. 160.

16 The Bodleian manuscript is mentioned, and the related line of argument supported, by Bruce Harbert, 'Chaucer and the Latin Classics', in *Writers and their Background*, ed. Brewer, pp. 137–53 (pp. 139–40). For Jankin's book, see Robert A. Pratt, 'Jankyn's Book of Wikked Wyves: Medieval Antimatrimonial Propaganda in the Universities', *Annuale Mediaevale*, 3 (1962), pp. 5–27. For John of Wales, see Robert A. Pratt, 'Chaucer and the Hand that Fed Him', *Speculum*, 41 (1966), pp. 619–42.

17 See Robert A. Pratt, 'Chaucer's Claudian', *Speculum*, 22 (1947), pp. 419–29 (p. 429). For a general study of the *Liber Catonianus*, see Paul M. Clogan, 'Literary Genres in a Medieval Textbook', *M&H* 11 (1982), pp. 199–209.

18 For emphasis on this aspect of Chaucer's education, see Richard Firth Green, *Poets and Princepleasers* (1980), p. 71. More generally, on the nature of the education provided for the younger members of a noble household, see Nicholas Orme, 'The Education of the Courtier', in *English Court Culture*, ed. Scattergood and Sherborne, pp. 63–85; Kate Mertes, *The English Noble Household 1250–1600* (1988), pp. 170–5.

19 Thomas Frederick Tout, *Chapters in the Administrative History of Mediaeval England*, Publications of the University of Manchester, Historical Series, 34–5, 48–9, 57, 64 (6 vols, Longmans, Green & Co., London, and The University Press, Manchester, 1920–33), III. 201–2; Tout, 'Literature and Learning in the English Civil Service' (1929), p. 382.

20 Richard Firth Green, 'Arcite at Court', *ELN* 18 (1981), pp. 251–7 (p. 253); Mertes, *The English Noble Household*, pp. 29–31.

21 Much in the preceding paragraphs is from Froissart's incomparable account of events in England and France between 1322 and 1400 in his *Chroniques*. Reference is to the volume of selections translated and edited by Geoffrey Brereton, *Froissart's Chronicles* (1968), namely pp. 105–10 (the burghers of Calais), 89–90 (King John of Bohemia), 140–2 (King John of France at Poitiers), 77 (purchase of ransoms), 143 (prisoners outnumbering captors), 147 (importance of ransoms to advancement), p. 187 (exchange of insults), 103 (agreeing on site for battle), 164 (the siege of Cormicy), 90, 98 (interest in feats of arms), 222 (story of Sir Robert Salle).

22 See e.g. Terry Jones, *Chaucer's Knight: The Portrait of a Medieval Mercenary* (Weidenfeld & Nicolson, London, 1980). Such a view neglects also the practical function of military chivalry in establishing some of the conventions of good behaviour between nations.

23 Geoffroi de Charny, *Livre de Chevalerie*, printed in *Oeuvres de Froissart*, ed. Kervyn de Lettenhove (1867–77), Vol. I (Part 3), p. 519.

24 See R. E. Kaske, 'The Knight's Interruption of the "Monk's Tale"', *ELH* 24 (1957), pp. 249–68.

25 Howard, *Chaucer and the Medieval World*, p. 271; Froissart, *Chronicles*, tr. Brereton, p. 343.

26 For discussion of the lack of interest in war in the poetry of Chaucer, as in 'Ricardian poetry' generally, see J. A. Burrow, *Ricardian Poetry* (1971), pp. 54–5, 93–102.

2 Early Career (the 1360s)

1 See e.g. Maurice Hussey, A. C. Spearing and James Winny, *An Introduction to Chaucer* (Cambridge University Press, Cambridge, 1965), p. 3; F. E. Halliday, *Chaucer and his World* (Thames & Hudson, London, 1968), p. 53.

2 See Richard Firth Green, 'Arcite at Court', *ELN* 18 (1981), pp. 251–7.

3 This is the traditional date of Thomas's birth, when any is quoted. It gains support from a record reported in Albert Croll Baugh, 'Kirk's Life Records of Thomas Chaucer', *PMLA* 47 (1932), pp. 461–515, where Thomas is mainpernor in a case in Buckinghamshire on 8 July 1389 (item 1, p. 463); he must presumably have reached his majority before that date.

4 This hypothesis is dismissed in the standard biography by Martin B. Ruud, *Thomas Chaucer*, Research Publications of the University of Minnesota, Studies of Language and Literature, 9 (1926), ch. 7, though it is reasserted with some vigour by Russell Kraus, *Chaucerian Problems: Especially the Petherton Forestership and the Question of Thomas Chaucer* (1932; repr. AMS Press, New York, 1973), pp. 50–6.

5 Andrew Breeze, of the University of Navarre, informs me that the authoritative *Historia Politica del Reino de Navarra* by the Spanish scholar Jose Maria Lacarra (Editorial Aranzadi, Pamplona, 1973) still refers to the record of 'Geoffroy de Sancerre, escudero inglés'; a little further on, equally unrecognizable, is 'Juan de Karzawal' (John Carswell).

6   *Life of the Black Prince, by the Herald of Sir John Chandos*, ed. Mildred K. Pope and Eleanor C. Lodge (Clarendon Press, Oxford, 1910), lines 3295–9.

7   For the argument that Chaucer was on some kind of diplomatic mission, see Albert C. Baugh, 'The Background of Chaucer's Mission to Spain', in *Chaucer und seine Zeit: Symposion für Walter F. Schirmer*, ed. Arno Esch, Buchreihe der Anglia Zeitschrift für Englische Philologie, Band 14 (Max Niemeyer Verlag, Tübingen, 1968), pp. 55–69. Chaucer's friend Sir Lewis Clifford was in Navarre in late 1366 and fought at Najera, but it is extremely unlikely that Chaucer was with him there, or was engaged in any military activity: see Thomas A. Reisner and Mary E. Reisner, 'Lewis Clifford and the Kingdom of Navarre', *MP* 75 (1978), pp. 385–90.

8   Gaston Phebus, *Livre de Chasse*, ed. G. Tilander, Cynegetica, 18 (Karlshamn, 1971), p. 52. For a brief account of the popularity of hunting at the court of Edward III, see pp. 61–3 in Given-Wilson, *The Royal Household and the King's Affinity* (1986), a book which is indispensable for the understanding of Chaucer's background as a court servant. For a discussion of literary uses of hunting imagery, esp. in erotic contexts, see Marcelle Thiébaux, *The Stag of Love* (Cornell University Press, Ithaca, NY and London, 1974).

9   C. S. Lewis, *English Literature in the Sixteenth Century, excluding Drama*, Oxford History of English Literature, 3 (Clarendon Press, Oxford, 1954), p. 61.

10   For *Guy of Warwick* and *Sir Tristrem*, see Pearsall, *Old English and Middle English Poetry* (1977), p. 115.

11   For female aristocratic ownership of 'romances', see Elizabeth Salter, 'England and the Continent during the Thirteenth Century: Royal and Aristocratic Patronage', in *English and International* (1988), pp. 75–100 (p. 75).

12   There are excellent chapters on 'The Game of Love' in John Stevens, *Music and Poetry in the Early Tudor Court* (Methuen, London, 1961), pp. 154–202, and in Green, *Poets and Princepleasers*, ch. 4, 'The Court of Cupid'.

13   See Richard Firth Green, *'Le Roi Qui Ne Ment* and Aristocratic Courtship', in *Courtly Literature: Culture and Context: Selected Papers from the 5th Triennial Congress of the International Courtly Literature Society, Dalfsen, The Netherlands, 9–16 August, 1986*, ed. Keith Busby and Erik Kooper, Utrecht Publications in General and Comparative Literature, 25 (John Benjamins, Amsterdam and Philadelphia, 1990), pp. 211–25 (p. 213).

14   Froissart's account of his arrival at Foix is in *Chroniques*, XI. 88. The dispute about a woman comes in *Chronicles*, tr. Brereton, p. 293.

15   *Les Enseignements d'Edouard III*, or *Instructio patris regis ad filium Edwardum*, printed (from Bodley MS 425, f. 107) in *Oeuvres de Froissart*, ed. Kervyn de Lettenhove, Introduction, Vol. I (Part 3), pp. 541–53 (p. 546).

16   See Derek Pearsall, 'The Alliterative Revival: Origins and Social Backgrounds', in *Middle English Alliterative Poetry and its Literary Background*, ed. David Lawton (D. S. Brewer, Cambridge, 1982), pp. 34–53 (p. 47).

17   The Paston story is in Ethel Seaton, *Sir Richard Roos: Lancastrian Poet* (Rupert Hart-Davis, London, 1961), p. 376; see also Pearsall, *Old English and Middle*

English Poetry, p. 221. For Froissart's story of Gaston, see *Chronicles*, tr. Brereton, pp. 264–5; the passage concerning Queen Philippa occurs in some manuscripts of the Prologue to Book IV of the *Chroniques*: see *Oeuvres*, ed. Kervyn de Lettenhove, XIV, p. 1.

18 *Of Arthour and Of Merlin*, ed. O. D. Macrae-Gibson, EETS 268 (1973), lines 23–4 (Auchinleck version); Usk, *Testament of Love*, in *Chaucerian and Other Pieces*, ed. Skeat, p. 2, lines 33–8. See further Pearsall, *Old English and Middle English Poetry*, pp. 85–9, 115–18, 189–91. A comprehensive survey of the subject is provided by Rolf Berndt, 'The Period of the Final Decline of French in Medieval England (Fourteenth and Early Fifteenth Centuries)', *Zeitschrift für Anglistik und Amerikanistik*, 20 (1972), pp. 341–69.

19 *Le Livre de Seyntz Medicines*, ed. E. J. Arnould, Anglo-Norman Texts, 2 (Basil Blackwell, Oxford, 1940), p. 239.

20 For a superb short sketch of Jean le Bon as a patron, and of the English court in the mid fourteenth century, see Elizabeth Salter, 'Chaucer and Internationalism', *SAC* 2 (1980), pp. 71–9, repr. in Salter, *English and International*, pp. 239–44. See also Nigel Wilkins, 'Music and Poetry at Court: England and France in the Late Middle Ages', in *English Court Culture*, ed. Scattergood and Sherborne, pp. 183–204 (pp. 190–97).

21 James I. Wimsatt, 'The *Dit dou Bleu Chevalier*: Froissart's Imitation of Chaucer', *MS* 34 (1972), pp. 388–400.

22 Froissart, *Chronicles*, tr. Brereton, p. 434 (Derby and Mowbray); 20–1, 158, 319 (views of peasants); 179 (sack of Limoges).

23 The quotation is from *Le Joli Buisson de Jonece*, where Froissart, encouraged by Philosophy to resume writing but (like Hoccleve, later) not too sure what to write, gives a list of the poems he has written: see lines 451–2 in the edn of the poem by Anthime Fourrier, Textes Littéraires Français (Librairie Droz, Geneva, 1975).

24 On Jean de la Mote and Philippe de Vitry, see James I. Wimsatt, *Chaucer and the Poems of 'Ch'* (1982), pp. 51–60. See also the important revisions of Wimsatt's interpretations of the two poems in F. N. M. Diekstra, 'The Poetic Exchange between Philippe de Vitry and Jean de la Mote: A New Edition', *Neophilologus*, 70 (1986), pp. 504–19.

25 There is discussion of the duke and *Merciles Beaute* in Wimsatt, *Chaucer and the Poems of 'Ch'*, p. 49. For Granson (paragraph following), see pp. 50–1, 69–74.

26 There is full discussion of the question of Chaucer's authorship in Wimsatt, *Chaucer and the Poems of 'Ch'*, pp. 1–8, followed by texts of all the poems of 'Ch'. Rossell Hope Robbins, in two essays published in the late 1970s, almost seems to prepare the way for the unveiling of 'Ch': see 'The Vintner's Son: French Wine in English Bottles', in *Eleanor of Aquitaine: Patron and Politician*, ed. William W. Kibler (University of Texas Press, Austin, 1976), pp. 147–72, and 'Geoffroi Chaucier, Poète Français, Father of English Poetry', *ChauR* 13 (1978), pp. 93–115. Robbins emphasizes, with a wealth of examples, the tenacity of French in court circles throughout the fourteenth

century, argues strongly that Chaucer's earliest poetry was in French, and suggests that the commissioning (or acceptability) of *The Book of the Duchess* is inexplicable unless Chaucer already had a reputation as a French poet.

27   'Chançon Royal', lines 1–6, in Wimsatt, *Chaucer and the Poems of 'Ch'*, p. 10.

28   On these poems, see ibid. pp. 44–6; for 'Cire Mire Bouf', see p. 46.

29   See Laura Hibbard Loomis, 'Chaucer and the Auchinleck Manuscript: *Thopas* and *Guy of Warwick*', in *Essays and Studies in Honor of Carleton Brown* (New York University Press, New York, 1940), pp. 111–28; also 'Chaucer and the Breton Lays of the Auchinleck Manuscript', *SP* 38 (1941), pp. 14–33; and the further discussion in the facsimile of *The Auchinleck Manuscript, National Library of Scotland Advocates' MS 19. 2. 1* (Scolar Press, London, 1977), Introduction (by Derek Pearsall and I. C. Cunningham), p. xi.

30   The quotations are from P. M. Kean, *Chaucer and the Making of English Poetry* (1972), I. 11, and J. A. Burrow, *Ricardian Poetry*, p. 12. For further discussion of Chaucer's debt to the popular romances, see Kean, pp. 5–23; Burrow, pp. 11–23; D. S. Brewer, 'The Relationship of Chaucer to the English and European Traditions', In *Chaucer and Chaucerians*, ed. Brewer (1966), pp. 1–38 (esp. pp. 4–15).

31   Burrow, *Ricardian Poetry*, p. 21.

32   *Sir Orfeo*, ed. A. J. Bliss, Oxford English Monographs (Oxford University Press, London, 1954), lines 544–52.

33   *Le Paradis d'Amour, L'Orloge Amoureus*, ed. Peter F. Dembowski, Textes Littéraires Français (Librairie Droz, Geneva, 1986).

34   See Wife of Bath's Prologue, III. 469–79, and cf. *Roman*, 12932–48; Franklin's Tale, V. 764–6, cf. *Roman*, 9424–42; General Prologue, I. 127–36 (Prioress), cf. *Roman*, 13408–32; General Prologue, I. 725–42 (calling a spade a spade), cf. *Roman*, 15159–92; *Roman*, 12761–4546 (La Vieille), 11065–11974 (Faux-Semblant), 5845–6900 (Fortune), 17039–874 (destiny), 18607–946 (*gentillesse*, cf. Chaucer's poem of *Gentilesse* and Wife of Bath's Tale, III. 1109–76), 5829–6901 (cf. Monk's Tale), 5589–658 (cf. Physician's Tale). The edn of *Le Roman de la Rose* used for citation is that of Ernest Langlois, SATF (5 vols, 1914–24).

35   Text and translation are from *Chaucer: The Critical Heritage*, ed. Brewer (1978), I. 39–42. In style, Deschamps's poem is remarkably similar to the bravura display pieces of Philippe de Vitry and Jean de La Mote, alluded to above.

36   See Caroline D. Eckhardt, 'The Art of Translation in *The Romaunt of the Rose*', *SAC* 6 (1984), pp. 41–63. There are some good pages on Chaucer's handling of the octosyllabic couplet in Howard, *Chaucer and the Medieval World*, pp. 143–7.

37   William Godwin, *Life of Geoffrey Chaucer*; George Williams, *A New View of Chaucer* (Duke University Press, Durham, NC, 1965). For record of payment of the annuity from Gaunt, see *Life-Records*, pp. 272–4. The relevant published records are *John of Gaunt's Register*, ed. Sydney Armitage-Smith, Camden Third Series, 20–1 (2 vols, London, 1911), covering the years

1371–5, and *John of Gaunt's Register, 1379–1383*, ed. Eleanor C. Lodge and Robert Somerville, Camden Third Series, 56–7 (2 vols, London, 1937).

38 For a discussion of this odd proceeding, see John Thompson, 'Textual Instability and the Late Medieval Reputation of Some Middle English Religious Literature', *Text*, 5 (1991), pp. 175–94 (pp. 178–80).

39 The best general account of Chaucer's debt to the French poets is given by James I. Wimsatt, *Chaucer and the French Love-Poets: The Literary Background of the Book of the Duchess*, University of North Carolina Studies in Comparative Literature, 43 (University of North Carolina Department of Romance Languages, Chapel Hill, NC, 1968). See also the valuable collection of translations by B. A. Windeatt, *Chaucer's Dream Poetry: Sources and Analogues*, Chaucer Studies, 7 (D. S. Brewer, Cambridge, and Rowman & Littlefield, Totowa, NJ, 1982).

40 Henry Miller, reported by Wayne C. Booth, *The Rhetoric of Fiction* (University of Chicago Press, Chicago, 1961), p. 367, and quoted by Elizabeth Salter, '*Troilus and Criseyde*: Poet and Narrator', in *Acts of Interpretation: The Text in its Contexts 700–1600: Essays on Medieval and Renaissance Literature in Honor of E. Talbot Donaldson*, ed. Mary J. Carruthers and Elizabeth D. Kirk (Pilgrim Books, Norman, Okla., 1982), pp. 281–91 (p. 282).

41 The phrase 'performing self' is from the very useful essay by Martin Stevens, 'The Performing Self in Twelfth-Century Culture', *Viator*, 9 (1978), pp. 193–212. There is sensible discussion of Chaucer's so-called 'persona', as a specially complex version of the normal practice of self-presentation in conversation, in Bertrand H. Bronson, *In Search of Chaucer* (University of Toronto Press, Toronto, 1960), pp. 25–32. It is the influence of E. Talbot Donaldson, and particularly of his famous essay on 'Chaucer the Pilgrim', *PMLA* 69 (1954), pp. 928–36 (frequently reprinted), that has been chiefly responsible for the proliferating discussion of the Chaucerian persona, as also for the spread of the rather impressionistic view of its social origins (see esp. pp. 935–6). Donald R. Howard, for instance, in 'Chaucer the Man', *PMLA* 80 (1965), pp. 337–43, speaks of the dynamic presence of Chaucer in his works as that of 'a bourgeois addressing his social betters' (p. 342).

42 Gaunt's will is printed in Sydney Armitage-Smith, *John of Gaunt* (Constable, London, 1905), pp. 420–36. The arrangements for Blanche's anniversaries are recorded in *Gaunt's Register*, ed. Armitage-Smith (above, n. 37), items 915, 918, 943, 1091, 1122, 1394, 1585, 1659.

43 See *Gaunt's Register*, ed. Armitage-Smith, items 1608, 1659. Constance bore him a daughter Catharine (Catalina) and a son who died soon after he was born in November 1376.

44 It was established by J. J. N. Palmer, 'The Historical Context of the *Book of the Duchess*: A Revision', *ChauR* 8 (1974), pp. 253–61, that Blanche died on 12 September 1368 and not, as previously thought, on the same date in 1369. Palmer argued that Chaucer's poem was written before November 1368, when the king was already planning a second marriage for his son, and certainly before Gaunt remarried in 1371. The arguments for a date in

1368 or 1369 are distinctly superior to those for a later date, such as those advanced by Edward I. Condren, 'The Historical Context of the *Book of the Duchess*: A New Hypothesis', *ChauR* 5 (1971), pp. 195–212. The argument that the reference to the black knight as a 'kyng' (line 1314) means that the poem was written after 1371, when Gaunt assumed the title of King of Castile and Leon, seems to strain a conventionally honorific form of poetic reference.

3   Advances (the 1370s)

1   For the suggestion of Gaunt's influence in 1374, which is developed in this paragraph, I am chiefly indebted to Ernest P. Kuhl, 'Chaucer and Aldgate', *PMLA* 39 (1924), pp. 101–22. Gaunt seems a likelier candidate than Alice Perrers, much favoured by Howard (*Chaucer and the Medieval World*, pp. 204–8), on the basis of some dubious evidence supplied by Haldeen Braddy, 'Chaucer and Dame Alice Perrers', *Speculum*, 21 (1946), pp. 222–8.

2   Hulbert, *Chaucer's Official Life*: 'The analysis of Chaucer's life does not confirm the theory that John of Gaunt exercised a ruling influence over his destiny' (p. 83); Manly, 'Three Recent Chaucer Studies': 'Geoffrey Chaucer's career was in no way exceptional for a faithful and efficient squire of the King' (p. 264).

3   J. A. W. Bennett, 'Chaucer's Contemporary', in *Piers Plowman: Critical Approaches*, ed. S. S. Hussey (Methuen, London, 1969), pp. 310–24 (p. 322). For the London book-trade, see C. Paul Christianson, 'Evidence for the Study of London's Late Medieval Manuscript-Book Trade', in *Book Production and Publishing in Britain 1375–1475*, ed. Griffiths and Pearsall (1989), pp. 87–108 (pp. 89–90).

4   John H. Schofield, *The Building of London from the Conquest to the Great Fire*, British Museum Publications in association with the Museum of London (Colonnade Books, 1984), ch. 4, 'The London of Yevele and Chaucer', p. 104. See also *Life-Records*, p. 171. The discrepancy between the documents reported in the *Life-Records* and the evidence of digging is not a matter for surprise.

5   Howard, *Chaucer and the Medieval World*, p. 188.

6   See J. A. Burrow, 'Bards, Minstrels and Men of Letters', ch. 10 in *Literature and Civilization*, ed. David Daiches and Anthony Thorlby, Vol. I: *The Mediaeval World* (Aldus Books, London, 1973), pp. 347–70. For Chaucer and his circle as the 'new men' of the age, men with fresh ideas on the social place and 'good' of literature, see D. S. Brewer, 'Class Distinction in Chaucer' (1968); Paul Strohm, 'Chaucer's Audience', *Literature and History*, 5 (1977), pp. 26–41; Anne Middleton, 'The Idea of Public Poetry in the Reign of Richard II' (1978). Middleton finds some 'new men' among the pilgrims in 'Chaucer's "New Men" and the Good of Literature' (1980).

7   Froissart, *Chronicles*, tr. Brereton, pp. 203–4.

8   See Robert A. Pratt, 'Chaucer and the Visconti Libraries', *ELH* 6 (1939), pp. 191–9. See further below, n. 19.

9   David Wallace, ' "Whan She Translated Was": A Chaucerian Critique of the Petrarchan Academy', in *Literary Practice and Social Change in Britain, 1380–1530*, ed. Patterson (1990), pp. 156–215.

10 The idea of 'medievalization' is from C. S. Lewis, who said of *Troilus* that 'the process which *Il Filostrato* underwent at Chaucer's hands was first and foremost a process of *medievalization*': see 'What Chaucer Really Did to *Il Filostrato*', *E&S* 17 (1932), pp. 56–75 (p. 56).

11 John Burrow draws attention to Pope's tactic in 'Poems without Endings', *SAC* 13(1991), pp. 17–37 (p. 29).

12 The arguments concerning 10 December are put forward, respectively, by David M. Bevington, 'The Obtuse Narrator in Chaucer's *House of Fame*', *Speculum*, 36 (1961), pp. 288–98, and by Larry D. Benson, 'The "Love-Tydynges" in Chaucer's *House of Fame*', in *Chaucer in the Eighties*, ed. Julian N. Wasserman and Robert J. Blanch (Syracuse University Press, Syracuse, 1986), pp. 3–22.

13 The phrase 'authenticating realism' is taken from the suggestive essay by Morton W. Bloomfield, 'Authenticating Realism and the Realism of Chaucer', *Thought*, 39 (1964), pp. 335–58. For Machaut and Froissart, see John M. Fyler's note in *The Riverside Chaucer*, p. 979 (line 63).

14 Richard J. Schoeck, 'A Legal Reading of Chaucer's *Hous of Fame*', *UTQ* 23 (1953), pp. 185–92.

15 For 'reception theory', see Hans-Robert Jauss, *Toward an Aesthetic of Reception*, tr. Timothy Bahti (University of Minnesota Press, Minneapolis, 1982). For the 'hermeneutic approach' see, generally, Richard Palmer, *Hermeneutics: Interpretation Theory in Schleiermacher, Dilthey, Heidegger, and Gadamer* (Northwestern University Press, Evanston, Ill., 1969), and, with reference to Chaucer, Judith Ferster, *Chaucer on Interpretation* (Cambridge University Press, Cambridge, 1985). For Chaucer's relation to the Ockhamite or nominalist tradition of scepticism, and to the *moderni* in general, see the stimulating book by Sheila Delany, *Chaucer's House of Fame: The Poetics of Skeptical Fideism* (Chicago and London, University of Chicago Press, 1972); also Laurence Eldredge, 'Chaucer's "Hous of Fame" and the "Via Moderna"', *NM* 71 (1970), pp. 105–19.

16 For Chaucer's knowledge of science, see Walter Clyde Curry, *Chaucer and the Mediaeval Sciences* (Oxford University Press, London, 1926; 2nd edn, revised and enlarged, Barnes & Noble, New York, 1960); also Mahmoud Manzaloui, 'Chaucer and Science', in *Writers and their Background*, ed. Brewer, pp. 224–61.

17 Giorgio Vasari, *Lives of the Most Famous Painters*, Introduction, quoted, with translation, in Erwin Panofsky, 'The First Page of Giorgio Vasari's Libro', repr. in his collection of essays, *Meaning in the Visual Arts* (Doubleday Books, New York, 1955; Penguin Books, Aylesbury, 1970), pp. 214–15.

18 See Laura Kendrick, 'Chaucer's *House of Fame* and the French *Palais de Justice*', *SAC* 6 (1984), pp. 121–33 (p. 123).

19 There has been some debate about this matter, with Robert A. Pratt, 'Conjectures regarding Chaucer's Manuscript of the *Teseida*', *SP* 42 (1945), pp. 745–63, arguing that Chaucer did not know the *Chiose*, and Piero Boitani, *Chaucer and Boccaccio*, Medium Ævum Monographs, ns 8 (Oxford, 1977), pp. 113–16, arguing that he did. Most recently, William E. Coleman has argued persuasively that the manuscript of the *Teseida* that Chaucer used belonged to a manuscript tradition that does not include the *Chiose* (and does not name Boccaccio as author): see 'Chaucer, the *Teseida*, and the Visconti Library at Pavia: A Hypothesis', *Medium Ævum*, 51 (1982), pp. 92–101 (pp. 97–9). Coleman has confirmed his view in 'Chaucer's Manuscript and Boccaccio's Commentaries on *Il Teseida*', *Chaucer Newsletter*, 9/2 (Fall 1987), pp. 1–6.

20 Matthew Arnold, 'The Study of Poetry', in *Complete Prose Works*, Vol. IX, ed. R. H. Super (University of Michigan Press, Ann Arbor, 1973), pp. 161–88 (p. 168). The line from Chaucer that Arnold does pick out (pp. 175, 181) is Prioress's Tale, VII. 579: 'O martyr souded to virginitee' (which Arnold misquotes, with *in* for *to*). Lewis's comment is in *The Allegory of Love*, p. 201.

21 John Keats, letter to John Hamilton Reynolds, 3 May 1818, Letter 64 in *The Letters of John Keats*, ed. Maurice Buxton Forman (Oxford University Press, London, 1931; 3rd edn, revised, 1947), pp. 143–4.

22 George Kane, *Chaucer* (Oxford University Press, Oxford, 1984), p. 56.

23 The phrase is from Paul Strohm's excellent book, *Social Chaucer* (1989), ch. 6, 'A Mixed Commonwealth of Style' (p. 144).

24 In Botticelli's *Birth of Venus*, says E. H. Gombrich, 'the image gained ascendancy over the text, Venus conquered her commentators' ('Botticelli's Mythologies: A Study in the Neoplatonic Symbolism of his Circle', *JWCI*, 8 (1945), pp. 7–60 (p. 43)). This essay is alluded to by Elizabeth Salter, *Fourteenth-Century English Poetry* (1983), p. 135; she gives a superb account (pp. 127–40) of Chaucer's handling of the whole scene and his subtle manipulations of Boccaccio and, equally, of the audience. For the medieval iconography of Venus, see Meg Twycross, *The Medieval Anadyomene*, Medium Ævum Monographs, ns 1 (Oxford, 1972), and, more tendentiously, Robert Hollander, *Boccaccio's Two Venuses* (Columbia University Press, New York, 1977).

25 See Henry Ansgar Kelly, *Chaucer and the Cult of St Valentine*, Davis Medieval Texts and Studies, 5 (University of California, Davis, and Brill, Leiden, 1986). Kelly's argument is that St Valentine's Day was actually 3 May, the day of St Valentine of Genoa, and that this was the date intended by Chaucer in all his references to St Valentine's Day and the mating of birds, an association which he himself invented; 14 February, the day of the other St Valentines, later took over this association.

26 There is approval of the mating habits of birds in the famous thirteenth-century encyclopaedia of Bartholomaeus Anglicus, *De Proprietatibus rerum*, cited from the 1582 print of John Trevisa's late-fourteenth-century English translation in *The Parlement of Foulys*, ed. D. S. Brewer, Nelson's Medieval and Renaissance Library (Thomas Nelson, London and Edinburgh, 1960), p. 114 (note to line 310).

27 See Larry D. Benson, 'The Occasion of *The Parliament of Fowls*', in *The Wisdom of Poetry: Essays in Early English Literature in Honor of Morton W. Bloomfield*, ed. Larry D. Benson and Siegfried Wenzel, Medieval Institute Publications (University of Western Michigan, Kalamazoo, Mich., 1982), pp. 123–44. Benson's essay is a skilful and convincing re-presentation of an argument first advanced by Koch in 1878.

4 Fame (1380–1386)

1 Those who have expanded on the role of the Princess Joan in Chaucer's career include Margaret Galway, 'Chaucer's Sovereign Lady', *MLR* 33 (1938), pp. 145–99 (among many other essays by the same scholar on the same theme), and John Norton-Smith, *Geoffrey Chaucer* (Routledge & Kegan Paul, London, 1974), pp. 62–3.

2 For a modern edition of *The Book of Cupid*, as well as of Clanvowe's other known work, a religious prose treatise, *The Two Ways*, see *The Works of Sir John Clanvowe*, ed. V. J. Scattergood (D. S. Brewer, Cambridge, 1975).

3 See the edition cited in ch. 2, n. 35; the ballade in praise of Chaucer is no. 285 in *Deschamps, Oeuvres*, ed. Saint-Hilaire and Raynaud, II. 138–9; the Flower and the Leaf poems are nos. 764–7, IV. 257–64. For a still-valuable discussion of the Deschamps connection, see G. L. Kittredge, 'Chaucer and Some of his Friends', *MP* 1 (1903), pp. 1–18; also John Livingston Lowes, 'Chaucer and the *Miroir de Mariage*', *MP* 8 (1910), pp. 165–86; 'The Prologue to the *Legend of Good Women* as related to the French *Marguerite* Poems, and the *Filostrato*', *PMLA* 19 (1904), pp. 593–683; 'The Prologue to the *Legend of Good Women* considered in its Chronological Relations', *PMLA* 20 (1905), pp. 749–864. The argument that the poetry of Deschamps has an affinity with Chaucer's, esp. in its embodiment of a new 'public' voice for the poet, that of neither court nor church (see the essays by Anne Middleton cited in ch. 3, n. 6), is interestingly put forward by Laura Kendrick, 'Rhetoric and the Rise of Public Poetry: The Career of Eustache Deschamps', *SP* 80 (1983), pp. 1–13. The affinity, one must remark, is very broad and depends on some selective comparison. The suggestion, frequently put forward elsewhere, that Deschamps knew other poems by Chaucer than the translation of the *Roman*, has little foundation. In particular, the opinion that the word 'pandras' in Deschamps' eulogy of Chaucer is an allusion to 'Pandarus', and shows that he knew Chaucer's *Troilus*, is mistaken: see Roy J. Pearcy, 'Chaucer, Deschamps, and *Le Roman de Brut*', *Arts: The Journal of the Sydney Arts Association*, 12 (1984), pp. 35–59, responding to Gretchen

Mieszkowski, ' "Pandras" in Deschamps's *Ballade for Chaucer'*, *ChauR* 9 (1975), pp. 327–36.

4 Deschamps, Ballade no. 536, *Oeuvres*, III. 375–6.

5 Ballade no. 893, *ibid.*, V. 79–80.

6 *Chaucerian and Other Pieces*, ed. Skeat, p. 123 (III. iv. 248–59).

7 For the Gower–Chaucer 'quarrel', see Fisher, *John Gower*, pp. 285–6.

8 That the William mentioned here was Cecily's father is a reasonable hypothesis based on the evidence of the records. The evidence that Alice Perrers was the second wife of William, and therefore Cecily's stepmother, is by contrast extremely flimsy. It is presented by Haldeen Braddy, 'Chaucer, Alice Perrers, and Cecily Chaumpaigne', *Speculum*, 52 (1977), pp. 906–11, who further speculates that 'the two females represented simply two court concubines of the lowest social status' (p. 908).

9 'Perhaps the one biographical fact everyone remembers about Chaucer, if one fact is going to be remembered, is that in 1380 Cecilia Chaumpaigne apparently threatened to accuse him of raping her' (Caroline Dinshaw, *Chaucer's Sexual Poetics* (1989), p. 10). The case was early examined by two legal historians, P. R. Watts, 'The Strange Case of Geoffrey Chaucer and Cecilia Chaumpaigne', *LQR* 63 (1947), pp. 491–515, and T. F. T. Plucknett, 'Chaucer's Escapade', *LQR* 64 (1948), pp. 33–6. The article by Watts is serious, and concludes that the act was one of rape.

10 Douglas, Prologue to Book I of his *Aeneid* translation, *Virgil's Aeneid, translated into Scottish Verse*, ed. David F. C. Coldwell, STS, 3rd series, nos. 25, 27, 28, 30 (4 vols, Blackwood, Edinburgh, 1957–64), Vol. II (no. 25) (1957), lines 410, 445–9.

11 Richard Firth Green, 'Chaucer's Victimized Women', *SAC* 10 (1988), pp. 3–21. See also Jill Mann, *Geoffrey Chaucer* (1991), ch. 1, 'Women and Betrayal'.

12 See John P. McCall, 'Chaucer and the Pseudo Origen *De Maria Magdalena*', *Speculum*, 46 (1971), pp. 491–509; also Margaret Jennings, CSJ, 'The Art of the Pseudo-Origen Homily', *M&H* NS 5 (1974), pp. 139–52.

13 See *The Peasants' Revolt of 1381*, ed. R. B. Dobson (Macmillan, London, 1970), pp. 162, 175, 210. Dobson's book provides an invaluable collection of contemporary records of the Rising, in translation, with full and expert commentary. For some further comment on the chronicle accounts, see Derek Pearsall, 'Interpretative Models for the Peasants' Revolt', in *Hermeneutics and Medieval Culture*, ed. Patrick J. Gallacher and Helen Damico (State University of New York Press, Albany, 1989), pp. 63–70.

14 E. P. Thompson, 'The Moral Economy of the English Crowd in the Eighteenth Century', *P&P* 50 (1971), pp. 76–136 (pp. 78, 136); *Peasants' Revolt*, ed. Dobson, p. 184 (from the Chronicle of Henry Knighton).

15 In his Latin *Vox Clamantis*, I. 652–3, Gower alludes to Jack Straw and Wat Tyler, using the common nouns for straw (*stramine*) and tile (*tegula*).

16 The idea expressed here, that Chaucer's articulation of social conflict was progressively depoliticized and privatized, is much indebted, though in the

context of a very different argument, to Lee Patterson, esp. his essay ' "No man his reson herde" ' (1987). He describes there how Chaucer customarily deflects the political into the transhistorically personal (e.g. p. 466), thus making 'what we have come to recognise as the characteristic liberal move' (p. 484). Paul Strohm (*Social Chaucer*) sees Chaucer's technique more positively as the creation of a fictional or dramatic 'space', an area of lessened risk, where confrontation can be worked out in conciliation. Of the passage in the Nun's Priest's Tale, he says: 'Chaucer's reference evokes the rising reassuringly, in a way that lessens its risk' (p. 165). John Ganim, in 'The Noise of the People', ch. 7 (pp. 108–20) in his *Chaucerian Theatricality* (Princeton University Press, Princeton, NJ, 1990), sees the passage, not dissimilarly – 'horror is rendered comic' (p. 114) – in a general context of the Bakhtinian and carnivalesque.

17 J. Leslie Hotson, 'Colfox *vs.* Chauntecleer', *PMLA* 39 (1924), pp. 762–81 (the cock and the fox of the Nun's Priest's Tale stand for Bolingbroke and Mowbray in referring to their famous encounter in 1398); '*The Tale of Melibeus* and John of Gaunt', *SP* 18 (1921), pp. 429–52 (*Melibee* was written to discourage John of Gaunt from going to war in Spain in 1386).

18 For the allusion to the tempest, see John Livingston Lowes, 'The Date of Chaucer's *Troilus and Criseyde*', *PMLA* 23 (1908), pp. 285–306 (p. 289). This is one of Lowes's less convincing dating arguments, but since so much of the accepted wisdom concerning the dates of Chaucer's middle-career poems is Lowes's wisdom, esp. as embodied in the two monumental articles on the date of the Prologue to *The Legend of Good Women* (above, n. 3), his argument is worth attending to. The allusion to 3 May is argued by Henry Ansgar Kelly, *Chaucer and the Cult of St Valentine* (ch. 3, n. 25), p. 125. There are many other explanations of the significance of 3 May in Chaucer's poetry, of which the best is that of John P. McCall, 'Chaucer's May 3', *MLN* 76 (1961), pp. 201–5, who explains it in relation to the Roman love-rites of Flora.

19 John Frankis, 'Paganism and Pagan Love in *Troilus and Criseyde*', in *Essays on Troilus and Criseyde*, ed. Salu, pp. 57–72, speaks of paganism in *Troilus*, and in the Knight's Tale and Franklin's Tale too (pp. 67–70), as 'a myth of mankind without God' (p. 72). A. C. Spearing, *Medieval to Renaissance in English Poetry* (1985), puts it thus: 'He needed to imagine pagan worlds in order to gain the impetus and the courage to interrogate his own God' (p. 57).

20 For an eloquent statement of this view, see Elizabeth Salter, *The Knight's Tale and the Clerk's Tale* (Edward Arnold, London, 1962), esp. pp. 33–5; also *Fourteenth-Century English Poetry*, pp. 141–81.

21 A very apt and clear statement by St Thomas Aquinas on the subject of planetary influences is quoted in Derek Brewer, *An Introduction to Chaucer* (1984), p. 98; see also Rosemond Tuve, *Allegorical Imagery: Some Mediaeval Books and their Posterity* (Princeton University Press, Princeton, NJ, 1966), p. 226. There is an elaborate, and rather overdone, account of the Knight's

Tale in terms of planetary influences in Douglas Brooks and Alastair Fowler, 'The Meaning of the Chaucer's *Knight's Tale*', *Medium Ævum*, 39 (1970), pp. 123–46.

22 Examples of homely images and proverbs, 1261, 1522, 1533, 1809–10. etc.; gossipy remarks, 1347, 1459–60, 2111, etc.; *abbreviatio*, 994, 1000, 1188, 1210, etc.; *transitio*, 1334, 1449, 1488, 1661, etc. For an example of 'mock-heroic absurdity' which turns out to be a perfectly straightforward piece of description, see ch. 1, p. 46.

23 See *Troilus*, i. 731 (Boece, I, pr. 4. 2–3), 786–8 (III, m. 12. 41), 848 (II, pr. 1. 113), 857–8 (I, pr. 4. 4–6), 960–1 (III, pr. 11. 56–73).

24 Translation in *English Historical Documents*, Vol. IV: *1327–1485*, ed. A. R. Myers (Eyre & Spottiswoode, London, 1969), p. 881. For some discussion of late-fourteenth-century vernacular response to the 'crisis' of free will, see Geoffrey Shepherd, 'Religion and Philosophy in Chaucer' (1974); Janet Coleman, *Piers Plowman and the Moderni* (Edizioni di Storia e Letteratura, Rome, 1981); John M. Bowers, *The Crisis of Will in Piers Plowman* (Catholic University of America Press, Washington, DC, 1986). There is a valuable brief discussion of the 'frontier' between late-medieval scholasticism (esp. nominalism) and vernacular literature in late-fourteenth-century England in Courtenay, *Schools and Scholars*, pp. 374–80. For the answer provided by a late-medieval theologian (God decided to give grace to those who do their best (*facere quod in se est*) and in so doing committed himself voluntarily to a limitation (*potentia ordinata*) upon his *potentia absoluta*), see Heiko A. Oberman, *The Harvest of Medieval Theology: Gabriel Biel and Late Medieval Nominalism* (Harvard University Press, Cambridge, Mass., 1963), pp. 245–6.

25 For a recent discussion of the kind of manuscript Chaucer may have used, see A. J. Minnis, '"Glosynge is a glorious thyng": Chaucer at Work on the *Boece*', in *The Medieval Boethius: Studies in the Vernacular Translations of De Consolatione Philosophiae*, ed. A. J. Minnis (D. S. Brewer, Cambridge, 1987), pp. 106–24.

26 Misreadings in the 'vulgate': II, m. 7. 28, pr. 8. 15; in Jean de Meun, I, pr. 4. 279, II, m. 5. 15, III, pr. 2. 3 (cf. m. 9. 40), m. 12. 59, IV, pr. 6. 243, m. 6. 51; in Chaucer's manuscript of Jean de Meun, III, pr. 12. 46. These examples are gathered from the excellent notes of Ralph Hanna III and Traugott Lawler in *The Riverside Chaucer*.

27 The quotation is from the valuable study by Mary J. Carruthers, *The Book of Memory: A Study of Memory in Medieval Culture*, Cambridge Studies in Medieval Literature (Cambridge University Press, Cambridge, 1990), p. 10.

28 Allusion to the events of 1398–9 is suggested by John Norton-Smith, 'Chaucer's *Etas Prima*', *Medium Ævum*, 32 (1963), pp. 117–24.

29 The interpretation in relation to the ordinance of 1390 was first offered by J. B. Bilderbeck, 'Chaucer's "Fortune"', *Athenaeum* (1902), pp. 82–3.

30 See V. J. Scattergood, 'Chaucer's Curial Satire: *Le Balade de bon conseyl*',

Hermathena, 133 (1982), pp. 29–45. A well-known poem in the tradition is Wyatt's 'Stond who so list upon the Slipper top / Of courtes estates' (adapted from Seneca).

31 Edith Rickert, 'Thou Vache', _MP_ 11 (1913), pp. 209–25.

32 Lewis John became seneschal and reeve of the duchy of Cornwall in 1423. The information about the poem's occasion is provided by John Shirley, the gossipy London scribe and book-handler of the fifteenth century, in one of his inimitable rubrics. See the edition of the _Moral Balade_ in _Chaucerian and Other Pieces_, ed. Skeat, pp. 237–44.

33 On Lydgate, see Pearsall, _John Lydgate_, pp. 204–10. In Trinity College, Cambridge, MS R. 3. 21, the Envoy to _Stedfastnesse_ is incorporated into Lydgate's _Prayer for England_, where it fits in very comfortably: see _Historical Poems of the XIVth and XVth Centuries_, ed. Rossell Hope Robbins (Columbia University Press, New York, 1959), p. 389. For some discussion of the genre of _Stedfastnesse_, see V. J. Scattergood, 'Social and Political Issues in Chaucer: An Approach to _Lak of Stedfastnesse_', _ChauR_ 21 (1987), pp. 469–75. Scattergood thinks the Envoy particularly appropriate to the king's situation in late 1387. In my view, the more point it might have, the less likely Chaucer is to make any.

34 The argument for formal revision was advanced by Robert K. Root, _The Textual Tradition of Chaucer's Troilus_, Chaucer Society, 1st series, 99 (1916). It is opposed by B. A. Windeatt, 'The Text of the _Troilus_', in _Essays on Troilus and Criseyde_, ed. Salu, pp. 1–22, as also in his important edition of _Troilus and Criseyde_ (Longman, London, 1984), pp. 36–54; also by Ralph Hanna III, 'Robert K. Root (1877–1950)', in _Editing Chaucer: The Great Tradition_, ed. Paul G. Ruggiers (Pilgrim Books, Norman, Okla., 1981), pp. 191–205. Root's view is reaffirmed by Charles A. Owen, '_Troilus and Criseyde_: The Question of Chaucer's Revisions', _SAC_ 9 (1987), pp. 155–72. See further, ch. 5, pp. 188–9, n. 20.

35 See the essay by C. S. Lewis cited in ch. 3, n. 10; also the discussion of _Troilus_ in Lewis, _The Allegory of Love_, pp. 176–97 (esp. p. 178), and a series of important essays by James I. Wimsatt: 'Guillaume de Machaut and Chaucer's _Troilus and Criseyde_', _Medium Ævum_, 45 (1976), pp. 277–93; 'Medieval and Modern in Chaucer's _Troilus and Criseyde_', _PMLA_ 92 (1977), pp. 203–16; 'Realism in _Troilus and Criseyde_ and the _Roman de la Rose_', in _Essays on Troilus and Criseyde_, ed. Salu, pp. 43–56; 'The French Lyric Element in _Troilus and Criseyde_', _YES_ 15 (1985), pp. 18–32.

36 For references to a listening audience, see i. 5, 450, ii. 30, 1595, 1750. Contrast the suggestions of a private reading audience in i. 6, 399, v. 270. For the narrator's activity, see i. 232–59 (vaunting), ii. 77 (encouraging), ii. 666–79 (reprimanding), ii. 1276, 1757, iii. 49, 56, 1058, 1385, 1400 (invocations), iii. 1193, 1224, 1319–37, 1372–93, 1408, 1681–94, 1804 ('embarrassment').

37 See iii. 1667, 1714, iv. 2 (references to Fortune), iv. 12–14 (narrator's

5   Reversals, New Beginnings (1386–1391)   331

helplessness), iv. 1415–21 (temporary comfort), v. 27, 469, 766, 1134, 1432 (prophetic tone), v. 505, 1172 (Pandarus).

38   Mark Lambert, 'Troilus, Books I–III: A Criseydan Reading', in Essays on Troilus and Criseyde, ed. Salu, pp. 105–25 (p. 119). Note, though, that Criseyde preserves still a certain degree of distance and non-commitment through the use of the passive 'ben yolde' (1211). See further the discussion in Derek Pearsall, 'Criseyde's Choices', SAC Proceedings, 2, 1986 (New Chaucer Society, Knoxville, Tenn., 1987), pp. 17–29.

39   These matters are well treated in A. J. Minnis, Chaucer and Pagan Antiquity, Chaucer Studies, 8 (D. S. Brewer, Cambridge, and Rowman & Littlefield, Totowa, NJ, 1982), pp. 93–107, and by Jill Mann, 'Chance and Destiny in Troilus and Criseyde and the Knight's Tale', in The Cambridge Chaucer Companion, ed. Piero Boitani and Jill Mann (Cambridge University Press, Cambridge, 1986), pp. 75–92. For the use of religious terms in erotic contexts, see e.g. i. 422, 464, 554–60, 932, 999, ii. 1503, iii. 1267, 1282, 1577.

40   The view that Troilus was written to urge the men of England 'to love as they should, not only for their own welfare, but for the welfare of England', is put forward by D. W. Robertson, 'The Probable Date and Purpose of Chaucer's Troilus', M&H ns 13 (1985), pp. 143–71 (p. 166).

5   Reversals, New Beginnings (1386–1391)

1   These, broadly, are the different points of emphasis, not in any way opposed, of those who have written best on Chaucer's audience, Paul Strohm and Dieter Mehl. See Strohm, 'Chaucer's Audience', Literature and History, 5 (1977), pp. 26–41; 'Chaucer's Fifteenth-Century Audience and the Narrowing of the "Chaucer Tradition"', SAC 4 (1982), pp. 3–32; Social Chaucer, ch. 3, 'Audience'; and Mehl, 'The Audience of Chaucer's Troilus and Criseyde', in Chaucer and Middle English Studies in honour of Rossell Hope Robbins, ed. Beryl Rowland (Allen & Unwin, London, 1974), pp. 173–89; 'Chaucer's Audience', LSE ns 10 (1978), pp. 58–73. In 'Chaucer's Audience(s): Fictional, Implied, Intended, Actual', ChauR 18 (1983), pp. 137–45, Strohm makes explicit some of the dictinctions between the two approaches, as between 'actual' and 'implied' audience. See also Walter J. Ong, 'The Writer's Audience is Always a Fiction', PMLA 90 (1975), pp. 9–21.

2   See Derek Pearsall, 'The Troilus Frontispiece and Chaucer's Audience', YES 7 (1977), pp. 68–74; also Elizabeth Salter, Introduction (with M. B. Parkes) to Troilus and Criseyde: A Facsimile of Corpus Christi College Cambridge MS 61 (D. S. Brewer, Cambridge, 1978); Elizabeth Salter and Derek Pearsall, 'Pictorial Illustration of Late Medieval Poetic Texts: The Role of the Frontispiece or Prefatory Picture', in Medieval Iconography and Narrative: A Symposium, ed. Flemming G. Andersen, Esther Nyholm, Marianne Powell and Flemming Talbo Stubkjaer (Odense University Press, Odense, 1980), pp. 100–23.

3   Machaut, Deschamps, Froissart, Christine de Pizan, Hoccleve and Lydgate

all make a point of referring to royal patrons, when they have them, in the text of their poems. See the essays cited in the previous note. Examples of English presentation pictures include British Library MS Cotton Augustus A. iv and Manchester, John Rylands Library MS 1 (both of Lydgate presenting his *Troy-Book* to Henry V), British Library MS Harley 2278 (Lydgate presenting his *Life of St Edmund* to Henry VI), and British Library MS Arundel 38 (Hoccleve presenting his *Regement of Princes* to Henry V).

4 See introduction, n. 12. On Richard's books, see Edith Rickert, 'King Richard II's Books', *The Library*, 4th series, 13 (1932–3), pp. 144–7; R. S. Loomis, 'The Library of Richard II', in *Studies in Language, Literature and Culture of the Middle Ages and Later*, ed. E. Bagby Atwood and A. A. Hill (University of Texas Press, Austin, 1969), pp. 173–8; Richard Firth Green, 'Richard II's Books Revisited', *The Library*, 31 (1976), pp. 235–9. On Richard II's patronage of the arts generally, see J. J. G. Alexander, 'Painting and Manuscript Illumination for Royal Patrons in the Later Middle Ages', in *English Court Culture*, ed. Scattergood and Sherborne, pp. 141–62. On Henry IV's education and love of books, see Gervase Mathew, *The Court of Richard II* (1968), pp. 32–3; K. B. McFarlane, *Lancastrian Kings and Lollard Knights* (1972), pp. 22–3, 116–17. The evidence that the handsome 'Stafford' manuscript of the *Confessio Amantis* (San Marino, Calif., Huntington Library MS Ellesmere 26. A. 17) was prepared as a presentation copy for Henry is questionable: see Peter Nicholson, 'Poet and Scribe in the Manuscripts of Gower's *Confessio Amantis*', in *Manuscripts and Texts*, ed. Pearsall (1987), pp. 130–42 (pp. 139–41).

5 For the Gloucester inventory, see V. J. Scattergood, 'Literary Culture at the Court of Richard II', in *English Court Culture*, ed. Scattergood and Sherborne, pp. 29–43 (p. 34). Scattergood gives a good general account of the literary interests of the aristocracy, as does K. B. McFarlane, 'The Education of the Nobility in Later Medieval England', in *The Nobility of Later Medieval England* (1973), pp. 228–47. The 'backswoodsmen' (below) are from another essay in the same collection (p. 161). For the Duke of York's reference to the *Legend*, see *The Master of Game*, ed. W. A. and F. Baillie-Grohman (Chatto & Windus, London, 1909), pp. 3–4: 'For as Chaucer saith in this prologe of the XXV good wymmen. Be wryteng have men of ymages passed for writyng is the keye of alle good remembraunce.'

6 See McFarlane, *Lancastrian Kings and Lollard Knights*, pp. 139–226. See the references in *Life-Records*, pp. 24, 50, 101, 104, 307, 343, 347, 492, 545. For reference in the present volume to these and other members of the Chaucer circle, see index.

7 Anne Hudson, *The Premature Reformation* (1988), pp. 392, 393. For the late-medieval 'fossilization' of the church, see Gordon Leff, 'Heresy and the Decline of the Medieval Church', *P&P* 20 (1961), pp. 36–51.

8 'Certis that prest is to blame that shulde so frely have the gospel, and leeveth the preching therof and turnyth hym to mannus fablis' (*De Officio Pastorali*),

quoted in Roger S. Loomis, 'Was Chaucer a Laodicean?' in *Essays and Studies in Honor of Carleton Brown* (New York University Press, New York, 1940), pp. 129–48 (p. 144). For the exclusion of *fablis* and even of moral exemplary tales from Lollard preaching, see Hudson, *Premature Reformation*, pp. 269–70.

9   This was presumably a book on hunting, and not, unfortunately, *Sir Gawain and the Green Knight*. See M. V. Clarke, *Fourteenth Century Studies* (Clarendon Press, Oxford, 1937), p. 120, and V. J. Scattergood, 'Two Medieval Book Lists', *The Library*, 23 (1968), pp. 236–9.

10   On the 'quality' of Chaucer's audience, and the subtlety of the demands that he makes upon the members of it, see Strohm, *Social Chaucer*, ch. 3, esp. pp. 72–5; also R. T. Lenaghan, 'Chaucer's *Envoy to Scogan*: The Uses of Literary Conventions', *ChauR* 10 (1975), pp. 46–61. Further information about Scogan is provided by May Newman Hallmundsson, 'Chaucer's Circle: Henry Scogan and his Friends', *M&H* 10 (1981), pp. 129–39.

11   The identification of Sir Peter is disputed, but the argument of E. P. Kuhl, 'Chaucer's "My Maistre Bukton"', *PMLA* 38 (1923), pp. 115–32, seems to me conclusive. The poem itself is in a well-established genre of antifeminist writing, and may owe a particular debt to the *Dissuasio Valerii ad Rufinum Philosophum ne uxorem ducat*, an epistle, which Chaucer knew well, inserted in the *De nugis curialium* of Walter Map (*c.* 1180).

12   Strode in his turn calls to mind the circle of Oxford scientists and astronomers with whom Chaucer certainly had some acquaintance (see the discussion on p. 217 of the *Treatise on the Astrolabe*). For Langland, see Nevill Coghill, 'Chaucer's Debt to Langland', *Medium Ævum*, 4 (1935), pp. 89–94; J. A. W. Bennett, 'Chaucer's Contemporary', in *Piers Plowman: Critical Approaches*, ed. S. S. Hussey (Methuen, London, 1969), pp. 310–24; Jill Mann, *Chaucer and Medieval Estates Satire* (1973), pp. 208–12; Helen Cooper, 'Langland's and Chaucer's Prologues', *YLS* 1 (1987), pp. 71–81 (concludes that Chaucer knew the A-text Prologue).

13   *Le Dit dou Florin*, 269–309, in Jean Froissart, *'Dits' et 'Debats'*, ed. Anthime Fourrier, Textes Littéraires Français (Librairie Droz, Geneva, 1979), pp. 183–4; *Chronicles*, tr. Brereton, p. 264. For other examples of the practice, see Green, *Poets and Princepleasers*, pp. 99–100. For examples of author-pictures, see the introduction by Elizabeth Salter to the facsimile of Corpus Christi College, Cambridge, MS 61 of *Troilus and Criseyde*, cited in n. 2 above; also the other authorities cited there.

14   See Phillipa Hardman, 'A Mediaeval "Library in Parvo"', *Medium Ævum*, 47 (1978), pp. 262–73.

15   Havelok is quoted here from *Medieval English Romances*, ed. A. V. C. Schmidt and Nicolas Jacobs (2 vols, Hodder & Stoughton, London, and Holmes & Meier, New York, 1980), I. 37–121.

16   See the discussion of 'Publication and Circulation', ch. 6 in H. J. Chaytor, *From Script to Print* (1945). For Petrarch and Boccaccio, see R. K. Root, 'Publication before Printing', *PMLA* 28 (1913), pp. 417–31, and for Chris-

tine, see esp. Sandra Hindman, 'The Composition of the Manuscript of Christine de Pisan's Collected Works in the British Library: A Reassessment', *BLJ* 9 (1983), pp. 93–123.

17   The standard works on the subject are Chaytor, *From Script to Print*, and Walter J. Ong, *Orality and Literacy: The Technologizing of the Word* (Methuen, London, 1982). There is useful analysis of Chaucer's style in terms of Ong's categories in Derek Brewer, 'Orality and Literacy in Chaucer', in *Mündlichkeit und Schriftlichkeit im englischen Mittelalter*, ed. Willi Erzgräber and Sabine Volk (Gunter Narr Verlag, Tübingen, 1988), pp. 85–119. See also Derek Pearsall, 'The English Romance in the Fifteenth Century', *E&S* 29 (1976), pp. 56–83 (esp. pp. 61–2, 67–75).

18   Petrarch's complaint about scribes is quoted in Robert Kilburn Root, *The Poetry of Chaucer: A Guide to its Study and Appreciation* (Houghton Mifflin, Boston, 1906; revised edn, 1922; repr. Peter Smith, Gloucester, Mass., 1950), pp. 69–70.

19   For discussion of Langland's practice of revision in the C version, see George H. Russell, 'Some Aspects of the Process of Revision in Piers Plowman', in *Piers Plowman: Critical Approaches*, ed. S. S. Hussey (Methuen, London, 1969), pp. 27–49, and 'The Imperative of Revision in the C Version of Piers Plowman', in *Medieval English Studies presented to George Kane*, ed. Edward Donald Kennedy, Ronald Waldron and Joseph S. Wittig (D. S. Brewer, Cambridge, 1988), pp. 233–44.

20   For some discussion of this question, in relation to the texts of the popular romances as well as those of Chaucer and Langland, see Derek Pearsall, 'Editing Medieval Texts: Some Developments and Some Problems', in *Textual Criticism and Literary Interpretation*, ed. Jerome J. McGann (University of Chicago Press, Chicago, 1985), pp. 92–106. On *Troilus*, see the authorities cited in ch. 4, n. 34.

21   From Christine's *Livre des fais et bonnes moeurs du sage roy Charles V*, quoted in translation in Green, *Poets and Princepleasers*, p. 204.

22   See Doyle, 'English Books in and out of Court', pp. 169–72; also A. S. G. Edwards and Derek Pearsall, 'The Manuscripts of the Major English Poetic Texts', in *Book Production and Publishing in Britain 1375–1475*, ed. Griffiths and Pearsall, pp. 257–78.

23   Nevertheless, Elaine Tuttle Hansen, 'Irony and the Antifeminist Narrator in Chaucer's *Legend of Good Women*', *JEGP* 82 (1983), pp. 11–31, argues with some force that the retelling of the legends, through omission and distortion, idealizes women in their 'pervasive and sometimes comic passivity, irrationality and stupidity' (p. 25), and thus demonstrates the true nature of the literary and social idealization of women and its consequences.

24   For this detail, see J. A. Tuck, 'Richard II's System of Patronage', in *The Reign of Richard II: Essays in Honour of May McKisack*, ed. F. R. H. Du Boulay and Caroline Barron (Athlone Press, London, 1971), pp. 1–20 (p. 5). The description of the events of the 1380s given in the following pages is much

indebted to the same author's *Richard II and the English Nobility* (Edward Arnold, London, 1973).

25 The emphasis here on the continuing reputation of crusading follows Maurice Keen, 'Chaucer's Knight, the English Aristocracy and the Crusade', in *English Court Culture*, ed. Scattergood and Sherborne, pp. 45–61. The chief representative of 'modern cynicism', of course (though it is a poor tribute to make to a stimulating book), is Terry Jones, *Chaucer's Knight: The Portrait of a Medieval Mercenary* (Weidenfeld & Nicolson, London, 1980). Keen is in part denying Jones's argument.

26 See Paul Strohm, 'Politics and Poetics: Usk and Chaucer in the 1380s', in *Literary Practice and Social Change in Britain, 1380–1530*, ed. Patterson, pp. 83–112. Strohm makes the further useful point that Usk's praise of Chaucer, in his *Testament of Love*, may be as much political as poetic, Chaucer being in 1386–7 'a successful adherent of the very faction to which he wished to belong'. For a more general account of Chaucer's tendency to withdraw from public life when there was trouble, see Strohm, *Social Chaucer*, pp. 36–41; also S. Sanderlin, 'Chaucer and Ricardian Politics', *ChauR* 22 (1988), pp. 171–84. The best recent discussion of party politics and 'the king's affinity' in Richard II's reign is in Given-Wilson, *The Royal Household and the King's Affinity*, pp. 203–57.

27 Compare the interpretation of Lynn Staley Johnson, 'Inverse Counsel: Contexts for the *Melibee*', *SP* 87 (1990), pp. 137–55. Johnson considers the translation very relevant to the events of 1387–8, and written by Chaucer specifically for the purpose of advising Richard.

28 *The History of the King's Works*, ed. H. M. Colvin, Vols. I and II: *The Middle Ages*, by R. Allen Brown, H. M. Colvin and A. J. Taylor (HMSO, London, 1963), II. 883.

29 For some comparison between Froissart's account of the Smithfield tournament (*Chroniques*, XIV. 253–65) and the description of the tournament in the Knight's Tale, with the argument that Chaucer made quite substantial revisions on the basis of personal experience of organizing the lists, see Stuart Robertson, 'Elements of Realism in the *Knight's Tale*', *JEGP* 14 (1915), pp. 226–55 (pp. 239, 251–3), and Johnstone Parr, 'The Date and Revision of Chaucer's *Knight's Tale*', *PMLA* 60 (1945), pp. 307–24 (pp. 317–24).

30 There is excellent discussion of the contrast between the medieval 'Book' and Chaucer's fictions in Jesse M. Gellrich, *The Idea of the Book in the Middle Ages: Language Theory, Mythology, and Fiction* (Cornell University Press, Ithaca, NY and London, 1985).

31 For the scholarship on these questions, and useful discussion, see Traugott Lawler, 'Chaucer', ch. 14 in *Middle English Prose: A Critical Guide to Major Authors and Genres*, ed. A. S. G. Edwards (Rutgers University Press, New Brunswick, NJ, 1984), pp. 291–313 (pp. 302–3), and the excellent apparatus in *The Riverside Chaucer* provided by John Reidy.

32   For the 'Merton school', see J. A. W. Bennett, *Chaucer at Oxford and Cambridge* (Clarendon Press, Oxford, 1974), pp. 58–85. For the interest in astrology at the court of Richard II, see Hilary M. Carey, 'Astrology at the English Court in the Later Middle Ages', in *Astrology, Science and Society: Historical Essays*, ed. Patrick Curry (Boydell Press, Woodbridge, 1987), pp. 41–56 (pp. 43–8). The *Kalendarium of Nicholas of Lynn* is edited by Sigmund Eisner, Chaucer Library, 2 (University of Georgia Press, Athens, 1980); see also his essay, 'Chaucer's Use of Nicholas of Lynn's Calendar', *E&S* 29 (1976), pp. 1–22. Linne R. Mooney, of the University of Maine at Orono, is preparing an edition of John Somer's *Kalendarium*, also for the Chaucer Library.

33   For the *Liber Uricrisiarum*, see Ralph Hanna III, 'Editing Middle English Prose: How Prior is the Source?' *Text*, 4 (1988), pp. 207–16. For the *Exafrenon*, see *Richard of Wallingford: An Edition of his Writings*, ed. J. D. North (3 vols, Clarendon Press, Oxford, 1976), I. 179–243, II. 83–126. The principal manuscript of the translation of the *Exafrenon*, Trinity College, Cambridge, MS O. 5. 26, is a compendium of late-fourteenth- and early-fifteenth-century English translations of scientific treatises. For further discussion of such writings, see Linda Ehrsam Voigts, 'Medical Prose' in *Middle English Prose*, ed. Edwards (n. 31 above), pp. 315–35; Laurel Braswell, 'Utilitarian and Scientific Prose', ibid., pp. 337–87; Linda Ehrsam Voigts, 'Scientific and Medical Books', in *Book Production and Publishing in Britain 1375–1475*, ed. Griffiths and Pearsall, pp. 345–402. For the quality of Chaucer's technical prose, see Sigmund Eisner, 'Chaucer as a Technical Writer', *ChauR* 19 (1985), pp. 179–201: Eisner shows that Chaucer's technical prose was much better than that of his contemporaries. Carol Lipson, ' "I n'am but a lewd compiler" ': Chaucer's "Treatise on the Astrolabe" as Translation', *NM* 84 (1983), pp. 192–200, points out that he still had his difficulties (and also that only about one-fifth of the work is directly translated from the Latin).

34   See *The Equatorie of the Planetis*, ed. Derek J. Price, with a Linguistic Analysis by R. M. Wilson (Cambridge University Press, Cambridge, 1955). The treatise was written soon after 31 December 1392, which is the date for which the instrument was constructed. Price's introduction is a model of judicious good sense and restraint, and remains extremely persuasive. For discussion of the *Equatorie*, see J. D. North, *Chaucer's Universe* (Clarendon Press, Oxford, 1988), pp. 156–81; M. L. Samuels, 'Chaucer's Spelling', in *Middle English Studies Presented to Norman Davis in Honor of his Seventieth Birthday*, ed. Douglas Gray and E. G. Stanley (Clarendon Press, Oxford, 1983), pp. 17–37 ('the *Equatorie* is in Chaucer's own spelling' (p. 28); 'this increases the likelihood that the *Equatorie* is an authentic and autograph work of Chaucer' (p. 35)); Pamela R. Robinson, 'Geoffrey Chaucer and the *Equatorie of the Planetis:* The State of the Problem', *ChauR* 26 (1991), pp. 17–30. All these argue (Samuels incidentally) that the *Equatorie* is Chaucer's holograph. Opposing arguments, on the basis of spelling and vocabulary, are put,

respectively, by Larry D. Benson, 'Chaucer's Spelling Reconsidered', and Stephen Partridge, 'Chaucer's Authorship of *The Equatorie of the Planetis*, both forthcoming in *English Manuscript Studies*, 3 (1992). In 'Is the *Equatorie of the Planets* a Chaucer Holograph?', *ChauR* 26 (1991), pp. 31–42, A. S. G. Edwards and Linne R. Mooney make it clear that the text in Peterhouse 75. I is not a holograph draft, and thus remove one of the principal arguments for Chaucer's authorship

6   Renewal (the 1390s)

1   Du Boulay, 'The Historical Chaucer', pp. 33–4.

2   Howard, *Chaucer and the Medieval World*, p. 426.

3   Dating of the General Prologue has traditionally rested on the reference to 'Middelburgh' (line 277), which was the port of Staple from 1384 to 1388; but there are other reasons, relevant at a later date, why the Merchant might have been keen to have the sea between Middelburgh and Orwell well policed (see the note to the line in the *Riverside Chaucer*). For arguments concerning the 'evolution' of the General Prologue, see Eleanor Prescott Hammond, *Chaucer: A Bibliographical Manual* (Macmillan, New York, 1908), pp. 254–5; Robert A. Pratt, 'The Development of the Wife of Bath', in *Studies in Medieval Literature in Honor of Albert Croll Baugh*, ed. MacEdward Leach (University of Pennsylvania Press, Philadelphia, 1961), pp. 45–79.

4   John S. P. Tatlock, *The Development and Chronology of Chaucer's Works*, Chaucer Society, 2nd series, 37 (London, 1907), p. 189.

5   Chaucer calls his translation 'Of the Wreched Engendrynge of Mankynde', a title which seems most appropriate to the opening chapters of the *De Miseria*, dealing with the miseries of sexual intercourse, pregnancy and birth and the general vileness of all bodily functions. However, Chaucer makes use of material from all three books in the Man of Law's Introduction and Tale and elsewhere. For full discussion, see the introduction to *Lotario dei Segni (Pope Innocent III), De Miseria Condicionis Humane*, ed. Robert E. Lewis, Chaucer Library (University of Georgia Press, Athens, 1978), pp. 17–30.

6   The argument that the Shipman's Tale was not originally intended for a female narrator has been supported, for instance, with the suggestion that the Shipman speaks 'in a piping falsetto', as if mimicking the kind of thing wives might say: see R. L. Chapman, '*The Shipman's Tale* was meant for the Shipman', *MLN* 71 (1956), pp. 4–5 (p. 5). There is an attack on 'the workroom view' of *The Canterbury Tales* in Howard, *The Idea of the Canterbury Tales* (1976), p. 22. The staunchest upholder in recent years of the idea of *The Canterbury Tales* as 'in process', albeit with some interpretative idiosyncrasies of his own, is Charles A. Owen, notably in *Pilgrimage and Storytelling: The Dialectic of 'Ernest' and 'Game'* (University of Oklahoma Press, Norman, 1977).

7   A full account of the presumed impact of the Wife of Bath on the development of the *Tales* is given in Owen, *Pilgrimage and Storytelling* (see above n. 6), and

in Pratt, 'The Development of the Wife of Bath' (see above, n. 3). The tales that allude to the Wife of Bath are of course those that figure largest in Kittredge's 'Marriage Group' (George Lyman Kittredge, 'Chaucer's Discussion of Marriage', *MP* 9 [1911–12], pp. 435–67), but one might prefer to think of them as 'the Wife of Bath Group', recognized as such by the editors of the Ellesmere manuscript and sensibly arranged in the order we now have them. For full discussion of the 'cancelled stanza' (IV. 1212a–g), see Manly and Rickert, *The Text of the Canterbury Tales*, II. 265. The lines presumed to be 'added' to the Wife of Bath's Prologue (III. 575–84, 609–12, 619–26, 717–20) appear in the Ellesmere manuscript but not in the Hengwrt manuscript (these are the two best and earliest manuscripts of *The Canterbury Tales*). See Manly and Rickert, *Text of the Canterbury Tales*, II. 191. This is the obvious but not the only possible interpretation of the textual variation here.

8   Several identifications of real-life models for the pilgrims are made by Manly, *Some New Light on Chaucer*. Manly's identifications have not been generally accepted, and I think they should not be. But his work on the kinds of identification that might have suggested themselves to a contemporary audience gives an essential historical dimension to our reading. Something further of this dimension of depth can be gained from reading in the Year Book law reports and Plea Roll law records, compiled in French for the use of practising lawyers: see W. F. Bolton, 'Pinchbeck and the Chaucer Circle in Law Reports and Records of 11–13 Richard II', *MP* 84 (1987), pp. 401–7.

9   There seems no reason to disagree with the opinion of Manly and Rickert: 'The evidence of the MSS seems to show clearly that Chaucer was not responsible for any of the extant arrangements' (*Text of the Canterbury Tales*, II. 475). For summary discussion of the order of the *Tales*, with extensive reference to the scholarship on the subject, see Pearsall, *The Canterbury Tales*, pp. 14–23. The opposed arguments about the authenticity of the manuscript ordering are set out by Larry D. Benson, 'The Order of *The Canterbury Tales*', *SAC* 3 (1981), pp. 77–120, and by N. F. Blake, *The Textual Tradition of the Canterbury Tales* (Edward Arnold, London, 1985). Who Chaucer's 'editors' may have been is not known. Thomas Chaucer, as his heir, may have had a role, as is suggested by John H. Fisher, 'Animadversions on the Text of Chaucer, 1988', *Speculum*, 63 (1988), pp. 779–93 (p. 789), and Thomas Hoccleve, who had a genuine care for Chaucer's memory (see appendix I, 'The Chaucer Portraits'), is another possibility.

10   For a detailed description of Hengwrt, and an account of the information to be derived from the physical evidence of the manuscript concerning the stages of copying, see the Introduction by A. I. Doyle and M. B. Parkes to *Geoffrey Chaucer, The Canterbury Tales: A Facsimile and Transcription of the Hengwrt Manuscript, with Variants from the Ellesmere Manuscript*, ed. Paul G. Ruggiers (University of Oklahoma Press, Norman, 1979). Doyle and Parkes assume that the Hengwrt and Ellesmere manuscripts were copied by the

same scribe, but R. Vance Ramsey, 'The Hengwrt and Ellesmere Manuscripts of the *Canterbury Tales*: Different Scribes', *SB* 35 (1982), pp. 133–54, has argued, on the evidence of spelling, that this is not so. His arguments are sufficiently refuted by M. L. Samuels, 'The Scribe of the Hengwrt and Ellesmere Manuscripts of *The Canterbury Tales*', *SAC* 5 (1983), pp. 49–65.

11 For a listing of the principal editions of *The Canterbury Tales*, together with a complete list of manuscripts, see Pearsall, *The Canterbury Tales*, pp. 321–6.

12 The 'Bradshaw shift' was incorporated by Furnivall in the influential *Six-Text Print of Chaucer's Canterbury Tales*, Chaucer Society (1868–77), and is still supported by some scholars. For further discussion and bibliographical references, see Pearsall, *The Canterbury Tales*, pp. 19–21.

13 David, *The Strumpet Muse*; Howard, *The Idea of the Canterbury Tales*; Patterson, ' "No man his reson herde" '; Dinshaw, *Chaucer's Sexual Poetics*, pp. 112–15.

14 *The Tale of Beryn*, ed. F. J. Furnivall and W. G. Stone, EETS, es 105 (1909); John Lydgate, *The Siege of Thebes*, ed. Axel Erdmann and Eilert Ekwall, EETS, es 108, 125 (1911, 1930 [for 1920]). It is interesting that both these poems work on the assumption that the pilgrimage is a round-trip (as described in the General Prologue) and not the one-way journey implied in the Parson's Prologue: see John M. Bowers, *'The Tale of Beryn* and *The Siege of Thebes*: Alternative Ideas of *The Canterbury Tales*', *SAC* 7 (1985), pp. 23–50.

15 The innovativeness of Chaucer's practice here has been noted by D. S. Brewer, 'Class Distinction in Chaucer' (it is 'not a true social placing but a moral comment' (p. 301)), and commented upon further by J. A. Burrow, *Medieval Writers and their Work: Middle English Literature and its Background* (Oxford University Press, Oxford, 1982), p. 80.

16 This argument is being differently and more subtly developed in a Harvard Ph. D. thesis by Leslie Dunton-Downer.

17 The 'dramatic' reading of *The Canterbury Tales* was first developed by George Lyman Kittredge, *Chaucer and his Poetry* (Harvard University Press, Cambridge, Mass., 1915), with a seductive lightness of touch; it lost some of its popularity after the overstatements of R. M. Lumiansky, *Of Sondry Folk: The Dramatic Principle in the Canterbury Tales* (University of Texas Press, Austin, 1955). For some sensibly expressed reservations about 'the dramatic principle', see C. David Benson, *Chaucer's Drama of Style: Poetic Variety and Contrast in the Canterbury Tales* (University of North Carolina Press, Chapel Hill and London, 1986), pp. 3–19.

18 Whether Chaucer knew the *Decameron* has been the subject of what may seem unnecessary debate; in a full discussion of the question, Donald McGrady, 'Chaucer and the *Decameron* Reconsidered', *ChauR* 12 (1977), pp. 1–26, concludes that he did know it.

19 *Middle English Romances*, ed. A. C. Gibbs, York Medieval Texts (Edward Arnold, London, 1966), introduction, p. 36.

20 The hypothesis concerning Gower is put forward by Peter Nicholson, *'The Man of Law's Tale*: What Chaucer Really Owed to Gower', *ChauR* 26 (1991), pp. 153–74. Gower's story of Constance is in *Confessio Amantis*, II. 587–1707.

Allusions to Gower's version of the story have been found in the Man of Law's Tale, II. 1009, 1086.

21 This account of the *Communiloquium* is based on Robert A. Pratt, 'Chaucer and the Hand that Fed Him', *Speculum*, 41 (1966), pp. 619–42 (pp. 619, 636). Pratt in his turn was indebted to the pioneering work of Beryl Smalley, *English Friars and Antiquity in the Early Fourteenth Century* (Basil Blackwell, Oxford, 1960). On the glosses to *The Canterbury Tales*, see Manly and Rickert, *Text of the Canterbury Tales*, III. 483–527, and the further references in Pearsall, *The Canterbury Tales*, p. 329, n. 22.

22 Of the three methods of organizing discussion of *The Canterbury Tales*, the first is used in my study of *The Canterbury Tales*, the second by P. M. Kean, *Chaucer and the Making of English Poetry*, and the third may be said to be the method of Charles Muscatine, *Chaucer and the French Tradition* (1957). Most studies of the *Tales* use one or other of the methods of organization I describe as impossible or pointless.

23 There is allusion here to the language of what has come to be called the 'new historicism', an approach to the study of the relationship between literature and history which is commented upon by Lee Patterson in ch. 2 of *Negotiating the Past* (1987) and variously practised in the essays collected by him in *Literary Practice and Social Change in Britain 1380–1530*. Most of the work of new historicism has been done in the field of Renaissance English literature, principally inspired by the writings of Stephen Greenblatt, especially *Renaissance Self-Fashioning: From More to Shakespeare* (University of Chicago Press, Chicago, 1980).

24 D. S. Brewer, 'Class Distinction in Chaucer', p. 304.

25 On this subject, see esp. Strohm, *Social Chaucer*, ch. 1.

26 The quotation is from Nigel Saul, 'The Social Status of Chaucer's Franklin', *Medium Ævum*, 52 (1983), pp. 10–26 (p. 23), who gives a summary of opinion on the matter and a judicious reassessment.

27 K. B. McFarlane, ' "Bastard Feudalism" ', *BIHR*, 20 (1947 [for 1945]) pp. 161–80 (p. 162). It was McFarlane who popularized the term and first gave a succinct account of the practice. Historically, of course, it is to be seen not as a 'degeneration' of feudalism but as the adaptation of feudalism to the changing conditions of a more fluid society.

28 See Michael Clanchy, 'Law and Love in the Middle Ages', in *Disputes and Settlements: Law and Human Relations in the West*, ed. John Bossy (Cambridge University Press, Cambridge, 1983), pp. 47–67 (p. 62). On the earlier history of and background to this process, see M. T. Clanchy, *From Memory to Written Record, England, 1066–1307* (Harvard University Press, Cambridge, Mass., 1979).

29 On the absence of father-figures in Chaucer, see Spearing, *Medieval to Renaissance in English Poetry*, pp. 92–103, and, for some aspects of his treatment of fathers, Jill Mann, 'Parents and Children in the "Canterbury Tales" ' (1983).

30 See Patricia J. Eberle, 'Commercial Language and the Commercial Outlook

in the *General Prologue*', *ChauR* 18 (1983), pp. 161–74. Eberle points out how rich the General Prologue is in the technical language of commercial practice (*purchas, rente, bargaynes, chevyssaunce*, etc.) and argues that 'Chaucer is building into his implied audience an awareness of the commercial realities with which his actual audience was involved' (p. 166).

31 See Britton J. Harwood, 'Chaucer and the Silence of History: Situating the Canon's Yeoman's Tale', *PMLA* 102 (1987), pp. 338–50.

32 E. Talbot Donaldson, *Chaucer's Poetry: An Anthology for the Modern Reader* (Ronald Press, New York, 1958), commentary, p. 932. Donaldson's essay on 'Chaucer the Pilgrim', frequently repr., was first published in *PMLA* 69 (1954), pp. 928–36. For a more genial view of the merchant of the Shipman's Tale, see V. J. Scattergood, 'The Originality of the *Shipman's Tale*', *ChauR* 11 (1977), pp. 210–31. See, further, Kenneth S. Cahn, 'Chaucer's Merchants and the Foreign Exchange: An Introduction to Medieval Finance', *SAC* 2 (1980), pp. 81–119.

33 See Kay E. Lacey, 'Women and Work in Fourteenth and Fifteenth Century London', in *Women and Work in Pre-Industrial England*, ed. Lindsey Charles and Lorna Duffin (Croom Helm, London, 1985), pp. 24–82 (esp. pp. 41, 53–6).

34 See Ernest P. Kuhl, 'Chaucer's Burgesses', *Transactions of the Wisconsin Academy of Sciences, Arts, and Letters*, 18, Part 2 (1916), pp. 652–75. Kuhl's arguments are qualified, but not substantially challenged, by Peter Goodall, 'Chaucer's "Burgesses" and the Aldermen of London', *Medium Aevum*, 50 (1981), pp. 284–92. The classic study of guild warfare in Chaucer's time is Ruth Bird, *The Turbulent London of Richard II* (Longmans, Green & Co., London, 1949).

35 Printed, with modern English translation, in *The Literary Context of Chaucer's Fabliaux: Texts and Translations*, ed. Larry D. Benson and Theodore M. Andersson (Bobbs-Merrill, Indianapolis and New York, 1971), pp. 101–15.

36 David Aers, *Chaucer, Langland and the Creative Imagination* (Routledge & Kegan Paul, London, 1980), p. 147.

37 See the excellent discussion in Jill Mann, 'Chaucerian Themes and Style in the *Franklin's Tale*', in *The New Pelican Guide to English Literature*, ed. Boris Ford, Vol. I: *Medieval Literature*, Part 1: *Chaucer and the Alliterative Tradition* (Penguin Books, Harmondsworth, 1982), pp. 133–53.

38 Such is the practice of 'Robertsonian' interpreters, e.g. W. F. Bolton, 'The "Miller's Tale": An Interpretation', *MS* 24 (1962), pp. 83–94; Paul A. Olson, 'Poetic Justice in the *Miller's Tale*', *MLQ* 24 (1963), pp. 227–36.

39 See the analysis of the Tale by Sheila Delany, 'Politics and the Paralysis of the Poetic Imagination in *The Physician's Tale*', *SAC* 3 (1981), pp. 47–60.

40 C. David Benson, 'The Aesthetic of Chaucer's Religious Tales', in *Religion in the Poetry and Drama of the Late Middle Ages in England: The J. A. W. Bennett Memorial Lectures, Perugia, 1988*, ed. Piero Boitani and Anna Torti (D. S. Brewer, Cambridge, 1990), pp. 101–17 (p. 116). See also Jill Mann, *Geoffrey Chaucer*, ch. 5, pp. 165–85, 'The Feminised Hero', and Jane Cowgill, 'Patterns of Feminine and Masculine Persuasion in the *Melibee* and the

Parson's Tale', in *Chaucer's Religious Tales*, ed. C. David Benson and Elizabeth Robertson, Chaucer Studies, 15 (D. S. Brewer, Cambridge, 1990), pp. 171–83 (p. 175).

41 Clerk's Tale, IV. 547–60; Man of Law's Tale, II. 834–40; Physician's Tale, VI. 238–50; Prioress's Tale, VII. 537–43.

42 Geoffrey Shepherd, 'Religion and Philosophy in Chaucer', p. 272.

Epilogue

1 See Patricia Eberle, 'The Politics of Courtly Style at the Court of Richard II', in *The Spirit of the Court: Selected Proceedings of the Fourth Congress of the International Courtly Literature Society (Toronto, 1983)*, ed. Glyn S. Burgess and Robert A. Taylor (D. S. Brewer, Cambridge, 1985), pp. 168–78. Eberle makes this argument in relation to Richard's assumption of magnificent clothing and other fashionable accessories.

2 For a brief, measured and up-to-date account of the deposition and the events leading up to it, see Caroline Barron, 'The Deposition of Richard II', in *Politics and Crisis in Fourteenth-Century England*, ed. John Taylor and Wendy Childs (Alan Sutton, Gloucester and Wolfeboro Falls, NH, 1990), pp. 132–49.

3 For this chronicle of events, see the important article by Sumner Ferris, 'The Date of Chaucer's Final Annuity and of the "Complaint to his Empty Purse"', *MP* 65 (1967), pp. 45–52, which supersedes the information in the *Life-Records*.

4 Armitage-Smith, *John of Gaunt* (see ch. 2, n. 42), Appendix 8 (4), pp. 463–4.

5 For a brief but characteristically incisive biography of Thomas Chaucer, see K. B. McFarlane, 'Henry V, Bishop Beaufort and the Red Hat, 1417–1421', *EHR* 60 (1945), pp. 316–48 (pp. 332–7). There are more circumstantial accounts in J. S. Roskell, *Parliament and Politics in Late Medieval England* (3 vols, The Hambledon Press, London, 1983), III. 151–91, and in the older book of M. B. Ruud, *Thomas Chaucer* (see ch. 2, n. 4). See also the printing by A. C. Baugh (see ch. 2, n. 3) of the records collected by Ernest F. Kirk. For more information on the most interesting of the later descendants, see J. A. F. Thomson, 'John de la Pole, Duke of Suffolk', *Speculum*, 54 (1979), pp. 528–42.

6 McFarlane, 'Henry V, Bishop Beaufort and the Red Hat', p. 336.

7 For discussion, see E. A. Greening Lamborn, 'The Arms on the Chaucer Tomb at Ewelme', *Oxoniensia*, 5 (1940), pp. 78–93; also *N&Q* 183 (1944), p. 287. The arms on Thomas Chaucer's tomb at Ewelme are now difficult to photograph well (plate 2), and so reference should be made to the detail in the 'Progenie' page of Speght's 1598 edition of Chaucer's *Workes* (plate 3).

8 John M. Bowers, 'Chaucer & Son: The Business of Lancastrian Poetry', presented at the conference of the Southeastern Medieval Association in

September 1990. I am grateful to Professor Bowers for sending me a copy of this paper.

Appendix I

1. For general accounts of the Chaucer portraits, see Aage Brusendorff, *The Chaucer Tradition* (Branner, Copenhagen, and Oxford University Press, London, 1925; repr. Clarendon Press, Oxford, 1967), pp. 13–27 ('The Chaucer Portraits'); Roger Sherman Loomis, *A Mirror of Chaucer's World* (Princeton University Press, Princeton, NJ, 1965), pp. 4–6 ('Portraits of Chaucer'), with 7 illustrations; Margaret Rickert, 'Illumination', in *The Text of the Canterbury Tales*, ed. J. M. Manly and Edith Rickert (8 vols, University of Chicago Press, Chicago, 1940), I. 561–605 (pp. 583–90); Michael Seymour, 'Manuscript Portraits of Chaucer and Hoccleve', *The Burlington Magazine*, 124 (1982), pp. 618–23, with 7 illustrations (including 5 of Chaucer); M. H. Spielmann, *The Portraits of Geoffrey Chaucer: An Essay Written on the Occasion of the Quincentenary of the Poet's Death* (privately printed, Adlard & Son, London, 1900, and simultaneously in three other publications, including Chaucer Society, 2nd series, 31), with 11 illustrations; Roy Strong, *Tudor and Jacobean Portraits* (National Portrait Gallery) (2 vols, HMSO, London, 1969), Vol. I: *Text*, pp. 46–8, Vol. II: *Plates*, pp. 82–5.

2. There are studies of the Ellesmere miniatures, including that of Chaucer, in Rickert, 'Illumination'; Edwin Ford Piper, 'The Miniatures of the Ellesmere Chaucer', *PQ* 3 (1924), pp. 241–56 (the Chaucer picture, pp. 249–52), with 23 half-tone illustrations; Herbert C. Schulz, *The Ellesmere Manuscript of Chaucer's Canterbury Tales* (The Huntington Library, San Marino, Calif., 1966), with colour reproductions of all the miniatures ('The Chaucer Portrait', pp. 6–8); Martin Stevens, 'The Ellesmere Miniatures as Illustrations of Chaucer's *Canterbury Tales*', *Studies in Iconography*, 7–8 (1981–2), pp. 113–34.

3. This is the view, generally accepted, put forward in Rickert, 'Illumination'.

4. For accounts of the Hoccleve portraits in particular, see Jeanne Krochalis, 'Hoccleve's Chaucer Portrait', *ChauR* 21 (1986), pp. 234–45; Jerome Mitchell, *Thomas Hoccleve: A Study in Early Fifteenth-Century Poetic* (University of Illinois Press, Urbana, Chicago and London, 1968), pp. 110–15 ('The *Regement* Portraits of Chaucer').

5. It would be relevant here to recall the rigour of both Henry IV and Henry V in their persecution of the Lollards, and to recall too Hoccleve's own poem of virulent anti-Lollard invective, the *Address to Sir John Oldcastle* (1415). For orthodox opposition to the Lollard attack on images, see G. R. Owst, *Literature and Pulpit in Medieval England* (Cambridge University Press, 1933; 2nd edn, Blackwell, Oxford, 1961), pp. 136–48, with particular reference to the treatise 'In Defence of Images' by Walter Hilton (pp. 137–9).

6. See Millard Meiss, 'The Smiling Pages', in Peter Brieger, Millard Meiss and Charles S. Singleton, *Illuminated Manuscripts of the Divine Comedy*, Bol-

lingen Series, 81 (2 vols, Princeton University Press, Princeton, NJ, 1969), pp. 31–80 (see pp. 42–4); Millard Meiss, *French Painting in the Time of Jean de Berry: The Late Fourteenth Century and the Patronage of the Duke* (2 vols, Phaidon, London, 1967), Vol. I, ch. 4, pp. 68–94 ('The Portraits of Jean de Berry').

7 A 'penner' was a writing-case containing pen, ink and other writing materials. It was carried by clerks and secretaries, usually at the girdle; Damyan has to borrow one in the Merchant's Tale (IV. 1879). The view advanced by R. Evan Davis, 'The Pendant in the Chaucer Portraits', *ChauR* 17 (1982), pp. 193–5, that the object is an *ampulla* or vial containing blood of St Thomas à Becket, is almost certainly mistaken.

8 David Wallace, 'Pilgrim Signs and the Ellesmere Chaucer', *Chaucer Newsletter*, 11 (1989), pp. 1–3.

9 However, the argument put forward by James H. McGregor, 'The Iconography of Chaucer in Hoccleve's *De Regimine Principum* and in the *Troilus* Frontispiece', *ChauR* 11 (1977), pp. 338–50, that the two pictures have a common interest in representing Chaucer as a wise counsellor of princes, is not persuasive. There has been much discussion of the *Troilus* frontispiece: see above, ch. 5, n. 2.

10 Despite the prominence of the gilt purse, the suggestion of Hilton Kelliher, 'The Historiated Initial in the Devonshire Chaucer', *N&Q* 222 (1977), p. 197, that this picture is meant to illustrate Chaucer as the author of *The Complaint to his Purse*, is most unlikely.

11 On this manuscript, see R. F. Yeager, 'British Library Additional MS. 5141: An Unnoticed Chaucer *Vita*', *JMRS* 14 (1984), pp. 261–81. The manuscript, which consists of a single leaf, has a brief and fanciful life of Chaucer on the verso, which Yeager shows to be indebted to Speght's 'Life' of 1598; but this does not determine the earliest date of the portrait.

12 There is excellent discussion of this question, and a valuable contribution to the scholarship on the whole subject of the later Chaucer portraits, in George L. Lam and Warren H. Smith, 'George Vertue's Contributions to Chaucerian Iconography', *MLQ* 5 (1944), pp. 303–22. Another person who had seen the Cotton picture, much earlier, was Sir Francis Kynaston, who describes it ('a high-priz'd iewell in the handes of my honor'd frend Sr. Thomas Cotton knt') in detail in his note to Book I, line 16, of his Latin translation of *Troilus and Criseyde* (1635): see Richard Beadle, 'The Virtuoso's *Troilus*', in *Chaucer Traditions: Studies in Honour of Derek Brewer*, ed. Ruth Morse and Barry Windeatt (Cambridge University Press, Cambridge, 1990), pp. 213–33 (p. 227). For a full account of Chaucer's tomb, see W. R. Lethaby, 'Chaucer's Tomb', *TLS* 21 February 1929 (p. 137).

13 Spielmann (see n. 1 above), p. 18.

14 On this picture, see Reginald Call, 'The Plimpton Chaucer and Other Problems in Chaucerian Portraiture', *Speculum*, 22 (1947), pp. 134–44 (with 2 illustrations).

Short Titles and Bibliography

Primary Sources

Benson, Larry D. (ed.), *The Riverside Chaucer*, 3rd edn (Houghton Mifflin, Boston, 1987).

Chaucer, Geoffrey, *The Riverside Chaucer*: see Benson

Chaucer Life-Records: see Crow and Olson

Crow, Martin M., and Olson, Clair C., *Chaucer Life-Records* (Clarendon Press, Oxford, 1966).

Deschamps, Eustache, *Oeuvres*, ed. Le Marquis de Saint-Hilaire and G. Raynaud, SATF (11 vols, Paris, 1878–1904).

Dobson, R. B. (ed.), *The Peasants' Revolt of 1381* (Macmillan, London, 1970; 2nd edn, 1983).

Froissart, Jean, *Chronicles*, tr. and ed. Geoffrey Brereton (Penguin Books, Harmondsworth, 1968).

—— *Chroniques*, in *Oeuvres de Froissart*, ed. Kervyn de Lettenhove (25 vols in 28, Devaux, Brussels, 1867–77; repr. Biblio Verlag, Osnabrück, 1967).

Gower, John, *Confessio Amantis*, in *The Works of John Gower*, ed. G. C. Macaulay (4 vols, Clarendon Press, Oxford, 1899–1902), Vol. I: *French Works*; Vols. II and III: *English Works* (also published as EETS, ES 81–2, 1900–1); Vol. IV: *Latin Works*. The *Mirour de l'Omme* is in Vol. I and the *Vox Clamantis* in Vol. IV.

Langland, William, *Piers Plowman: An Edition of the C-Text*, by Derek Pearsall, York Medieval Texts, 2nd series (Edward Arnold, London, 1978).

Life-Records: see Crow and Olson.

Manly, John Matthews, and Rickert, Edith (eds), *The Text of the Canterbury Tales, Studied on the Basis of All Known Manuscripts* (8 vols, University of Chicago Press, Chicago, 1940).

The Riverside Chaucer: see Benson.

Sir Gawain and the Green Knight, ed. Malcolm Andrew and Ronald Waldron, in *The Poems of the Pearl Manuscript*, York Medieval Texts, 2nd series (Edward Arnold, London, 1978).

Skeat, Walter William (ed.), *Chaucerian and Other Pieces*, Vol. 7 of the Oxford edition of *The Complete Works of Geoffrey Chaucer* (Oxford University Press, London, 1897).

Secondary Sources

Brewer, Derek (ed.), *Chaucer and Chaucerians: Critical Studies in Middle English Literature* (Nelson, London and Edinburgh, 1966).

—— 'Class Distinction in Chaucer', *Speculum*, 43 (1968), pp. 290–305.

—— (ed.), *Writers and their Background: Geoffrey Chaucer* (G. Bell, London, 1974).

—— (ed.) *Chaucer: The Critical Heritage* (2 vols, Routledge & Kegan Paul, London, 1978).

—— *An Introduction to Chaucer* (Longman, London, 1984).

Burrow, J. A., *Ricardian Poetry: Chaucer, Gower, Langland and the Gawain Poet* (Routledge & Kegan Paul, London, 1971).

Chaytor, H. J., *From Script to Print: An Introduction to Medieval Literature* (Heffer, Cambridge, 1945).

Courtenay, William J., *Schools and Scholars in Fourteenth-Century England* (Princeton University Press, Princeton, NJ, 1987).

David, Alfred, *The Strumpet Muse: Art and Morals in Chaucer's Poetry* (Indiana University Press, Bloomington, 1976).

Dinshaw, Carolyn, *Chaucer's Sexual Poetics* (University of Wisconsin Press, Madison, 1989).

Doyle, A. I., 'English Books In and Out of Court', in *English Court Culture in the Later Middle Ages*, ed. Scattergood and Sherborne, pp. 163–81.

Du Boulay, F. R. H., 'The Historical Chaucer', in *Writers and their Background*, ed. Brewer, pp. 33–57.

Fisher, John H., *John Gower: Moral Philosopher and Friend of Chaucer* (New York University Press, New York, 1964).

Given-Wilson, Chris, *The Royal Household and the King's Affinity: Service, Politics and Finance in England 1360–1413* (Yale University Press, New Haven, Conn. and London, 1986).

—— *The English Nobility in the Late Middle Ages: The Fourteenth-Century Political Community* (Routledge & Kegan Paul, London, 1987).

Godwin, William, *The Life of Geoffrey Chaucer, the Early English poet: Including Memoirs of his Near Friend and Kinsman, John of Gaunt, Duke of Lancaster* (2 vols, Phillips, London, 1803).

Green, Richard Firth, *Poets and Princepleasers: Literature and the English Court in the Late Middle Ages* (University of Toronto Press, Toronto, 1980).

Griffiths, Jeremy, and Pearsall, Derek (eds), *Book Production and Publishing in Britain 1375–1475* (Cambridge University Press, Cambridge, 1989).

Howard, Donald R., *The Idea of the Canterbury Tales* (University of California Press, Berkeley, Los Angeles and London, 1976).

—— *Chaucer: His Life, his Works, his World* (E. P. Dutton, New York, 1987); published in the UK as *Chaucer and the Medieval World* (Weidenfeld & Nicolson, London, 1987).

Hudson, Anne, *The Premature Reformation: Wycliffite Texts and Lollard History* (Clarendon Press, Oxford, 1988).

Hulbert, James Root, *Chaucer's Official Life* (The Collegiate Press, Menasha, Wis., 1912; repr. Phaeton Press, New York, 1970).

Kean, P. M., *Chaucer and the Making of English Poetry* (2 vols, Routledge & Kegan Paul, London, 1972), Vol. I: *Love Vision and Debate*: Vol. II, *The Art of Narrative*.

Lewis, C. S., *The Allegory of Love: A Study in Medieval Tradition* (Oxford University Press, London, 1936).

Manly, John Matthews, *Some New Light on Chaucer* (Holt, New York, and G. Bell, London, 1926).

—— 'Three Recent Chaucer Studies', *RES* 10 (1934), pp. 257–73.

Mann, Jill, *Chaucer and Medieval Estates Satire: The Literature of Social Classes and the General Prologue to the Canterbury Tales* (Cambridge University Press, Cambridge, 1973).

—— 'Parents and Children in the "Canterbury Tales"', in *Literature in Fourteenth-Century England: The J. A. W. Bennett Memorial Lectures, Perugia, 1981–2* (Gunter Narr Verlag, Tübingen, and D. S. Brewer, Cambridge, 1983), pp. 165–83.

—— *Geoffrey Chaucer*, New Feminist Readings (Harvester Wheatsheaf, London, 1991).

McFarlane, K. B., *Lancastrian Kings and Lollard Knights* (Clarendon Press, Oxford, 1972).

—— *The Nobility of Later Medieval England* (Clarendon Press, Oxford, 1973).

Mathew, Gervase, *The Court of Richard II* (John Murray, London, 1968).

Mertes, Kate, *The English Noble Household 1250–1600: Good Governance and Politic Rule* (Basil Blackwell, Oxford, 1988).

Middleton, Anne, 'The Idea of Public Poetry in the Reign of Richard II', *Speculum*, 53 (1978), pp. 94–114.

—— 'Chaucer's "New Men" and the Good of Literature in the *Canterbury Tales*', in *Literature and Society*, ed. Edward W. Said, Selected Papers from the English Institute [1978], NS 3 (Johns Hopkins University Press, Baltimore, Md. and London, 1980), pp. 15–56.

Muscatine, Charles, *Chaucer and the French Tradition: A Study in Style and Meaning* (University of California Press, Berkeley and Los Angeles, 1957).

Patterson, Lee, *Negotiating the Past: The Historical Understanding of Medieval Literature* (University of Wisconsin Press, Madison, 1987).

—— '"No man his reson herde": Peasant Consciousness, Chaucer's Miller, and the Structure of the *Canterbury Tales*', *South Atlantic Quarterly*, 86 (1987), pp. 457–95; repr. in *Literary Practice and Social Change*, ed. Patterson, pp. 113–55.

—— (ed.), *Literary Practice and Social Change in Britain, 1380–1530* (University of California Press, Berkeley, Los Angeles and Oxford, 1990).

Pearsall, Derek, *John Lydgate* (Routledge & Kegan Paul, London, 1970).

—— *Old English and Middle English Poetry*, The Routledge History of English Poetry, Vol. I (Routledge & Kegan Paul, London, 1977).

—— *The Canterbury Tales*, Unwin Critical Library (Allen & Unwin, London, 1985).

—— (ed.), *Manuscripts and Texts: Editorial Problems in Later Middle English Literature*, Essays from the 1985 Conference at the University of York (D. S. Brewer, Cambridge, 1987).

Robertson, D. W., *Chaucer's London* (John Wiley, New York, 1968).

Salter, Elizabeth, *Fourteenth-Century English Poetry: Contexts and Readings* (Clarendon Press, Oxford, 1983).

—— *English and International: Studies in the Literature, Art and Patronage of Medieval England* (Cambridge University Press, Cambridge, 1988).

Salu, Mary (ed.), *Essays on Troilus and Criseyde*, Chaucer Studies, 3 (D. S. Brewer, Cambridge, and Rowman & Littlefield, Totowa, NJ, 1979).

Scattergood, V. J., and Sherborne, J. W. (eds), *English Court Culture in the Later Middle Ages* (Duckworth, London, 1983).

Shepherd, Geoffrey, 'Religion and Philosophy in Chaucer', in *Writers and their Background*, ed. Brewer, pp. 262–89.

Spearing, A. C., *Medieval to Renaissance in English Poetry* (Cambridge University Press, Cambridge, 1985).

Speght, Thomas, 'Chaucer's Life', in *The Workes of our Antient and Lerned English Poet, Geffrey Chaucer, newly Printed*, ed. Thomas Speght (London, 1598); conveniently accessible in *Geoffrey Chaucer: The Works 1532*, a facsimile edition by D. S. Brewer, with supplementary material from the editions of 1542, 1561, 1598 and 1602 (Scolar Press, London, 1969).

Strohm, Paul, *Social Chaucer* (Harvard University Press, Cambridge, Mass., 1989).

Thrupp, Sylvia L., *The Merchant Class of Medieval London [1300–1500]* (University of Chicago Press, Chicago, 1948).

Tout, Thomas Frederick, 'Literature and Learning in the English Civil Service in the Fourteenth Century', *Speculum*, 4 (1929), pp. 365–89.

Wimsatt, James I., *Chaucer and the Poems of 'Ch' in University of Pennsylvania MS French 15*, Chaucer Studies, 9 (D. S. Brewer, Cambridge, and Rowman & Littlefield, Totowa, NJ, 1982).

Index